* *

IRELAND'S OPPORTUNITY

**GLUCKSMAN
IRISH DIASPORA**

IN THE GLUCKSMAN IRISH DIASPORA SERIES

Kevin Kenny, General Editor

Nicholas Wolf, Associate Editor

America and the Making of an Independent Ireland: A History
Francis M. Carroll

The Coffin Ship: Life and Death at Sea during the Great Irish Famine
Cian T. McMahon

Changing Land: Diaspora Activism and the Irish Land War
Niall Whelehan

*Homeward Bound: Return Migration from Ireland and India at the
End of the British Empire*
Niamh Dillon

Young Ireland: A Global Afterlife
Christopher Morash

Aiding Ireland: The Great Famine and the Rise of Transnational Philanthropy
Anelise Hanson Shrout

The Green Space: The Transformation of the Irish Image
Marion R. Casey

Hereafter: The Telling Life of Ellen O'Hara
Vona Groarke

The Irish Revolution: A Global History
Edited by Patrick Mannion and Fearghal McGarry

Ireland's Opportunity: Global Irish Nationalism and the South African War
Shane Lynn

* *

Ireland's Opportunity

Global Irish Nationalism and the South African War

Shane Lynn

* * *

NEW YORK UNIVERSITY PRESS

New York

* *

NEW YORK UNIVERSITY PRESS
New York
www.nyupress.org

© 2025 by New York University
All rights reserved

Please contact the Library of Congress for Cataloging-in-Publication data.

ISBN: 9781479835607 (hardcover)
ISBN: 9781479835652 (library ebook)
ISBN: 9781479835638 (consumer ebook)

This book is printed on acid-free paper, and its binding materials are chosen for strength and durability. We strive to use environmentally responsible suppliers and materials to the greatest extent possible in publishing our books.

The manufacturer's authorized representative in the EU for product safety is Mare Nostrum Group B.V., Mauritskade 21D, 1091 GC Amsterdam, The Netherlands.
Email: gpsr@mare-nostrum.co.uk.

Manufactured in the United States of America

10 9 8 7 6 5 4 3 2 1

Also available as an ebook

For Catherine Bernadette

CONTENTS

List of Figures ix

Preface xi

Note on Terminology xiii

Introduction: Ireland's Opportunity 1

PART ONE: TRANSATLANTIC REVOLUTIONARIES

1. "The Hour of Destiny": The Nationalist Resurgence
   in Ireland 25

2. "Physical Farce": Transatlantic Fenianism and the
   Dynamiting of the Welland Canal 49

PART TWO: AMERICAN PRO-BOERS

3. "Either Irish or German, or a Very Bad Mixture of Both":
   Agent X and the Pro-Boers of San Francisco 75

4. "Petty Injuries": The Limits of Irish American Agitation . . . 104

PART THREE: DIVIDED LOYALTIES

5. "Jingoistic Hysteria": James Grattan Grey and the War in
   New Zealand 133

6. "Strictly Constitutional": Australia's Irish Nationalists
   Juggle Loyalty and Dissent 153

7. "A Few Idiots"? Irish Nationalists in Canada Mention
   the War 179

PART FOUR: FENIANS, SPIES, AND THE LEGACY OF WAR

8. "Ha! Ha!" Unmasking Agent Z (and Uncaging
   Luke Dillon) 211

   Conclusion: The "Beginning of the End"? 245

   Acknowledgments 255

   Notes 257

   Bibliography. 303

   Index 323

   About the Author 337

LIST OF FIGURES

I.1 Tom Clarke, 1899. Public Domain. 8

I.2 "A Mhidsummer Noight's Dhrame," *Punch*, 14 Feb 1900. 10

I.3 "Too much for him!", J. S. Pughe, centerfold in *Puck*,
21 Mar 1900, Library of Congress.. 14

1.1 Pro-Boer protest at College Green, Dublin, on 17 Dec 1899.
In *Le Petit Journal: supplement illustré*, 31 Dec 1899,
Bibliothèque nationale de France.. 32

1.2 Maud Gonne, 1900. J. E. Purdy & Co, Boston, Library of
Congress. 36

1.3 Michael Davitt, 1895. Charlie Farr, Maryborough, State
Library of Victoria. .39

1.4 "Outflanked, be Jabers!" *Punch*, 14 Mar 1900.. 45

2.1 Welland Canal dynamiters. Information wanted poster,
April 1900, CBS 22397/S, National Archives of Ireland.. . . .51

2.2 James Mullett and James "Skin-the-Goat" Fitzharris, 1883,
NLI NPA INV15. Courtesy of the National Library
of Ireland.. 67

3.1 "The Boers as they really are," San Francisco *Call*,
29 Oct 1899, Chronicling America, Library of Congress. . . .77

3.2 "Politics makes strange bedfellows," Louis Dalrymple,
Puck, 5 May 1899, Library of Congress. 79

4.1 Irish American Transvaal Ambulance Corps departing
New York, *Irish World*, 24 Feb 1900.. 107

4.2 William Bourke Cockran, ca. 1903–1905, C. M. Bell, Washington, DC, Library of Congress. 110

4.3 W. J. Bryan election poster, 1900, NPG.83.177, National Portrait Gallery, Smithsonian Institution. 115

4.4 "He won't go off his beat," J. S. Pughe, *Puck*, 7 Mar 1900 122

5.1 James Grattan Grey and his wife, Jane, *Irish World*, 13 Oct 1900. 135

5.2 Henry William Cleary as Bishop of Auckland, 1910–, 1/2–024702, Alexander Turnbull Library, Wellington, New Zealand. 149

6.1 Dr. Nicholas O'Donnell and his son, 1897, O'Donnell Family Photographs, State Library of Victoria. 158

6.2 Arthur Lynch, ca. 1910–1915, Bain News Service, Library of Congress.. 162

6.3 Patrick Francis Cardinal Moran, ca. 1900. Public Domain. 171

7.1 John Devoy, 1916, Bain News Service, Library of Congress.. 184

7.2 Charles Fitzpatrick, ca. 1890–1902, Montminy & Cie, Quebec, P551, Archives of the Law Society of Ontario. . . . 198

8.1 Joseph McGarrity, ca. 1910, OM II 5/25/4, Joseph McGarrity Collection, Digital Library@Villanova University.. 213

8.2 John Nolan and Luke Dillon in Kingston Penitentiary, 1910. Correctional Service of Canada fonds, RG73-C-6, Vol. 558, e010995338 & e010995296, Library and Archives Canada. 227

8.3 Luke Dillon interviewed in Atlantic City, *Washington Times* (DC), 26 Jul 1914, Chronicling America, Library of Congress.. 234

PREFACE

In the modern world, wars can have a profound influence on political thought and social movements thousands of miles distant from the fighting. This book uncovers the impact of the South African War (1899–1902) on Irish nationalism. It is not a history of events in South Africa; rather, it is a study of how perceptions of the war acted as a catalyst for dramatic and transformative developments in Irish nationalism. These developments were not confined to the island of Ireland. The distinguishing characteristic of Irish nationalism was the presence of millions of adherents strewn across Ireland's vast global diaspora. Although they shared much in common, local conditions decisively influenced these scattered communities' perceptions of Irish issues and their preferred solutions to the "Irish question." Until now, their response to the South African War has received little attention. This book addresses that gap.

Opposition to Britain's war on the Boer republics had a unifying and revitalizing effect on Irish nationalism around the world after a decade of disharmony. Many considered the war fundamentally unjust and believed the Anglo-Boer and Anglo-Irish relationships to be analogous. Irish nationalists and Boers had, however, little in common besides their enemy. This misidentification was enabled by a fuzzy understanding of South African realities and a reflexive white supremacism. There was, in the era of "high imperialism," no shortage of conquered peoples with whom Irish nationalists could choose to identify. But sporadic affinities for these largely nonwhite candidates never rivaled the deluge of popular sympathy directed at the Boers.

The pro-Boer outlook of Irish nationalists did not represent what we would today consider a coherent anti-colonial or anti-imperial worldview. Theirs was a highly selective solidarity with a clear racial criterion. Ireland and its diaspora were, after all, almost entirely contained within the British and American empires, and Irish political culture at home and abroad was deeply imbricated in empire. With few exceptions, Irish nationalist "anti-imperialism" at the turn of the twentieth century echoed the basic assumption underlying much of western imperial thought: that political sovereignty was the domain of white men. Among the most radical Irish nationalist critics of the war and of imperialism in the United States, for example, were men and women who were comfortable with, or who had themselves participated in, the conquest of Native American land. Many had also, only a year previously, cheered the American acquisition of Cuba and Puerto Rico. Boer sympathies could also be entirely compatible with enthusiasm for the British empire. Irish nationalists in Britain's Dominions who opposed the war (and many did not even go that far) presented themselves as the guardians of a more virtuous sort of empire—one in which autonomy for its white constituents would be repaid handsomely with loyalty, and in which the subordinate position of nonwhite subjects was seldom questioned. Empire was, for both its supporters and opponents, the ineluctable framework through which Ireland's futures, and the futures of its diaspora communities, were imagined.

From the late eighteenth century, nationalists enlisted foreign governments, British political parties, and other diaspora and settler groups—all with varying levels of enthusiasm—as "friends of Ireland." During the South African War the Boers, naturally, occupied top spot on the list of nationalist Ireland's designated allies. But in coordinating a nationwide pro-Boer movement, Irish nationalists in the United States also kindled a friendship with German Americans and, eventually, the German government, that would prove fateful. Those at the radical end of the nationalist spectrum were particularly interested in the opportunities for revolutionary action that these new cross-ethnic and international combinations could produce during "England's difficulty" in South Africa. The impact of the war on physical force nationalists was, this book stresses, especially profound. But their fortunes were highly sensitive to the shifting intelligence landscape, the strategic interests of the great powers, and the momentum of the mainstream moderate nationalist movement. The missed opportunities of 1899–1900 would convince certain key Fenian leaders to act decisively during the Great War.

NOTE ON TERMINOLOGY

In line with recent scholarship, "South African War" is used here instead of "Boer War" or "Second Anglo-Boer War." Those latter descriptions obscure the complexities of the conflict and the involvement of other groups—particularly native Africans.

"Afrikaner" has lately emerged as the preferred term for the Afrikaans-speaking descendants of the largely Dutch, Huguenot, and German colonists in South Africa. The Irish observers who are the subject of this book, however, exclusively used the term "Boer" to describe this group. Because contemporary references to "Boers" and "pro-Boers" are quoted and paraphrased extensively here I have, for the sake of consistency and the avoidance of confusion, preferred the term "Boer" over "Afrikaner" throughout.

"Fenians" were the advocates of Ireland's separation from the United Kingdom by physical force if necessary. This shorthand was popularized by (and outlived) the Fenian Brotherhood, an Irish American revolutionary organization founded in 1858 and named for the *Fianna* warriors of Gaelic legend. "Fenianism" refers broadly to this philosophy.

"Home Rule" was a proposed form of limited self-government for Ireland based on a devolved Dublin parliament within the United Kingdom. It was the preferred option of the popular mainstream constitutional nationalist movement.

Introduction

Ireland's Opportunity

"England's difficulty has at last come," proclaimed a circular of the Clan na Gael—the North American sister organization of the Irish Republican Brotherhood—in November 1899. The outbreak, six weeks earlier, of war between the British Empire and the Boer republics of South Africa presented a "splendid opportunity" for the supporters of revolutionary Irish nationalism to "deal England a deadly blow in her hour of peril and thus prepare the way for the freedom of our motherland." For almost a decade, transatlantic Fenianism had been hobbled by a bitter feud between two rival factions. But as Anglo-Boer relations lurched towards war during the summer of 1899, reconciliation became a matter of urgency. The "union of the two wings of the organisation," the authors of the circular congratulated themselves, "did not come a moment too soon."[1] Within months, Fenians attempted to sabotage imperial infrastructure with dynamite attacks, traveled to South Africa to fight alongside the Boers, launched a campaign to oppose enlistment in the British army, and lobbied Britain's rivals to intervene in the war with the promise that an uprising in Ireland was imminent.

The South African War also excited a spirit of unity within the constitutional nationalist movement. The once punctiliously whipped Irish Parliamentary Party had, from 1890, dramatically disintegrated following the fall and death of its leader, Charles Stewart Parnell. But in 1899, opposition to the war created new common ground between its squabbling factions and, in combination with a renewed campaign for land reform, paved the way for the party's reunification under John Redmond the following year. As the prominent nationalist MP, Michael Davitt, explained it:

> This comradeship of combat in a common cause of liberty against the criminal aggression of a great empire upon two little republics finally broke down

the barriers which nine years of sectional strife had set up between Irish nationalists.[2]

The South African War was a major global event. Its deeply controversial origins and the unusual spectacle of white, Christian colonies becoming the targets of imperial expansion triggered a popular anti-British and anti-imperialist backlash—especially in continental Europe and North America.[3] Although "Boer fever" subsided within a year, its legacy was enshrined in seminal works on imperialism by J. A. Hobson and V. I. Lenin.[4] For Britain's supporters, a series of early reverses and the fear that a rival great power would intervene on the Boer side made the war seem almost a defensive one. As the world watched and peril loomed, loyalists felt keenly the need to demonstrate the cohesiveness of the empire. Thirty-five thousand volunteers from the white settler colonies answered the call, joining an imperial mobilization of 450,000 troops—Britain's largest in the century between the Napoleonic Wars and the Great War.[5] The uproarious empire-wide celebrations following the relief of besieged British garrisons at Kimberley, Ladysmith, and Mafeking, meanwhile, became synonymous with jingoism—the militaristic popular patriotism that came to pervade Britain and its Dominions during this era of high imperialism.[6] But the pounding of the jingo drum faltered as the conventional war transitioned to a grinding guerrilla conflict. The romance of desperate charges, close scrapes, and daring rescues was replaced by the tedium of blockhouses and unsettling reports of scorched earth and concentration camps.

The war was, as Roy Foster has pointed out, "nearly as crucial an event for Irish nationalism as the death of Parnell."[7] Irish nationalists saw Britain's treatment of the Boers as analogous to Ireland's own experience of conquest and colonization. In their eyes the Boers were another small, largely agrarian nation whose right to self-determination was being stamped out by an acquisitive British neighbor. This reconstruction of the Boers in the Gaelic image was influential despite its inconsistencies: the most glaring of which were the Boers' Calvinism and the presence of large and diverse native South African populations on whose lands they had settled. Such details were overshadowed in nationalist minds by the profoundly troubling precedents the war appeared to be setting. If the empire could not tolerate two tiny Boer statelets on the other side of the world, then what hope was there for an independent or autonomous Ireland on Britain's doorstep? If the great powers and even the United States stood idly by while the Boer republics were crushed, then who would stand with Ireland in its hour of need? Hope occasionally burst through the fog of outrage; each upset the Boers inflicted on their opponent produced moments of euphoria among sections of the Irish audience. Maybe a clever and determined David could go it alone against the imperial Goliath? These questions brought Irish nationalism buzzing to life with anxious energy. This galvanic effect has been noted by historians of Ireland; so too has the injection of anti-imperialist language into certain quarters of nationalist discourse, and the war's psychological legacy on some future nationalist leaders. Few, however, have examined its impact in depth.[8] Only Donal P. McCracken has produced book-length studies on the subject, and while these remain essential reading, they are confined to the island of Ireland and to South Africa.[9] This book adopts a wider lens.

Irish nationalism was, after all, a global phenomenon. By the outbreak of the South African War, two in five Irish-born people lived beyond the island's shores. Ireland's rate of emigration during the 1890s was "easily the highest in Europe"—three times greater than the nearest competitor.[10] These emigrants were among the six million who, during the nineteenth century, left Ireland behind. They settled chiefly in the United States, Britain, and the white settler colonies of North America and Australasia. This movement of people had its roots in the mid-eighteenth century, picked up pace following the Napoleonic Wars, and accelerated dramatically with the Great Famine of 1845–1852. The emigrants and descendants of emigrants that made up Ireland's global diaspora far exceeded the population of the island, which by 1901 stood at 4.4 million and continued to shrink.[11] They were a complex and heterogenous group whose experiences, attitudes, and political allegiances could vary greatly according to religion, class, time of emigration, point of origin, and place of settlement, as well as between generations.[12] The cases of an Ulster Protestant settler in Appalachia, a Munster-born Catholic fleeing famine to Toronto, and a second-generation Melbourne barrister may bear little mutual resemblance. Despite this diversity, for many Irish Catholic (and some Protestant) emigrants and their descendants, nationalism remained a stubbornly persistent pillar of ethnic identity well into the twentieth century. The belief in some form of Irish self-government as the solution to Irish problems had arrived on the same boats that carried the trickle of banished United Irishmen in the 1790s, and the floods of emigrants from the Ireland of Daniel O'Connell between the 1820s and the 1850s.[13] It took hold in emigrant communities and was sharpened by the bitter legacy of famine, the perception of emigration as a form of exile, and first-hand experience of practical independence—whether in Britain's self-governing settler colonies or the republican United States.[14] It was sustained by a steady stream of new arrivals, an activist press, and the tours of peripatetic agitators raising funds and support for nationalist movements at home. Diaspora nationalism tended to wax and wane according to the fortunes of these movements, but local conditions could also be a decisive influence, nudging it towards loyal moderation or republican revolution depending on the prevailing political culture or the personalities of local powerbrokers.[15]

Historians of Ireland increasingly agree that "island-centric" histories of nationalism are incomplete, and that contemporaries commonly saw themselves as part of a "Greater Ireland" spanning several continents.[16] From the earliest days of O'Connell's repeal campaign to the nod to "exiled children" in the Proclamation of the Irish Republic, the diaspora was a recurring motif in nationalist polemic.[17] It was portrayed as simultaneously the nation's deepest wound and its greatest asset. But diaspora nationalism was more than just a rhetorical staple or a badge of identity for emigrant communities. Through their influence on their own governments, the value of their financial contributions, their participation in revolutionary violence, and their sheer weight of numbers, Irish nationalists abroad directly influenced the movements at home. By the same token, developments in one node of the diasporic web could shape those of another, sometimes quite independent of Ireland.[18] If the British and American empires were a "patchwork quilt" of connected but distinct *milieux*, then global Irish nationalism crossed its seams in all directions and with sometimes unpredictable results.[19] The histories of Ireland and its diaspora communities were not simply "parallel"; they were, as practitioners of the "new imperial history" have observed of settler societies generally, "dynamically inter-connected and thus mutually formative."[20] To repurpose a phrase from J.G.A. Pocock: they "interacted so as to modify the conditions of one another's existence."[21] We can trace these interactions by looking closely at people whose movements and ideas crossed oceans and borders.[22] In this case: people whose lives were transformed by the South African War.

This book shows that the fin-de-siècle was a turning point in the history of global Irish nationalism. Despite the period's reputation in the canon of Irish political history as "a sort of crease in time, a featureless valley" between the fall of Parnell and the Home Rule crisis, in fact the war years witnessed a burst of activity marked by a sudden revival of separatism and a resurgent Irish Party buoyed by a new grassroots machine.[23] The impact of the South African War rippled across "Greater Ireland," re-energizing diasporic nationalism after a decade of decline. If we follow these ripples through Ireland itself and five sites of settlement—the eastern United States, the western United States, New Zealand, Australia, and Canada—clear patterns emerge: patterns that reveal much about the nature of global Irish nationalism; patterns that both predate the South African War and can be seen to repeat during the revolutionary period a decade later. We see how global Irish nationalism could be jolted out of dormancy by dramatic external stimuli, and how it could just as quickly implode in a mess of infighting. We see Irish nationalists in the white settler colonies struggle to balance an often sincerely felt duty of loyalty to the empire with their sympathy for its enemies. We see revolutionaries despair at their struggle to mobilize while many times their number don British uniforms. We see the importance of the unceasing intelligence war between Fenians and spies in determining the fortunes of the movement. And we can detect the complex tensions and seeming contradictions intrinsic to global Irish nationalism and its relationship to empire that would later be dramatically exposed by the Anglo-Irish Treaty and its fallout. The South African War was not, as some nationalists hoped, the catalyst that dissolved the Union settlement in Ireland. But it foreshadowed the events that would ultimately produce this outcome. And, this book suggests, it set at least some of them in motion.

* * *

The conspirators behind the revolutionary street theater of Easter 1916 made no secret of the influence the South African War had on their thinking. "Whenever England goes on her mission of empire, we meet and we strike at her," Patrick Pearse warned in 1914. "Yesterday it was on the South African veldt, tomorrow it may be on the streets of Dublin."[24] Pearse and many of his fellow insurgents took to those streets sporting "De Wet" or "Cronje" caps—Boer-style slouch hats. Michael Collins, a veteran of the rising, was later nicknamed the "Irish De Wet" for his role in coordinating guerrilla operations during the War of Independence. In 1921 he confided to the real Boer General Christiaan de Wet that "Your great fight against the same foe was the earliest inspiration of the men who have been fighting here for the past two years."[25] The analogies, as historians Donal Lowry, Bruce Nelson, and others have pointed out, did not stop there, and were not confined to the physical force end of the nationalist spectrum.[26] But the South African War made an especially deep impression on the mind of Tom Clarke, the senior figure in the secret IRB council behind the rising. "Clarke's greatest regret," explained one historian of the rebellion, "was the failure to rise during the Boer War."[27] Clarke was the living link between the skirmishing Fenianism of the dynamite war and the resurgent insurrectionary variety of the Great War. In his life, and in the movement to which his life was devoted, the excitement, frustration, and disillusionment elicited by the South African War would prove transformative.

Clarke had joined the Irish Republican Brotherhood in Dungannon, Co. Tyrone, as a young man. But after an altercation with police during the Land War—the period of agrarian protest and disturbance aimed at transforming Ireland's quasi-feudal land system—he fled to New York in 1880. There he joined the Clan na Gael, and in 1883 was dispatched on a bombing mission to London.[28] Some Fenians had answered the call, most commonly associated with the Skibbereen-born Brooklyn journalist Jeremiah O'Donovan Rossa, to harness the new military science of "infernal machines"—dynamite bombs—to bring the fight for Irish independence to the British mainland.[29] But Clarke's mission, like many others of the Dynamite War between 1881 and 1885, was watched by spies and betrayed by informers before a fuse could be lit. Clarke was caught in possession of explosives and spent fifteen years in English prisons before his release, on amnesty, in September 1898.[30] He returned to Ireland but struggled to find work, his hopes of a job at Dublin Corporation and of an American lecture tour both failing to materialize. His achievements during his first year of freedom came through his old friend and fellow Fenian inmate John Daly, the Mayor

of Limerick, who awarded Clarke the freedom of that city and introduced him to his niece, Kathleen Daly. Tom and Kathleen's courtship
is documented in a series of tender letters that provide glimpses of the
nationalist world through which both moved as it was reshaped by
the outbreak of the South African War.

Clarke emigrated to New York for the second time in October 1899,
joking that nothing could induce him to return "except I was going
to fight [. . .] John B[ull]."[31] War erupted while he was at sea; as he
crossed the Atlantic, Boer troops crossed the borders into Natal and
Cape Colony. Arriving in New York he was struck by how "[t]he Boer
War is occupying everyone's thoughts around here."[32] He worried that
if his brother Joseph did not also quit Ireland soon then "he may be
dragged off by the English to fight against the Boers," so he sent him
a steamship ticket and money to induce him to move to America.[33]
Clarke had seen his family uprooted by the military before. His father
had been a British Army sergeant. A year after Tom's birth in Hamp-
shire, England, his father was posted to South Africa and the family
followed; Tom spent his early childhood there before they returned to
Ireland.[34] Clarke was thrilled by the Boer successes in his former home
during the early months of the war and participated with enthusiasm
in the American pro-Boer movement. What Clarke saw as the Boers'
brave patriotism in arms against overwhelming military odds resonated
deeply with him. He wrote to a friend in Dublin:

> We are going to have a big Boer meeting tomorrow in the Grand Central
> Palace. Of course I'll be there, occupying a back seat but as hearty & earnest
> a sympathizer with the gallant farmers of the Transvaal as will be in the Hall.
> Holy God but aren't they surprising the world! Yes almost as much as they
> are surprising the English. Talk of Washington & the American patriots of
> the Revolution. These Boers & their old Oom Paul [Kruger, President
> of the Transvaal] are knocking them completely into the shade. Washington
> and the United States of America are "not in it" with my brave, old Oom
> Paul and his United States of Africa. Success to him & them & the prayer
> of every exiled Irishman here in these States.[35]

This feeling was not confined to Fenians. John Redmond made his
maiden Commons speech as leader of the reunited Irish Parliamentary

Figure 1.1. Tom Clarke, 1899. Public Domain.

Party the occasion for a philippic against the imperial government's actions in South Africa. "The sympathy of Ireland is with the two South African Republics," he declared. "We abhor this war; we call for its stoppage, and we declare our intention to do all that in us lies to maintain the independence of these two little Republics, which was won by untold sacrifices, and defended by a heroism which is without parallel in the history of the world." The conquest of the Boers, he claimed, would only create another Ireland in South Africa.[36] The sympathies Clarke and Redmond described were sincerely felt across the nationalist spectrum. They were rooted, however, in a flimsy and sometimes willfully distorted understanding of South Africa's reality. Like many observers who had an axe to grind with imperial Britain, Irish nationalists held a mirror to themselves and called it "the Boers."[37]

* * *

In some respects, the Boers more closely resembled Ireland's Protestant planters than the indigenous Gael of the nationalist imagination.[38] They were the descendants of the largely Calvinist Dutch, German, and Huguenot colonists who settled the Cape in the mid-seventeenth century. Following Britain's seizure of the Dutch colony at the Cape during the Napoleonic Wars, friction grew between the new colonial administration and the Boer settlers. The breaking point was Britain's abolition of slavery in 1833. In protest against these and other perceived acts of interference, a large migration of around 13,000 Boers to the interior northeast of the Orange River, known as the Great Trek, commenced in 1835.[39] Through the violent displacement of native African nations, these "Voortrekkers" founded and settled a series of independent colonies, the largest and most abiding of which were the Orange Free State and the South African Republic—the latter known typically as "the Transvaal." British expansion followed close behind. A diamond boom near Kimberley led to the creation of the British colony of Griqualand West, bordering the Orange Free State. Some instances of British encroachment occurred on the invitation of the Boers. Financial vulnerability and a fear of being overwhelmed by the Zulu military threat led the Boer colony of Natal to request British annexation in 1843 and the Transvaal to accept, albeit grudgingly, its own annexation in 1877. But the British victory over Cetshwayo's Zulu

"A MHIDSUMMER NOIGHT'S DHRAME."
Oom Eottom and the roival Toitanias—unoited at last. (How long will it last?)

Figure 1.2. "A Mhidsummer Noight's Dhrame," *Punch*, 14 Feb 1900.

Kingdom in 1879 encouraged the Transvaal Boers to reassert their sovereignty in arms the following year.[40] The resulting First Anglo-Boer War lasted just three months and culminated in an embarrassing defeat for British forces at Majuba Hill in late February 1881. Prime Minister William Gladstone, unwilling to commit to a protracted conflict, offered peace on favorable terms: Transvaal independence under limited British suzerainty. The war indefinitely stalled British designs to create a Canadian-style South African federation.

Irish nationalists had, since 1877, made their own contribution to the frustration of that project. It was in debates over the South Africa Confederation Act that the radical wing of the Home Rule Party, including a young Charles Stewart Parnell, carried out some of its most infamous exercises in parliamentary obstruction. While slowing the proceedings to a crawl, Parnell compared the annexation of the Transvaal with the Act of Union: "As it was with Ireland," he told the House of Commons, "so it was with the South African colonies."[41] Colonial analogies between Ireland and South Africa were also made outside of Parliament. When the Land League was launched at a mass meeting at Irishtown, Co. Mayo, in April 1879, cheers were raised for the Transvaal Boers as a fellow small nation resisting British imperial domination.[42] The Zulus were cheered, too, although, as with subsequent sporadic gestures of superficial sympathy with the Egyptian Arabi Pasha or the Mahdi of Sudan, this amounted more to a gibe at the British government, recently embarrassed by defeat at Isandlwana, than any sincere identification.[43]

The discovery of extensive gold deposits on the Witwatersrand in 1886 transformed the Transvaal from a colonial backwater into a site of global economic significance, shifting the region's center of gravity away from the British Cape. A massive gold rush brought tens of thousands of foreign miners to work in the capital-intensive goldfields of Johannesburg. This flood of so-called *uitlanders* threatened to submerge the small Boer population. There were Irish sojourners among them—notably Arthur Griffith, who edited the small Middelburg *Courant* before joining the Fenian John MacBride in the gold mines.[44] The government of wartime hero Paul Kruger imposed a fourteen-year residency requirement on the diverse *uitlanders* to preserve the dominance of ethnic Boers over the electoral franchise and, he believed, to secure the Transvaal's independence. (The mining business depended on even larger numbers of Black African and some Indian laborers, but there was little expectation among western observers that they be afforded equal citizenship.)[45] The *uitlander* question presented a useful lever in the hands of those who wished to see the Transvaal brought under formal British control. Chief among them was Cecil Rhodes, mining magnate and Prime Minister of the Cape Colony. In 1895 he conspired with Colonial Secretary Joseph Chamberlain to launch a private filibustering expedition, composed of employees of Rhodes's British South Africa Company and led by Leander Starr Jameson, which was intended to support a simultaneous *uitlander* uprising in Johannesburg and bring about the overthrow of Kruger's government. (A plan which, it must be said, bore some resemblance to the much-lampooned Fenian raids on British North America almost three decades previously.) The "Jameson Raid," as it became known, was a farcical failure, and the rebellion never materialized. The affair convinced the Boer republics that Britain could not be trusted to deal in good faith and that preparations would need to be made to resist future aggression.[46] In London, a desultory parliamentary inquiry into the raid received the minimum cooperation required from Rhodes and Chamberlain and absolved the ringleaders of wrongdoing. Irish Canadian Home Rule MP Edward Blake resigned his seat on the select committee in protest against Rhodes's refusal to produce certain incriminating telegrams. Irish nationalists were roundly critical of parliament's auto-absolution. "English freebooting is a virtue," the New York *Irish Republic* announced acerbically in the wake of the inquiry's report.[47]

The *uitlander* question was the official pretext for war in 1899. In September, Chamberlain issued an ultimatum to Kruger, effectively threatening invasion unless his government satisfied *uitlander* grievances, including their admission to the electoral franchise. Most scholars agree that Britain's regional strategic and economic interests outweighed its ostensible concern for *uitlander* rights, but whether gold and international capital were important factors (as contemporary critics of the war insisted) has been a matter of considerable debate.[48] In any case, Kruger refused Chamberlain's ultimatum as expected, and on 9 October he sent a purely symbolic counter-ultimatum demanding that British troops withdraw from regions bordering his state within forty-eight hours. It was, of course, rejected. On 11 October 1899 the South African Republic, joined by the Orange Free State, formally declared war on Britain.[49]

Chamberlain and Lord Alfred Milner, the British High Commissioner for Southern Africa, had hoped the Transvaal would back down when threatened with force. If necessary, they reckoned the tiny Boer republics could be easily overwhelmed in a matter of months.[50] Imperial morale was, at the time, riding high. The previous year at Omdurman, in Sudan, a British-led force commanded by Irish-born General Herbert Kitchener had annihilated a Sudanese Mahdist army twice its size in a devastating demonstration of modern military technology. But the Boers, spirited by memories of Majuba Hill and the hope that a rival great power could be induced to intervene against Britain, resolved to fight.[51] They struck quickly, driving into British territory and besieging the towns of Ladysmith to the east, Mafeking in the west, and the diamond town of Kimberley to the southwest, where Cecil Rhodes found himself trapped. Boer commandos stunned the world by inflicting a series of defeats on British relief forces at Stormberg, Magersfontein, and Colenso between 10 and 15 December 1899. The reversals of this "Black Week" and the uncertain fates of the besieged garrisons were brought vividly to life in newspapers across the empire by a legion of war correspondents that included a young Winston Churchill. The bleak situation raised the specter of a possible British defeat, especially in the event of an opportunistic intervention by France or Russia. To loyalists the war became a great emergency that would require all the attention and resources of the empire.

The Boer successes proved short-lived. From February 1900 growing British forces under Lord Roberts gradually overwhelmed the static Boer positions through sheer weight of numbers. By June the Roberts "steamroller" had driven its way north to the Transvaal capital of Pretoria, relieving the besieged garrisons at Kimberley, Ladysmith, and Mafeking along the way. News of each rescue sparked jubilant, sometimes riotous street celebrations across the empire.[52] The Boer governments fled into exile in Europe, but commandos of *bittereinders* remained to prosecute a guerrilla campaign against the British occupation of the republics. During this "second phase" of the war the British Army, now under Lord Kitchener, intensified its controversial use of scorched earth tactics and concentration camps to pressure the Boer insurgents to submit. An estimated 27,000 people, mostly women and children, died in these disease-ridden camps—a number four times higher than the estimated 7,000 Boer combat deaths. These figures combined represented about 17.5% of the total Boer population.[53] Pro-Boers had long abandoned hope of British defeat, but as reports of the human cost of "Kitchener's War" filtered home through journalists such as Emily Hobhouse, loyalist enthusiasm waned. Of the 450,000 British troops that served in the conflict—around 6,500 of which were from New Zealand, 7,000 from Canada, 20,000 from Australia, and 30,000 from Ireland—an estimated 22,000 died. Britain also made extensive use of over 100,000 native African "auxiliaries," at least 10,000 of them armed.[54] A volunteer ambulance corps of 1,100 Indian stretcher-bearers was created in Natal by a young Mohandas K. Gandhi, then eager to demonstrate Indian loyalty to the British empire.

Figure 1.3. "Too much for him!", J. S. Pughe, centerfold in *Puck*, 21 Mar 1900, Library of Congress.

The pressures of war in a multiracial environment made short work of the prevailing belief that the conflict should be a white man's affair. Some British commanders were reluctant to accept Gandhi's assistance until heavy casualties at Spion Kop forced their hand. Opponents of the war, for their part, were ostentatiously aghast at Britain's supposed "unleashing" of natives upon the precarious Boer minority. But Africans were abundantly represented among the combatants, workers, and casualties on both sides and, indeed, on neither. Kitchener's scorched earth policy immiserated tens of thousands of native people, and approximately 20,000 died in segregated British-run concentration camps.[55] Recent research has suggested that Black Africans comprised perhaps a quarter of Boer manpower.[56] African nations acted in their own interests, sometimes independently of either side, taking advantage of the upheaval caused by the war to settle old scores with white colonists.[57] Boer loyalties were also more diverse than some contemporary observers allowed. Some served on the British side, and those living in the British Cape Colony were divided on the question of the war.[58] A mutual desire to contain native Africans and prevent neighboring Swazi and Zulu kingdoms capitalizing on the vulnerability of the colonies was a crucial factor in bringing about peace negotiations in 1902.[59] Milner and Kitchener offered generous terms, hoping to reconcile the Boers to life in a united, white South African polity. A general amnesty, £3 million in reconstruction aid and future self-government, was offered, while the question of Black enfranchisement was postponed indefinitely. These complex and racially heterogeneous aspects to the period are why scholars have come to prefer the term "South African War" to the narrow, older formulation, the "Second Anglo-Boer War" or simply "Boer War."

* * *

To Irish nationalist pro-Boers, Britain's early defeats were thrilling; here was a lesson in jingo hubris. The "pirate empire" had fatally underestimated a small but determined minority. Right, it seemed, was prevailing over might. In their eagerness to re-create the Boers in their own image, however, Irish nationalists willfully overlooked the complex realities of the situation in South Africa. The simplified binary of evil Briton versus virtuous Boer had no more enthusiastic exponent than Michael Davitt, who resigned his parliamentary seat in protest against the war and traveled to South Africa to chronicle what he called *The Boer Fight for Freedom* (1902). Despite having previously defended the Zulus and criticized the mistreatment of Australian aborigines, Davitt dismissed indigenous South Africans as "Kaffirs" and "savages" and condemned Britain's arming of them. Although he would later earn a reputation as a critic of anti-Semitism in Russia, he endorsed the conspiratorial view that "Anglo-German Jewry" had helped to foment the war. Having lost an arm to a machine in a cotton mill as a child, Davitt was a lifelong supporter of labor rights, but his criticism of mine owners did not translate to sympathy for exploited Black laborers on the Rand.[60] Davitt may, consciously or not, have been overcompensating for British propaganda that presented the war as, in part, a defense of native rights against backward and bigoted Boers. But as Bruce Nelson has argued, "Davitt's refusal to see black Africans as fully formed human beings with their own legitimate grievances and aspirations" was informed by a contemporary disposition to express anti-colonial or self-determinationist thinking in the language of "white entitlement."[61]

White supremacy was not just an accidental by-product of the strained analogy between Gaels and Boers. It was a central feature of the contemporary imperial world; and "[e]mpire," as Paul Townend points out, was "the pervasive and formative context of, and no mere exotic backdrop for, Irish politics in the last quarter of the nineteenth century."[62] Global Irish nationalism was as much a product of empire as it was a reaction against it. Although some committed anti-imperialists dotted their ranks, for most Irish nationalists at the turn of the twentieth century the British empire's greatest crime was its continued refusal to allow Ireland to assume its rightful place among the self-governing white races of the world. For colonial settlers of Irish origin desiring to be held in equal esteem to their neighbors of Anglo-Protestant descent, Ireland's subordinate position within the United Kingdom and the insinuations of racial inferiority that undergirded the union were deeply frustrating. Many, particularly in Britain's Dominions, would have been content with the limited autonomy of Home Rule, promising as it did a semblance of equal partnership within the empire and a measure of racial redemption.[63] Irish Americans, wedded to a colonial mythology of their own, tended to desire a fuller measure of independence, and to imagine themselves, Ireland, and the Boer republics as part of an anti-British republican axis. For them, Paul Kruger was the George Washington of a United States of Africa and the Boers colonial patriots fighting for liberty from a capricious empire, sturdy pioneers outnumbered by dangerous natives.[64] Tom Clarke, who embraced this comparison, put his own racist attitudes bluntly in a letter of March 1900 to Kathleen. He was dissatisfied with his Upper East Side neighborhood, complaining that "there are any amount of niggers living here abouts & we Irish as a rule don't care for coming too much in contact with the coloured folks."[65] That the Boers were more deserving of sympathy than the nonwhite victims of imperialism was something on which moderate and advanced nationalists could both agree. The question of what to do next, however, caused a boiling over of tensions that had simmered since the Parnell split.

Moderate nationalists were typically content for their protests against the war to be heard from the streets, the newspapers, and the House of Commons, and to harness pro-Boer feeling in service of the United Irish League. For Fenians like Tom Clarke, Boer fever was all well and good, but direct action was essential to succor the Boers and to provide the spark needed to reignite the national spirit. But before it could "make itself felt," transatlantic Fenianism needed to overcome a decade of disorganization. As Ireland's opportunity slipped away, Clarke found progress achingly slow. "Things here," he complained to a friend in Dublin, "are not satisfactory—by no means."

> I am sick of a good deal of what I see. The same demoralization has taken place here as on your side, & here we are "getting ready"—making preparations—when we should be acting. But where's the good—a fellow can do nothing but keep on churning his wrath.[66]

Time was working against Fenianism. So too was another formidable adversary. The Clan na Gael circular of November 1899 had warned that "England's secret service was never more active than now, and its agents will strain every nerve to gain admission to our ranks."[67] They did not, in this case, need to strain too hard. An informant already in the ranks supplied a copy of the circular to his handler in New York, who forwarded it to Whitehall. In January 1900 it was printed in full— along with the story of the Clan's reunification and the names of every member of the new joint executive—in *The Times*.[68] The message to the Clan was clear: "they cannot trust the veil of secrecy upon which they rely to protect them from the consequences of their crimes."[69] The Clan na Gael was a masonic-style revolutionary secret society with a fluctuating membership generally in the thousands; regional camps were organized into around forty local districts, and a national executive was elected by delegates at a biennial convention.[70] Infiltration by British secret police had long constrained the Clan's attempts to foment revolutionary upheaval in Ireland. Fear alone of spies and informants could create chaos in its ranks. Suspicion and distrust had been instrumental in dividing the Clan throughout the 1880s and 1890s but it also, as we shall see, inadvertently contributed to its reunification in 1899—a development that caught the directors of the intelligence system off guard. Leaking the November circular to the *Times* was a bluff; for the first time in a decade, the secret police had no one inside the new Clan executive and they were scrambling to keep up. The Clan's leaders did not know it, but at the outbreak of the South African War they had the upper hand in the intelligence game. The shape of Ireland's supposed "opportunity" would be determined by whether Fenians could convert that advantage into the direct action they sought, or whether spies could close the gap in time to frustrate them.

Irish pro-Boers, and Fenian observers in particular, took special comfort in the presence of two small Irish brigades fighting alongside the Boers. Not since the Fenian raids had Irish soldiers faced British troops across the battlefield. If the glowing reports in nationalist papers like the New York *Irish World* were to be believed, then they were acquitting themselves more like General O'Neill's victorious Irish Republican Army at Ridgeway than other, less glorious attempts at filibustering and insurrection. Tom Clarke considered them "a credit to Ireland in every way," and described "Major" John MacBride, talisman of the larger of the two outfits, as "a first class fellow."[71] In April 1900 Clarke seriously considered heading to the Transvaal to join up with them—although his devastation at the Daly family's denying him permission to marry Kathleen was undoubtedly clouding his thinking.[72] Wisely, he demurred, remaining in New York as a personal secretary to John Devoy, an old stalwart of the Clan na Gael's secret executive. Clarke was present in the city to provide a hero's welcome to MacBride and his Irish brigade in November 1900. When Kathleen was, finally, able to join Clarke there in July 1901, he arranged for MacBride and the Fenian firebrand Maud Gonne to attend their wedding "as Best man & Best woman or whatever they call it."[73] Gonne agreed but had to back out when other commitments arose; she and MacBride would soon commence an ill-fated marriage of their own.[74] Despite all the excitement, the talk of revolution, and a handful of abortive codas to the dynamite war, the actions and support offered to the Irish brigades stood as the only real achievements of radical nationalists during the war. But these did little to materially advance the national question, and organized Fenianism could claim scant credit for events at the front. Disillusionment spread through the ranks, and leading Fenians defected to the United Irish League.

It was mainstream nationalists, even more so than the secret police, who fixed the boundary to the march of Fenianism—something that was illustrated starkly by the ill-fated attempt to get John MacBride elected *in absentia* to the House of Commons at the February 1900 by-election for South Mayo (the seat that Michael Davitt had resigned in protest against the war). The Irish Party and United Irish League refused to support the Fenian-run MacBride campaign on their own turf. While demonstrating their great esteem for "Major" MacBride himself, they put forward their own, more practical, pro-Boer candidate. MacBride was duly trounced at the polls. "'Tis disgusting," Clarke griped to Kathleen after the election, "to find how rotten the spirit of our people has become through the teaching of the Parliamentarian moral force man."[75] This bitterness would help to make opposition to constitutional agitation an official pillar of Fenian policy by 1902, and create the widest gulf between Fenians and the Irish Party since the days of Isaac Butt. "Our organization," explained the report of the 1902 Clan na Gael convention, "gave parliamentary agitation a full, fair trial." But "men cannot fight under two flags that represent opposing principles."[76] This new position came at the cost of considerable influence and popular support. But it placed men committed to "Revolution and Revolution alone," men like Tom Clarke, in control of what remained of the Clan and the IRB after the war.[77]

As Donal McCracken has pointed out, "[i]n Ireland there was no hazard in being a pro-Boer."[78] The same was true in the United States. Not so in Britain's white settler colonies, where loyal majorities identified as subjects of the empire or, as James Belich has argued, "Better Britons" than the Britons themselves.[79] The Irish nationalist preference for constitutional methods had always been most pronounced in the Dominions.[80] Ireland, these colonial activists argued, simply desired the same measure of responsible government that the colonies enjoyed. There was no disloyalty in seeking constitutional redress for Ireland's legitimate grievances. On the contrary, Dominion-style self-government for Ireland would bring harmony to the Anglo-Irish relationship and help strengthen the empire. But the South African War posed a problem for the Irish nationalists of Australia, New Zealand, and Canada. At its outbreak a wave of popular jingoism swept the colonies; parliaments pledged volunteer contingents to support the imperial war effort; suspected disloyalists were subject to the scrutiny of neighbors and journalists.[81] The umbrella of "constitutionalism" offered only flimsy shelter to Irish nationalists in Melbourne, Auckland, or Toronto when the Irish Party sympathized as openly as the most diehard Fenians did with the empire's Boer enemies. Following the Party line meant risking accusations of disloyalty and Fenianism, sparking a sectarian backlash, and jeopardizing the progress they had made in integrating with colonial society over the previous decade. Breaking with the nationalist leaders at home, on the other hand, meant being labeled a "Jingo," a "shoneen," or a "West Briton" by some in their own camp. Bitter disputes erupted over how best to navigate these twin hazards in responding to the war. Attitudes varied regionally, shaped by local cultures, the density of the Irish Catholic population, the influence of the Catholic clergy, and the strength of local and cross-border nationalist networks.

During a period when Irish nationalists in the colonies were becoming increasingly accommodated to the orthodoxy of high imperialism, the South African War stood out as a moment of crisis. If supporting the empire meant trampling on the independence of small white nations and breaking with the nationalist leaders at home, then clearly something was wrong. But anti-imperialism was often a step too far for communities that were, at some level, aware that they owed their existence to conquest and colonization, and whose prosperity seemed proof of the genius of empire. The real problem, they decided, was not empire as such. Rather, it was unnecessary expansion and the Jingo excess that fueled it. From the moral high ground of "good" imperialism, they deplored the South African War as a vanity project of Chamberlain and his Tory friends, a misadventure for which brave Irish and colonial soldiers and plucky Boers would needlessly fight and die. Although there were nationalists in the Dominions who strongly supported the war and others who openly supported the Boers, this was the attitude that pervaded the nationalist and Catholic press across the colonies. Irish nationalists in the United States, for their part, drew a similarly arbitrary distinction. The American "imperialism" they criticized pertained exclusively to overseas expansion. The conquest of contiguous North America, by contrast, was only right and proper, while aggressive adherence to the Monroe Doctrine in Latin America was preferable to cutting any deals with Britain.[82]

Chapter 1 of this book shows how the South African War sparked a nationalist resurgence in Ireland, especially at the separatist end of the nationalist spectrum. Despite enjoying several advantages, however, transatlantic Fenianism was too disorganized to seize its "hour of destiny."

The Clan na Gael and the IRB's spectacular attempt to dynamite the Welland Canal in Ontario, Canada, detailed in Chapter 2, backfired badly. A plot hatched by Irish and Dutch pro-Boers in San Francisco to destroy a Royal Navy base on Vancouver Island was foiled, as Chapter 3 reveals, by a most unusual informant. Chapter 4 argues that failures such as those, in combination with the rise of the United Irish League, took a disastrous toll on the unity that an anti-imperialist moment, triggered by the South African and Philippine Wars, had temporarily restored to Irish nationalism in the United States. Chapter 5 examines the complicated firing of the Irish nationalist New Zealand Hansard chief reporter James Grattan Grey to show how starkly different the nationalist response could be in a British colony experiencing war fever. Chapter 6 follows Grey to Australia, where a more robust nationalist culture openly criticized the war but drew the line at sympathizing with Fenians or anti-imperialists. A similar pattern of cautious criticism expressed through loyal and clerically mediated nationalism was evident in Canada but, as Chapter 7 argues, radical influences percolated north from the United States and could find a sympathetic audience among certain hardliners in Montreal. The final chapter traces the legacies of the war, culminating in the release of the Welland Canal dynamiters and the unmasking of Britain's top spy in America just as the Great War broke out in Europe.

That war would test, once again, global Irish nationalism's relationship to empire. For men like Tom Clarke it represented a fresh opportunity. They would be determined not to repeat the mistakes of the South African War years. As Clarke's friend Sean McGarry later explained:

He never understood it and never gave up thinking of it . . . The feeling of humiliation at the failure of his generation (as he called it) during the Boer War was still with him and he wanted to do all that one man could do to ensure that should another war come, it would be proved to the world that there were still in Ireland men who were willing to fight and die for Irish freedom.[83]

PART ONE

Transatlantic Revolutionaries

"The Hour of Destiny"

The Nationalist Resurgence in Ireland

During the summer of 1899, Major Nicholas Gosselin had reason to be pleased. A stream of reports crossed his desk at Palace Street, Westminster, announcing the seemingly terminal decline of radical nationalism in Ireland. County Inspector Samuel Waters, Dublin Castle's adviser on Fenianism in the southern half of the country, reported in May that secret societies there had "been entirely inactive" and would probably remain so. It was, he wrote, generally believed that "the Government have such a staff of informers on hand that no sensible man would trust himself in any unlawful secret organisation."[1] In the northern counties, participation in secret societies continued to dwindle as attentions were absorbed by local government elections, the Ancient Order of Hibernians, and the growing United Irish League.[2] In Ballina, the unveiling of a monument commemorating General Humbert's invasion in 1798 was marred by the outbreak of a quarrel between Fenians leading the ceremony. "[T]he spectacle of one leader throwing a jug of water over another," Gosselin smirked, "was an edifying one for the French visitors who were present."[3]

Nicholas Gosselin missed few opportunities to claim credit for this quiescence. For sixteen years, he had been at the heart of the British state's efforts to contain the transnational Fenian threat. Born to an Anglo-Irish gentry family with roots in Cavan, Gosselin spent over two decades in the British Army and a short stint as an Irish Resident Magistrate before taking up spycraft. In 1883, as the government scrambled to respond to the shocking Phoenix Park Murders and a dynamite bombing campaign targeting British cities, he was hired by a shadowy new intelligence department tasked with overseeing counter-Fenian operations. In its unassuming letterhead, the department announced itself as the "Home Office Crime Department—Special Branch"; although officially it did not exist. Despite its controversial use of *agents provocateurs*, a sometimes-turbulent relationship with its police collaborators, and an overzealousness in its efforts to topple Charles Stewart Parnell, the "Special Branch"—and Gosselin—proved effective at disrupting, demoralizing, and dividing transatlantic Fenianism.[4] As his boss and mentor, the former Indian Civil Service officer Edward George Jenkinson, once boasted to a Home Secretary: "No [Fenian] feels sure that his most intimate friend is not a traitor, and they find it exceedingly difficult to get workers."[5] By 1890, as Irish nationalist movements imploded, Gosselin was promoted to head up the Special Branch.[6] For the rest of that decade, he sat atop the pyramid of agencies responsible for ensuring that the extremism of the 1880s did not resurface.[7]

It was with some concern, then, as summer turned to autumn in 1899, that Gosselin observed the tenor of the reports filtering through from Ireland change dramatically. In September, Inspector Waters told that the "excitement occasioned" by the anticipation of war in South Africa and the reunification of the Clan na Gael in America had provided a "powerful stimulus" to secret society organizers.[8] In October, he warned that news of early Boer successes had "so inflamed the minds of Irish extremists that they are ripe for revolutionary organisation."[9] His northern counterpart described the prevalence of "a strong undercurrent of disloyalty" aroused by agitators who "openly preached sedition in connexion with the Transvaal War."[10] In January 1900 the Deputy Inspector General of the RIC remarked that IRB men in the west "undoubtedly contemplate armed insurrection as quite a possible event under certain contingencies."[11] And Gosselin was confronted with distinctly unedifying spectacle of Fenians in Paris lobbying the French government to intervene in the war on the Boer side (pointing, as the United Irishmen once had, to rebellious Ireland as a front waiting to be opened). Even if a revolution, a French invasion, or a British defeat in South Africa were unlikely to occur, a budding belief in these possibilities had the power to revitalize Fenianism—with potentially dangerous results. Sir David Harrel, the Under-Secretary for Ireland, worried that if the war and the land question could bring Fenians and Home Rulers to coalesce around the United Irish League—as they had around the Land League two decades before—then the government would be facing a grave situation.[12] How had the picture suddenly become so dire?

And why did the outcome feared by the authorities ultimately fail to come about?

* * *

Gosselin had seen off previous attempts to reignite the so-called national spirit. When he inherited the Special Branch at the turn of the 1890s, organized Irish nationalism was in disarray. The fall and death of Parnell left the constitutional movement in pieces. The Clan na Gael was cleft in two by the fallout from the murder in Chicago of Patrick Henry Cronin, a leading Fenian wrongly suspected of being a British spy.[13] A decaying IRB, starved of American money, lived on scraps from the Gaelic cultural revival but its numbers and political influence had declined considerably. By the middle of the decade, however, a new force had emerged in the United States that sought to revitalize nationalism in part through radical action: the Irish National Alliance. The INA was, in practice, a front organization for the anti-Croninite wing of the Clan na Gael, intended to fill the void left by the decay of the Irish Party's grassroots machinery and to absorb the remnants of the IRB.[14] Its leader was the wealthy Roscommon-born Brooklyn building contractor, William Lyman, a man Gosselin described as "rich, sober, determined, and a fanatic in his hatred of England."[15] Lyman sunk $5,000 of his own fortune per year in a radical weekly, *The Irish Republic*, to promote this "new movement."[16] "England knows not mercy, and she must be treated accordingly," his paper reminded its readers. "Whether she be laid in ashes, or whether her Statesmen be slaughtered in the streets like pigs, a cheer must go up from Irishmen all over the globe."[17] Lyman's INA sought to make itself the transatlantic standard-bearer of an uncompromising new separatism. But its message did not resonate widely, and its growth proved sluggish.[18] Desperate to gain traction, Lyman encouraged bombings in Dublin, tried to launch a new bombing campaign in Britain with dynamite smuggled via Antwerp, and attempted to assassinate Joseph Chamberlain.[19] But these efforts were repeatedly frustrated by Gosselin's spies—on one occasion in spectacular fashion from the witness stand.[20] Unable to deliver, Lyman's reputation tanked. "We want no associates of spies," cried Irish New Yorkers when he was nominated as Grand Marshal of the city's St. Patrick's Day parade in 1897.[21] By mid-1899 Lyman was ousted, and Gosselin happily reported that the INA was "practically extinct" in Ireland.[22]

Hope remained that the centenary year of the 1798 rebellion would help bring about the national revival that Lyman had failed to achieve.[23] But the preparations for the commemoration events were marred by faction fighting on both the moderate nationalist and Fenian sides.[24] The planned visit to Ireland of an Irish American delegation, slated to number in the thousands, was derailed by the outbreak of the Spanish-American War. "[E]ager as we have been to participate," the American leaders explained, "we believe the seat of war is the proper destination for every Irish American who leaves the country."[25] Just as republican France had assisted the United Irishmen, they believed, so must the United States and Irish Americans help Cuba shake off the Spanish yoke.[26] The lacklustre '98 centenary events were generally felt by advanced nationalists to have been a disappointment.[27] "[T]he whole thing," as the business manager of the *Independent* newspaper and member of the IRB Supreme Council Fred Allan had worried, went little further than "speech-making, demonstrating & flag waving." "Still," he shrugged to John Devoy, "it may put a little national spirit in the young men here, & Lord knows they want it."[28]

There was no guarantee, however, that those young men would gravitate towards Allan and Devoy's end of the nationalist spectrum. Alarmingly for them, the parliamentarians seemed to have gained most from the centenary. William O'Brien MP laid claim to the United Irish brand through his United Irish League (UIL), launched in Westport, Co. Mayo, in January 1898. Although it emerged initially from a local agrarian crisis, within two years the UIL grew to become a national movement spearheading a new phase of land agitation. Its immediate goal was a speedier transition from landlordism to peasant proprietorship, in part through the breaking up of large grazier holdings in favor of small farmers. In the process it also aimed to revive and reunite the demoralized and fragmented Irish Party through pressure from below. The UIL quickly won the support of prominent Irish MPs and former Land Leaguers such as Michael Davitt and the leader of the anti-Parnellites, John Dillon.[29] It also, according to RIC reports, drew some support from the younger generation of advanced nationalists.[30] Similarly, the creation of new representative county and borough councils by the Local Government (Ireland) Act of 1898 threatened to draw the Fenian base into electoral politics.[31] Increasingly it seemed that there was no place for revolutionaries in nationalist politics and vanishingly little popular interest in secret societies and their organs. Several advanced nationalist journals, including Lyman's *Irish Republic*, folded in 1898 and 1899, and a takeover of the Dublin *Independent* resulted in the purging of the IRB element from its staff—Fred Allan with them.[32] At Dublin Castle it was observed that with "nothing but distrust and discord" in America and the distraction of local politics in Ireland, "the IRB is likely to die of inaction."[33]

Two interventions rescued Fenianism from that fate—at least for the moment. The first, ironically, was the success of Gosselin's Special Branch in bringing down William Lyman. In March 1899 his embarrassed lieutenants opened secret negotiations with John Devoy to discuss the potential reunification of the Clan na Gael.[34] Disagreement over whether P. H. Cronin had been a spy had been central to the decline and division of the Clan after his murder in 1889. Ten years later, with the anti-Croninite wing reeling from the realization that their own leader's inner circle had been fatally compromised by informers, the "distrust and discord" over the Cronin dispute seemed redundant. Both wings were ready to bury the hatchet; and they buried it in William Lyman. At an emergency convention at Buffalo in May 1899, Lyman was expelled by his followers for spending recklessly and allowing the "secrets of the organization" to be "disclosed to the British Government."[35] The way for unity was now clear. On 4 September 1899—four days before Chamberlain's ultimatum to Kruger—the negotiations between the two wings concluded in Philadelphia. A circular announcing the establishment of a provisional united executive and the end of the decade-long feud was issued to the membership of the newly consolidated Clan na Gael.[36] This came, as a subsequent circular added, "not a moment too soon."[37] Because the second intervention that rescued Fenianism from irrelevance was the South African War.

* * *

Passions in Ireland were running high for most of the war's opening year. Veterans of the Irish revolution would later point to the great impression this period left on them as younger men, and the galvanizing effect that Boer sympathies could have on nationalist feeling. Joseph V. Law-less, for example, claimed that the war "excited the interest of Irishmen all over the world" and "was something to awaken more than a passive sympathy in Ireland."[38] Frank Henderson said that in Dublin "feeling was very pro-Boer."[39] The same was true in London according to Hugh Hehir, where "the Irish exiles were strongly pro-Boer and I fully shared that feeling."[40] Seumas Robinson, whose family had "become convinced that the British Empire was invincible," described the excitement provoked by news of British defeats in the first months of the war: "Heavens! what thrills we got out of that great struggle. Bonfires in the streets on the news of a Boer victory, complete disbelief in Boer reverses!"[41] Mary Clancy told how her husband George "met a group of Trinity College students on O'Connell Bridge, Dublin, shouting and waving a Union Jack in celebration of a Boer defeat." George "rushed the crowd," wrestled the flag from them and threw it into the river, escaping "bruised but victorious."[42]

Students of Trinity College—a unionist stronghold—were involved in other skirmishes with Boer sympathizers during the opening months of the war. At the *Independent* offices on Trinity Street, near College Green, a nightly magic lantern display was projected on the opposing façade. Large crowds gathered to see snippets of war news and to cheer (or jeer) pictures of leading figures from the Boer and British sides. On the evening of 19 October, mobilized by a loyalist placard titled "Wake up Trinity!", a group of about one hundred students made a sortie to heckle the largely pro-Boer crowd at the lantern display and sing loyalist songs. The groups exchanged insults, and the *Independent* staff taunted the students with messages on the lantern display such as "Have you awakened yet, Trinity?" The confrontation shortly devolved into what Dublin Metropolitan Police (DMP) Commissioner J. J. Jones described as "a regular pandemonium." Fist fights broke out, windows were smashed, soldiers in the area were "hustled" by the pro-Boer crowd, and the students were chased back to the college where they carried on the fight by hurling objects from their windows. When similar scenes were repeated the following night, police demanded the *Independent* cease the nightly magic lantern displays owing to the "probability of serious rioting," and the Dean of Trinity College was asked to forbid students demonstrating from its windows.[43]

An even greater provocation to civil unrest, it turned out, was Joseph Chamberlain's visit to Dublin in December to accept an honorary doctorate from Trinity College. A pro-Boer demonstration scheduled to be held at Beresford Place to coincide with the visit was proclaimed by the DMP. In defiance, the protestors went ahead with the meeting but found Beresford Place cordoned off by over one hundred police officers who seized the brake (an open horse-drawn wagon) carrying the organizers and led it to Store Street police station. This confrontation only excited the large crowd. When the socialist republican James Connolly, one of the brake's passengers, grasped the reins and escaped, the demonstration became a haphazard procession pursued by police to O'Connell Street and then south of the river to College Green. Transvaal flags and green banners were waved outside Trinity College, while nationalist songs and "We'll hang Joe Chamberlain up a sour apple tree" were sung by the crowd. When the procession made its way down Dame Street to Dublin Castle, mounted police arrived to reinforce those on foot. Although Connolly's wagonette broke through the cordon again, the horses split the crowd. Some police were injured attempting to seize the flags, while pro-Boers hurled mud and "ginger beer bottles."[44] Several arrests were made—including Connolly's. With their audience finally dispersed, the remaining organizers retreated indoors to deliver their speeches.[45]

Feeling in the country was nevertheless more complex than these dramatic scenes in Dublin would suggest. A future Trinity College graduate and legal adviser to revolutionary Sinn Féin, Kevin O'Shiel, recalled the response to the war during his childhood in Omagh, County Tyrone. Nationalist opinion couldn't be reduced to a simple "bigoted or intensely-felt pro-Boerism" and was, he claimed, less pronounced than the sympathy expressed for Catholic Belgium during the Great War. Part of the reason for this was that the "upper stratum" of Catholics, including the clergy, had heard that the Boers "were nearly worse than the Orangemen" in their anti-Catholicism. Local nationalist leaders supported charitable funds for British and Irish soldiers, widows and orphans "side by side with a vague pro-Boerism, generally ventilated in varying degrees of emphasis, according to the nature and object of the speakers on political platforms." He recalled "hundreds of Catholics and Nationalist 'townees' and agricultural labourers," classes in which Fenianism and agrarian radicalism were well-represented, "taking the

Figure 1.1. Pro-Boer protest at College Green, Dublin, on 17 Dec 1899, *Le Petit Journal: supplement illustré*, 31 Dec 1899, Bibliothèque nationale de France.

Queen's 'shilling' and enlisting." But when cheered by loyalist crowds on their way to the front, these were known to respond with their own "loud cheers for 'Krudger an' the Boers.'"[46]

Several instances of Irish militia companies publicly cheering for the Boers in defiance of their commanding officers were reported during the first year of the war. When marching out of the barrack gate in January 1900 to relieve a regular regiment at Aldershot which had been dispatched to South Africa, the Wexford militia reportedly played the rebel song "The Boys of Wexford" and gave "lusty 'Cheers for the Boers' and 'Hurrahs for Kruger.'"[47] The North Cork Militia at Kanturk and the Louth militia put on similar displays within weeks of this event.[48] On 25 July a fracas broke out between the Cork Militia and the Dorset Regiment billeted together at the fort on Spike Island in Cork Harbour. In the canteen the Cork men gave "cheers for Kruger and the Boers" and sang "God Save Ireland" and "The Boys of Wexford." The Dorsets shot back with lusty renditions of "God Save the Queen" and "Rule Britannia." The singing provoked a brawl, culminating in an attack on the Dorsets' regimental quarters. Windows were broken and a sergeant major of the Dorsets was seriously injured after receiving a brick to his head. Order was reportedly only restored when the Dorsets were ordered by their non-commissioned officers to fix bayonets.[49] When in March 1900 the Clare Militia marched through Milltown Malbay "carrying a green flag and shouting and cheering for Kruger" at the alleged instigation of local IRB men, Major Gosselin was informed. "[N]otwithstanding their shouting and cheering," he responded, "[I] would chance leading them against the Boers. [I] will, however, inform the Adjutant, who is [my] son."[50]

Gosselin may have been right to smirk at these stories. Sporadic displays of defiance from within the ranks paled beside the considerable Irish contribution to the British war effort. Between thirty and fifty thousand Irish men are estimated to have fought on the imperial side during the South African War, the largest ever mobilization of Irish troops until the Great War.[51] Volunteers of Irish birth and descent were also among the contingents dispatched from Canada, Australia, and New Zealand. A disproportionate number of the war's leading British generals were of Irish birth or origin, including Roberts, Kitchener, Rudolph Lambart, Francis Clery, Fitzroy Hart, Thomas Kelly-Kenny, and the director of British Military Intelligence, John C. Ardagh.[52] The 2nd Royal Dublin Fusiliers were given the honor of leading the relief column into Ladysmith on 3 March 1900 in recognition of their bravery during the Tugela campaign. That same month Queen Victoria announced that Irish soldiers would be permitted to wear the shamrock on St. Patrick's Day. The "shamrock concession," it was hoped, might go some little way toward alleviating anti-war sentiment and encouraging further recruitment in Ireland. Service in an imperial war did not necessarily equal a wholehearted endorsement of its aims or methods. Doubtless many volunteers believed the empire to be a force for good and enlisted out of a sincerely felt sense of duty; others may have thought rather more of adventure than politics. Professional soldiers' first loyalties may have been to the job and to their comrades in arms. Whatever songs were sung on the march to the boat, the experience of war could change a soldier's tune in either direction. Take Colonel Maurice Moore, scion of a Galway Catholic landowning family and brother of the novelist George, for example. He was honored with a C. B. (Companion of the Order of Bath) for his service as a Connaught Ranger during the war. What his superiors did not know was that he had all the while been leaking secrets to the prominent British anti-war journalist W. T. Stead. Moore had become disgusted by Kitchener's dirty tactics during the second phase of the war, and quietly risked court martial and execution in his efforts to expose the horrors of scorched earth and concentration camps to the British public.[53] By the same token, some of the empire's loudest critics during the South African War—including some who fought on the Boer side—emerged as its staunchest defenders during the Great War.

Whatever the private feelings of Irish soldiers, there was no escaping the fact that tens of thousands of them were in South Africa fighting against the Boers. This reality was deeply aggravating to advanced nationalists. At a secret IRB meeting in Longford in January 1900, speakers attempted to explain away this troublesome incongruity by portraying Irish soldiers as dupes. It was economic "necessity," the attendees heard, that "drove even worthless Irishmen into the English army." Once these alleged victims of British misgovernment reached South Africa, it was claimed, they were used as cannon fodder by their British masters and could reliably be found in the most dangerous positions on the frontline.[54] In October 1899 thousands of green placards were posted throughout the country carrying the warning that "ENLISTING IN THE ENGLISH ARMY IS TREASON TO IRELAND." The placard advised that recruiting sergeants should be watched and followed to prevent them from "trying to entrap thoughtless Irish Boys." "Remember Ninety-Eight," it entreated. "Remember the Penal Laws. Remember the Famine."[55] Police were ordered to tear down the posters wherever they were seen.[56] A note at the foot of each bill announced that they had been printed "by order of the Irish Transvaal Committee."

* * *

The Transvaal Committee was established in Dublin on 30 September 1899 to oppose enlistment and coordinate the pro-Boer movement in Ireland. It was the most visible token of the renewed sense of purpose that the war bestowed on advanced nationalists. "They are," Commissioner Jones complained of its members, "Fenians of the worst type."[57] In fact they were a mix of leading IRB men such as John O'Leary, ex-INA figures like James Barrett of Manchester, some more advanced Irish Party MPs including William Redmond, and a few hangers-on: notably W. B. Yeats.[58] The Committee was behind a mass pro-Boer demonstration at Beresford Place on 1 October. Thousands were in attendance. Michael Davitt MP delivered a forceful oration, arguing that the *uitlander* question was merely a pretense for a gold-grab by capitalists, and expressing his hope that Britain would be defeated.[59] This was not the first pro-Boer demonstration Dublin had seen—as early as 27 August the Irish Socialist Republican Party held a rally to oppose the prospect of war. Its leader, James Connolly—though not a formal member of the Transvaal Committee—was an important ally and a frequent presence on the platform at Dublin's anti-war demonstrations.[60]

Of the Committee's permanent organizers, preeminent were its secretary, Arthur Griffith, and treasurer, Maud Gonne. Griffith, as political editor of Ireland's only remaining Fenian organ—the *United Irishman*—and having just returned from a sojourn in South Africa where he met the men who would organize the first Irish Transvaal Brigade, found himself in a position of some authority in the creation of pro-Boer opinion.[61] Gonne's wealth, energy, and formidable talent

Figure 1.2. Maud Gonne, 1900. J. E. Purdy & Co, Boston, Library of Congress.

as an agitator, meanwhile, placed her at the center of the transatlantic Irish pro-Boer movement.

Though best known today as the object of Yeatsian onanism—literary and otherwise—Gonne was, during the South African War, a far more important figure in her own right than her bespectacled devotee. She was the daughter of an English Colonel stationed in Ireland, heiress to a London merchant fortune, and a convert to radical Irish national-ism in adulthood. In 1887, aged nineteen, she commenced a long affair with the prominent right-wing French revanchist, Lucien Millevoye.[62] Through the 1890s her reputation for beauty and theatrical talent was overtaken by the notoriety of her anti-British agitation—funded in part by her substantial inheritance. She was suspected to have paid the passage of Irish dynamiters to the United States, and to have urged the bombing of vessels carrying troops to South Africa.[63]

Besides her contributions to conventional Fenianism, Gonne's ability to enlist women to the radical cause was particularly concerning to the authorities. When the McGillicuddy sisters of Ballina were found to be distributing seditious leaflets and collecting funds for the Transvaal Com-mittee at the suggestion of Maud Gonne, the matter reached the highest level of Irish government. Their father's position as an Inland Revenue of-ficer was used to pressure him to "restrain his daughters"—who had by De-cember 1899 raised all of eight pounds. Under-Secretary Sir David Harrel informed the Secretary of Inland Revenue that the Lord Lieutenant himself considered it "most unseemly" that the family members of an employee of the government should be engaged in such activities. McGillicuddy was promptly warned that unless he kept his daughters under control "steps will have to be taken for removing him from Ireland."[64] He did as he was asked.

In April 1900 Gonne was at the fore of the opposition to the visit of Queen Victoria—the first to Ireland since 1861.[65] Gonne's controversial "Famine Queen" article was one of a series of inflammatory pieces ap-pearing in the *United Irishman* that resulted in its temporary suppres-sion by the government. In the piece she excoriated moderate nationalist leaders who claimed the Queen's visit was "not political." She insisted that Victoria had really come to Ireland "to ask for soldiers" to crush the Boers. With characteristic belligerence, Gonne took aim squarely at the Queen herself:

And in truth, for Victoria, in the decrepitude of her eighty-one years, to have decided after an absence of half-a-century to revisit the country she hates and whose inhabitants are the victims of the criminal policy of her reign, the survivors of sixty years of organised famine, the political necessity must have been terribly strong; for after all she is a woman, and however vile and selfish and pitiless her soul may be, she must sometimes tremble as death approaches when she thinks of the countless Irish mothers who, sheltering under the cloudy Irish sky, watching their starving little ones, have cursed her before they died.[66]

Inghinidhe na hÉireann (Daughters of Ireland) emerged in part from Gonne's opposition to the "children's picnic" hosted by Victoria at the Phoenix Park. Initially comprising nationalist women members of the Celtic Literary Society, the Inghinidhe, with Gonne as president, organized a successful counter-picnic with an anti-enlistment theme. The Inghinidhe—or Cumann na mBan (the Women's Council) from 1914—became an important force in advanced nationalist politics and attracted the membership of the most influential women activists and intellectuals of the Gaelic revival and the revolutionary period.[67] Nevertheless, despite the determined opposition of Gonne, Griffith and their allies, the Queen's visit was, by any measure, a success, and her public appearances drew huge crowds. Dublin Corporation resolved to present a loyal address to Victoria—a process in which Fred Allan, in his capacity as Lord Mayor Thomas Pile's private secretary, was intimately involved. Remarkably, Allan was simultaneously secretary of the IRB's Supreme Council. In a demoralizing defeat for the hardliners, a slim majority of the Supreme Council voted against censuring him for his professional responsibilities.[68]

Although her romantic affair with Millevoye ended in 1900, Gonne remained the predominant figure in the Parisian nexus between French nationalists and Irish radicals. Until October 1898 she had run a radical journal, *L'Irlande Libre*; in November 1899, together with the Irish Australian adventurer Arthur Lynch, she founded the Boer Franco-Irish Committee to lobby for various forms of French intervention in the war.[69] Paris, long a hub for Irish revolutionists in exile, was the site of an important Fenian conference in the summer of 1900, about which little is known.[70] By the end of that year, at Gosselin's encouragement, British military intelligence had worked a spy named De Brandt into "an excellent position" to provide "valuable information respecting the Paris gang of Irish Nationalists."[71] Gonne was chief amongst them. It was discovered that her pet project was, in imitation of Theobald Wolfe Tone, to secure backing for a French invasion of Ireland in the event of an Irish wartime uprising. A secret memo by Director of Military Intelligence John C. Ardagh warned that "although sensible and moderate people in

Figure 1.3. Michael Davitt, 1895. Charlie Farr, Maryborough, State Library of Victoria.

France are unlikely to place a very high value on the assurances of Miss Maud Gonne," nevertheless he felt that such a scheme was "rather more probable now in the event of war, than it has been at any time during the last forty years."[72] He was not wrong. French military intelligence agents were active in Ireland during the South African War, compiling reconnaissance reports on the strength of various nationalist organizations and surveying landing zones for an invasion force. Irish republicans also provided the French military with a ten-page dossier on how best to coordinate with Irish rebels in the event of an invasion.[73]

As British opinion backed the Dreyfusards in criticism of the French authorities' handling of that notorious affair, advanced Irish nationalists reflexively rallied behind the French government. Even Michael Davitt—known for his support for Zionism and his outspoken criticism of anti-Semitism in Russia and the Limerick Pogrom of 1904—preferred to defend France from Anglo-American aspersions than to sympathize with Dreyfus.[74] The chimera of a special relationship with a great continental republican patron was too valuable to Irish revolutionary mythology to jeopardize. Gonne's Fenian circle had little in common with the French right they attempted to cultivate— besides a penchant for Anglophobia and anti-Semitism. Gonne had long shared the anti-Semitism espoused in Millevoye's *La Patrie*. The belief held by many pro-Boers in Ireland, France and elsewhere, that the South African War was the result of a conspiracy of capitalists, miners, and financiers commonly carried an anti-Semitic corollary— sometimes quiet, sometimes emphatic. Arthur Griffith readily indulged such polemic in the columns of the *United Irishman*, both from himself and, more commonly, from contributors.[75] Most virulent of these was the ex-Irish Party MP and notorious crank, Frank Hugh O'Donnell, whose correspondence from London contained poisonous tirades against the "swarming Jews of Johannesburg."[76]

O'Donnell—probably through the influence of his friend Mark Ryan, the chief physical force organizer in London—had by 1900 secured the position of IRB liaison to Dr. Willem Johannes Leyds, the Boers' European representative headquartered at Brussels. This made O'Donnell the conduit for Boer money intended to assist the IRB in undermining the British war effort and destabilizing Ireland. Gonne, who probably desired the role for herself, was furious at this development. How, she protested, could a loose cannon like O'Donnell represent the IRB when he was not even a member? O'Donnell shot back with accusations that Gonne could not be trusted: "If she is not a spy she is almost one and her bragging is more dangerous than treachery itself."[77] This was rich coming from O'Donnell, whose reputation as a wrecker had several times made him the subject of similar suspicions.[78] When O'Donnell issued a series of pamphlets attacking Theobald Wolfe Tone—and Gonne's attempts to ape Tone's Parisian plotting—Griffith apologized to readers of the *United Irishman* "for having allowed Mr. O'Donnell to write in the columns" and dropped him as a contributor.[79] This rift ensured the prospect of putting Leyds's patronage of the IRB to use was sorely diminished. O'Donnell was subsequently accused of having pocketed the £12,000 he received.[80]

Griffith spent a good deal of energy defending Gonne's reputation. Michael Davitt, for example, had long distrusted her, and he repeated his suspicions in November 1899.[81] This position earned him some hostile treatment in the columns of the *United Irishman*—even though Davitt was perhaps the most influential of all the Irish pro-Boers.[82] When Ramsey Colles, the editor of the *Irish Figaro*, ridiculed Gonne for claiming that Irish soldiers were shipped to South Africa with "manacled wrists," an incensed Griffith showed up at his office and physically assaulted him. Griffith earned a two-week prison sentence for the attack.[83] Colles then went further and accused Gonne of being in receipt of a large government pension. Gonne brought criminal libel charges against him in retaliation. At the police court hearing, Colles's attorney brought up Gonne's "shocking" record of attacking the Queen, soldiers, and the police—which only served to convince the presiding justice that a libel must have occurred. "Nothing could be imagined more mean," he remarked, "than for a person to be abusing the Government as she had been, and at the same time to be taking a pension from it."[84] Colles retracted the claim and apologized before the case went to trial.[85]

Gonne was vindicated, but repeated accusations of spying had a habit of sticking. For an aspiring Fenian leader whose gender, antecedents, and overzealousness were already off-putting to many of her contemporaries, the charge of "informer" was damaging. It was also unfounded. From January 1900 the customs authorities were ordered by the Special Branch to search Gonne's luggage whenever she entered the United Kingdom.[86] Her anti-enlistment campaign was so bothersome to Dublin Castle that by November 1900 Under-Secretary Sir David Harrel began pestering the Home Office to do more to contain her. He asked Gosselin to have agents watch her more closely in Paris. "I had in former days an agency in Paris and had a lady in my employment who lived in a 'flat' directly under Miss Gonne and was well up in all her doings," Gosselin replied, "but in those days she was not looked on seriously, and 'My Lady' has been lost sight of for years."[87]

Although he was unable to help, and the Foreign Office and the CID were unwilling, Gosselin assured Harrel that De Brandt, Sir John Ardagh's military intelligence agent in Paris, was making good progress with Gonne. Meanwhile Sir Kenelm Digby, Under-Secretary at the Home Office, acceded to Harrel's request to explore the feasibility of bringing Gonne before a jury on charges of sedition.[88] That this course was not pursued was probably prudent. Handing Gonne a shot at martyrdom in a British courtroom may only have lifted the pall of suspicion that helped to both stymie her ambition and divide her friends from her opponents within the movement.

It is difficult to assess the success of Gonne and her allies' anti-enlistment campaign. Certainly, it had little or no material effect on the war's outcome. Britain's superiority in numbers over the Boers was overwhelming, and the colonies produced a surplus of volunteers. Any scattered victories over the recruiting sergeant in Ireland were chiefly symbolic. That is not to say they were insignificant—advanced nationalism was sustained by miniature triumphs and its opponents were acutely sensitive to the small shifts in momentum they could produce. The campaign certainly troubled the authorities. At the turn of 1900 General Hugh McCalmont complained that in the Cork district, owing to a "strong undercurrent of disloyal feeling" there had been a "serious falling off in the recruiting for the line and militia."[89] The police were concerned at rumors that large numbers of young men were emigrating to America for fear of being conscripted. They also received reports that Boer agents were active in Ireland and secretly recruiting for the enemy.[90] These rumors were just that. What was known for certain was that the Transvaal Committee was openly carrying out its own recruitment drive.

The possibility of forming an ambulance corps to travel to the front under the banner of the red cross was first proposed at a Transvaal Committee meeting on 14 October 1899. One month later the project was officially launched, and a subscription fund opened. The ambulance corps was to attach itself to the Irish Brigade fighting on the Boer side. The fund attracted subscriptions from Michael Davitt, several MPs, and prominent Fenians in Britain and Ireland. Despite a promising start, the project failed to generate much interest. The fund stalled at around £300 and attracted just twenty-three volunteers. Remarkably, in contrast with the later all-male Irish American corps, six of these were women.[91] The project was ultimately abandoned, and no ambulance corps ever left Ireland. But the money raised was quietly used to pay the passage of individual volunteers to South Africa. Dublin Castle intelligence reports noted that "small batches of Irishmen" had been sent to Paris, where Gonne's Boer Franco-Irish Committee arranged for them to travel to South Africa via Antwerp or Marseilles as "ordinary emigrants."[92] We know at least one of the listed volunteers for the ambulance corps made it to South Africa in this fashion—Dr. Michael S. Walsh of Swords. He found the Irish Brigade near Pretoria in early March 1900 and remained treating the wounded until later that year. "The war is an awful game," he wrote home. "[I]f the English people could only see & hear the wounded the wars would be few."[93] Another small party of Irishmen found "Major" John MacBride the same month and handed him a letter of introduction from Anna Johnston of Belfast, former coeditor of the *Shan Van Vocht*. "We could send a large number—hundreds in fact—if the means to do so were forthcoming," she explained. "But you know how it is with us."[94]

* * *

Advanced nationalists had the most to gain from harnessing popular pro-Boer sentiment in Ireland. The spectacle of the Boers taking up arms to resist oppression and the British reversals of "Black Week" undoubtedly assisted in "resurrecting," as M. J. Kelly has noted, "the moth-balled adage 'England's difficulty, Ireland's opportunity.'"[95] Frustratingly for agitators like Gonne, however, it did not necessarily follow that organized Fenianism would rise Phoenix-like from the ashes of the past decade. Two significant obstacles stood in the way. One was the burden of disorganization and decay inherited by the splits and failures of the 1890s. Efforts to harness the radical revival sparked by the outbreak of the war and the reunification of the Clan na Gael simply could not keep pace with developments in South Africa. Attempts to reorganize the IRB and the remnants of the INA along American lines were still ongoing when Pretoria fell in June 1900.[96] County Inspector Waters—who had been deeply concerned during the opening months of the war—was by July 1900 satisfied that Fenian leaders had still "failed utterly to establish any general secret organisation" in Ireland. The movement in the southern counties, he informed the Special Branch, was "absolutely disorganised and impotent."[97]

The other obstacle was that Irish nationalist pro-Boer feeling had no shortage of outlets that were safer and more appealing than those offered by secret societies. The new system of local government was one. On 7 September 1899 Limerick Borough Council passed a resolution expressing "sympathy with the plucky Boer farmers in their fight against the English" and "a hope that if war takes place it may end in another Majuba Hill."[98] This resolution was circulated to local councils throughout Ireland and similar expressions of sympathy were adopted by at least thirty-three such bodies—including Cork, Mayo, and Kildare County Councils.[99] The Transvaal Committee's attempted foray into this sphere went poorly. Its members agitated for the adoption of a pro-Boer resolution by Dublin Corporation, and managed to secure the support of Lord Mayor Daniel Tallon, who rose to speak in the resolution's defense at City Hall. "The present war was undertaken on the instigation of Mr Chamberlain," he told the chamber, "and the capitalists who are greedily longing to grab the gold mines." Although doubtless sympathetic to this interpretation, the corporation's Labour members absented themselves from the vote so as not to upset their allies in Britain. A group of moderate nationalists did the same. Without a quorum, the motion collapsed—to the delight of the unionist members and to the outrage of the nationalist crowd in the gallery who heckled the proceedings with cheers for Maud Gonne, Kruger, and the Boers.[100]

The constitutional nationalist movement was enjoying a revival of its own and was able to absorb much of the ardor that Fenians sought to capture. Irish Party MPs had been vocal critics of the first Anglo-Boer War of 1880–81, as well as the Jameson Raid of 1895–6. With the Liberal Party divided over the South African War, the Irish nationalists became the main voice of opposition to the war in Parliament.[101] None protested more spectacularly than Michael Davitt. On 25 October 1899 he rose in the House of Commons to condemn the war for the third time—but on this occasion announced the resignation of his seat "as a personal and political protest against a war which I believed to be the greatest infamy of the nineteenth century." Accepting that the Irish

Figure 1.4. "Outflanked, be Jabers!" *Punch*, 14 Mar 1900.

Party's opposition to the war could delay the granting of Home Rule, he declared he "would not purchase the liberty of Ireland at the base price of voting against liberty in South Africa."[102]

In February 1900 Davitt traveled to South Africa as a war correspondent. He spent just under two months there, meeting Boer leaders and the Irish commandos, attending the last session of the Volksraad and gathering material for a book on the war.[103] His correspondence from the front was a central feature of the pro-Boer coverage of newspapers such as the *Freeman's Journal* in Dublin, the *Irish World* in New York, the *Melbourne Advocate*, and occasionally Millevoye's *La Patrie*. Though an ex-IRB man with lingering revolutionary sympathies, Davitt had been estranged from the transatlantic Fenian leadership since the Parnell split. By 1899 he had thrown his support, and his formidable experience of coordinating "land wars," behind the United Irish League. It was the UIL that enjoyed the dividend of Davitt's pro-Boer advocacy. In some quarters little distinction was drawn between support for the UIL and for the Boers. When Patrick Ford—another ex-Fenian turned pragmatic moderate—opened his New York *Irish World*'s "UIL Fund" to North American subscriptions, many donations came with explicitly pro-Boer sentiments attached. Mary Hennessy of New Orleans sent her three dollars "hoping England's difficulties will increase, and hoping God may direct the Boer bullets."[104] Patrick Kelleher of Butte asked that his two dollar subscription be used to "buy bullets for the Boers or dynamite to blow up the English House of Lords."[105] Ford had previously insisted that the Boers needed men and Ireland needed money, but after months of noncompliance he caved to the will of his subscribers and opened a dedicated Boer Fund.[106]

By the turn of 1900 the United Irish League had over 400 branches, more than 60,000 members, and was still growing.[107] The UIL's success was the catalyst for the reunification of the Irish Parliamentary Party. The leaders of the rival factions, each concerned at the League's potential to absorb or eclipse their following, recognized the necessity of bringing it under the Party's control.[108] John Redmond, leader of the small Parnellite grouping, was chosen in compromise as the united Party's president. Redmond's first speech in parliament in this new position was an attack on the South African War. Pro-Boer resolutions were frequently passed at local UIL meetings.[109] But the focus of the united Party and its new national grassroots organization was to be the land question. In recognition of this commitment, when Michael Davitt's vacated seat in the UIL heartland of South Mayo came to be filled, the Parliamentary Party gave the UIL the freedom to select their own candidate to contest the by-election.[110] They chose the League's secretary John O'Donnell, then in prison for his role in land agitation. During electoral contests in previous "land wars," a candidate like O'Donnell might have safely counted on Fenian support. But the transatlantic Fenian leadership was ambivalent about the UIL, and the ugly spectacle of the Parnell split had turned many against cooperation with parliamentarians. The IRB and the Transvaal Committee saw the election as an opportunity to embarrass the British government and to score a victory for advanced nationalism by capitalizing on pro-Boer feeling.

As early as January they had decided that Major John MacBride of the Irish Brigade—though still fighting on the Boer side in South Africa—ought to assume the vacancy. Because MacBride would naturally be ineligible to take his seat if elected, the police suspected his candidacy was only being used as cover for IRB meetings. But the Fenians took the contest seriously. MacBride—a native of Westport whose exploits with the Irish Brigade had been lionized in the nationalist press for months—was hardly a weak candidate. When Arthur Griffith learned that the UIL intended to contest the election, he tried to persuade John O'Donnell to let MacBride have it first, then take it for free after MacBride was declared ineligible. But William O'Brien, convinced the contest was pivotal to the UIL's future and worried that his Healyite rivals had their eye on the seat, was unwilling to take the risk.[111] At a mass meeting at Ballyhaunis in February, he told his followers that it was no insult to MacBride or the Boers to support O'Donnell and the League—"the only organisation at the present moment giving Dublin Castle one hour's uneasiness"—in a case such as this:

> Cheers for the Boers are all very well. Yes: but work for Ireland is still better . . . Why we would be the derision of the world if we were to show ourselves such a race of idiots as to be ready to ruin the Irish cause in order to make a demonstration that would be as useless to the Boers as if we spent our last shilling in drinking their health (loud cheers and laughter). They are engaged much more sensibly in fighting for their own cause, as we should be engaged in fighting for ours (cheers).[112]

It was pointed out that, unlike MacBride, John O'Donnell could (once he was out of jail) go to Westminster and tell the British government "to their faces" that the people of South Mayo backed the Boers.[113] The by-election was to be a harsh reminder of the subordinate position advanced nationalists held in Irish politics. Even had they not been so deftly outmaneuvered on the Boer question, they could not have competed with the machinery of a thriving UIL, the momentum of a reunited constitutional movement, and a candidate endorsed by Davitt, O'Brien, and the clergy. After a bitter campaign, during which the Fenian activists John Daly and James Egan were on one occasion stoned by a crowd of UIL supporters, O'Donnell beat MacBride easily by 2,401 votes to 427.[114]

The affair cemented the animosity between Fenian leaders and the UIL.[115] Unwilling to join the moderates and—as the Queen's visit and the Mayo by-election proved—unable to beat them, the Fenians had

backed themselves into a corner. Their hopes were pinned on cooperation with allies outside of Ireland. Frank Hugh O'Donnell may have
soured the partnership with W. J. Leyds, but ongoing negotiations
with agents of France and Russia kept alive the belief that those powers
would intervene in the war, or at least provide direct support for Irish
revolutionary activity. The United States—where pro-Boer feeling
was strong, the Clan na Gael was united, and a presidential election
was imminent—was also central to Fenian calculations. "Do the children of the 'Mother of Exiles' realise," Maud Gonne asked via the
columns of the *United Irishman* in January, "that the hour of destiny,
which, if wasted, can never be recalled, is perhaps passing?"[116] Fenians,
if they were to galvanize the transatlantic movement and prove their
use to Britain's rivals, urgently needed to strike a blow that would make
their presence felt. Not for the first time, Canada would be their target.

"Physical Farce"

Transatlantic Fenianism and the Dynamiting of the Welland Canal

In the early evening of Saturday 21 April 1900, sixteen-year-old Euphemia Constable crossed the bridge over the Welland Canal near Lock 24 at Thorold, Ontario. She was on her way to visit a friend. As she walked, she spotted two men at either side of the lock, each lowering a valise along its hinges using a length of rope. One of the men cried "Hurry on, Jack, or it'll go off!" and ran in the direction of the Niagara Falls Road. The other scrambled to drop his valise in place before pursuing his friend. Two explosions followed, the first of which knocked Euphemia to the ground, unconscious. The blasts, caused by dynamite inside the valises, sent water into the air, smashed nearby windows and damaged the canal banks and the lock hinges. But the lock remained intact. Engineers later noted that had the explosives been placed "into the gate pits instead of into the chain holes," the lock would not have held. Twelve million cubic feet of water would have been suddenly unleashed downstream, washing away a Grand Trunk Railway station and causing loss of life and property in the town of Merritton.[1] The lock's destruction would also have paralyzed Canada's inland shipping network; the Welland Canal served as the vital link between Lakes Erie and Ontario, carrying over five million tons of freight annually.[2]

The two men hurried eastward on foot towards Niagara Falls. They were overtaken by a cab carrying the Mayor of Thorold and some witnesses to the explosions, rushing to inform the police. By the time the two men arrived at Niagara Falls that night, they had been identified as suspects and were quickly arrested. The first man was revealed to be John Walsh of Dublin, described variously as a "vacant face[d]" and "soft fellow, very unlike a conspirator."[3] The second was the stout, hard-drinking ex-boxer John Nolan, a notorious operative in Dublin's Irish Republican Brotherhood. A third man who had been seen several times in their company was arrested at a local hotel. He gave his name as Karl Dallman, a fifty-year-old English-born Methodist living in Buffalo who had met the other two men while on a drinking "spree." He claimed to know nothing of any dynamite attack.[4] He was not believed. Police suspected—correctly—that he was the ringleader of the plot. It would eventually be discovered that Dallman's true identity was Luke Dillon of Philadelphia—a former president of the Clan na Gael executive who had once planted a bomb in the chamber of the House of Commons at Westminster. But what were these men doing in southern Ontario? Years later, Luke Dillon explained that their intention was to assist the Boers:

> The object of the dynamiting was not so much to inflict injury to lives or property but to create the condition by which the Canadian Government would be compelled to keep its troops at home to protect the country rather than send them abroad to help the English fight the Boers.[5]

The dynamiting of the Welland Canal was the latest in a long series of attempts by Irish revolutionaries in the United States to strike at Britain through Canada, a place they had for generations considered the empire's soft underbelly.[6] Until the bombs exploded, Dillon, Nolan, and Walsh were able to carry their plot through to its unsuccessful completion without detection by British secret police. Despite the warning attached to the leaked Clan na Gael circular of November 1899 in the *Times*—that Fenians could not "trust the veil of secrecy upon which they rely"—it seems Major Nicholas Gosselin and his colleagues were none the wiser.[7] The toppling of William Lyman had inadvertently paved the way for a new leadership, uncompromised by spies and informers, to assume control of a freshly unified Clan na Gael just as war erupted in South Africa. "I have been unable to get inside the new Executive," Gosselin admitted in June 1900, "and I have failed to obtain an exact knowledge of what the Executive's aims are." One of the few things he could be sure about was that "the Welland Canal fiasco was their doing."[8]

And a fiasco it was. The Welland Canal plot was intended to be the means through which the revived physical force movement would "make itself felt."[9] It was a transatlantic affair, conceived, funded, and

Figure 2.1. Welland Canal dynamiters. Information wanted poster, April 1900, CBS 22397/S, National Archives of Ireland.

executed jointly by the Clan na Gael and the IRB, intended as a message to London and to Ottawa that distance could not preserve the empire from the violence it had unleashed in South Africa. They dispatched two of their most experienced dynamiters, Luke Dillon and John Nolan, to do the work. But the plan backfired badly. The humiliating failure and capture of hardened operators severely demoralized the transatlantic revolutionary movement. A lingering suspicion that Luke Dillon must have been betrayed would haunt Philadelphia Fenian circles for years. The South African War had made revolution seem a possibility to radical Irish nationalists. But the fiasco at the Welland Canal only appeared to confirm pre-war suspicions that Fenianism was moribund after all, and that the Clan na Gael and IRB were indeed the "physical farce" party their critics alleged.[10]

* * *

Since at least the War of 1812, the idea that "Ireland will be rescued from British bondage on the plains of Canada" held some purchase in the imaginations of Irish nationalists in the United States. To generations of aspiring revolutionaries, crossing the British North American border looked simpler than crossing the Atlantic. Whether by simply creating a distraction or, better yet, sparking an Anglo-American war, they hoped to provide insurrectionists back home an opportunity to strike for freedom. At the very least, harassing Canada could help Irish American revolutionary leaders show their followers (on whose subscriptions they depended) that they meant business. The Welland Canal repeatedly surfaced as a potential target for these raiders and saboteurs. Following the failed rebellion of 1837, the Canadas were subjected to cross-border raids for several years by Patriot exiles and their American sympathizers.[11] On 9 September 1841 an explosion caused by gunpowder damaged the locks at Allanburg, just south of Thorold. The blast was believed to be the work of the infamous Benjamin Lett, a Kilkenny-born guerrilla whose actions earned him the epithet "the Rob Roy of Upper Canada."[12] By 1848, a different set of revolutionaries operating south of the border set their sights on Canada East. The Irish Republican Union, based in New York City, seriously contemplated a filibuster into the colony in the hopes of assisting a rebellion of the Young Irelanders back home. Despite offers of assistance from a radical

Irish nationalist fringe within the colony, nothing came of their bluster besides a few spiked cannon in Quebec City.[13]

1848—the year of revolution—also, fittingly, saw the birth of Luke Dillon in Leeds, England. His parents appear to have left Sligo during the Famine. Six years later Luke and his family moved to Trenton, New Jersey, before eventually settling in Philadelphia. He was eighteen years old when, in 1866, the Fenian Brotherhood made good on the Irish Republican Union's threats of 1848 and launched a series of raids across the British North American border. An attack on the Welland Canal was briefly considered by the raiders. On 9 April 1866 William E. Leonard wrote to General Thomas William Sweeny, one of the leaders of the "Senate" wing of the Fenian Brotherhood, suggesting that the canal's destruction should form part of the invasion strategy. "[T]he canall is 25 miles long with 26 locks on it," wrote Leonard. "[Y]our point is the gard lock by destroying this lock and the one below it you destroy the whole canal."[14] Though a small victory was won over Canadian militia by the invading Irish Republican Army on 2 June 1866 at Ridgeway, less than twenty kilometers east of the canal, the canal survived unscathed through the raids that ended in 1871.[15]

Luke Dillon did not participate in the Fenian raids. In August 1867 he enlisted in the 27th Infantry Regiment of the United States. He served a three-year term at the rank of corporal, fighting in Red Cloud's War in Montana and Wyoming. He later told his friend, the prominent Philadelphia Fenian Joseph McGarrity, that he "liked the Indians, and very soon learned sufficient of their language to speak with them in their own tongue."[16] Whether he had any qualms about his active part in their expropriation was not mentioned. Two Irish fellow soldiers supposedly converted Dillon to Fenianism. In August 1870, when his term expired, he returned to Philadelphia, took up shoemaking and married Mary Shields, another emigrant of English birth and Irish parentage, with whom he would raise four children. Not, however, before being sworn in as the 448th member of the Free Soil Club, a "district" of the recently founded Clan na Gael.[17]

According to Joseph McGarrity, the Junior Guardian (vice president) of Dillon's district was James "Red Jim" McDermott, a man who would later become known as one of the most infamous *agent provocateurs* on Britain's payroll.[18] At the time of Dillon's swearing-in McDermott may not have been among their number, but there was no shortage of spies and informants in the Fenian ranks. The best known and most success-ful of them was Henri Le Caron (real name Thomas Billis Beach) who, from his position as Adjutant-General of the Fenian Brotherhood, fed crucial information to the British and Canadian authorities and helped to undermine the raids of 1870. These failures finally discredited the filibustering strategy and helped bring about the disintegration of the Fenian Brotherhood.[19] Le Caron carried his spying career into the Clan na Gael, which grew through the 1870s to take the Brotherhood's place as the engine of the transatlantic separatist movement. By 1882, he estimated that Luke Dillon was among the eighteen most influential men in the organization.[20]

Dillon was a hardline revolutionist, a "man of iron nerve, cool and determined."[21] The compromise with constitutionalists implicit in the "New Departure" policy did not sit well with him. So he gravi-tated, for a time, towards the faction of the Clan na Gael that advo-cated "skirmishing"—taking the Irish question to the heart of Britain through the "scientific warfare" of dynamite bomb attacks.[22] In 1884 he was among several dynamitards responsible for explosions in London that damaged the Conservative Party's Junior Carlton Club, the intel-ligence department of the War Office at Adair House, and the Criminal Investigation Department (CID) office at Scotland Yard.[23] These were symbolic targets chosen pointedly to embarrass Britain's apparatus of state security. Dillon returned to London the following year with an even more spectacular landmark in mind. On 25 January 1885 he and fellow Philadelphian Roger O'Neill entered Westminster Palace. It was a Sat-urday, and the buildings were open to public visitors. O'Neill placed a black bag full of dynamite in the crypt of Westminster Hall. Its explosion filled the Hall with dust and caused panic among the crowds of visitors. Taking advantage of the disturbance, Dillon entered the chamber of the House of Commons and placed a parcel of dynamite along the govern-ment benches. The blast tore up the seats, twisted the wood panelling and damaged the Speaker's chair. At least five people were seriously injured by the explosions. Police sealed off the buildings in the immediate aftermath of the attack, but Dillon and O'Neill managed to escape undetected, al-legedly blagging their way out by masquerading as detectives.[24]

Dillon made it safely back to Philadelphia. But most Fenian dynamiters were less fortunate. A month before Dillon's attack on the House of Commons, another party of dynamiters led by the veteran Fenian William Mackey Lomasney, formerly of Toronto, met a dramatic end when attempting to destroy a buttress of London Bridge from a rented skiff. Their bomb exploded prematurely, instantly killing Lomasney and his two companions, and leaving the bridge undamaged.[25] More often, however, dynamiters were arrested before they had an opportunity to light a fuse. Between 1882 and 1885 twenty-five of them, including Tom Clarke and John Daly, were caught and imprisoned in Britain.[26] The evolving intelligence system, spearheaded by the new Special Branch, was key to the frustration of the dynamite campaign. In 1883, for example, "Red Jim" McDermott—formerly of Luke Dillon's Philadelphia camp—helped the Special Branch obtain the imprisonment for life of five Cork Fenians by roping them into a bogus dynamite plot.[27]

Four years of "skirmishing" ultimately achieved little but the arrest of conspirators and the injury of innocents. In the eyes of many Irish nationalists, the dynamite war only damaged the cause of independence which, by contrast, appeared to have been advanced with far greater success by the Land War and the Irish Parliamentary Party under Charles Stewart Parnell. By 1885 the Supreme Council of the IRB announced its official opposition to the dynamite policy. But the so-called Triangle faction—the three-man cabal that dominated the Clan na Gael—remained invested in it and opted to cut ties with the IRB rather than preserve the transatlantic connection. Luke Dillon returned from England incensed by this development. He had already grown disillusioned with the Triangle's management of the dynamite campaign. Dynamiters, he complained, were sent to Britain virtually penniless; those departing via New York were arrested with suspicious regularity, and the families of those imprisoned or killed in the course of their work were not given the financial support they were owed.[28] To make matters worse, serious financial irregularities had emerged in the Triangle's books. In 1886 Dillon joined forces with John Devoy and Dr. Patrick Henry Cronin to lead a split in the Clan. Their secessionist faction adopted the somewhat ironic title "United Brotherhood" (UB). Dillon became its first President.[29]

The dynamite war collapsed in this atmosphere of dissension and mutual distrust. But the useful trick of the bogus dynamite plot was retained by British intelligence agencies in their ongoing efforts to neutralize Parnellism. In 1887 the *agent provocateur* Frank Millen, working with the Special Branch, cooked up a sham conspiracy to assassinate Queen Victoria by blowing up Westminster Abbey during her Golden Jubilee celebration. Senior Parnellite MPs were canvassed by the plotters to imbricate them in the conspiracy. Luke Dillon was also approached; presumably, he told Devoy, because he was "not entirely ignorant of the manner those things are done." But something about the plot felt off to Dillon, and he sent the men packing. Nothing, in the end, came of the Jubilee Plot besides the imprisonment of two of Millen's dupes. The attempts to connect the affair to Parnell's party were not convincing.[30] The Special Branch, then under the direction of CID chief Robert Anderson, would have another go through the Special Commission on Parnellism and Crime, a judicial inquiry triggered by letters published in the *Times* which appeared to connect Parnell with the Phoenix Park Murders. During its dramatic proceedings the letters were discovered to be forgeries and, despite a sensational appearance in the witness stand by Henri Le Caron, who revealed his long career as a spy at the heart of North American Fenianism, Parnell was vindicated. But Le Caron's testimony sent a fresh spy panic through the Clan na Gael. The organization had been briefly reunited in 1888. But Luke Dillon's old Triangle faction enemies became convinced that his friend Patrick Henry Cronin was another spy, just like Le Caron. When in May 1889 Cronin's body was found stuffed in a suitcase in a Chicago sewer the Clan was plunged into turmoil. The lurid details of the murder shocked the American public, and the highly publicized trial shed an unflattering light on the Clan na Gael's seedy world of squabbling factions.[31]

Luke Dillon stepped forward as the embattled Clan's public spokesperson in the wake of the murder. He insisted it was "not an organisation of thugs" and that it could never condone the murder of an American citizen. Ostentatiously cooperating with the police investigation, he publicly declared that no "pledge of secrecy" should prevent Clan members coming forward with information. "Our first allegiance," he told the press, "is to the law of this country as citizens"—although like a good Fenian he made an exception for America's neutrality laws which, he stipulated, "we could violate."[32] But there was no papering over the cracks that the murder had exposed. The Clan ruptured in two again. The "Croninite" wing, led by Dillon and Devoy, began once again calling themselves the UB, while the anti-Croninites came under the sway of William Lyman and his "new movement." Parnell, meanwhile, was eventually brought down not by Robert Anderson, but by the revelation of his extra-marital affair. Disorganization would prevail until the outbreak of the South African War.

* * *

Dynamite may have fallen out of favor for a time in the United States and Britain, but a small cadre of extremists in Dublin clung on to the skirmishing strategy. John Nolan was, in the eyes of Dublin Castle and the Special Branch, perhaps the most dangerous of the lot. He was a known associate of men involved in the Phoenix Park murders of 1882 and may himself have been a member of the Irish National Invincibles, the secret society to which the murderers belonged.[33] By the 1890s some remnants of the Invincibles conspiracy coalesced around the P. W. Nally Club, named after a prominent IRB man and Gaelic athlete who, in November 1891, died in Mountjoy Prison, allegedly owing to his severe mistreatment.[34] The Nally Club was a front for a Fenian cell suspected of being behind a series of minor explosions and arson attempts in Dublin from October 1891. John Nolan was usually found in the company of his friend and fellow Nally Club member, John Merna, a sometime bartender and grocer's assistant.[35] The pair were watched closely by John Mallon, the Armagh-born Catholic detective who had risen to the rank of Assistant Commissioner of the DMP and head of the plainclothes G Division, and who served as the chief conduit for anti-Fenian intelligence in Ireland.[36] Mallon thought little of Merna. He described him as "almost illiterate," chronically out of work, and "weak"; without Nolan at his side, he wrote, "there is not much in him."[37] But Nolan, who Mallon considered "very nimble and destitute of feeling," was a different matter.[38] As a pair they could, and did, cause both Mallon and Gosselin's secret police frequent headaches.

Nolan and Merna were among those suspected of planting a dynamite package outside Dublin Castle's Detective Office, the blast from which fatally wounded one of Mallon's detectives on Christmas Eve of

1892.[39] After being examined in March 1893 by a secret inquiry established under the Explosives Act to investigate the attack, Nolan and Merna fled to New York.[40] There they were rumored to have received instruction in the use of explosives from experienced Irish Americans.[41] On 24 November they returned to Dublin; in the two days that followed an unexploded device was discovered at Aldborough Barracks and a small explosion occurred at Tyrone Place just off O'Connell Street.[42] When their friend, Walter Sheridan, was arrested with detonators on his person, Nolan and Merna suspected his accomplice Pat Reid had betrayed him to the police.[43] On 27 November, shortly before boarding a steamer to Liverpool, Pat Reid was shot dead on Cardiff Lane near the Grand Canal Docks. Mallon, certain that Nolan and Merna were the assassins, arrested them both. "Nolan," he was alleged to have screamed during their interrogation, "I'll hang you if I can!"[44] Yet despite witness testimony, the extraordinary powers conferred by a Special Inquiry, and a remand period of unprecedented length, the Crown's case against Nolan and Merna fell apart at police court.[45] The two men had a powerful ally in Fred Allan, a leading member of the IRB Supreme Council and the business manager of the *Independent*. He organized and funded their defense, personally swore himself their alibi before the Special Inquiry, and according to a later rumor even hid the murder weapon in his own safe.[46]

Following their release, Nolan and Merna returned to New York. There they were welcomed into William Lyman's confidence and helped to found another branch of the Nally Club, which was soon penetrated by spies.[47] In October 1894, Gosselin was convinced that the two were tasked with carrying out some dynamite outrage on Lyman's orders. When Merna returned to Dublin that month, his luggage was searched; among his belongings was an apron "evidently bought for the purpose of wearing over the ordinary clothes when working with chemicals."[48] Gosselin tailed Merna himself and wrote reproachfully of the "self-satisfied smirk on his cunning face." When Nolan and Merna returned to America later in 1895, Lyman selected them to carry out an attack in Canada: to blow up the Welland Canal. Little information survives about this plot. Gosselin caught wind of it and warned the Colonial Office. Later reports indicate simply that the plot failed owing to "the agent's want of nerve."[49] In 1896 one of Gosselin's American spies implied that Nolan and Merna had "disappointed" Lyman "and that if they ever returned he would make it damn hot for them."[50]

As the INA collapsed through 1897 and 1898 the pair remained in Dublin, where Fred Allan found them work as compositors at the *Independent* offices. By early 1899 they were among the IRB element purged during the paper's reorganization by its new owners, the Harmsworths of the *Daily Mail*. In March a notice was posted barring from the premises "John Merna and other ex-employees of whom the English hands, lately imported, are becoming afraid."[51] It was rumored that Nolan had hidden dynamite in the offices before his dismissal, and guns were later found concealed in the building.[52] Their patron, Fred Allan, was also sacked. When he found work as Lord Mayor Thomas Pile's private secretary, police believed that he could no longer be involved in secret society business.[53] So when they learned that Allan had, with the help of Maud Gonne, purchased a transatlantic fare for the hard-up Nolan and Merna in October 1899, they wrongly assumed it was little more than a personal favor.[54] In fact, the outbreak of the South African War and the reunification of the Clan na Gael had revived their dynamiting careers. Together with John Walsh and a fourth man, a Dublin fitter named John Rowan, they traveled to make a second attempt at destroying the Welland Canal. This time, Luke Dillon's oversight would ensure that "want of nerve" could pose no obstacle.

* * *

Their mission encountered an inauspicious start. On the day of their intended departure from Liverpool they were scheduled to meet with William McGuinness of Preston, a leading Lancashire IRB man, at Tom MacDermott's pub on Marybone. But McGuinness failed to show up, and the four Johns missed their sailing on the S. S. *Belgenland*.[55] They had to wait two weeks to travel on the S. S. *Rhynland*, on which they endured a miserable passage. Severe storms confined the passengers below deck for almost the entire voyage. Barely able to make headway against a swell which twice submerged the bridge, the ship ran out of coal; the engine crew was forced to burn wood on the final stretch. The *Rhynland* arrived at Philadelphia after sixteen days at sea—more than twice the length of a typical passage.[56] The four Johns proceeded a few days later to New York—the *Rhynland*'s manifest shows that each had given various addresses in Brooklyn and east Manhattan as their destinations.[57] Merna returned to an address on Peck Slip where he had previously lived in 1894. They may have visited Tom Clarke at his flat on West 94th Street.[58] In December John Rowan dropped out of the picture, possibly returning to Dublin, and was not seen in connection with the other suspects again. His role in the affair, and indeed whether this was the real John Rowan or another man using an assumed name, was never clear. Within a few weeks the three men had left New York for Washington, DC. Merna and Walsh found work as bartenders at Joe McInerney's Saloon on 9th Street NW. Nolan was hired as a fitter at a foundry one hundred miles to the south in Richmond, Virginia. These were peculiar choices for men who had spent prior sojourns in New York and Philadelphia, where they had no shortage of friends and connections. Neither Washington, DC, nor Richmond were typical destinations for recent Irish emigrants and were far from being hubs of Fenianism. It is quite likely the men were laying low.

If so, they did not do a particularly good job of it. On the night of 12 March 1900, John Merna was found lying dead on the floor of the staff bedroom above McInerney's saloon. Walsh was interviewed by police. He told them that Merna had been in good spirits that evening, and when his shift ended around eight o'clock, he had retired to his room and shot himself through the heart with the .38 caliber revolver McInerney kept behind the bar. The coroner, finding no evidence to suggest Merna had been murdered, submitted a verdict of death by suicide. Later, following the arrest of Nolan and Walsh in Canada, it was rumored that Merna had been "removed by his comrades."[59] It was considered suspicious that Merna had in his possession a receipt for a $10 bank draft from Dublin, as well as a note implying he had a brother serving in the Prince of Wales's Leinster Regiment based at Halifax and active in the South African War.[60] One scholar has argued that Merna had been a spy since the early 1890s.[61] But there is no clear or convincing evidence that this was the case. Certainly, like many Fenians, he was in proximity to known spies and informants. Yet he was so frequently a subject of surveillance and police correspondence that if he was an agent then Gosselin and Mallon went to extraordinary lengths to feign ignorance; they spilt a great deal of ink speculating about his movements and intentions.

Merna's Fenian "comrades" would need to be charged with a similarly elaborate bluff if they are to be painted as his assassins. By all accounts Merna's death left them genuinely shocked and saddened. William Crossin wrote to John Nolan on 19 March telling him that he was "stunned by the act. His mind must have been affected. Poor Jack, I am sorry that he died in that way." Crossin was a member of the ten-man joint executive of the united Clan na Gael, and the highest ranking Fenian in Philadelphia besides Luke Dillon.[62] Crossin told Nolan he would arrange to have the executive "pay the bill" to have Merna "buried decently"—not a gesture the Clan was in the habit of making for suspected traitors. He added that "[Fred] Allan will be shocked when he hears this."[63] In a letter to his wife, John Walsh wrote that they were "all knocked about" by the news and that "[i]t must have been a terrible shock to Merna's wife when she heard of what Jack had done."[64] John Nolan appears to have lost his job at the foundry the week following Merna's death, having presumably been absent to arrange and attend the funeral in Washington. Joe McInerney decided to sell his saloon and head home.[65] There is no evidence—besides the singular timing of his death—that points to betrayal on Merna's part or foul play on the part of his associates.

Of the four Johns, only two remained.

* * *

At some point in March 1900, as Bloemfontein, the capital of the Orange Free State, fell to the British and the Boer armies retreated northwards, Nolan and Walsh met with Luke Dillon in Philadelphia.[66] Dillon had spent much of the 1890s working at the city's Dime Savings Bank, and serving on the executive of the UB, the Clan's Croninite wing.[67] He had not yet fully retired, however, from the "active work" through which he had made his name. According to Joseph McGarrity, Dillon crossed the Atlantic in the early 1890s with the intention of assassinating Henri Le Caron. He made it as far as Paris before the plot was called off, word having allegedly been leaked to the British authorities.[68] By 1897, to his embarrassment, Dillon found himself in financial trouble. His friend John Devoy arranged a testimonial to assist him in the payment of his debts and appears to have met with some success; one respondent praised "the splendid service rendered and the enormous sacrifice made by [Dillon] in the cause."[69] His misfortune does not appear to have dented his prestige among Irish-Philadelphians. He rose to the position of President of the Dime Savings Bank, served as Grand Marshal of the city's 10,000-strong 1798 centenary parade, was treasurer of the Irish Political Prisoners' Fund, and was on the reception committee for the visit of John Redmond and Lord Mayor of Dublin Daniel Tallon in November 1899.[70] But the testimonial was likely the occasion for his departure from the executive of the UB. He was not involved in the negotiations with the anti-Croninites after Lyman's fall, nor was he a member of the provisional joint executive of the united Clan na Gael announced in September 1899 following the success of the unity talks.[71] By the outbreak of the South African war Dillon was around fifty years old, and absent from the Clan executive for the longest period since leading the split in 1886. He was free for other business.

On 22 March 1900 Dillon traveled with William Crossin to Buffalo and stayed briefly at a local hotel before returning to Philadelphia.[72] By 15 April he was seen back in the same establishment drinking with Nolan and Walsh. The three men registered under the false names Karl Dallman of Trenton, John Smith of New York, and Thomas Moore of Washington, DC. The next morning before setting off for Niagara Falls, New York, Dillon gave each of his companions a canvas valise packed with cakes of dynamite.[73]

They booked two hotels, one on either side of the Falls, and carried the valises to the Canadian side on separate trips a day apart. Blending with the crowds of London or Dublin was one thing; plotting a terror attack in rural Canada was another entirely. The dynamiters had a hard time not standing out. They were seen crossing the suspension bridge several times over the course of three days, attracting the suspicion of a United States Treasury agent posted at the border.[74] On two occasions the plotters reconnoitered the Welland Canal at Thorold, where locals noticed them lurking about. On 20 April Fred Latta of Niagara Falls, Ontario, was walking behind Dillon and Walsh for two blocks and overheard their conversation:

"Do you know where Jack [Nolan] is?"

"I suppose he is getting drunk," replied Walsh.

"If we don't keep that ----- sober we will never be able to pull off that job," was Dallman's answer.

"How are we going to keep him sober?" said Walsh.

"If we can't do it any other way we will have to lock him in a room."[75]

Dillon later vehemently denied this exchange ever took place. Indignant, he challenged a reporter: "Do you suppose that if I were a conspirator I would allow anyone within three feet of me while I was speaking of a matter of that kind?"[76] But Nolan had a reputation in Dublin for being a heavy drinker; it was plausible that his habit might have posed problems for Dillon.[77] True or not, Latta's story was to prove persuasive later in court.[78]

On 21 April another witness saw Walsh visit the local tailor's shop and buy a length of rope while Nolan stood waiting outside. This was the same rope Euphemia Constable saw Nolan and Walsh using to lower the valises of dynamite into the gate pits of lock 24 of the Welland Canal at Thorold, later that day. With ample witnesses to their suspicious movements in both Thorold and Niagara Falls, they were arrested almost immediately upon their return. A local police detective connected Dallman with the two men and apprehended him at his hotel before he could escape the country.[79] Walsh and Nolan's hotel room on the New York side was searched; a rubber bag filled with fuses was discovered and turned over to the Canadian authorities.[80] The three men were held at the Welland gaol. It did not look good for them.

* * *

It was at this point that Canada's celebrity detective, Scottish-born John Wilson Murray—who bore the cumbersome title of Chief Inspector of the Criminal Investigation Branch of the Department of the Attorney General of Ontario—took up the investigation of the affair.[81] His account appears in his *Memoirs of a Great Detective* (1904), co-authored by Buffalo journalist Victor Speer. The two had first cooperated in 1902 when Speer interviewed Murray for a ten-chapter feature for the *Buffalo Express* on Luke Dillon's career and the Welland Canal explosion.[82] Speer's fustian style and Murray's vanity combined to make the *Memoirs* often unreliable, but the chapter on the Welland affair, based largely on police and court reports only four years older than the book itself, is reasonably accurate. Still there are some flourishes, such as this doubtful passage where Murray describes his first encounter with the dynamiters:

I had them photographed in the Welland gaol. Dallman smashed the camera and made a break for liberty. I pulled my revolver and we had quite a tussle. Dallman strove to dash through the door. I halted him and forced him back and then locked him in a cell. Nolin [sic] and Walsh stood together as if Dallman were a stranger to them.[83]

Dillon was still operating under the alias "Karl Dallman." He claimed complete ignorance of any dynamite plot, insisted he was not a member of any Fenian organization, and said he had never seen Nolan and Walsh before he spent a few days drinking with them in Niagara Falls. It is highly unlikely that he attempted, like a dime novel villain, to make a break on foot from the Welland gaol.[84] Instead word was sent to Philadelphia, where William Crossin arranged for Dillon to be represented at trial by William Manley German, a prominent barrister and Liberal MPP for Welland.[85] No arrangements were made for Nolan and Walsh, who offered no defense. Even when the police quickly established that no such person as Karl Dallman ever lived in Trenton or Buffalo, Dillon and German remained sanguine. The Crown, they believed, had no evidence "to show actual complicity" on his part.[86] Their strategy depended, however, on keeping Dillon's revolutionary resume a secret. He explained to the police court that he maintained his anonymity simply because he had "a wife and family and the notoriety of all this might break her heart."[87]

The three were committed for trial without the Crown establishing Dallman's real identity or even a motive. In the days following the explosion it had been widely rumored that the attack was part of a scheme hatched by Buffalo "scoopers"—workers who shoveled freight grain—to shut down grain shipping on the Welland canal and divert work to their port.[88] It was reported that hundreds of raiders would soon cross the border to rescue the prisoners and finish the job. A combined force of over two hundred Canadian police and militia was stationed at the border crossings to guard against any such attempt.[89] But J. W. Murray never doubted the attack was the work of Fenians. Within days the grain-handler conspiracy was dismissed.[90] The descriptions and likenesses of the dynamiters were sent to the United Kingdom, where Gosselin and Mallon confirmed the identities and Fenian background of Nolan and Walsh.[91] In a sign of their temporary blindness to the workings of transatlantic Fenianism, it was generally believed, for at least a month, that Dallman must be John Rowan.[92]

During the police court hearings, Murray took his investigation to the United States, traveling to New York, Philadelphia, Washington, DC, and Richmond. Several leads in the documents found on Nolan and Walsh gave him, with the assistance of the Special Branch, a reasonably clear picture of the American movements of Nolan, Walsh, and Merna after their arrival in mid-November 1899.[93] A letter written by William Crossin that mentioned Fred Allan made clear the dynamiters' connection to the Clan na Gael and the IRB. But Murray failed to establish Dallman's identity in time for the trial. In his memoirs he claimed that "in due time" he learned that Dallman was Luke Dillon, and that men who knew him "went to see him" and "identified him positively," but does not specify when.[94] The Pinkerton Detective Agency had been contracted by Commissioner of Dominion Police Arthur Percy Sherwood to investigate rumors of Fenian designs against Canada since January 1900.[95] On 30 April Sherwood asked the Agency to conduct its own investigation—parallel to Murray's—into the dynamiters' antecedents; but this too failed to uncover Dallman's identity.[96] Murray was back in Canada by 17 May; his findings were immediately released to the press. Newspapers carried details of Nolan's Fenian career, Merna's suicide, the connection with the Clan, and their movements with Dallman after their meeting in Buffalo.[97] The leaked story appears to have been the manoeuvre of the Crown Prosecutor in charge of the case, E.F.B. Johnson. Sherwood wrote to Johnson on 18 May complaining about the publication of these details "which we agreed should have been kept . . . till such time as we could have surprised them with it."[98] Days later Johnson told reporters that, at trial, he had "no intention of introducing evidence relating to any secret society" or any possible motive.[99] With only circumstantial evidence against Dallman, attempting to prove beyond doubt that he had masterminded a Fenian plot would be a tricky move in the courtroom. Letting the press freely proclaim the Fenian connection ahead of time, however, could only help the Crown's case.

The trial commenced at an inauspicious time for the Fenian dynamiters. On 23 May Empire Day was marked in Canadian schools; on 24 May, while loyal Canadians celebrated Queen Victoria's birthday, the prisoners entered the dock.[100] Nolan and Walsh were doomed, but at stake was whether the Crown could demonstrate that Dallman was the "guiding hand" behind the plot. An impressive tally of thirty-eight witnesses were called to this effect, testifying to having seen the three men behaving suspiciously together at the Falls and the Canal in the days approaching the explosion. For the prosecution, Johnson told the jury that this act of "terrorism . . . strikes at her Majesty the Queen" and warned that "[t]oday the attack is on the Welland Canal, tomorrow it may be on the railway bridges, the next day on the Houses of Parliament"—clearly oblivious that Dillon was working in the opposite order! William Manley German attempted to highlight inconsistencies in the witness testimony and establish an alibi for Dallman. He argued that there was no "material evidence" to connect Dallman with the explosion, and that his guilt should not be inferred merely by his association with Nolan and Walsh. After a two-day trial and thirty-five minutes of deliberation, the jury returned a unanimous guilty verdict against all three prisoners. The judge, describing the bombing as "a crime against civilization" motivated by "hate," sentenced each of them to life in prison.[101]

The three men were visibly shaken. Interviewed after the sentencing, Nolan admitted that he had expected he and Walsh would get fifteen years and that Dallman, against whom he felt there was "no case," would be acquitted. Dallman was despondent. He told a reporter that "it would be better if [he] had been hanged" than to know the worry that his slow death in prison would cause his family.[102] The next day, as the three men were conveyed north to Kingston Penitentiary, they put on a brave face. They smoked cigars and "cracked jokes all the way." To the sheriff accompanying them they warned that although their attempt to blow up the canal had failed, "other and more successful attempts" might soon follow.[103]

* * *

There may well have been another attempt in the works. In 1899, two Invincibles who had served sixteen years in Dublin prisons were pardoned and released. One of them, James Fitzharris—who bore the nickname "Skin the Goat" for selling a pet animal's hide to fund his drinking habit—had driven a getaway cab for the Phoenix Park

Figure 2.2a, 2.2b. James "Skin-the-Goat" Fitzharris (left) and James Mullett (right), 1883, NLI NPA INV15, 18. Courtesy of the National Library of Ireland.

murderers in 1882. The other, Joseph Mullet, had been convicted for attempting to murder a member of the jury at his fellow Invincibles' trial.[104] Mullet was frail of health and suffered from a hunched back, but was sharp. His brother James was a high-ranking Dublin IRB man, at whose pub extremists like John Nolan were known to congregate.[105] In January 1900 the Mullets were suspected of involvement in a plan to dynamite a military barracks in Dublin; a few months later they were believed to be plotting an outrage in connection with the Queen's visit.[106]

By late April 1900, police caught wind that Joseph Mullet and Skin-the-Goat Fitzharris were intending to sail to New York. According to some accounts they were to settle there as ordinary emigrants; by others they were to undertake a lecture tour on their experiences of prison. This struck John Mallon as odd because Skin-the-Goat, he felt, "could only be used for show, just like a bear. He has no intelligence and is nearly always drunk."[107] Unlike the higher class of Fenian ex-convict such as John Daly, conspirators in the Phoenix Park murders were not typically held up as objects of sympathy to Irish American audiences. The apprehension of their peers John Nolan and John Walsh at Niagara Falls suggested to police that the movements of Mullet and Fitzharris had a more sinister objective than lecturing. Mallon's suspicion deepened when an informant produced a letter from Transvaal Committee member J. F. McCarthy to Arthur Griffith. "Dear Arthur," it read:

> I would hardly credit my eyes when I saw about F[itzharris] & M[ullet]'s proposed visit to the states, how in the name of common sense did it creep into the papers, it might have upset our project completely & everything has been going on so smoothly lately, but [cryptic symbols] I know for a fact have not taken any notice yet . . . I have got the samples of [cryptic symbols] they only came this morning, will you come over tonight as I want to select them as they have made arrangements to leave for New York next week.[108]

Mullet and Fitzharris's American connections were also troubling. They had attended the Manchester Martyrs celebration in Glasgow on 24 November 1899 and probably met William Crossin of Philadelphia there.[109] The passage of the two ex-convicts to New York was to be paid by Patrick "Rocky Mountain" O'Brien.[110] Gosselin considered O'Brien a "dangerous man." He spent much of 1900 working as a Clan na Gael emissary in Ireland and in Paris and was believed to have knowledge of Fenian designs against Canada and their negotiations with the French government.[111]

Mullet and Fitzharris left Dublin on 19 May, sailing for New York via Queenstown. During their passage their drinking and anti-British talk riled fellow passengers and reportedly landed them in some fights. Meanwhile the US Immigration Commissioner at New York had, either by press reports or a nudge from British authorities—been alerted to the pair's approach and intimated to reporters that they would be detained.[112] Upon their arrival on 26 May, this is precisely what happened. Rocky Mountain O'Brien protested; Jeremiah O'Donovan Rossa personally attempted to visit them at Ellis Island but was turned away.[113] Under US immigration law, ex-convicts could be refused landing. Political crimes were the exception. Mullet and Fitzharris argued—and their friends echoed—that like many admitted Fenian visitors before them, the offenses they committed had been political and, what's more, that they had been released with a pardon.

Their case was heard by a Board of Special Inquiry, which ruled that their convictions in relation to the Phoenix Park affair had not been political but ordinarily criminal, and that any pardons they received did not expunge their criminal record where American law was concerned.[114] Given the visitors' dubious intentions, this decision was probably prudent but was no less extraordinary for that. Never before had Fenians been denied entry to, or deported from, the United States. Mullet and Fitzharris appealed to the Department of the Treasury, with representations made on their behalf by ex-judge George Curtis strongly disputing the legality of the decision.[115] By 20 June the Assistant Secretary of the Treasury announced that the ruling of the New York Board was upheld. They were to be sent home.[116] Outrage was expressed in the columns of the *Irish World*. The decision was portrayed as yet another example of McKinley's America kowtowing to the British.[117] The pair themselves complained they had been treated even worse by America than they had by Britain. As onlookers gathered to witness their deportation, Fitzharris reproached the crowd:

> "And to think we were detained right under the shadow of the Statue of Liberty."
> "Oh, sit down, Jim," remarked Mullett. "The thing is hollow."[118]

* * *

Canadian fears that further dynamite attacks were being planned, and that the Clan na Gael intended to break the Welland Canal dynamiters out of prison, prompted the government to take heightened security measures.[119] Commissioner Sherwood set aside $31,000 for the protection of the canals at Welland, Lachine, Soulanges, Sault Ste. Marie, and Cornwall, and swore in around sixty special constables to guard them throughout the summer and autumn of 1900.[120] The Canadian Secret Service Agency had men placed on passenger vessels traveling on the Lachine Canal at Montreal.[121] On two separate occasions, sentries guarding the Welland Canal exchanged fire with strangers approaching the locks at night.[122] Dynamite was discovered in an unmarked box on the canal wharf at Cornwall.[123] Undercover detectives were stationed in Kingston and extra guards were posted around the penitentiary walls.[124] All this served only to make Dallman, Nolan, and Walsh's sentence more miserable, as they were placed in the maximum security "prison of isolation" and allowed contact with no persons save "the high officials of the institution."[125]

The immediate response of the Clan to the failure of the Welland Canal bombing is difficult to establish. There was a Convention held at Atlantic City in July 1900 at which the provisional executive was replaced by an elected one, but no record of that meeting survives.[126] John Devoy could not be reached by reporters for comment and neither his personal papers nor his subsequent writings contain any mention whatever of the affair. Nor do comments appear in the letters of Tom Clarke or in those of any other significant republican figure on either side of the Atlantic. Maud Gonne was the only one to break the silence. She issued a public statement in response to rumors that she had funded the bombing. These were "totally untrue," she said; it would be unprincipled to "ask others to go into danger which I do not share." She made it quite clear that in denying her own involvement, however, she was not "in any way condemning or disapproving the action of brave men" who were striking "a blow against that monstrous iniquity the British Empire."[127] Another sort of denial came from an unnamed "close friend of John Devoy" interviewed in New York, who likely persuaded nobody in declaring that the whole affair was a "Scotland Yard plot . . . devised to cast a slur on the Irish people."[128]

The silence of Dillon's colleagues was prudent. There was no sense incriminating Dillon or themselves by putting anything in writing, and little to be gained by claiming ownership of such a fiasco. What is certain is that the embarrassing failure at the Welland Canal and the imprisonment of Dillon severely demoralized the newly reunited Clan na Gael and the transatlantic Fenian movement generally. "[I]t is most extraordinary," observed John Mallon, "what a damper the conviction of Nolan and Walsh has put on extreme politics in Dublin."[129]

Gosselin also noted this development with satisfaction.[130] But the Welland affair was something of an embarrassment for his department, too. Immediately after the bombing Gosselin wrote his superiors at the Home Office drawing their attention to a January 1896 memo from his American agent regarding Lyman's plot to sabotage the canal. "I think it right," Gosselin said, "to call attention to the fact that this Department is not altogether in the dark as to the designs of the enemy it is paid to combat."[131] Yet the truth was that his department was very much in the dark about the designs that brought Dillon, Nolan, and Walsh to Ontario. As Fenians scrambled to seize Ireland's "hour of destiny," the Special Branch found itself scrambling to keep up. It was luck and the dynamiters' own incompetence, rather than any intervention by secret intelligence, that saved the canal and led to the plotters' imprisonment.

Years later, when it became public knowledge that prisoner D294 at Kingston Penitentiary was in fact Luke Dillon, the persona of Karl Dallman was finally dropped. There was no longer any point in acting like an innocent holidaymaker who chose the wrong drinking partners, so Dillon's story adjusted accordingly. From then on, he insisted that the Welland Canal plot was entirely his own doing, and that he had personally recruited Walsh and Nolan to assist him.[132] Taking responsibility for the plot's failure and in so doing shielding both "the cause" and his "comrades" from blame was, in Dillon's mind, the honorable and sensible course. It was not until his death in 1930—by which time Crossin, Devoy, and most other prominent Clan leaders during the South African War had also expired—that his friend Joseph McGarrity felt it appropriate to set the record straight. In a circular McGarrity stated that "[t]he Clan na Gael may well be proud of the fact that every blow our beloved patriot struck at the enemies of Ireland was the official act of our organisation."[133] In an obituary for the *Irish World* he added that "[t]he explosives necessary were secured by William Crossin, Luke's co-worker in Philadelphia, and were conveyed to the Canadian border."[134] Crossin was a member of the united executive in 1900.[135] Dillon, who had made financial support for the families of Fenians killed or imprisoned a special cause of his, would not have taken unilateral action that could leave his wife without a pension in the event of his capture.[136] The Welland Canal attack was neither a solo mission nor a "Scotland yard plot" but, as Gosselin feared, it was an authorized act of the Clan na Gael.

The role of Nolan, Merna, and Walsh suggests that the IRB had almost as much a hand in the affair as the Clan. The departure of two of Dublin's most notorious Fenian operatives for Philadelphia immediately following the outbreak of the South African War was hardly a coincidence—especially given that these same men had been involved in a previous plot to sabotage the canal in 1896.[137] The apparent funding of their passage by Fred Allan and Maud Gonne, and their meeting with William McGuinness in Liverpool points to the complicity of senior republican figures in Dublin and northern England.

As Dillon later explained, the goal of the dynamiting was to force Canada "to keep its troops at home" rather than send them to South Africa.[138] If the Clan could not send a thousand men to fight with the Boers in South Africa, so the thinking went, it could produce the same effect by tying down a thousand Canadian troops to guard against dynamiters. The crippling of the Welland Canal just as spring shipping was set to resume on the Great Lakes system would have been a hugely expensive obstacle to Canadian trade and the eastward flow of provisions—some of which went to supporting the war effort. It would have been a spectacular demonstration of Fenian potential, and may have had an inspirational effect on advanced Irish nationalism and the Boer war effort alike. Just as the Fenian Brotherhood of the 1860s had hoped their raids might help spark an Anglo-American conflict, the Clan na Gael's targeting of Canada during the South African War was partly intended to drive a wedge between the two empires.

In the event, none of this happened. The damage to the lock was trivial, and quick repairs meant the canal was fit to be reopened on 25 April as previously scheduled. The dynamite scare engendered by the bombing did divert some Canadian manpower to guard duty. Two hundred militia and police were posted at the Niagara frontier in late April, and twenty-four soldiers watched the Welland Canal.[139] Sixty special constables guarded Canadian canals throughout the summer of 1900.[140] But these numbers hardly represent a meaningful loss to the imperial war effort in South Africa, which saw about 450,000 troops deployed.[141]

One historian has described the Welland Canal attack as "[t]he final blast of the skirmishing campaign."[142] Not quite. There would be further attempts during the War, and at least one blast. Radical Irish nationalist Boer sympathizers had another Canadian target in mind. Two thousand miles to the west, on Vancouver Island, lay the Royal Navy's Pacific squadron base at Esquimalt.

PART TWO

American Pro-Boers

"Either Irish or German, or a Very Bad Mixture of Both"

Agent X and the Pro-Boers of San Francisco

In the autumn of 1899, a nineteen-year-old operatic singer named Sannie Kruger arrived in San Francisco. After securing work at the Tivoli Opera House, she authored a front-page special for the *San Francisco Call*'s Sunday magazine titled "The Boers as They Really Are." In it she explained that she was the Transvaal-born grand-niece of the famous Boer patriarchs President Paul Kruger, former Vice-President General Piet Joubert, and General Christiaan De Wet. On this authority she set out to counter what she felt were widespread American misconceptions about Boer society and especially Boer women. The piece was festooned with photographs of Sannie Kruger in various dramatic outfits and poses, including one of her in military attire aiming a pistol. She wrote with a calculated, self-aggrandizing flourish. "Like all Boer girls," she explained, "I am an excellent shot and fervently wish that I were back in the Transvaal that I might defend our land." She stressed that Boers were not "semi-savage," and she took particular pains to "stoutly deny" that there was any habitual "intermingling" of blood between Boers and natives. "The Hottentots, the Kaffirs and the Zulus are our servants," she wrote.[1] Like most opponents of the war in the United States, she understood that among the greatest barriers to sympathy for the Transvaal and the Orange Free State was the suspicion that Boer people did not occupy the same status in the imagined racial hierarchy as northern Europeans. The more closely the Boers could be brought to resemble the ideal of the American frontiersman or the colonist of the revolutionary period, the better pro-Boers could compete with the increasingly popular notion that the United States and the United Kingdom shared a common "Anglo-Saxon" identity and were, therefore, natural partners in empire. Her message fell on receptive ears.

Irish nationalists in the United States were deeply troubled by the rise of transatlantic Anglo-Saxonism. It seemed to many to be the latest incarnation of the fiercely anti-Catholic and nativist Know-Nothing movement that had been firmly, and sometimes violently, hostile to Irish immigration during the mid-nineteenth century. Exalting the Anglo-Saxon as the archetypal American, they felt, erased the historic contributions of other white ethnic groups to American society and marginalized American Catholics in the present. Thus Thomas Paine's shibboleth that "Europe, not England, is the Mother Country of America" was pointedly enshrined in the banner of John F. Finerty's *Chicago Citizen*, one of the country's preeminent Irish newspapers.[2] Equally disturbing was the mutually reinforcing relationship between popular Anglo-Saxonism and the McKinley administration's policy of rapprochement with Britain. As far as many Irish American nationalists were concerned, the cosier the Anglo-American partnership, the steeper Ireland's path to independence. For them, the South African War represented a test of American commitment to the principles of republican liberty and the sovereignty of white peoples.[3] An American polity that could be brought to identify with the white, Christian Boers resisting British imperialism could also, they hoped, be persuaded to support an independent Ireland should the need arise. The value of the pro-Boer movement in the United States to Irish nationalists was therefore threefold. First was its core function as an outlet for genuine sympathy with the Boer underdog in what was widely felt to be an unjust and asymmetrical conflict. Second, it provided a platform for cross-ethnic cooperation with other white ethnic groups opposed, for their own reasons, to the related issues of Anglo-Saxonism, rapprochement, and imperialism. And finally, for a minority of extremists, it offered new partners in their efforts to commit meaningful direct action.

German Americans—many of whom were Catholic and many nervous of an Anglo-American combination against their *vaterland*—were natural allies in this. Indeed, across much of the eastern seaboard and Midwest, Irish and German communities were the engines of the pro-Boer movement. In San Francisco, however, it was the local Netherlands Society that provided the impetus. A club for largely well-to-do residents of Dutch birth and descent, it was founded in September

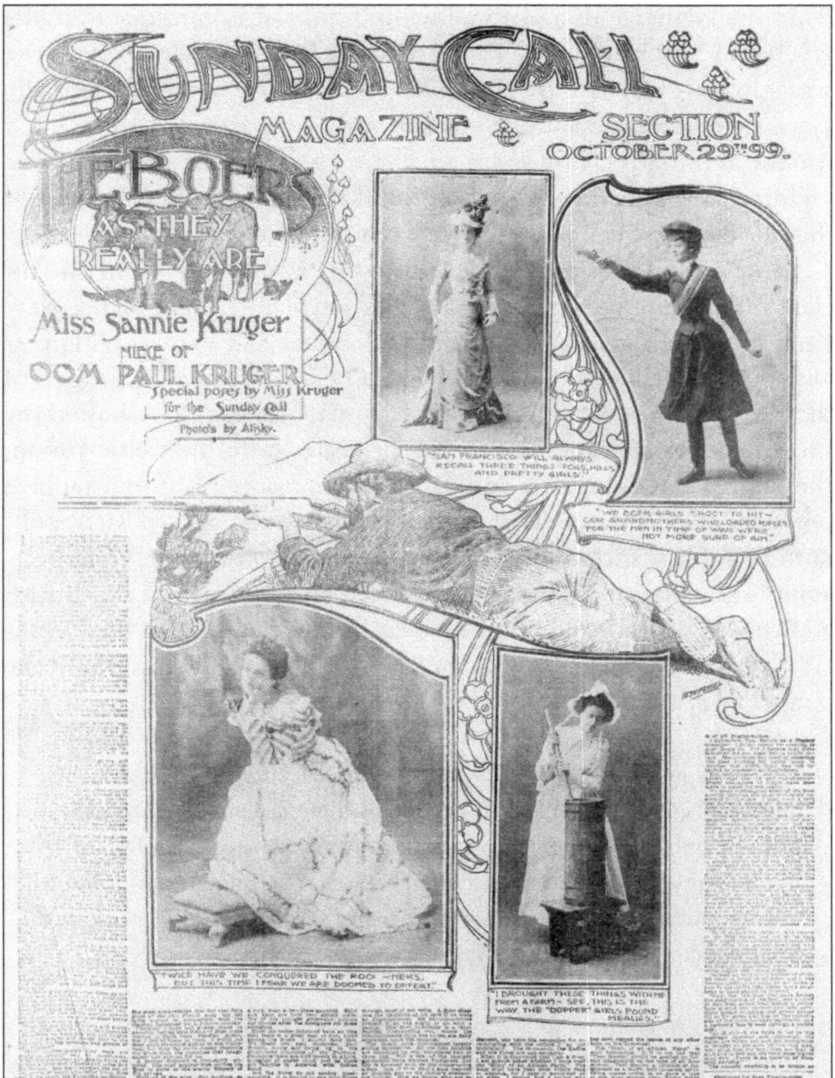

SUNDAY CALL

MAGAZINE SECTION

OCTOBER 29TH 99.

THE BOERS AS THEY REALLY ARE

BY Miss Sannie Kruger

NIECE OF OOM PAUL KRUGER

Special poses by Miss Kruger for the Sunday Call

Photo's by Alisky.

"SAN FRANCISCO WILL ALWAYS RECALL THREE THINGS-FOGS, HILLS AND PRETTY GIRLS"

"WE BOER GIRLS SHOOT TO HIT-OUR GRANDMOTHERS WHO LOADED RIFLES FOR THE MEN IN TIME OF WAR WERE NOT MORE SURE OF AIM"

"TWICE HAVE WE CONQUERED THE ROOI-NEKS, BUT THIS TIME I FEAR WE ARE DOOMED TO DEFEAT"

"I BROUGHT THESE THINGS WITH ME FROM A FARM- SEE, THIS IS THE WAY THE "DOPPER" GIRLS POUND MEALIES."

Figure 3.1. "The Boers as they really are," San Francisco *Call*, 29 Oct 1899, Chronicling America, Library of Congress.

1898 to celebrate the inauguration of the young Queen Wilhelmina.[4] By 24 October 1899 the society had followed the example of several cities in the Netherlands and appointed a Transvaal Committee to transmit resolutions to the local papers wishing Paul Kruger victory in the struggle with Britain.[5] Belgian, French, Scandinavian, and especially German ethnic associations became early supporters of this Dutch American initiative. But it was an alliance with San Francisco's Celtic Union that transformed the small social club into the nerve center of the pro-Boer movement on the west coast of America.

Representing fifteen of San Francisco's Irish societies—from the Ancient Order of Hibernians and its ladies' auxiliaries to the high-society Knights of St. Patrick—the Celtic Union was San Francisco's largest and most influential ethnic association. On 3 November the Knights of the Red Branch—the city's leading Clan na Gael chapter—hosted the first of a series of meetings between delegates from the Celtic Union, the Transvaal Committee, and other ethnic associations to arrange a pro-Boer demonstration later that month.[6] Before a packed Metropolitan Hall, this first mass meeting experimented with a tone of respectability and restraint that was flatly rejected by the stridently anti-British audience. One of the evening's orators, former chairman of the Democratic Party of California William H. Alford, especially misjudged the temper of the crowd:

> The Boers may be narrow, they may be bigoted, they may not always be just, but they have right on their side in this contest. As an individual I have believed and still desire to believe in the ultimate justice of Great Britain. (A storm of hisses.) I have seen peace reign wherever her drumbeats were heard. (Hisses until the speaker was forced to stop.) I have seen slavery banished from her shores. (Pandemonium.)[7]

Alford was not invited to speak at any further pro-Boer events.

Better received were the more trenchant resolutions presented by Irish American Thomas F. Barry, another Democrat and a colonel in the National Guard. He denounced the "cruel and wanton invasion" of the Boer republics carried out "for purely commercial and mercenary purposes." The "blood-guilty rapacity of Great Britain," he warned, threatened to "absolutely exterminate a brave race."[8] The

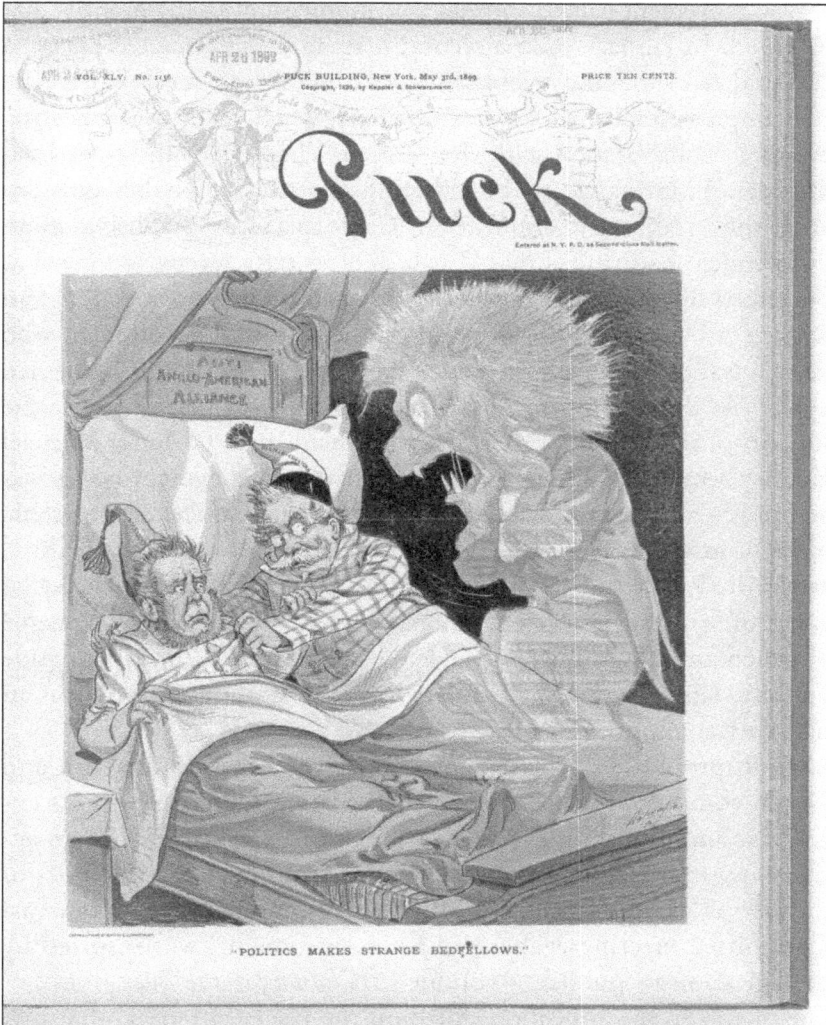

Figure 3.2. "Politics makes strange bedfellows," Louis Dalrymple, *Puck*, 5 May 1899, Library of Congress.

meeting was successful enough to convince the Transvaal Committee that public opinion would support a sustained agitation and more besides. The following week the Committee invited subscriptions to a fund that would finance the sending of "material aid" and an "ambulance corps to the scene of the fighting."[9]

The movement gained considerable momentum in the months that followed. In January 1900 a second mass meeting attracted between two and ten thousand people.[10] The Dutch American hotelier Carrie Cnopius established a ladies' auxiliary, which soon began hosting events in collaboration with the women's chapters of the city's Irish societies.[11] Having clearly outgrown its roots in the Netherlands Society, the "Transvaal Committee of California" was established as an independent body in February.[12] Much of its early success was owed to the efforts of its energetic secretary and chief propagandist, L.K.P. Van Baggen, a Dutch-born former clerk in the Transvaal government who had moved to San Francisco in 1898 upon the death of his Californian wife.[13] As the Committee expanded, Van Baggen helped secure the support of influential patrons, many of them Irish. Ex-Judge Michael Cooney became its president and most active public figure. Cooney was an old Fenian known for assisting in the famous *Catalpa* prison rescue of 1876, in which Fenian convicts in Western Australia were spirited across the Pacific to freedom in San Francisco.[14] Charles B. Flanagan, editor of San Francisco's Irish nationalist weekly *Nation* (only fragments of which are still extant), was an active committee member alongside his wife. James Duval Phelan, the city's Irish Catholic Mayor, was an honorary committee member.[15]

High-profile sympathizers also came from outside the Irish and Dutch communities. Professor David Starr Jordan, the famous eugenicist and founding President of Stanford University, was an active supporter; so too was the celebrity frontiersman and "poet of the Sierras," Joaquin Miller.[16] Miller, whose appearances at Transvaal Committee meetings generated great excitement, was inspired by the agitation to publish a volume of *Chants for the Boer* (1900).[17] The poems in the collection called on the Boers to repeat "that red, dread day at Bunker Hill," and urged Paul Kruger to "stand firm, grim shepherd-hero, stand!"[18] Miller's best work was, however, long behind him; the volume made little impact. The *Chicago Tribune*'s review charitably concluded that Miller's *Chants* "make up in passion what they lack in poetic art."[19]

San Francisco's most influential pro-Boer had both Dutch and Irish roots, but never formally joined the Transvaal Committee. Father Peter C. Yorke was born in Galway, grandson to a Dutch immigrant. He trained for the Catholic priesthood at Maynooth and was posted to San Francisco in 1887. As editor of the archdiocesan newspaper, the *Monitor*, and president of the Gaelic League of California, Yorke rose to local prominence during the 1890s as a labor advocate and an eloquent proponent of advanced Irish nationalism.[20] Many pro-Boers, especially in America's gateway to the Pacific, could be hesitant to equate US imperialism with British jingoism; the Transvaal Committee, for example, generally avoided directly addressing the ongoing war in the Philippines. But Yorke bitterly denounced both in the same breath. On 13 March 1900 he delivered the principal oration at San Francisco's Robert Emmet anniversary celebration. He told the audience that although Britain was undoubtedly "the biggest, brutalest, bloodiest bully that stalks the earth," American hands were also "stained with blood" by their actions in the Philippines. Imperialism in both cases, he claimed, was propelled by the fallacy of the "divine right of races." It made Christians only "at the point of the sword" while depriving its victims of "the inalienable right of nationality." For Yorke, Irish and Boer were united by a "bond of natural sympathy" in the shared imperative to resist imperialism and fight for freedom "by force of arms."[21] His speech was printed in pamphlet form and circulated as far as Ireland, where extracts from it were used in pro-Boer handbills.[22] His advocacy of physical force made him so popular with the Clan na Gael that they debated changing the rules to allow him to attend as the delegate for San Francisco and address their 1902 convention—despite the fact that, as an ordained priest, he was unable to swear the required oath.[23]

It did not take long for Sannie Kruger, the glamorous young Boer singer and activist, to be drawn into the Transvaal Committee's agitation. She appeared as "an interested spectator" at the first mass meeting in November.[24] On Christmas Eve 1899 the *Call* published "Oom Paul and Gen. Joubert as I knew them"—a lavish recollection of her childhood encounters with her famous uncles.[25] By the second mass-meeting in January she was one of the principal attractions. Her rendition of the "Transvaal national hymn" earned an ovation that was "thrilling in its intensity."[26] Through the first three months of 1900, the zenith of the pro-Boer movement, she performed at every mass meeting and benefit concert in San Francisco and Oakland. She assisted Van Baggen in publishing an English translation, with music, of the "Transvaal national hymn," copies of which were sold throughout the west coast "in aid of the Boer ambulance fund."[27]

The anthem booklet was launched on St. Patrick's Day, 1900. That year's celebrations in San Francisco were Boer-themed, and all proceeds were given over to the Transvaal Committee. Between speakers that reminded the crowd that "these Boers are fighting your fight," and that "opinion overturns empires," Sannie Kruger performed "to cheers and applause" and was pictured in the press coverage.[28] The organizers stressed that San Francisco and "every quarter of the globe" was a front in the war against "England's oppression"; if "opinion overturns empires," then the multi-ethnic Transvaal Committee was to the battleground of opinion what the celebrated international volunteer brigades were to the Boer frontline. For those thousands of miles from the fighting who wanted to feel as though they were in the thick of the struggle, Sannie Kruger was invaluable. In addition to her singing talent, "interesting personality," and good looks, she presented herself as Boer royalty—an authentic slice of the Transvaal and a means of feeling closer to Kruger and his generals. The *Chronicle*, in recognition of her talismanic importance, described her as "the Maud Gonne of the Boer cause in Western America."[29]

∗ ∗ ∗

Sannie was not the only Kruger produced by west coast Boer sympathizers to galvanize their following. Pro-Boer feeling was strong in Washington state.[30] Fundraisers were held in Spokane and Tacoma, but the largest mass-meeting took place in Seattle.[31] There the organizers produced a man named Reverend Paul Kruger, a United Brethren minister living in remote Huntsville in the southeastern extreme of the state. Inspired, perhaps, by Sannie, this man claimed to be a grandnephew of the President of the Transvaal himself. In his speech to the crowd, he "referred to a letter which he said he had recently received from Oom Paul." Neither of these claims is likely to have been true. The reverend was born in Germany to German parents, and never visited South Africa—making him a doubtful relative or correspondent of Kruger's. Nevertheless, his presence and his insistence that "the Boers were fighting for the principles of the American revolution" produced the intended enthusiasm among the audience. On his return to Huntsville, he even organized a pro-Boer meeting at nearby Colfax, but subsequently took no further part in the agitation.[32]

The Transvaal Committee had nominal "jurisdiction" over the Pacific coast, but it had little hand in the agitation in Washington. Despite attempts to coordinate a national day of action, the pro-Boer movement remained largely spontaneous and decentralized. Nevertheless, the San Francisco committee successfully organized meetings at Oakland, Sacramento and Hayward and took credit for others in Stockton and as far along the coast as Los Angeles and Portland.[33] Neither of those latter cities—each about one-third the size of San Francisco and with relatively small Irish communities—proved able to sustain an agitation to rival the Bay Area's. The *Los Angeles Times* was strongly pro-imperialist in tone, describing Kruger's government as a "medieval despotism" and claiming stories of atrocities in South Africa and the Philippines alike were the fabrications of "agitators and partisans."[34] The British Consul at Portland, James Laidlaw was quite satisfied with the pro-British "tenor" of *The Oregonian*, Portland's paper of record.[35] He reported that a benefit concert for British widows and orphans had been more successful than a subsequent pro-Boer meeting, and remarked that "the composition of the [latter] assemblage was not such as to lead one to believe that the sentiment of the respectable people here is anti-British."[36]

Still, the Bay area's pro-Boers did not have it all their own way. Passions aroused by the war could produce bitter public feuds with local supporters of Britain's cause. In January an argument between the wealthy English-born politician, bookmaker, and horse-breeder Caesar Young and another "prominent racetrack [man]," Irish-born pro-Boer G. T. Murphy, on the subject of the war boiled over into a street brawl outside an Oakland post office.[37] On 30 March a concert for the benefit of British soldiers was held at the Metropolitan Temple, chaired by the prominent Donegal-born businessman and author, William Greer Harrison. The Boers were dismissed as "an intolerant, dirty people"; their sympathizers condemned; and the audience joined in a rousing rendition of "God Save the Queen." Across the street, a pro-Boer counterdemonstration on the steps of the City Mint (a traditional venue for protests) was blocked by nine police

officers posted on the orders of its McKinley-appointed Superintendent, Frank A. Leach. Several showdowns over the use of the Mint
steps unfolded over the following months, with Leach insisting that
he had a right to ban discussion of an "international question" from
government property, and the Transvaal Committee attacking him
for what they considered a "pusillanimous and contemptible surrender to imperial England." By June, former Republican congressio-
nal candidate-turned anti-imperialist Transvaal Committee member
Thomas O'Brien was arrested for attempting to speak from the steps
and jailed for two days. O'Brien proceeded to sue Leach for having
falsely imprisoned him; when Leach bizarrely failed to respond to the
suit, a default judgment was entered against him for $25,000—then
the largest sum ever awarded in California.[38]

Mass meetings and minor acts of civil disobedience may have been
enough to satisfy most Boer sympathizers on the west coast. But the
most committed among them sought to help the Boers directly. First,
financial aid was remitted to W. J. Leyds, the Boer representative at
Brussels.[39] Next the Transvaal Committee attempted to follow the example of Irish nationalists in Chicago and Boston by raising an ambulance corps which, it was openly suggested, would be free to join the
fighting once it arrived at the front.[40] While some individuals may have
received assistance in travelling to South Africa, there is no evidence
that this corps ever took shape, let alone departed. A Boer widows and
orphans fund was established, though it is unclear whether this money
ever found its way to any South African civilians.[41] What is clear is
that from mid-December 1899 a cabal of Dutch hardliners and Fenians
within the Transvaal Committee had secretly decided to pursue extra-
legal forms of assistance. But they were being watched.

* * *

The local pro-Boer movement initially attracted the attention of the
British authorities ahead of its first mass-meeting in November 1899,
when the organizers invited every consul in the city except the British. William Clayton Pickersgill, a career diplomat who had previously
served in Madagascar, Portuguese West Africa, and the Congo, had been
the British Consul General at San Francisco since October 1898.[42] The

European consuls all politely declined the invitation, and Pickersgill laughingly told a reporter that he had been "conspicuously ignored."[43] He wrote of the "amusing" affair to his immediate superior Lord Julian Pauncefote, the first British ambassador to the United States, and remarked that the principal figures behind the meeting "were either Irish or German, or a very bad mixture of both."[44]

Within a few weeks Pickersgill's dismissiveness gave way to anxiety about the Transvaal Committee's intentions. In mid-December he was approached by an informant named "Saunders" who claimed that "a car load of war materiel" had been purchased by the Committee and was to be shipped to South Africa via train to Seattle. Pickersgill alerted the British consuls at Portland and Seattle. He engaged the consulate's attorneys—the firm of T.E.K. Cormac, Denis Donohoe, and Alexander R. Baum (apparently a more agreeable mixture of Irish and German)—to investigate Saunders's credibility. Ultimately, no evidence could be found of munitions either passing Portland or arriving at Seattle, and the attorneys determined that Saunders was a man with a "bad reputation" who was attempting to sell bogus information for a profit.[45] In the course of investigating his allegations, however, Cormac, Donohoe & Baum secured a source who would prove to be both reliable and valuable. This informant, who was acquainted with and apparently trusted by the leading figures in the Transvaal Committee, was engaged on a monthly salary of $150 and assigned the codename "Agent X."[46]

Pickersgill's reliance on his attorneys to manage intelligence gathering—and his new star informant—was unusual and something of a bone of contention with Pauncefote. The firm's legal fees effectively doubled the cost of the consulate's secret inquiries. It may be that Pickersgill, having been in the city only a year and having no experience monitoring Fenianism or engaging private detective agencies such as Pinkerton's, considered the hands of Cormac, Donohoe & Baum more reliable than his own in a matter so delicate. This degree of separation was also, it seems, intended to preserve Agent X's cover. When Pauncefote pressed his concerns about the mounting costs, Pickersgill claimed it would be impossible for "any public official being able to deal directly with a spy engaged in such work as that which X is doing."[47] If Agent X was to be retained, the Foreign

Office simply had to stomach the attorneys' fees. Pickersgill assured Pauncefote of his confidence in the arrangement:

> It was not possible except through their intermediary to secure the services of Agent X, of whose identity even I am supposed to be ignorant, but whom I have recognised accidentally and whom I consider to be a person extremely well qualified for the part of private detective.[48]

In case assurances alone did not persuade Pauncefote of the necessity of the added expense, Pickersgill also transmitted ample reports describing the project's success. As a result, there survives a detailed—if at times selective—record of the firm's investigations in Foreign Office papers.

Agent X was trusted by certain leading figures in the pro-Boer movement. The Vice President of the Transvaal Committee, Louis Christian Cnopius, and his wife Carrie—President of the Ladies' Auxiliary—were Agent X's chief sources of information. In company with "the Cnopiae" (as they were dryly dubbed in the reports), Agent X could also participate in unguarded conversations with men such as Van Baggen.[49] The details of these exchanges were then relayed through oral interviews and written reports to Cormac, Donohoe & Baum, who forwarded the highlights to the consul. Agent X does not appear to have been a permanent officer of the movement, but attended occasional committee meetings concerning the organizing of pro-Boer meetings and concerts, as well as some gatherings of the ladies' auxiliary.[50] Luncheons and trips to the theater— expenses covered by the consulate—could be equally fruitful.[51] While not typically privy to the finer points of Transvaal Committee planning, Agent X had abundant access to conversations touching obliquely on plots and the movements of suspects. This access gave Pickersgill enough information to put the appropriate authorities—and where necessary, Pinkertons—on the scent. At first, the reports related to shipments of supplies—possibly arms—to South Africa, which Agent X repeatedly heard had been accomplished at least once through Portland. A subsequent attempt at smuggling was frustrated when Pickersgill, having learned from X the name of the shipping company being contracted, sent private detectives to warn the agency against collaborating with the Transvaal Committee.[52] But concerns soon shifted to the movement's potential to bring the violence of the war to North America.

* * *

From late December 1899 newspapers across the United States contained a rash of reports that American Fenians intended to assist the Boers by striking at Canada. Men were allegedly mustering from Nebraska to Massachusetts, and "vast quantities of dynamite, lyddite ammunition and supplies" were supposedly being stored in remote areas of Vermont and Maine in preparation for an invasion.[53] Colonel Roger F. Scannell of Boston, a veteran of the Fenian raids of the 1860s, told reporters that "an army of 100,000 Irish Nationalists" would invade Canada and "make things interesting for the English government."[54] The rumors of an invasion were generally received—correctly—by the State Department and the British Embassy as no more than deliberate misinformation intended to "frighten the Canadians into keeping their soldiers at home."[55] It did not have the desired effect; rather it was reportedly "laughed at by the militia department, the Government, and the people generally" in Canada.[56]

Still, British authorities were alert to the possibility that Fenians might attempt to cause mischief in Canada on a smaller scale. Commissioner of Dominion Police A. P. Sherwood, as we have already seen, hired Pinkertons to watch American Fenians from January 1900.[57] Captain Fagen, acting Senior Officer at the Royal Navy base at Esquimalt on Vancouver Island asked Consul Laidlaw at Portland to pay special attention to any suspicious activity in the Pacific northwest. When an Irish-Liverpudlian military veteran named Edward Magee told a reporter that he had raised a pro-Boer military company of forty-six men in Seattle, Laidlaw had him watched.[58] Nothing came of Magee's corps; it was by his own admission established "to intimidate principally."[59] The most danger was to be apprehended from schemes that did not appear in the newspapers first—the Welland Canal bombing being a prime example.

A similar plot to destroy strategic infrastructure appears to have been underway on the west coast, and Agent X was the first to detect it. On 16 January 1900, when attending a branch meeting of the Ladies' Auxiliary at which leading members of the Transvaal Committee and "some Fenians" were present, Agent X learned from Van Baggen that "there was talk of blowing up" part of the Royal Navy base at Esquimalt on Vancouver Island. The Knights of the Red Branch—the front organization for San Francisco's Clan na Gael—were pressing the Dutch side of the pro-Boer agitation for a volunteer to send north to help carry out the attack.[60]

Pickersgill immediately communicated his concerns about the possible unfolding plot to the United States Attorney for northern California but found him disinclined to spend money on an investigation unless directed to do so by Washington, DC.[61] While offering every assurance that violations of neutrality would not be tolerated, the US government scrupulously evaded assisting British or Canadian authorities in the politically precarious enterprise of spying on Irish American nationalists—much to the frustration of Pickersgill and Pauncefote.[62] In late January Agent X had another conversation with Van Baggen and learned that although the plot against Esquimalt was progressing, the Irish were reluctant to move ahead until the Dutch side had contributed a volunteer.[63] There was, for the moment, little to distinguish this plot from other fantastical rumors of Fenian activity picked up by British consulates throughout the United States at the turn of 1900. Then on 5 February, Pickersgill received the following letter:

> British Consul,
> Dear Sir, I am in a position to give you the most valuable information that will save several millions of dollars, for a consideration. Please use none of your official envelopes.
> Yours, J.F.M.[64]

Two days later T.E.K. Cormac of Cormac, Donohoe & Baum met with "JFM," whom he described in his report to Pickersgill as a "small, thin . . . shabbily dressed" man in his late twenties. JFM seemed "exceedingly anxious concerning his own safety" throughout the course of the interview. Extracting specific details from him required "considerable fencing and cross-questioning." He claimed to be on the inside of the pro-Boer movement and to know that the Transvaal Committee had at least $1,100 deposited in one bank. There was, he said, an ongoing disagreement within the movement over whether the funds should be applied to "legitimate Red Cross purposes" or to "the destruction of Government buildings in Canada," but the "inner ring" of leading members who controlled the funds were in favor of physical force. He claimed that on 4 February two men had left the city for Victoria, via Seattle, to coordinate the dynamite attacks and would go to Chicago once the work was done. One was a Dutchman named Van Der Line. The other was an Irish New Yorker calling himself Francis Scanlan, a thirty-five-year-old blacksmith-turned-electrician who "fears neither God nor devil." JFM explained he had come forward because he did not want to see lives lost and property destroyed in Canada. But he admitted he was hard up. Cormac added his own suspicion that "his object was probably revenge." JFM agreed to continue attending pro-Boer meetings and provide more information if possible. Cormac had him tailed by Pinkertons immediately after leaving the meeting.[65]

Agent X was supplied with JFM's description and on 15 February encountered him at a Transvaal Committee meeting. His real name, it emerged, was M. F. Jordan—JFM were his initials in reverse—one of the Knights of the Red Branch who had become actively involved in the pro-Boer agitation.[66] As his lackluster alias suggested, Jordan was not cut out to be a spy. He quickly became convinced that he was being shadowed by Fenians investigating his treachery; in fact, the men following him were Cormac's Pinkertons. This mix-up, Cormac lamented, had put Jordan in a "paroxysm of terror." On one occasion when Jordan noticed the detectives watching the front entrance of a barber shop he had visited, he fled out the back door and jumped over a fence.[67] Pickersgill, already stretched to cover the fees of Agent X, his attorneys, and the Pinkertons, insisted that the British Columbia Government should pick up the tab for Jordan's "consideration." Negotiating this arrangement meant a considerable delay in payment—which only further convinced Jordan that informing was not worth the risk.[68] Aside from a chance meeting with Cormac on 1 March, Jordan was in too great a "state of terror" to cooperate with the consulate.[69] On 22 March, in his last communication with Pickersgill, he asked to be left alone:

I had hoped my last letter would end the matter. In the event of interception no paltry consideration would ever satisfy my conscience, and you place yourself in my position and I think you would feel likewise. Let those people be watchful.[70]

The consulate may have lost a potentially important source, but the Jordan episode served to reinforce Pickersgill's confidence in Agent X. With the agent's information on a BC dynamite plot corroborated by Jordan's, the threat posed by the Transvaal Committee assumed a graver aspect. Pickersgill cabled Captain Fagen at Esquimalt and the Lieutenant Governor at Victoria to be on alert for persons with "hostile intentions."[71]

* * *

In the months that followed, strange incidents took place at Esquimalt that seemed to vindicate suspicions that it was being targeted. On 26 February two miners visiting from the Yukon gold-rush town of Dawson were found wandering around the naval base, having walked in along the beach at low tide. They were interrogated and their rooms in Victoria searched, but with nothing to contradict their story of a Sunday stroll gone awry, they were released with a warning.[72] M. F. Jordan told Cormac that he believed these men to have been "sub-agents of the San Francisco emissaries," and Agent X was given the impression that Louis Cnopius thought the same.[73] The guard at the fort was doubled. Around this time "a man who desired to work mischief" was seen clambering over the *chevaux-de-frise* into the base but escaped after warning shots were fired.[74] In April the paymaster at the base, Lieutenant James Clarke, deserted with thousands of pounds in his possession.[75] Days later a sentry noticed the figure of a man walking through the fort in low light and stormy weather. When the figure did not respond to the challenge the sentry opened fire—as the heightened security protocol required. The man turned out to be the garrison's own Lieutenant Reginald Scott on patrol duty, and the two bullet wounds he sustained to his chest proved fatal. It was supposed that Scott could not hear the sentry's voice through the blowing gale.[76] The specter of Fenianism was proving deadlier than the real thing.

Security concerns were raised even higher after the Welland Canal bombing of 21 April. Major Bennett of the Duke of Connaught's Own Rifles told reporters in Vancouver that on 16 May two "supposed Fenians" attempting to sneak into the fortifications at Esquimalt were repulsed under fire and escaped under cover of darkness. He explained that "ultra-Boer sympathisers" from San Francisco were known to have traveled to Victoria "with the avowed intention of blowing up the Esquimalt fortifications with dynamite."[77] As a precaution, plans to hold a firework display near the fort for Queen Victoria's birthday on 24 May were canceled lest the event provide cover for explosions of a different sort.[78]

It is unclear how many of these incidents represented false alarms or, conversely, near misses. Leading figures on both sides appeared convinced the threat to Esquimalt was real. Montagu White, former consul of the South African Republic in London and unofficial representative of the Transvaal in the United States, was interviewed in Washington, DC, in mid-April 1900. He argued that the longer the war went on, the more hope there would be for the Boers as Britain's vulnerabilities elsewhere in the empire could be exposed. "Not long ago there was a little flurry on the Canadian border at Esquimalt" he said, which "showed how many things might occur which might trouble Great Britain."[79] Captain Fagen at Esquimalt admitted to Pickersgill that his own superiors were skeptical about the "reality of the danger" on the west coast. But Fagen himself stressed his gratitude to Pickersgill for the intelligence work at San Francisco which he believed "probably saved us from dangers which few can be brought to believe in until too late." "As a fellow-countryman of the chief conspirators," remarked Pickersgill, "[Fagen] realises, no doubt more than most Englishmen do, the temptation which an unprotected head offers to an Irishman playing with a stick."[80]

When word reached San Francisco in late February that the guard at Esquimalt had been doubled and that intruders had been apprehended, members of the Transvaal Committee began to suspect that one of their number was giving information to the British consulate.[81] This heightened anxiety made Agent X's job difficult. Sources became more circumspect. Louis and Carrie Cnopius were particularly rattled by the possibility of exposure and quarreled with Van Baggen over the risks of his physical force policy.[82] It would be safer, they felt, to focus on sending men and materiel to South Africa instead.[83] But as these pet schemes of the Cnopius couple failed to get off the ground—thanks in part to Agent X's spying—they stepped back from pro-Boer agitation in April. The man who emerged to take their place was someone whom Agent X had first met at luncheon with "the Cnopiae" in late March—a Fenian who called himself "Donovan."[84]

A thirty-five-year-old engineer from Syracuse, New York, Donovan very closely matched the description of the "Francis Scanlan" whom Jordan claimed had been sent north to Victoria in February.[85] Agent X won him over quickly, and in a series of conversations over three months he divulged a considerable amount of information. He told the agent that he had been waiting in Portland until February when he received instructions from some Chicago Fenians to proceed to British Columbia. He and a companion were tasked with managing three men who would do the real work. But when the guard was doubled, it became too difficult to approach the naval complex; the plan was put on hold and he came to San Francisco to await further orders. In April he was ordered back to Chicago "to report fully the condition of Coast affairs" and was still, despite the now formidable obstacles, sanguine about the prospect of success at Esquimalt.[86] But in May he told X that one of the men in Victoria had to be removed for "drinking and talking."[87] By June talk of Esquimalt had ceased and Donovan intimated that locks of Canadian canals such as those at Lachine and Sault Ste. Marie would likely be targeted next.[88] Agent X's reports frequently stressed that Donovan was "dangerous," and one of them contained information about his background:

> He says that he is the son of one of the Fenians who were executed in Ireland and his family expelled, all their property stolen from them, and he does not think anything is quite bad enough for the English . . . [He is] ready to throw away his life or anyone else's if he can accomplish anything.[89]

Donovan's true identity was a mystery to the consulate and remains so. It was briefly suspected that he might have been the same person as the "Karl Dallman" arrested in connection with the Welland Canal explosion, and photos were sent to San Francisco so that Agent X might identify him.[90] It was quickly discovered that this could not be the case as Donovan appeared again in San Francisco while "Dallman" was in custody in Canada.[91] Copies of Agent X's reports containing Donovan's description were sent north to Victoria, but his movements did not follow a predictable pattern and proved difficult to track.[92] In late April, after a visit from Donovan, X attempted to telephone Cormac, Donohoe & Baum to inform them which ferry he was taking across the Bay so that they could put Pinkerton detectives on his trail. But the call could not be made in time and Donovan slipped through the net.[93]

In some ways Donovan seems too good to be true. The convenient timing of his arrival on the scene, his unusual candor, and the sensational nature of his revelations, combined with the apparent failure of the consulate to track or properly identify him, is strange. Indeed, there may be grounds to question the reliability of Agent X's reports from April onward. Citing "considerations of economy," Pickersgill discontinued the agent's monthly salary of $150 from 15 April and thenceforth paid for information only as it arose. With previous sources drying up, this new arrangement may have encouraged Agent X to exaggerate both the danger posed by Donovan and the value of his disclosures. For example, when Pickersgill fell seriously ill in early June 1900, the agent claimed Donovan had insinuated in conversation that the consul had been poisoned.[94] When Cormac, Donohoe & Baum met with Pickersgill's physician to investigate this possibility, they were assured that the consul had typhoid fever. The attorneys found that the poisoning story "was doubtless the idle boast of a depraved man," but they were forced to reckon with the uncertain accuracy of X's reports. They decided that:

> It does not follow, however, in our judgment, that the balance of D[onovan]'s disclosures should necessarily be regarded as false. The value of the disclosures obtained by X from him in the past, as far as the same related to plots against Canada, has been fully proved.[95]

It might be reasonable to wonder whether Agent X had invented Donovan entirely, had "a member of [the] firm" of attorneys not personally seen him on at least one occasion in July.[96]

More questions were raised about the Agent's response to a photograph of the mysterious Welland Canal bombing suspect "Karl Dallman." X claimed to have met the man at a Transvaal Committee meeting around 23 March at the office of Charles Flanagan, but could not remember anything more about him.[97] We know, however, that "Dallman," or Luke Dillon, was in Buffalo on 22 March. The misidentification may have been an honest mistake on Agent X's part; it may equally have been an effort to remain in the consulate's pay. There is no evidence that Pickersgill or the attorneys ever doubted their agent's intentions; the surviving correspondence in the Foreign Office papers gives the opposite impression. Both parties repeatedly affirmed their confidence in Agent X as an "excellent source of information."[98] Superintendent Frank Hussey of the Victoria Police did not trust J.F.M., but he believed Agent X had done "considerable work" under the direction of Cormac, Donohoe & Baum, whose "loyalty is unquestionable." Chief of Dominion Police A. P. Sherwood similarly believed the attorneys were trustworthy, but wondered whether they were "being imposed upon" by X.[99] The BC government nevertheless took the extra precaution of hiring Pinkerton men to investigate Agent X.[100] No report survives, but had they discovered anything to discredit the agent, it would most likely have been brought to the consulate's attention. As late as 20 July 1900 Wellesley Moore, acting consul during Pickersgill's illness, believed that their mole "may still prove useful."[101] But that was to be the final mention of Agent X.

* * *

The identity of Agent X was a closely guarded secret; no names were mentioned in official correspondence. We do know, however, that X was a woman. Pickersgill let it slip in a handwritten note to Pauncefote at the foot of one of X's reports. Referring to the "Saunders" affair and the rumored arms shipment to South Africa, Pickersgill explained that while that particular case had proven bogus there was reason to believe another scheme had since succeeded: "X heard from those who had arranged for the shipment that it had been safely accomplished, and here she refers to it again."[102] The agent's sex was confirmed from another source entirely—Superintendent Frank Hussey of Victoria. Hussey traveled to San Francisco in April 1900 for treatment of an eye condition, and while there he met with Pickersgill. In a letter written from the McNutt Hospital, Hussey told the Attorney General of British Columbia that "Special Agent X is a woman employed by Mr Cormack [sic]—Mr Pickersgill has only recently ascertained this fact—I shall see her before I leave this city."[103]

Agent X's reports and the correspondence between Cormac, Donohoe & Baum, Pickersgill and Pauncefote are rich in clues about her life. They detail the events she attended, the circles in which she moved, her perspective on the politics underlying the movement and even aspects of her family life. She spent more time with the women of the movement—notably Carrie Cnopius, Cora Driffield (in whose house lodged two suspicious Belgian-born sympathizers) and the wife of Charles Flanagan—than she did with the men.[104] It is also clear that Agent X belonged to the Dutch side of the movement. Before meeting Donovan through "the Cnopiae," she encountered the Irish side of the movement only at meetings and events, and the vague terms in which she described it convey little familiarity with Irish American associations or politics. The reports point to a young, educated, middle-class woman who was highly regarded by some of the leading figures in the Transvaal Committee, and who helped organize several events between January and late March 1900. Even these broad parameters narrow things down considerably. The comprehensive coverage of the San Francisco pro-Boer movement in the local newspapers shows that only a handful of women had access to the meetings that Agent X attended.[105] One of them was Sannie Kruger, "the Maud Gonne of the Boer cause in Western America."[106]

* * *

Sannie Kruger was a liar. For a start, that was not her real name. She was born Mercedes Estelle Woodford in South Africa in 1880. Her father, Ethelbert George Woodford, was a New York-born mining engineer who achieved some prominence on the Rand. Her mother was the South Africa-born Susanna "Sannie" De Wet, a relative of Generals Christiaan and Piet De Wet, Piet Joubert, and, so she claimed, of Paul Kruger—although the latter connection is dubious.[107] She and Ethelbert had two sons after Mercedes—Washington Wyman and Lincoln De Wet Woodford. At some point in the early 1890s, their marriage failed. Susanna received a lump sum settlement and moved to London with the children. The boys attended boarding school in Croydon, and Mercedes was educated in Brussels.[108] There she met and befriended a daughter of apostle John Willard Young—son of the famous Mormon prophet, Brigham Young. This, it seems, is where the trouble began.

Young, then also living in London, became acquainted with Susanna through their daughters' friendship. He persuaded Susanna to purchase

$20,000 worth of stock in an American venture in which he was in-
volved. The money shortly disappeared. Susanna sued, alleging she had
been swindled; in 1897 a London court awarded a judgment in her
favor, but Young did not honor the damages owed.[109] That year, probably for reasons connected to these financial troubles, Susanna and the
children relocated to Denver, Colorado, where Susanna secured a divorce from Ethelbert.[110] Mercedes, then seventeen, soon eloped with her
father's private secretary, Frank E. Newsam, against her father's wishes.
The two married in Tucson, Arizona, and were joined by her mother
and brothers; her disapproving father returned to South Africa.[111] With
no support forthcoming from Ethelbert, the family's financial circumstances continued to deteriorate; Washington was forced to take work as
a steam locomotive fireman, then later at a copper mine with his brother
Lincoln.[112] Mercedes later alleged that her husband Frank was failing to
provide.[113] Sometime around October 1899, aged 19, Mercedes ran away
again—this time alone—to San Francisco. She found work as an operatic singer at the Tivoli Opera House, but not as Mercedes Woodford or
Mrs. Newsam. Instead, she took her mother's name—Sannie—and the
surname of her famous purported granduncle: Kruger.[114]

This new persona proved a hit in a San Francisco experiencing "Boer
fever" during the opening months of the South African War. But, cut
off from her father and her husband and a long way from South Africa,
she remained in financial trouble. A performer's wage and whatever
consideration she received for her articles in the *Call* could not have
been enough to maintain "Sannie Kruger"—let alone her family—in
circumstances approaching the comfort they enjoyed before their fortunes turned. She needed money and she needed a divorce. As the
Chronicle later remarked:

> The divorce prayed for explains the reasons for Sannie Krueger's [sic] public
> career and brings out some family history. She was without means, her hus-
> band having utterly failed to support her, and as her father and mother were
> separated and their fortunes about dissipated she could get but little from
> the sources to which she would naturally have looked in her trouble.[115]

Under such circumstances, a monthly salary of $150 for passing in-
formation on the pro-Boer movement to the British consulate must

have looked an enticing proposition. It may be that Sannie Kruger encountered Cormac, Donohoe & Baum while in the market for a divorce attorney. Sadly there is no record of how exactly the firm engaged Agent X, or who approached whom.

Agent X's contract began in mid-December 1899, the month after Sannie Kruger attended her first pro-Boer meeting.[116] Sannie Kruger, like Agent X, was naturally closest to the Dutch side of the pro-Boer movement. In the 1900 United States census she was enumerated at the same residence as Louis and Carrie Cnopius—friends and confidants of Agent X.[117] Agent X and Sannie Kruger were both most actively involved in the Transvaal Committee between January and March 1900, notably at meetings where arrangements were made for the pro-Boer themed St. Patrick's Day celebration.[118] Sannie Kruger was the main performer at that event. In one report Agent X mentioned that she was expecting a personal visit from Van Baggen on 18 February, explaining obliquely: "He has literary aspirings."[119] One month later the "Transvaal National Hymn" appeared in booklet form, published by Van Baggen with lyrics provided by Sannie Kruger.[120]

It was not long before things began to unravel, however. On the evening of 23 March, a man showed up at the Tivoli Opera House and asked to see Mrs. Newsam. When told there was no such lady working at the theater, he pointed to Sannie Kruger's photo and insisted there was. Sannie emerged and admitted that the unnamed visitor was an old friend, that she had indeed married Frank Newsam, and that she had been living under an assumed name. She lied, however, in claiming that the marriage had been arranged against her will and that she had since "got an absolute divorce." The scandal immediately reached the local newspapers under such headlines as "SANNIE'S SECRET STUNS THE JOHNNIES."[121] Three days later Pickersgill wrote to Pauncefote mentioning that he had "accidentally" discovered the identity of Agent X.[122] On 1 April Frank Newsam himself arrived in San Francisco, and as the story of her false identity and failed marriage appeared in newspapers throughout the country, Sannie Kruger was granted a month's leave of absence from the Tivoli.[123] Newsam returned to Tucson a few days later—it is possible that Sannie followed him to visit her family. Certainly, in the weeks that followed she was conspicuous by her absence from the pro-Boer scene. She was billed to perform at a pro-Boer meeting at Hayward on 7 April, but the organizers announced that she was "unable to be present on account of illness."[124] Neither was she anywhere in the program or reports of the pro-Boer benefit concert held at the Metropolitan Hall on 24 April.[125] It is probably no coincidence that the consulate received no information from Agent X between 28 March and 24 April. Her full monthly salary was not renewed on 15 April, and she received only a "half month salary" of $64 for the period between 15 April and 11 May.[126] The records contain no explanation for this change. But we can hazard a guess.

* * *

In the meantime, Sannie's father had returned to the United States, together with several other American citizens resident in South Africa. Their visit was undertaken in support of the US Consul at Pretoria, Charles Macrum, who had discovered that his consular dispatches were being intercepted, delayed, and opened by the British military censor. In December 1899, unable to properly perform his duties, Macrum had left for Washington, DC, to report personally on what he claimed were violations of US neutrality. The State Department opted to suppress the affair lest it fuel opposition to its policy of rapprochement with Britain. Upset, Macrum turned to the press in February; his story was taken up by anti-imperialists and pro-Boers as proof that the United States was conducting a secret alliance with Britain. Ethelbert and his fellow Americans were back in the United States to defend Macrum's conduct in the controversy and to support his calls for an inquiry.[127]

When asked in Washington whether the San Francisco stage performer mentioned in the papers was really the niece of "Oom Paul," Ethelbert replied that he had never heard of a Sannie Kruger. Suspicious, he wrote her a letter asking whether she was family or a fraud; the response confirmed that she was in fact his daughter. This communication was the catalyst for a reconciliation between Ethelbert and his estranged family.[128] It may have been Ethelbert who sent the "old friend" to the Tivoli to find Mrs. Newsam. He also sent Carrie Cnopius a letter encouraging the pro-Boer movement and condemning the McKinley administration's support for Britain, the "pirate in a dress suit."[129] For Sannie this détente with her father meant the return of some financial stability for the first time in three precarious years.

In mid-April Ethelbert told reporters he would henceforth "pay the expenses" of his daughter's operatic training.[130]

Sannie Kruger was back on the San Francisco stage by May. She performed at some small non-political events at which fellow pro-Boer, Professor David Starr Jordan, lectured on natural history. But she did not feature at any further Transvaal Committee meetings or concerts. At some point in mid-1900 her mother joined her in San Francisco.[131] Agent X's circumstances changed around the same time. From May her description of Donovan's visits to her, en route to San Francisco, imply that she was living across the Bay.[132] In July Cormac, Donohoe & Baum explained that "X's residence is a private house situated in a suburb and occupied solely by X and family."[133]

Agent X did not see Van Baggen or attend any Transvaal Committee meetings from May onward, and her information now came chiefly from conversations in her house with Donovan. Reporting on one such conversation, she noted the following exchange: "D[onovan] said 'Do not let Mrs. De Wet know I have been here she is too smart for you to deal with.' I showed him her photo and he knew it immediately. I do wish it were possible to identify D. He will be 'wanted' some day."[134] Mrs. De Wet was Sannie Kruger's mother. It is unlikely that many people in San Francisco would have in their home a photograph of this middle-aged South African woman, only recently arrived in the area. Except, perhaps, her daughter.

It should be noted that there are two fragments of evidence that could be presented against the case that Sannie Kruger was Agent X. Letters and invoices from the attorneys indicate that Agent X attended (and claimed expenses for) a pro-Boer rally hosted by the Robert Emmet Club at Sacramento on 8 February.[135] But in neither the promotional press release ahead of the meeting, nor the brief local news report after, was Sannie Kruger's name mentioned. Others of the San Francisco delegation likely in attendance also went unreported, however, and there is no evidence that Sannie was anywhere else at the time of this meeting.[136] Another strike against Sannie Kruger is a line in a receipt for Agent X's expenses for the period 15 March—15 April which reads: "Conopius [sic], F. and Kruger—$3.00." The line appears between charges for "entertaining," and probably refers to a luncheon or theater visit involving Carrie Cnopius, Mrs. Flanagan, and Sannie Kruger. It would be sloppy indeed for the individual typing the invoices to include the surname of Agent X anywhere. How might this be explained? A box office receipt for tickets reserved in the women's names, for example, might have been submitted by Agent X.[137] If a secretary unaware of Agent X's identity was tasked with compiling the summary of expenses, he or she may not have known what names to obscure. The mention of her name may, in other words, be an administrative error. It is worth noting, however, that aside from this invoice Sannie Kruger was *never once* mentioned in Agent X's reports or in any of the exchanges between the attorneys, Pickersgill or Pauncefote. This is a peculiar omission. A person with her prominence and her Boer connections—someone who had been publicly likened to Maud Gonne—ought to have been central to the consulate's inquiries.

The balance of evidence leans persuasively towards the conclusion that Sannie Kruger was Agent X. She had a clear financial motive. She was not averse to deceit or juggling multiple identities. She had twice already defied her pro-Boer parents. Her role as a performer and a symbol of the movement, along with her collaboration with Van Baggen on the "Transvaal National Hymn," aligns with Agent X's status as a trusted associate of leading figures and an occasional member of committees, rather than a full-time organizer. Like Agent X, she assorted chiefly with the Dutch side of the movement, was no expert on Irish politics, and was especially close to the Cnopius family. Apart from Sacramento she can be positively placed at some of the same meetings as Agent X; her absences also align. Agent X's disappearance and pay-cut in April correspond exactly with the scandal over Sannie Kruger's real identity and her leave of absence from the theatre. Her reduced participation in the movement after her return in late April seems to match that of Agent X. Finally, the evidence that Agent X appeared to be living in a suburban house with a Mrs. De Wet, of whom she possessed a picture, is difficult to discount. The female informant who was instrumental in foiling a joint Fenian–pro-Boer dynamite plot on Vancouver Island was almost certainly the nineteen-year-old grand-niece of the Boer generals Joubert and De Wet.

* * *

There is an extraordinary irony in the likelihood that the talisman of the pro-Boer movement in California, the token Boer herself, was quietly selling its secrets to the local British Consul. At least the pro-Boers and Irish nationalists of San Francisco were spared the pain of knowing. Sannie Kruger and Mrs. Sannie De Wet stepped quietly to the fringes of the scene after the spring of 1900. On at least two occasions, Mrs. De Wet gave a public lecture on "South Africa and Boer life," with an accompanying musical performance from her daughter, but these events were not held under the auspices of the Transvaal Committee.[138] Sannie Kruger focused on her operatic training; she acquired a reputation as an impressive soprano and enjoyed a relatively successful career that included a European tour.[139] Despite turning away from politics, her family life remained characteristically dramatic. Sometime after 1903 she married again. Her husband was Grant Carpenter, twin brother of famous Californian artist and ethnographer Grace Carpenter Hudson. Grant, a lawyer, reporter, and by the 1920s one of Hollywood's most prominent screenwriters, was fifteen years Sannie's senior and had children from a previous marriage. Their reportedly turbulent relationship was at one point particularly strained when Sannie's brother Lincoln—following his sister's example—eloped with Grant's daughter against the family's wishes.[140]

Ethelbert remarried and had three children in Seattle. After the earthquake in 1906, Susanna "Sannie" De Wet moved back to Colorado and married a rancher. The family was in the newspapers again in 1910 and 1913 when mother and daughter filed suit to enforce payment of the settlement awarded against John Willard Young by a London court in 1897.[141] Whether they succeeded is unclear. Following the failure of her marriage to Grant Carpenter in 1916, Sannie Kruger re-joined her mother in Colorado, married again, changed her name back to Mercedes, and found work as a music teacher. In 1955 after the death of her husband, she visited South Africa for the first time since her childhood; four years later she died in San Francisco.[142]

The Transvaal Committee of California remained active—albeit on a reduced scale—for the duration of the war. Schemes to assist the Boers were abandoned in favor of simple propaganda and anti-imperialist lobbying. For example, the Committee organized receptions for prominent pro-Boers passing through San Francisco. James Grattan Grey, the

Irish-Australian pro-Boer dismissed from the New Zealand Hansard staff, was feted by the society on his arrival in September 1900.[143] Commandant Willem Snyman and American adventurer Francis John Turner, who had fought on the Boer side, gave lectures on their experiences in 1901.[144] Another benefit concert was held in December 1901, and Father Yorke addressed the final pro-Boer mass meeting at the Metropolitan Hall in February 1902.[145] The Irish connection survived the Esquimalt plot failure, with Fenians Michael Cooney and Jeremiah Deasy occupying the Committee's presidency in the two years that followed. At Cooney's funeral in February 1901, Van Baggen and the German American suffragist Theodore Pinther were among the Committee men who carried his coffin.[146] Van Baggen and Pinther also became frequent contributors to Patrick Ford's *Irish World* (New York). Their articles criticizing Rand mining interests and Britain's conduct of the war were for some months a central feature of the anti-war coverage in the United States' most prominent "Irish" weekly.[147] The cross-ethnic cooperation that characterized the Transvaal Committee's agitation was echoed in the eastern states. It would resurface to challenge the "great rapprochement" in various forms until 1917, when the US entry into the Great War on the Allied side spelled the end of the Hiberno-German anti-British lobby.

The South African War provoked a storm of feeling in San Francisco, whipped up by a resurgent Irish nationalism and an anti-imperialist outcry in which groups of Dutch and German Americans, among others, shared. The Transvaal Committee emerged to stage-manage this theatre of indignation. For a time, Sannie Kruger was its star performer. But the "inner circle" of hardliners within the Committee were unable to turn harmless ovations into meaningful material contributions to either the war or, as the Fenians among them would have hoped, to the Irish question. Distance militated against them. Ireland and South Africa were on the other side of the world; even British Columbia was almost a thousand miles to the north. The remote Pacific coast may have been safely beyond the reach of the Special Branch. But in the end, no expertise was necessary to thwart their plans. The ad-hoc espionage of the local British consulate proved to be enough. Pickersgill and his attorneys were able to persuade Sannie Kruger, the "Maud Gonne of the Boer cause in Western America," to inform on her admirers (unlike her namesake, whatever her reputation). Like the Welland Canal attack before it, the Esquimalt plot's failure demoralized its backers. But there was life in the movement still. There were other means, besides dynamite, by which Irish nationalist pro-Boers could seek to frustrate British ambitions. There was no shortage of opportunities for cross-ethnic cooperation; there was even another Boer celebrity onto whom they could latch. Irish nationalists in the eastern states might seize "the hour of destiny" yet—if they could only set aside their differences and act quickly. If indeed.

4

"Petty Injuries"

The Limits of Irish American Agitation

The fragile unity restored to Irish nationalism in the United States by the outbreak of the South African War was shattered before the return of peace. For a time, Irish nationalists appeared to be of one voice in condemning British imperial aggression and in sympathizing with the Boers. They cultivated alliances with Dutch, German, and other Americans in burgeoning pro-Boer and anti-imperialist movements and sought to pressure the American government to intervene—either materially or in spirit—on the Boer side, and to turn away from its own recently adopted policy of overseas imperial expansion. The newly reunited Clan na Gael was at the forefront of this agitation. But the Clan's repeated failure to strike a meaningful blow against Britain during the war sorely diminished its standing. After the fiasco at the Welland Canal and the rumbling of the Esquimalt plot, the Clan scrambled to claim credit for the exploits of the Irish Transvaal Brigade and was able to score some symbolic victories against the British remount service operations at New Orleans. But this was all too little, too late. When the pro-Boer and anti-imperialist movements foundered in the wake of the fall of Pretoria and the re-election of President William McKinley, the cracks began to surface. Many leading American Fenians seceded from the Clan na Gael and cast their lot with the flourishing United Irish League. There was nothing unusual about the mainstream pragmatic separatists of Irish America pledging their support for the Home Rule cause and its parliamentary champions. What was novel was the culture of intransigence that came to define the Clan na Gael which, by 1900, was firmly in the hands of a hard core of revolutionists increasingly convinced that rebellion with foreign support was the only viable path to Irish independence. They spurned the "provincialists" of the UIL, choosing instead to lurk about the embassies and consulates of Britain's rival great powers and the clubrooms of the Gaelic League. This militant set, the self-appointed defenders of true nationality, may have bungled "Ireland's opportunity" during the South African War. But their fixation with the idea would be pointedly—and fatefully— revived after 1914.

* * *

The spirit of unity achieved in 1899 was remarkable given how endemic faction fighting was to Irish nationalism in the United States. Perhaps unsurprisingly, it was to prove short-lived. The old patterns reasserted themselves soonest in Chicago, where once again a local power struggle between leading Fenians foreshadowed a schism at the national level. "Colonel" John F. Finerty had emerged as that city's most influential Irish nationalist since the murder of P. H. Cronin. Born in Galway, Finerty fought in the Union army during the Civil War and was afterward involved in the Fenian raids on Canada.[1] He served briefly as a Democratic congressman between 1882 and 1884, was a high-ranking member of the Irish National League of America during the 1880s, and was a strong supporter of William Lyman's Irish National Alliance from 1895.[2] Part of Finerty's influence came from his editorship of the *Chicago Citizen*, established by him in 1882, and by the end of the century the leading Irish newspaper in the Midwest. The other part came from his position as a powerbroker within the United Irish Societies of Chicago (UISC), a large confederation of over one hundred of the city's Irish organizations. Finerty founded the UISC in 1876 and frequently served as its president.[3] With the outbreak of the South African War, Finerty comfortably incorporated a strident pro-Boerism to his philosophy of physical force nationalism and Anglophobia.[4] When interviewed in late December 1899 about rumors that the Clan intended to strike at Canada, he responded with classic Fenian bombast:

[I]f Canada becomes too aggressive in sending volunteers [to South Africa] it is not at all improbable that a counteracting move will be made here . . . Any country that is spoiling for a fight, as Canada seems to be, usually is accommodated . . . If this government becomes involved with Canada there will be 250,000 Irish-Americans to enter the army and fight Canada and England.[5]

Finerty's bluster was at around this time electrifying audiences at a series of UISC-organized pro-Boer mass meetings.[6] He was also the key figure in the creation of the physical force movement's proudest contribution to the South African War: the Irish American Transvaal Ambulance Corps. In contrast to the Dublin and San Francisco efforts, which failed to get off the ground, the project launched in Chicago by the UISC was a notable success. Finerty was credited with helping to raise almost $15,000. Thirty-eight volunteers signed up in Chicago, including seven physicians and many others with military training. They were joined by sixteen men from several cities in Massachusetts. The corps of fifty-four paraded under a red cross flag in New York, accompanied by various nationalist leaders, before embarking on 15 February.[7] Upon their arrival in South Africa in April, however, the majority immediately took up arms and joined in the fighting alongside the existing Irish Brigades.[8] The "ambulance corps" label was largely a ruse to skirt US neutrality laws. The impact of this small group on the fighting was of course negligible. But getting men to the front was, for advanced nationalists in America, a precious tangible achievement in what was otherwise a year of frustrations.

Finerty's reputation may have been riding high, but his ascendancy in Chicago was under threat. From the autumn of 1899 John T. Keating, a Cork-born whisky wholesaler, attempted to wrest control of the UISC from Finerty.[9] Keating was a formidable challenger. Not only was he a prominent member of the united Clan na Gael's new executive; he was also the sitting national president of the Ancient Order of Hibernians (AOH) which, at over one hundred thousand members and growing, was the largest Irish fraternal organization in North America.[10] His Chicago backers included the veteran Fenian Ricard O'Sullivan Burke. But Finerty was no pushover. He raised a furor in the press against Keating and his "Cork Cabal," accusing them—as was traditional in Irish American faction quarrels—of misappropriating funds and putting their selfish political ambitions above the national struggle. Finerty ultimately defeated the coup attempt, but the power struggle created a fresh split among Irish nationalists in Chicago—and these had a history of spreading. When twenty-one members of the Boer ambulance corps arrived back in Chicago in November 1900, they were greeted by a spectacle of the disunity that had arisen in their absence. At the

THE IRISH-BOER HOSPITAL CORPS ON FIFTH AVENUE, N. Y., GOING TO THE STEAMSHIP.

Figure 4.1. Irish American Transvaal Ambulance Corps departing New York, *Irish World*, 24 Feb 1900.

train station, a "lively skirmish" took place as two competing reception committees—one led by Finerty, the other by O'Sullivan Burke—hustled members of the corps to rival banquets. The "score," according to a reporter, "was 16 to 5 in favour of the Finerty faction."[11]

* * *

By challenging Finerty and losing, Keating had earned the new Clan executive a powerful enemy. The rupture in Chicago was to have grave consequences for the unified nationalist movement in the United States. But for most of 1900 these were not immediately apparent. Opposition to the wars in South Africa and the Philippines, and the heated campaign preceding the November presidential election, all helped paper over the cracks. Leading Irish nationalists of every type—from Maud Gonne and John Devoy to Finerty and Patrick Ford—were frequent attendees of pro-Boer meetings across the United States. Most ubiquitous was US Congressman for East Manhattan, William Bourke Cockran. Born in Sligo, Cockran was a career Democrat known as one of the greatest political orators of his time.[12] A noted progressive, Cockran had a brief love affair with Jennie Churchill and was considered a mentor by her son Winston (who shared his talents, if not his politics).[13] At the outbreak of the South African War, Cockran threw himself into the pro-Boer and anti-imperialist movements in the US. He was chosen as chairman of the National Boer Relief Fund Association, an alliance of largely Dutch, German, and Irish Americans based in New York.[14] This delighted Patrick Ford, who believed Cockran's election "identifies the Irish race with the twofold cause of nationality and universal liberty."[15] Cockran was beloved of Fenians, too. He delivered the principal address at the united Clan na Gael's Robert Emmet anniversary celebration at New York in March. "Emmet's legacy," he told the audience of three thousand at the Academy of Music:

> was why the sympathy of Irish hearts went out to South Africa, where brute force mocks at justice and tyranny attempts the extermination of the small, scanty band of Boer patriots struggling for their independence . . . [T]he enemies of Ireland had boasted that factional differences had ended the fight of her people for freedom, but the war upon the South African Republics

had reunited them. Irish opposition to the Boer war was justified by duty to civilization, to American citizenship, and to the Irish race.[16]

Cockran also lent his talents as a speaker to the American Anti-Imperialist League. Founded in Boston in 1898 to oppose the annexation of the Philippines, the League was a federation of progressive politicians and intellectuals. Among its prominent members were millionaire philanthropist Andrew Carnegie, labor leader Samuel Gompers, and author Mark Twain. Although less conspicuously Irish or German, the League had in common with the pro-Boer movement a revulsion of McKinley's policies of expansion and Anglo-American rapprochement. Securing the election of the anti-imperialist Democratic candidate William Jennings Bryan in McKinley's place was the obvious solution—but Bryan's unpopular opposition to the gold standard was an obstacle to his electability. Cockran was personally opposed to Bryan's bimetallism but felt that imperialism was the greater threat. Another victory for McKinley, he warned, and "imperialism will be so firmly imbedded in our political life that it can never be expelled."[17]

The popularity of the pro-Boer movement brought many Irish Americans to cast a more critical eye on their own government's attempt to annex the Philippines. The rhetoric of anti-imperialism increasingly featured in Irish newspapers and meetings.[18] At the UISC convention of June 1900, at which John Finerty was re-elected president, resolutions were passed sympathizing with the Boers, "vehemently" protesting any Anglo-American alliance, and expressing "disgust" at the American policy in the Philippines. "[W]e should blush for the great republic," declared one resolution, "if it should grow greater in extent, although smaller in moral power, by imitating the robber tactics of the British empire."[19] For many Irish Americans, opposition to the war in the Philippines was motivated less by concern for the inhabitants of the islands than by the violation of an imagined principle of American republicanism.[20] Their opposition to "expansionism" was strictly an overseas concern and did not apply to the conquest of the contiguous United States. Finerty, for example, was known for his work as a war correspondent and historian of the Sioux Wars—an exercise, as he described it, "in advancing our banner in the wilderness of the West and in subduing the savage and sanguinary tribes that so long barred the path of progress

Figure 4.2. William Bourke Cockran, ca. 1903–1905, C. M. Bell, Washington, DC, Library of Congress.

in our Territories."[21] A letter to the editor of the Chicago *Inter-Ocean* called attention to this inconsistency in rather unsympathetic terms:

> Memory runneth back with easy effort to the time when this same orator was an expansionist of the most radical sort—when he charged over the Western plains, eager to demonstrate that the only "good Indians" were dead Indians, regardless of the fact that, according to Democratic logic of today, these Indians were being robbed of the same rights that now sets all Democracy boo-hooing in sympathy for the Filipinos.[22]

Elements of this tension seem to have occurred to Finerty, and he snatched rather weakly at a thesis that would reconcile anti-imperialism with the ongoing Catholic and Irish participation in empire. The problem, he proposed, was one of style. Catholics intuitively beat a gentler and more benevolent path to civilization and progress. The Catholic explorers who discovered the New World and the early French missionaries who penetrated its interior, he claimed, "did not approach the Indian in the offensive attitude of conquerors and masters, but as benefactors and brethren." It was the arrival of Protestant settlers and Anglo-Saxon imperialism that turned the "cross of Christ" into "the hilt of a conqueror's sword."[23] All this could plainly be seen to be unfolding anew in the formerly Spanish Philippines, where majority-Protestant American soldiers were reported to be pillaging the natives' Catholic chapels. As this rather tortured reasoning suggests, sympathy for the nonwhite victims of empire often came a distant second to the domestic projects of Irish nationalists. The need to restrain the voracious conquering impulse of the Anglo-Saxon overseas became, ultimately, just another argument for greater Catholic representation in American politics.

Analogies with the conquest of North America could also serve to unite Catholic and Protestant Americans' perspectives on the South African War. Most observers were generally ignorant of, or indifferent to, the war's impact on the native African population. Even the *Indian Chieftain* of Vinita, Oklahoma, passed over native Africans to instead side wryly with the Boer as the "barbarian" who, as in Edward Gibbon's histories of Rome, would be the downfall of decadent empires, the "less civilized man . . . whom history should have taught [Britain] to let alone."[24] The racist oppression inflicted by the Boers upon native Africans was occasionally raised by supporters of Britain as a justification for the invasion of the two republics—an argument some African American observers found persuasive. Pro-Boers, however, were quick to scoff at the idea that the British Empire, with its unsavory record in India and elsewhere in Africa, had natives' interests at heart.[25] White Americans were more readily swayed by popular analogies between the *voortrekker* and the white pioneer, and between the Boer republics and the colonial revolutionaries. In this paradigm, native South Africans assumed a menacing aspect in the white American imagination. Newspaper reports and pro-Boer agitators stoked fears that Britain was preparing to arm and unleash natives upon the outnumbered Boers—just as she had once allied with American Indians in her wars against the United States.[26] A resolution passed at a pro-Boer meeting at Portland, Oregon, described this bugbear vividly:

> [T]he precipitation on [the Boers] of savage foes in alliance with trained soldiery threatens the repetition of the horrors of Wyoming, Fort Darien and other events bitterly remembered by the American people as ruthless instances of British perfidy and dishonour.[27]

Maud Gonne made a similar argument in her speech at a pro-Boer meeting at the New York Academy of Music in February 1900. "England's methods of warfare have not changed," she howled, "since she turned loose the red savages armed with scalping knife and tomahawk to make savage war on the American colonists."[28] Meanwhile, another white American insecurity was targeted by L.K.P. Van Baggen of San Francisco in his contributions to the *Irish World*: British control of the Rand, he argued, would mean the ejection of white miners in favor of cheap Black labor.[29]

Flattening out the complexity of the situation in South Africa by relying on a simplified racial identification with the Boers, ornamented with reminders of Britain's historical "perfidy," both reinforced Irish American pro-Boerism and enhanced its appeal to white American society more broadly. For Irish Americans the pro-Boer movement was about more than just befriending their enemy's enemy; in combination with the anti-imperialist movement, it provided a platform from which to project their vision for the United States' role in the world, and for the Catholic role in the United States, at a time when they believed Anglo-Saxonism and the great rapprochement were leading the country astray. Ireland, too, stood to benefit. As one Irish American correspondent of John Redmond put it, "This movement is of course serving the cause of Ireland indirectly, because it is extending the spirit of hostility to England among a large element of our citizenship not heretofore especially sympathetic with Ireland."[30] Even if the Boer cause proved to be a lost one, Americans who could be convinced that Britain was the villain in South Africa—as she had once been in America—might also be persuaded that Britain was the villain in Ireland.

Despite the impressive showing of pro-Boerism in major urban centers, many Americans nevertheless did not share the Irish nationalist perspective on the war. Indifference to, even satisfaction with, British and American imperialism was widespread. Many openly supported the war. Pro-British societies throughout the United States cheered on imperial victories and encouraged Anglo-American friendship.[31] Some accepted the version of the Boers advanced by the pro-war British press: that they were half-civilized and not quite white, that they had oppressed the *uitlanders* and had themselves been the aggressors in the conflict with Britain. A letter to the *Philadelphia Bulletin* described them as "a backward, uncouth and offensive lot."[32] William Bourke Cockran received letters from some of his constituents who were displeased with his pro-Boer activism. One criticized the Boers' "corrupt oligarchy" and accused their American supporters of "arous[ing] political enmities and race hatreds."[33] Another explained that he was "solicitous that the Boers should derive equal benefits from the second freest government in the world, namely England, even if these good things of life have to be forced upon them by a good trouncing."[34]

That McKinley's government seemed to share in this view and give Britain its silent blessing in South Africa—while caving on the Alaska boundary dispute and gobbling up the Philippines—was proof to many Irish Americans that US imperialism and "Anglomania" were two sides of the same coin. McKinley had to go, for the sake of the United States, Ireland and the Boers alike. With the conventional phase of the war over by the summer of 1900, lingering hopes for international intervention on the Boer side—or at least a mitigation of the terms of their defeat—were vested in a Bryan victory.[35] Bourke Cockran, who had supported McKinley against Bryan in 1896 over the currency issue, returned to the Democratic fold in 1900, believing this election represented a choice between "republic or empire."[36] Prominent Irish nationalist Republicans dramatically switched allegiance in August 1900, forming the "Irish American Union" to "resist imperialism and militarism in every form, and to bring about the election of a President who will stand by American institutions and traditions." Patrick Ford and John Devoy were among its members.[37] John Finerty and his *Chicago Citizen* also ditched McKinley for Bryan, complaining that "[w]e have no American foreign policy; our policy is the policy of England."[38] Reports to the Special Branch observed that the Bryan campaign "absorbed all the energy of the Clan na Gael" and speculated that "the future activity and importance of Irish American conspiracy depends largely on the result."[39]

The result was not favorable to the conspirators. McKinley won by an even greater margin than he had in 1896. A despairing Patrick Ford insisted that the election result did not constitute a mandate for imperialism, which he believed most Americans still opposed. Rather, the Republican campaign's focus on the return of economic prosperity after the depression of the mid-1890s, represented by the "full dinner pail" slogan, had muddied the waters and prevented the election from being a plebiscite on imperialism. Whatever the explanation, the outlook for Irish nationalists and their allies was suddenly gloomy. "[I]mperialism in its most aggressive form" was imminent. "England's Candidates Triumphed," ran the headlines in the *Irish World*. "Defeat for the Irish."[40]

* * *

The determination to unseat McKinley had temporarily shielded Irish American nationalists from the new rivalries crystalizing in Ireland since the Mayo by-election and the Queen's visit. Amid the bitter disappointment following Bryan's defeat, American politics were set aside, and divisions among Irish Americans were free to take shape. The United Irish League had been preoccupied for much of 1900 with expanding its organization throughout Ireland, as well as helping to cement the reunification of the Irish Parliamentary Party. In the so-called "khaki election" of October 1900, which returned Salisbury's Unionist alliance

Figure 4.3. W. J. Bryan election poster, 1900, NPG.83.177, National Portrait Gallery, Smithsonian Institution. Note the Boer, Cuban, and Filipino saluting the Statue of Liberty with their national flags.

to power, the IPP made a reasonably strong showing. The UIL was confirmed in its position as the grassroots engine of the constitutionalist movement, but its leaders were disappointed that they had not succeeded in radically transforming the composition of the parliamentary party itself.[41] The UIL was, however, helping to rehabilitate the IPP's reputation—particularly in the United States. Patrick Ford's *Irish World* had combined support for the UIL with open hostility to parliamentarians for the first half of 1900, but as the alliance matured the paper's position on the IPP softened.[42] Finerty and the United Irish Societies of Chicago also expressed satisfaction at the unity achieved in Ireland.[43] By the end of 1900, with elections in the United Kingdom and the United States concluded, the way was clear for the expansion of the UIL to America.

Finerty and his allies in Chicago, already estranged from the Clan executive over the quarrel with Keating, were among the first prominent American Fenian leaders to come out in support of the UIL. In November 1900 they sent a $500 donation to the *Irish World's* UIL fund.[44] Around the same time Michael J. Ryan of Philadelphia, once a prominent ally of Luke Dillon, Devoy, and Cronin against the Triangle, also declared his support for the League. These moves were in flagrant defiance of Clan policy. Cooperation with parliamentarians had been officially proscribed by the convention of July 1900; those present pledged themselves "to the principle that physical force is the only engine a revolutionary organisation can consistently and successfully use." Faced with the insubordination of Finerty and Ryan—who had actually chaired the July convention—the Clan executive reaffirmed this position. The "bitter but instructive" experience of years past, it was argued, proved that "men cannot fight under two flags that represent opposing principles."[45] The strategy they had embraced, in alliance with the IRB, of seeking the military cooperation of foreign powers required that there be no ambivalence about their commitment to physical force. Despite the outward appearance of polarity, the relationship between constitutional and physical force nationalism had for decades been fluid and often complementary. This new policy of strict segregation was a break with convention. By the turn of 1901 Devoy, once the architect of the New Departure, was less interested in the question of land reform than he was in sending the Irish American inventor John

Philip Holland to impress the French government with his Fenian submarine designs.[46]

In early 1901 Maud Gonne and Major John MacBride—back from South Africa—made a lecture tour of the United States at the Clan's invitation. Devoy and Tom Clarke took up the organizing duties. Clarke's friend and former fellow prisoner, the Fenian Mayor of Limerick John Daly, also traveled to the United States to complement their efforts with a lecture tour of his own.[47] The intention was to bolster the Clan's exclusive revolutionist policy by demonstrating to American audiences that Ireland's leading Fenians vehemently opposed the UIL and the IPP. But "the opposition," Devoy warned MacBride, was "hard at work . . . The cry of 'disunion' which they have raised goes a long way."[48] An intransigent Clan, which had achieved little during the first year of the South African War, could easily be attacked for obstructing the first popular Irish nationalist movement to gather real momentum in over a decade. The *Irish World* carried numerous letters from subscribers rebuking Gonne and MacBride for "preaching disunion."[49] Ford himself described their tour as "evil," and insinuated that Gonne was "doing the enemy's work." Repudiating her claims that parliamentarism had achieved nothing in thirty years, he asked the same question of the Clan na Gael:

> What has it even attempted to do? Nothing. The Clan na Gael has been called Ireland's "standing army," and in a sense the title is well earned, for it has done nothing and is doing nothing but standing. What is the matter? Has the man who claims to own the Clan na Gael entered into a treaty of amity with England? Certainly it is the most peaceable and quiescent military body in all the world, except when it is attacking some other Irish organisation, and then the directing genius is fierce.[50]

While Gonne, MacBride, and Daly toured, John Finerty reached out to Michael Davitt, inviting him to assist in arranging the visit of a parliamentary delegation later in the year to lay the groundwork for the establishment of the UIL in the United States.[51] Independent branches had already been formed in several cities, but no formal national organization yet existed. Roderick Kennedy of New York, a recent member of the UB executive, was similarly in touch with John Redmond. In June

1900 he had optimistically reported that "All over this country unity is the word all along the line." But by January 1901 he told Redmond he was among those in the Clan na Gael taking a stand against the prohibition on supporting parliamentary methods. By June, he and the other UIL supporters were officially expelled from the Clan.[52] When Michael J. Ryan attempted to secure re-election as the Clan's District Officer for Philadelphia—threatening to bring the organization and its assets in that city under the control of secessionists—William Crossin resigned his seat on the executive in order to run against him. After a rancorous campaign Crossin succeeded, but Ryan and his followers could not be reconciled.[53] Neither could Finerty, Kennedy, or others late of the Clan who were prepared to ally with the UIL and launch a new "New Departure." The "united" Clan na Gael had survived less than two years.

∗ ∗ ∗

Throughout these upheavals, Irish nationalists in the United States remained active in pro-Boer agitation and conspiracy, albeit with diminishing intensity. The American visit and tour of three Boer envoys in May and June 1900 was the occasion for a fresh round of mass meetings.[54] The envoys were awarded the freedom of New York, and the United Irish Societies of that city issued them a gushing address of sympathy with their struggle against England, "this oppressor of all mankind, this scourge of humanity."[55] The envoys' attempt to secure American arbitration of the war failed, as expected, after a frosty meeting with Secretary of State John Hay—an event the *Irish World* contrasted pointedly with Benjamin Franklin's reception in Paris.[56] The visit also wound up damaging the reputation of the National Boer Relief Fund when it emerged that money supposedly raised for Boer widows and orphans was instead spent enhancing the envoys' comfort.[57] When asked by William Bourke Cockran to conduct an audit of the fund, Patrick Ford reported a "lamentable extravagance in the expenditure of monies" by the fund's Dutch American treasurer, George William Van Siclen.[58]

Secret conspiracies were also afoot, although it remains difficult to parse genuine plots from rumors and disinformation. Despite a rash of stories at the turn of 1900 about planned raids on Canada and the stockpiling of weapons near the border, it is highly unlikely anything of the sort was ever seriously contemplated. But Theodore Roosevelt, then still Governor of New York, reported being sounded out by a delegation of Fenians as to whether he would stand in the way of any such attempt. He responded that he would "promptly call out the militia and clap them all in jail."[59] Wilfrid Laurier received, via Ambassador Pauncefote and Governor General Minto, a report from an informant in Lawrence, Massachusetts, providing details of plans to raid Canada and even a map showing the location of an alleged cache of weapons on the Niagara frontier.[60] We know that in 1900 the "military" section of the Clan na Gael was reformed and renamed the "Irish Volunteers," but whether those involved saw Canada as a potential battleground is doubtful.[61] Using rumors to generate a border scare was probably seen as a cheap way of tying down Canadian manpower and resources that might otherwise find their way to South Africa.

Some rumors could be quite exotic. The cabinet at Ottawa was alerted to the possibility that Canadian troop and munition ships could be targeted by American pro-Boer privateers.[62] The British Consul General at Boston heard that the Clan na Gael intended to dynamite a Cunard Line steamship at New York.[63] Later in 1901, Fenians were suspected of being involved in a conspiracy to exploit the sensitive Alaska boundary issue.[64] A revolutionary secret society of American gold miners named the "Order of the Midnight Sun" reportedly operated in Skagway and in the Yukon town of Dawson. Their intention, it was feared, was to launch a revolt that would bring the Yukon goldfields under American jurisdiction.[65] Some observers had already commented that the Klondike was full of "American *uitlanders*" and that the United States might reasonably apply similar measures to protect their wellbeing as those taken by Britain on behalf of its own subjects in the Transvaal.[66] The affair was taken seriously enough by the Canadian government that the Mounted Police and the Dominion Police both launched investigations, sending detectives as far south as San Francisco. The Order, such as it was, collapsed after its objectives became public knowledge.[67]

Still, other more plausible forms of interference in Canada were anticipated. Percy Sanderson, the British Consul General at New York, warned Lord Salisbury in June 1900 that leading Fenians planned to break the Welland Canal dynamiters out of Kingston penitentiary.[68] A few weeks later the British Consul at Chicago, William Wyndham, was informed that Ricard O'Sullivan Burke, a veteran of certain notorious and ill-fated prison rescues, was supervising the plot. Pinkerton detectives discovered, however, that Wyndham's Chicago informants were simply on the make.[69] Nevertheless reports on a planned prison break continued to reach British authorities from various sources throughout 1900. In December, Gosselin claimed to have reliable information that the Clan was cultivating a member of prison staff who would assist in Luke Dillon's escape. He asked Kenelm Digby to stress to the Colonial Office and the Canadian Government "the importance of the prisoner and the necessity of extreme vigilance."[70] Devoy, in a letter of March 1901 to MacBride, alluded dismissively to an "offer to rescue the prisoners of war," but whether this referred to the men in Kingston or captured members of the Irish Brigade in British camps in Ceylon and elsewhere is unclear.[71]

The Clan na Gael's most concrete achievements during this period concerned the Irish and Irish American veterans of the fighting in South Africa. Despite the brewing conflict over the UIL, the Clan cooperated with Finerty and his followers to pressure the McKinley administration to request the release of a handful of Irish American prisoners of war held in British camps—and in at least one case succeeded. John Keating played a prominent part in the joint efforts of the Clan and AOH to pay for the passage and resettlement of Irish and Boer combatants in the United States—at the cost of over five thousand dollars.[72]

Besides the ambulance corps, it is difficult to know how many of these men were assisted in reaching the front in the first place by Irish nationalist organizations. From the outbreak of the war, the *Irish World* printed in its editorial page a notice titled "Ho for the Transvaal!" encouraging readers to travel to South Africa by means "other than English ships" for reasons implied rather than specified.[73] Reports that hundreds of volunteers were making their way to South Africa by various routes appeared from late 1899 through to April 1900, but many were likely false or greatly exaggerated.[74] Rumors of active recruiting for the Boer army in American cities troubled British consulates throughout the United States. Investigations in Kansas City, Chicago, San Francisco, and elsewhere as a rule found reports of recruiting to be no more than saloon talk.[75] The same can be said for rumors of arms shipments to the Boers; consulates kept a continuous watch on major American weapons factories and ports and Percy Sanderson compiled a monthly report to the Foreign Office on the movement of munitions.[76] These inquiries were overwhelmingly conducted by hired Pinkerton detectives—a practice Gosselin questioned. That agency, he warned, was "permeated with members of the Clan na Gael and cannot be trusted." Sanderson could only shrug in response. True, he admitted, the Pinkertons employed "many Irishmen, some of whom are no doubt members of [the] secret society." But "[t]he same is the case with the local police and all detective agencies."[77] The consulates had little choice but to trust them to report on suspicious activity.[78] Ultimately, if Irish nationalists did send volunteers or supplies to South Africa, they did so on too insignificant a scale to be detected—or to boast about later.

* * *

While British consulates were anxiously monitoring rumors that war materiel was being secretly shipped to the Boers, British military attachés operating in southern and western states were organizing "the largest horse and mule purchasing business the world had ever seen."[79] From the beginning of the war the British army turned to American stock—larger, cheaper, and more abundant than other options—as the source for its "remount service."[80] Agents operating from Ohio to Oregon purchased the animals, which were conveyed to a "mammoth" British-leased facility in Lathrop, Missouri, then transported by rail to New Orleans. There they were loaded on steamships bound for South Africa.[81] Over 1,000 animals per week were shipped this way. By April 1902 it was estimated that the British government had transported around 200,000 animals from the United States at a cost of almost $50 million.[82]

If the McKinley administration's neutrality was frustrating for pro-Boers, this program of furnishing the British army with the sinews of war was scandalous. Not only was the United States standing by while the Boer republics were crushed—it was providing crucial assistance and profiting in the process. As the scale of the remount service began attracting attention in 1901, it became a target for opponents of the war. Most prominent among these was a self-styled "Boer representative" named General Samuel Pearson. Born in Durban in 1862, Pearson was an engineer and businessman who reportedly acted as "assistant head

Figure 4.4. "He won't go off his beat," J. S. Pughe, *Puck*, 7 Mar 1900.

commissary general for the South African Republic" during the first year of the war.[83] He fled to Europe following the fall of Johannesburg and in November 1900 made his way from Rotterdam to New York. His wife and children were imprisoned in Barberton concentration camp in the eastern Transvaal.[84] Stocky, mustachioed, and impetuous, Pearson spoke with "a distinct English accent" and wore military attire and a slouch hat.[85] When Winston Churchill lectured in New York on his escape from Boer captivity, Pearson was in the audience and attracted some attention for claiming he had been involved in Churchill's pursuit.[86] He shot to prominence when, in March 1901, he secured a temporary injunction from a United States District Court at New Orleans to halt the shipment of horses and mules to South Africa.[87]

Pearson argued in court that he had property in the Boer republics which was at risk of destruction by the continued sale of horses and mules to the British army. The suit, when heard, was promptly thrown out by the judge and the temporary delay in shipments was lifted. In reality the suit was a publicity stunt intended to create a platform from which Pearson could allege the remount service violated US neutrality laws. The judge directed Pearson to take it up with the president.[88] Over the following year he did precisely that.[89] In the meantime, some Boer sympathizers explored other means of targeting the remount service.

Just after midnight on 10 August 1901, a "dynamite torpedo" exploded against the hull of the steamship *Mechanician*. The large vessel sat moored at New Orleans's Stock Landing pier where, in the morning, it was to load one thousand horses for Cape Town. Crew sleeping near the site of the explosion were thrown from their bunks. Their cabins were first scorched by the blast then drenched with seawater launched fifty feet in all directions. One officer, the contents of whose cabin were rearranged by the shock, awoke with "an electric fan for a bedfellow"—still spinning. The bomb had been attached by cotton rope to the anchor chain, floated at the waterline and detonated by a time fuse. Because it floated alongside a section of layered, convex iron plates, the damage was not sufficient to sink the ship. By listing to starboard, the breech was kept above the waterline and any water taken in was promptly pumped out.[90] Three days later the *Mechanician* was repaired and fit to sail.[91] The threat of a repeat attack was taken seriously. In future all vessels supplying

British remounts would be loaded at the more secure dock at Chalmette, east of the city. Nightly patrols of twenty constables, armed with revolvers, watched the water.[92]

The ship's crew and New Orleans police agreed that the dynamiters must have approached the *Mechanician* on a skiff, but none were spotted on the night. The only potential witness was a bartender at a nearby saloon who claimed to have seen a hatless and coatless man running up the levee ten minutes before the explosion.[93] The local British Consul went straight to the superintendent of New Orleans police to demand the arrest of Samuel Pearson, insisting the Boer representative must have been behind the plot. The request was declined. There was no evidence to connect Pearson to the explosion. Indeed, Pearson was confident enough in his innocence to sue the Consul for $20,000 in damages for having slandered him by the accusation.[94]

A Chicago detective was sent to assist the New Orleans police and the British authorities undertook an investigation of their own, but the mystery does not appear to have been solved. Some speculated that the explosion may have been an act of revenge by American muleteers unhappy with their treatment by their British paymasters on the return trip to South Africa.[95] But the strategic target, the amateurish placement of the dynamite against a reinforced section of the hull, and the possible cooperation with the Boer agitator Pearson all bear comparison with the Fenian plots against Esquimalt and the Welland Canal the year before. In June 1900, reflecting on what the Clan na Gael might still have in store, Gosselin had written:

> I fear they have some big design on foot possibly against some of our ships of war, I know this has been mooted before, and the blowing up of a ship in the Spanish war has shown its possibility.[96]

It may be that the Clan na Gael hoped sinking the *Mechanician* at New Orleans would produce a similar effect on Anglo-American feeling as the sinking of the *USS Maine* in Havana Harbor had on Spanish-American relations just three years earlier.

In a book of 1972 on the Fenian career of Joseph McGarrity, Sean Cronin—a journalist and for a time IRA Chief of Staff in the 1950s—claimed that William Crossin was behind the dynamiting of the *Mech-*

anician. "Crossin and his two companions," he wrote, "were almost swept over the falls in their tiny boat but they managed to damage the vessel."[97] Cronin's source is not provided. What we do know is that Samuel Pearson was in touch with the Clan na Gael generally and with William Crossin personally. In response to a letter of December 1901 Pearson thanked Crossin for his "efforts" and complained that he was "exceedingly hard up for money." The "1 dollar & 10 cents" to his name was not, he wrote, "a very big fund to carry on a 'war.'"[98] The British authorities appear to have been aware of this connection. Two weeks after the dynamiting of the *Mechanician,* a British spy in Philadelphia was urged to "[c]ultivate Crossin all you can as he is *most important,*" and in November was ordered to report "[a]nything you see or hear about Pearson."[99]

Pearson's rising popularity among the Clan na Gael appears to have inspired another Boer veteran to ingratiate himself with the Irish pro-Boers. Captain Louis de Villiers, described in the papers as "the celebrated Cape rebel," took to American stages in khakis and high boots to deliver lectures on the ongoing Boer resistance. On one occasion, he and Pearson shared the stage in a double bill at New Orleans.[100] American pro-Boers wrote de Villiers asking for advice on how to travel to South Africa to fight against the British, and a Colorado man approached him with a proposal to poison mules bound for South Africa.[101] "The plan seemed so absurdly impracticable," de Villiers told a reporter, "that I at first considered him a spy who had come to propose a plan to see if I could not suggest a better one."[102]

In February and March 1902, de Villiers made a lecture tour of New England, meeting with local Clan na Gael leaders and marching as a guest of honor in the Pawtucket St. Patrick's Day parade.[103] In Boston he encountered the recently returned leader of the New England Irish ambulance corps, Richard J. Barry, whose experience of the war led him to suspect that something about de Villiers was not quite right. Barry wrote to the acting consul of the Orange Free State at New York requesting information on de Villiers's antecedents. It emerged that the "Captain" had indeed fought in South Africa—just not on the right side. He was no "Cape rebel" but was reportedly a French Canadian who had served in Strathcona's Horse. The Clan immediately concluded that he was a British spy. They were probably correct. De Villiers promptly disappeared. "If we had known," Clan members told a reporter in Hartford, Connecticut, "he would never have left the hall alive."[104]

After de Villiers was exposed, Samuel Pearson was interviewed at Washington, DC. He said that de Villiers had given him money and had tried to persuade him to sneak into the British facility at Chalmette. Pearson claimed this was to have him "hustled aboard" a British transport and taken prisoner; it was more likely intended to implicate him in the *Mechanician* explosion. He bragged unconvincingly that he knew de Villiers was a spy immediately "but pretended to put faith in him." More credible was his explanation of de Villiers' mission:

> As the Irish League [sic] is in sympathy with the Boers, and the British are fearful of a Fenian plot, they think that by assuming the role of Boer officers they can ingratiate themselves with the Irish and learn their plans.[105]

They thought right.

Pearson's political campaign proved considerably more frustrating to the British than the threat of dynamiting. When polite audiences—first with McKinley and then with Theodore Roosevelt after his assumption of the presidency in September 1901—produced nothing, Pearson decided to force the issue with another stunt. In February 1902 he wrote to Roosevelt insisting that the hundred-acre British-leased facility at Chalmette port, staffed by dozens of British military attachés, amounted to a base of military operations actively engaged in the prosecution of war against the Boer republics.[106] If the United States was truly committed to neutrality, it should close the facility or extend the same courtesy to the Boers. What was sauce for goose, he contended, was sauce for the gander:

> Will I be permitted to strike these with the force I might assemble here? I pray your excellency to either put an end to this state of affairs or permit me to strike here one blow . . . [M]ay I not consider your silence or inaction the equivalent of consent for me to stop the further violation of the neutrality laws at this port, or to carry on war here for the burghers?[107]

Roosevelt had Secretary of State John Hay warn Governor of Louisiana William Wright Heard to take steps to prevent this threatened breach of the peace. But Heard, a Democrat, took Pearson's side. Without endorsing Pearson's hollow threat to "strike a blow," Heard agreed that the British "base of war supplies" at Chalmette must be considered a violation of neutrality. He kicked the matter back to Hay, explaining that "[t]he burghers of South Africa are making a fight for their homes and their liberties," that the animals shipped from Chalmette were "indispensable to the operations of the British army," and that they must therefore "be considered as contraband of war, of greater value than arms or soldiers that England can so easily furnish from within her borders."[108] When word of the disagreement reached the prominent pro-Boer Congressman William Sulzer, he pushed a resolution through the House requiring that Hay furnish Congress the correspondence with Heard, along with dozens of other files documenting controversies surrounding the shipping of horses and mules.[109]

These developments placed the remount service in the headlines once again. Stories emerged of American muleteers working on transport vessels being pressured to enlist in the British army through tactics such as the denial of wages, shore time, or return passage.[110] Papers reported the horrific conditions on board the cramped livestock transports, and the routine loss of ten percent or more of the animals per voyage.[111] That Chalmette, once the site of Andrew Jackson's famous victory over the British at the Battle of New Orleans in 1815, now possessed a British "atmosphere" was deplored.[112] The cabinet bowed to pressure to launch an investigation, through the War Department, of the allegations that the Chalmette base violated American neutrality.[113]

Pearson was confident that the report of the federal investigator would produce a satisfying result.[114] He may have been correct. The report was submitted to the cabinet at the end of April, but the Attorney General sat on it for two weeks.[115] On 15 May Roosevelt briefly announced that no action would be taken against the British operations at Chalmette.[116] Despite pressure from Pearson the cabinet refused to make the report public.[117] But by this time the shipments of horses and mules had already been quietly halted. A member of the British Remount Commission staff later wrote that his superiors had received "an intimation of a diplomatic nature that it was best that our work should cease."[118] Roosevelt's government had, it seems, taken appropriate steps to spare themselves and their British counterparts the embarrassment of a defeat at Pearson's hands. In any case, the closing of the remount service came too late to matter. Peace negotiations were already well underway. On 31 May 1902 Kitchener, Milner, and delegates representing the Transvaal and Orange Free State signed the Treaty of Vereeniging. The war was over.

* * *

Pearson's pyrrhic victory notwithstanding, the burst of Irish nationalist activity in the United States during the South African War was all sound and fury. For transatlantic Fenianism in particular, the litany of setbacks chipped away at the unity and optimism that had characterized the war's opening months. In Ireland, the failure to send an ambulance corps to the Transvaal, the meager resistance to the Queen's visit, and John MacBride's defeat at the South Mayo polls had all been demoralizing enough. Across the pond the arrest of the Welland Canal dynamiters, the abortive attempt to bomb the Royal Navy's base at Esquimalt, and the deportation of Joseph Mullet and James Fitzharris, together with the recrudescence of factional strife, left the revolutionary movement in disarray. As the war progressed, the momentum appeared to swing decidedly in favor of the growing United Irish League and the reunited Irish Parliamentary Party. But momentum was just that. Although a new land settlement was on the horizon by the close of 1902, the resurgent constitutional nationalist movement was still in no position to bargain for Home Rule or influence imperial policy on either side of the Atlantic. This was small solace for the Clan na Gael. The official report of its 1902 Convention at Washington, DC, tried to explain away its failures. The timing and the circumstances had been all wrong: the newly reunited organization was not ready for any major operations; the fighting in South Africa was "thousands of miles distant"; and "no foreign power" could be enlisted to threaten Britain. "It would," the report stated, "be vastly different if the war was between England and a continental power."[119] Next time, the report implied, they would be ready.

At the outset of the South African War, the leaders of the Clan na Gael had announced their determination to go beyond "the infliction of petty injuries that can exert no influence on the ultimate result of the struggle."[120] By the war's end, however, petty injuries—both to their opponents and to each other—were all Irish nationalists in the

United States had accomplished. Those in Britain's Dominions, by contrast, were inclined to see the war itself as injurious to the empire. They shirked the language of anti-imperialism and instead attacked the culture of jingoism they believed was corrupting an empire that could, and should, enshrine a more equal partnership among its white nationalities.

PART THREE

Divided Loyalties

5

"Jingoistic Hysteria"

James Grattan Grey and the War in New Zealand

There are two conflicting versions of the events that took place on the SS *Moana* during its three-week voyage from Auckland to San Francisco in September 1900. Both involve the Irish-born Australasian journalist James Grattan Grey and his wife Jane, née O'Keane. One story, told by Irish nationalist journals, alleged that Jane was harassed and insulted by "a gang of British cowards and lickspittles, headed by a North of Ireland Presbyterian parson." The reason for this mistreatment was reported to be her husband's reputation as a critic of New Zealand's participation in the South African War. Grey's Boer sympathies, it was said, had caused him to be sacked from his job as head of New Zealand's Hansard staff and his departure from the colony represented a sort of exile. The loyalist passengers on board the *Moana* sent a deputation to the captain requesting that the Greys be banished to steerage. But they found, to their chagrin, that the captain was "an Irishman named Carey" who, siding with his countrymen, "sent the fellows about their business very quickly."[1]

The other story claimed that Jane had become exasperated with repeated renditions of "God Save the Queen" at the close of each night's entertainment. She stormed out once and eyebrows were raised. On the second occasion she was challenged by some fellow passengers, and while explaining her distaste for the proceedings, she insulted "that dirty old woman," Queen Victoria. Jane apologized to Captain Carey in the morning, but the offended passengers demanded that she apologize to them all or be relegated to steerage. Jane refused, so the Captain arranged a compromise: the Greys could remain in saloon but would have to take their meals separately from the other passengers.[2]

The second account may have been closer to the truth, but it was the first that was believed and repeated by Irish nationalists and opponents of the South African War in the global English-language press. The ostracism on the *Moana* was taken as the latest in a series of persecutions suffered by James Grattan Grey for speaking out against jingoism. In Melbourne, the newly established Peace and Humanity Society endorsed Grey as a victim of "the frenzy of jingo militarism which has recently run riot in our colonies."[3] On their arrival in San Francisco, the Greys were visited by representatives of the city's Transvaal Committee.[4] Its president, Judge Michael Cooney, provided them with a letter of introduction to John Redmond that praised Grey's "manly and independent advocacy of the Boer cause" and complimented his "patriotic wife."[5] Patrick Ford's *Irish World* of New York used characteristically effervescent language in its coverage of the Greys' case. In a "grotesque display of Anglo-Saxon intolerance," it explained, James had been "driven out of [New Zealand] for expressing sympathy with the Boers."[6] Ford hired Grey as the *Irish World*'s correspondent on the November 1900 Irish National Convention at Dublin's Rotunda, and provided him with introductions to more Irish Party leaders, including John Dillon.[7] The *New York Times* reported a rumor that Grey's sacrifice was to be rewarded by the Irish Party with a seat at Westminster.[8] Grey's supporters considered him a martyr for freedom of speech, anti-imperialism, and Irish nationalism, and seized on his experiences as a parable on the dangers of "jingoistic hysteria."[9]

As with the events on the *Moana*, however, the nationalist version of Grey's treatment in New Zealand omitted important details. Popular investment in the idea of imperial unity loomed large in the political culture of the Australasian colonies, and this militated against the expression of anti-war dissent that was commonplace even in the respectable press and parliament of the United Kingdom.[10] But painting an exaggerated picture of colonial loyalist intolerance helped some Irish nationalists explain away the weakness of the anti-war and Home Rule movements in the Dominions. This interpretation was encouraged by Grey himself, a talented propagandist who appeared to relish his newly acquired celebrity. The real situation was, of course, more complex. Through the 1890s, with nationalist movements in the doldrums at home, interest in the Irish question had retreated since the high-water mark of the Parnell era. Irish Catholics in the colonies were encouraged by an increasingly self-assured and distinctly Irish hierarchy to

MR. AND MRS. J. GRATTAN GREY

Figure 5.1. James Grattan Grey and his wife, Jane, *Irish World*, 13 Oct 1900.

embrace the empire and to carve out a place for themselves in the new national identities that were emerging within it.[11] Loyal Irishness was a complementary phenomenon to the "Better Britonism" that motivated Australasian colonies to compete in their contributions to the imperial war effort. There was a widespread belief, encouraged from the pulpit and the clerical nationalist press, that performing model citizenship in the colonies was the surest way for the Dominion Irish to advance the cause of Home Rule. An important component of this belief was that Home Rule was not an end in itself. As colonial Irish nationalists insisted—and visiting Irish Party delegations seeking donations gladly echoed—Home Rule would serve to strengthen the bonds of empire.[12] Unsolved, the Irish question posed a major obstacle to imperial harmony; solved, the energies once consumed by the struggle for self-governance could be harnessed to the empire's benefit. The spectacle of a thriving Ireland freed from the shackles of the Union to pursue its potential (vaguely defined, but always tremendous) would, it was assumed, carry the added benefit of elevating the colonial Irish in the eyes of their neighbors.[13] And Home Rule would represent an important step towards the kind of imperial system they had long preferred: one defined less by Britishness and more by the voluntary collaboration of autonomous white communities.[14]

The nationalist revival sparked by the South African War occurred on terms that were difficult to reconcile with this consensus. The Irish Party's unseemly disintegration had dismayed Australasia's Irish nationalists, but a clerically enforced policy of neutrality had done much to prevent the contagion of factionalism from spreading to the colonies through most of the 1890s.[15] Now, ironically, the Irish Party's reunification at home—facilitated as it was by a common abhorrence of Britain's South Africa policy—caused cracks to appear abroad. Mainstream colonial Irish nationalism had laid claim to respectability by repudiating Fenianism and insisting on the imperial benefits of Home Rule.[16] But with the Irish Party joining Fenians in openly sympathizing with the empire's enemies, Irish nationalists in the colonies were placed in a difficult position. Divisions over how to interpret the situation in South Africa were compounded by disagreements about how to juggle seemingly incompatible loyalties to Ireland, their host societies, and the empire.

The variations in Irish nationalist responses to the South African War across the British Dominions demonstrate the importance of local conditions—including settlement patterns, political culture, and transnational networks—in shaping diaspora politics. The transatlantic Fenian revival sparked by the war did not reach the antipodes; the vigilance of the clergy and the loyalist majority, as well as the sheer distance from the site of any potential revolution, meant organized Fenianism had always struggled to gain—or indeed to desire—a foothold there.[17] Responses to the war instead tended to conform to three broadly moderate and often overlapping patterns. There were Boer sympathizers like James Grattan Grey who followed the Irish Party line and accepted confrontation with jingoes. Crushing the sovereignty of small white nations was not, they argued, the right sort of imperialism. There were some who attempted a difficult balancing act—disapproving of the war's origins while pointedly disdaining the Boers; criticizing jingoism while hoping for a speedy British victory; insisting that dissent did not equal disloyalty. These moderate critics were as likely to cite Gladstone and Bright or contemporary British liberal critics of the war as they were to quote Michael Davitt. Finally, many were swept up in the popular enthusiasm for the imperial war effort, and seized on the war as an opportunity to demonstrate Greater Ireland's value to the empire. What better evidence of this than the leadership of the Anglo-Irish Generals Roberts, French, and Kitchener, the exploits of the Royal Irish Fusiliers, or the Irish volunteers among the more than twenty thousand men who enlisted in Australasian contingents?

Pro-Boer sentiments were most likely to be recorded in big cities with higher concentrations of Irish Catholic settlers, established networks of nationalist organizations, and livelier connections to the movements in Ireland. Irish nationalist pro-Boerism was therefore at a distinct disadvantage in New Zealand where, as Patrick O'Farrell pointed out, the Irish population "tended to be dispersed, scattered, and rural, lacking the concentration of America, even Australia."[18] In 1901, the number of Irish Catholics spread across the entire colony of New Zealand was not much greater than those residing in Melbourne alone. Sydney's Irish Catholics easily outnumbered the total population of New Zealand's most populous city: Auckland.[19] The flow of new emigrants from Ireland (often vital in sustaining advanced diaspora nationalism) had slowed with the end of assisted migration schemes in 1891, and so by the turn of the century New Zealand's Irish population was older on average than other white settler groups.[20] The relative absence of sectarian antagonism until the early twentieth century obviated, at least in part, some of the local utility of nationalist organizations as a means of buttressing Catholic confessional identity.[21] A remote and quiescent colony with a relatively small, aging, and diffuse Irish Catholic population, New Zealand could seldom sustain the more robust levels of nationalist agitation that can be identified in other diaspora communities.

Grey's sympathizers were correct to observe that the South African War helped to lend certain strains of popular imperialism a more narrowly British and Protestant aspect—a process that would reach its zenith during the Great War and the immediate postwar years. This pressure could impede Irish nationalist expression everywhere in the Dominions, but it was particularly pronounced in New Zealand where, as Oliver MacDonagh noted, the attachment to Britishness was "considerably more pervasive, enduring, and powerful" than in Australia or Canada.[22] As this stifling atmosphere acquired an increasingly sectarian edge, it would eventually produce, in combination with the stimuli of the 1916 rebellion and the rise of Sinn Féin, a backlash among Irish nationalists in New Zealand that more resembled the "aggressive" and "confrontational" tradition across the Tasman.[23] But the conditions in 1899 were conducive only to a relatively subdued revival of interest in Irish nationalism. Whereas in Ireland and in the United States something approaching a pro-Boer consensus meant that debate centered around what, if anything, should be done about Ireland's opportunity—in New Zealand and Australia, Irish nationalists debated what they should think about England's difficulty.

* * *

According to James Grattan Grey and his supporters, his troubles started with an article appearing in the *New York Times* of 26 November 1899. Grey was the author. The article condemned the injustice of Britain's war on the Boer republics and attacked the decision by the colonial governments of Australasia to dispatch contingents to assist the mother country. Australians and New Zealanders had "no quarrel with" the Boers, Grey argued, and it was "odd" that "they should think it necessary to assist in the subjugation of a people who claim the right of self-government the same as they do." The empire, he stressed, was not in danger; Britain could easily beat the Boers alone; the colonies' wealth and manpower could be put to better use at home than "in crushing poor old Oom Paul." Grey alleged that the contingents were being used chiefly to advertise imperial unity to rival great powers, and to set a precedent for colonial participation in future wars. But it was, he insisted, impossible to get a fair hearing on this issue because "the jingoistic spirit at the Antipodes is too inflamed just now to care anything about the rights or wrongs of the question."[24]

Grey was born to a Catholic family in Downpatrick, County Down, in 1847. He spent some time in Belfast as a young man, reporting for Dublin papers on "sectarian feuds"—which he later described as the "shame and disgrace" of "the Black North."[25] He emigrated first to Australia, and by 1876 was in Wellington working as a parliamentary reporter on the New Zealand Hansard staff. Between sessions he supplemented his income by writing for a range of papers in Australia and New Zealand. By 1896, at the nomination of Premier Richard Seddon, Grey was promoted to Chief Reporter, the most senior position in the Hansard service. His contract awarded him a salary of £400 per year—below the usual going rate for his position, but guaranteed him "liberty . . . to take outside work."[26] It was with this understanding that he became a regular contributor to the *New York Times* on New Zealand affairs.

Two months passed before Grey's anti-war *New York Times* article was noticed in New Zealand. The Dunedin *Evening Star* first broke the story on 29 January 1900, and a week later Seddon wrote to Grey asking him to confirm whether he was indeed its author.[27] Grey responded that he was, elaborating on his opposition to the Premier's policy and the "hideous tragedy" unfolding in South Africa at the behest of "greedy and grasping capitalists."[28] In March Seddon was in Dunedin to help see off New Zealand's fourth volunteer contingent to South Africa. When quizzed by an *Evening Star* reporter on the subject of Grey's article, he provided copies of their correspondence and confided that Grey's dismissal would likely be considered at the next parliamentary session. The *Star* made the most of this scoop, publishing the details under the sensational headline: "The Chief of Hansard avows himself a pro-Boer and glories in his rank republicanism."[29]

Grey was no republican, but to many New Zealanders it was no less scandalous that the colony's chief parliamentary reporter was an un-apologetic Boer sympathizer drawing a state salary while undermining the government in foreign newspapers. As the story spread, Grey acted quickly, reaching for his pen to assert some control over the narrative. On 2 April he published the first of two pamphlets titled *Freedom of Thought & Speech in New Zealand: A Serious Menace to Liberty*. In these he forcefully set out his interpretation of the affair. He claimed that the timing of the Dunedin *Star*'s scoop—amid the "whirl of warlike excitement" of the fourth contingent's departure—was no accident. It showed it to be a calculated hit by Seddon and the jingo press on a journalist who dared to speak out against the war.[30] He insisted that the strictures on political speech enforced in the civil service did not apply to him because he was not a civil servant—but rather a journalist engaged by the government on a contract that explicitly entitled him to continue his profession.[31]

Within a month, Grey followed up with a second pamphlet on his case. Taken together, these pamphlets provided readers with around one hundred pages of evidence in support of Grey's position on the war and his right to express it. Eight pages contained letters received by Grey from sympathizers across New Zealand appearing to represent a range of political backgrounds. Some testified to having themselves been abused for criticizing the war. One correspondent from New Plymouth griped that it was "unjust to be classed with those who are real traitors to the Empire, while in truth it is because we love the Empire more than they, that we cry out against her real enemies, those who are responsible for the war."[32] A correspondent from Taupiri grumbled, "I came to what I thought was a free country. I have been deceived."[33] An Auckland sym-pathizer quoted Michael Davitt's criticism of the war, before complain-ing "I have been denounced as a 'traitor,' as 'impertinent,' 'imprudent,' etc., for expressing my opinions in a colony that is always boasting of the glories of British freedom."[34] Fred Zeltner, an American immigrant, told the Wellington *Evening Post* that he had been "insulted, dragged into fights, and have suffered all kinds of indignities simply because I sometimes say that the war is unjust."[35] The pamphlets contained similar extracts from New Zealand newspapers reporting on other cases of individuals and families being intimidated, assaulted, boycotted, or fired for holding—or being suspected of holding—Boer sympathies.[36]

Grey's pamphlets were designed to serve as a digest of anti-jingo public discourse in New Zealand, and to demonstrate that this minority position cut right across colonial society. Women's voices appear to have been more prominent than their Australian or Canadian counterparts. An "Auckland Lady" born in Britain told Grey that it was "a horrible thing to see people *volunteering* to go and kill inoffensive people." "I am" she wrote, "ashamed and disgusted for my race daily."[37] In May 1900 the Women's National Council of New Zealand signaled its opposition to the war with a unanimous resolution in favor of peace and arbitration and against "militarism."[38] Louisa Blake, a liberal suffragist from Christchurch, pointed out in the *Lyttelton Times* that while the Boer treatment of native Africans had been held up as a reason for supporting the war, the Boers were hardly "exceptional" in this behavior: "Britishers, when a little off the track of civilization, are not only immoral, but unspeakably cruel to their victims."[39]

Wartime dissent against imperialist orthodoxy in the colonies could mean, as one of Grey's correspondents claimed, being labeled "traitors or Fenians."[40] Grey argued that in Australasia popular jingoism had been "worked up" by politicians seeking "favours and distinctions." The colonial press had allegedly sustained this feeling by under-reporting the extent of anti-war sentiment in Britain. As a corrective, Grey listed prominent British politicians, clergymen, journalists, and intellectuals who opposed Chamberlain's "policy of conquest and blood" and asked whether they should "be stigmatized as 'traitors' to Great Britain."[41] He provided dozens of pages of excerpts critical of the war from British newspapers and journals and organizations like the Stop the War Committee that he claimed had been "suppressed in the colonies."[42]

The pamphlets sought to create the impression that even supporters of the war were behind Grey. They included letters from correspondents respectfully disagreeing with his opinion but admiring him for, as one put it, his "courage in these days of servility."[43] Some pro-war New Zealand newspapers did indeed express reservations about the government's move to fire Grey. The *New Zealand Times* of Wellington considered Seddon's handling of the case as "undignified," and the Christchurch

Press called the idea of punishing him for his opinions "monstrous"—
even if they were "incorrect."[44] But the government had made up its
mind. On 20 July Grey's contract as Chief Reporter of the Hansard
Staff was terminated.[45]

Grey's dismissal turned a New Zealand controversy into international news. As his widely circulated pamphlets provided such a neat
and forcefully argued account, they became the chief source for most
of the reporting done on his case outside of the colony. Grey reaped
the benefits. He received a letter of congratulations from the famous
English journalist and Stop the War Committee founder W. T. Stead.
"I am delighted to know," Stead wrote, "that you have kept your
head steady in the midst of the semi-delirious sentiment which has
submerged common sense, reason, justice and humanity."[46] The ac-
claimed Cape Boer author and anti-war activist Olive Schreiner also
publicly praised Grey. In a letter to the *New York World*, she urged
Americans to welcome him and his wife for the contribution they had
made in the efforts "to arrest the hand of England in the commission
of the crime of the century."[47]

Grey's decision to leave New Zealand helped to reinforce the theme
of martyrdom and exile that he and his supporters cultivated. A ball-
and-supper testimonial was held in his and Jane's honor in Wellington on 20 August 1900, with sympathetic MPs John Hutcheson and
A. R. Atkinson present. Grey told those in attendance that he had been
denied compensation by the government for the termination of his
contract because he refused to apologize for his convictions. His supporters duly handed him "a cheque for a substantial amount."[48] Another send-off banquet was held in Auckland, at which the couple were
presented with "a purse of sovereigns" before boarding the SS *Moana*
to San Francisco.[49]

Yet Grey's version of events, and the international reporting that
echoed it, did not quite provide the full picture. His posturing as a martyr to jingoism depended to some extent on winning the sympathies
of progressives, socialists, and anti-imperialists who were more likely
to oppose the war. These were unusual bedfellows for a man like Grey.
From March 1899 he had published a series of articles in the *New York
Times* attacking what he described as the "labour tyranny" under which
New Zealand had suffered since a cabal of "Radicals" had captured the

Liberal government earlier in the decade. He condemned New Zealand's experiments in old age pensions, labor arbitration, women's suffrage, and "one man one vote" as failures and "solemnly warn[ed] the American people against these innovations."[50]

These attacks on the government had already been raised in the House of Representatives—two months before his article on the South African War first appeared in print. Arthur Morrison, the Liberal MP for Caversham, read extracts from Grey's columns and asked whether the house should consider applying "the good old rule of one man one job" to the Hansard chief. Grey was criticized from both sides of the floor for his "injudicious" comments on the government's progressive social policies. The Ulster-born leader of the conservative opposition, William Massey, believed Grey "had made a most serious mistake." The young Liberal Patrick Joseph O'Regan—who would later become New Zealand's most prominent Irish nationalist—felt that Grey's actions "could not be too strongly condemned." Even John Hutcheson, who six months later would be among Grey's loudest defenders, believed he "had committed a very grave indiscretion, and that no member of the staff should in his official capacity write strong partisan articles." In April 1900 Grey painted Premier Seddon as a vindictive tyrant. Yet in the August 1899 debate Seddon explained that he "held a very high opinion" of Grey and admitted he had personally recommended his appointment as Chief Reporter in 1896. As Seddon saw it, it was perfectly acceptable for members of the Hansard staff to supplement their income with ordinary reporting. However, public confidence in the impartiality of the service was undermined when its Chief attached his name to such obviously hostile and partisan columns.[51] The matter was referred to the parliamentary Reporting Debates and Printing Committee, which took the view that while "reporting and literary work" was permissible, "in future, members of the Hansard staff should not actively participate in New Zealand politics."[52] Grey got off lightly. Rather than punishment, he received the benefit of the doubt. The Committee recognized that there had been some ambiguity in the terms of his contract and clarified their future expectations.

This earlier affair was the key factor in Grey's dismissal for his criticism of the government's war policy. With parliament finally back in session, Grey was once more summoned before the Reporting Debates and Printing Committee on 17 July 1900. In a terse exchange, the chairman reminded Grey of the Committee's finding in his previous case. Grey claimed it carried "no significance whatever" to him. Seeing that his fate was sealed, he took the opportunity to grandstand, shirking the Committee's focus on technical points and shifting the discussion to the war and freedom of conscience. "I do not withdraw one-thousandth part of an inch from the position I have taken up," he insisted. "[T]he threat of dismissal has no terrors for me." Finding Grey in contempt of its authority, the Committee recommended the termination of his contract.[53]

As Grey was an employee of Parliament, rather than of the government, the Committee's recommendation needed the approval of the House of Representatives to take effect. On 19 July Seddon moved a resolution to adopt the Committee's report, stating he "deeply regret[ted]" its necessity. This was not about punishing Grey for criticizing the South African War, he insisted, but about satisfying public expectations of impartiality in an important office of parliament. "I do not care whether it was an article in regard to the removal of the disabilities of women, or in regard to the elective executive, or any other question," he told the House. A long debate followed. Most speakers did not question the standard to which Grey was being held, but whether it was being applied evenly to other state employees engaging in political speech. For example, George Warren Russell, the radical Liberal member for Riccarton, pointed out that another member of the Hansard staff actually owned the Auckland *Observer*. "[F]ish is being made of one man and flesh of another," he complained. The only difference in Grey's case was that his published opinions were clearly labeled with his name and title. Nevertheless, there was a general cross-partisan consensus on the specifics of Grey's case. The Printing Committee's report was adopted by 47 votes to 11.[54] The following day the speaker of the House, Galway-born George Maurice O'Rorke, informed Grey that he was out of a job.[55]

This aspect of the affair—which casts the Seddon government's actions in a more reasonable light—was glossed over in Grey's self-mythologizing. It is not addressed until the seventy-fourth page of his second pamphlet, where it appeared under the heading "A Former Attempt to Prevent Freedom of Opinion." In four carefully curated pages,

Grey presented cherry-picked extracts from sympathetic speeches and editorials and omitted any mention of the substance of his offending articles and the report of the Printing Committee. Shorn of inconvenient complexities or of details that might offend otherwise sympathetic liberals and radicals, Grey's account posed as a useful parable for any who sought to criticize militarism, imperialism, Anglo-Saxonism, or the Seddon government. In reality, Grey's firing was not the smoking gun of jingoistic intolerance he claimed it to be. But his campaign helped shed light on the issue, and the stories contained in the letters and newspaper cuttings assembled in his pamphlets reveal the pressures exerted on some New Zealanders to adhere to the pro-war consensus.

* * *

Grey had clear reasons for keeping quiet about his conservatism and prior warning from parliament—reasons which likely also explain his reticence about his denomination and his Irish nationalist politics. He was a Catholic and a staunch Home Ruler but made nothing of this in his pamphlets. It is noteworthy that his religion and his support for Home Rule were very seldom mentioned by others in the colony. No member of the House of Representatives—of whom fourteen out of sixty-eight were Irish-born—considered them relevant.[56] In the newspaper reporting it did not come up until August 1900, when rumors first began circulating that Grey would be considered for a parliamentary seat in Ireland. The *Lyttelton Times* mused that Irish electors would be easily persuaded by his martyrdom as they were "often too ready to credit the tales of the man with a grievance."[57] A correspondent signing himself "Irishman" took exception to this, pointing out the contribution of Irish soldiery to the war and adding "I have known Mr Grey for over thirty-five years, and I don't think he has the ghost of a show of ever representing an Irish constituency."[58]

In any case, there is no evidence that a political career for Grey was ever seriously entertained in Ireland—or among Irish nationalists in New Zealand for that matter. Remarkably, no Irish or Catholic organizations in the colony came out in support of Grey. This may have been owing to Grey's disinclination, before he left New Zealand, to connect his criticism of the war with his Irishness. But his overseas sympathizers and his New Zealand detractors readily highlighted the association where it suited them.[59] Grey's decision not to court this languishing constituency spared New Zealand's Irish nationalists the difficult prospect of having to declare for or against him.

Organized Irish nationalism had been largely dormant in New Zealand since the Irish party's collapse in the early 1890s. The revival sparked elsewhere by the South African War and the reunification of constitutional and advanced movements was least pronounced in that colony. During the war years, the Wellington and Auckland branches of the Irish National Federation (INF)—an old Home Rule organization represented on both sides of the Tasman Sea—were briefly reactivated to little consequence.[60] In January 1901 the Auckland branch sent £30 and a letter to John Dillon explaining that they could now make a "fresh start" after ten years of "heartrending" division that made organizing and fundraising impossible.[61] In June 1902 the Wellington branch sent £50.[62] These paltry figures paled in comparison to the sums raised in previous tours by Irish Party delegates to the colony—the most recent being that of John Dillon, Thomas Grattan Esmonde, and John Deasy in 1889, who left with £6,000.[63] The picture might have been different had the colony not been neglected by Irish nationalist organizers since. In January 1902 the founder of the United Irish League William O'Brien, then in Australia, declined an invitation from the Auckland INF to visit New Zealand.[64]

The INF avoided making any public statement on either the war or on the treatment of James Grattan Grey. Instead, the Wellington branch congratulated the Queen on her visit to Dublin in April 1900, and in February 1901 the Auckland branch sent condolences on her death.[65] In this they were in line with the leadership of the Irish Party. But their silence on the war was at odds with the Party, whose vociferous opposition was noted in the loyalist newspapers of New Zealand.[66] The Christchurch *Press* scorned the Irish Party's pro-Boerism as "a purely fictitious sympathy and admiration for a race absolutely alien to them in religion and political ideals." It noted with satisfaction that, by contrast, the "honest Home Rulers" of the "Hibernian societies in the colonies" had sent addresses to the Queen expressing gratitude for the shamrock concession and the royal visit to Dublin, even though "many of them deplore the war, just as many Englishmen do."[67] It is difficult to establish the proportion of Irish nationalists who supported the war and those who kept their reservations private. "J. O'C." of North Gisborne wrote to the New York *Irish World* in October 1900 claiming that "there are a great many pro-Boers here" but "we have got to hold our tongues."[68] The following year, M. J. Sheahan of Dunedin told Irish Party deputy leader John Dillon much the same thing: "[o]ur people here to a man almost are with the Boers, but are compelled to keep their opinions, as several have suffered locally for giving vent to them."[69]

Whatever their numbers, the pro-Boers evidently held little sway. New Zealand's most important Irish Catholic organization was the Hibernian Australasian Catholic Benefit Society (HACBS). Although technically a nonpolitical friendly society, in 1900 its branches throughout the colony participated in events with unambiguous pro-war messaging. On 14 March the Wellington branch sent an address to the Queen which included a wish for "every success to the British arms in South Africa," and its St. Patrick's Day festivities included a brief reception to the Fourth Contingent ahead of its departure for South Africa that evening.[70] The Christchurch Hibernians also sent an address to the Queen, and celebrated St. Patrick's Day with a concert and cinematograph show at which images of Lord Roberts and the New Zealand Contingents were met with singing of "Soldiers of the Queen" and Kipling's music hall war anthem "The Absent-Minded Beggar."[71] The Auckland festivities were less overtly loyal and featured "The Wearing of the Green" rather than "God Save the Queen." This did not go unnoticed. A correspondent named "Irish Nationalist" explained to the *New Zealand Herald* that "no disrespect was intended" by the musical program, and that he was sure "there is not an Irishman alive who does not, down in his deep Irish heart, admire [the Queen's] womanly virtues."[72]

While James Grattan Grey's friends in Wellington and Auckland presented him with a purse of sovereigns without the help of any Irish organizations, the HACBS of Dunedin was busy organizing a testimonial and gift of £30 to Father Henry William Cleary.[73] Born in Wexford in 1859, Cleary trained for the priesthood at St. Patrick's College Maynooth, the Roman Seminary, and the Seminaire de Saint Sulpice in Paris, before emigrating to Ballarat, Victoria. He spent a decade there sharpening his considerable literary ability. His tracts against anti-Catholic prejudice in Australia secured his appointment in 1898 as editor of Dunedin's *New Zealand Tablet*—the colony's preeminent Catholic journal and the closest thing to an Irish nationalist newspaper that it possessed.[74] Under past and future editors—such as the ardent Home Ruler Bishop Patrick Moran, and the Sinn Féiner Father James Kelly—the *Tablet* explicitly identified Irish Catholic interests in New Zealand with Irish nationalist politics at home.[75] Under Henry Cleary, the *Tablet*'s position on the Irish question was more subdued. Cleary unequivocally supported Home Rule but was wary of the Irish question's potential to obstruct Irish Catholic integration into New Zealand society. He preferred to be combative and uncompromising on issues of local Catholic interest—especially denominational education—while emphasizing Catholic loyalty to the empire.[76]

Cleary later became well-known for demonstrating this loyalty through serving, while Bishop of Auckland, a three-month stint as a chaplain on the western front during the winter of 1916–17. He was awarded an OBE in 1919 in recognition of his contributions to the war effort.[77] His response to the South African War, however, was markedly different. He believed it was "avoidable and unnecessary." He scoffed at justifications based on the question of the *uitlander* franchise, insisting that the war was really the outcome "of the clamour of the capitalists," and that the "working classes" would ultimately bear its financial and physical cost. "And yet," he lamented, "the worker huzzas the sword that is sharpened to slit his carotid artery, and applauds the ringed finger that picks his pocket."[78] In essays on the horrors of modern warfare, Cleary expressed disgust at how jingoism elevated the "wholesale man-butchering in the open-air shambles known as battlefields."[79] Yet he made it emphatically clear that he was not a pro-Boer. Some Catholic publications skeptical of the war published mixed reports about the legal position and alleged mistreatment of Catholics in the Boer republics.[80] But Cleary's *Tablet* was immediately adamant that Catholics and Jews were persecuted in the Transvaal, and that the Boers were an "obstinate" minority, "Protestant of Protestants," who may not have deserved invasion but who certainly did not merit Catholic support.[81]

The fact that criticism of the war's origins—especially when it came from Irish Catholics—tended to be met with accusations of pro-Boerism or anti-imperialism deeply irritated Cleary. It was, he pointed

Figure 5.2. Henry William Cleary as Bishop of Auckland, 1910–, 1/2–024702, Alexander Turnbull Library, Wellington, New Zealand.

out, a view widely held among British liberals that "this miserable war [was] for the sake of a handful of capitalists." Nevertheless, he argued, now that it had become an imperial crisis, any sensible subject could see it was imperative that Britain's defeat be averted; indeed, a Boer victory would be "a great calamity for Catholic interests in South Africa." Cleary agreed with another critic of the war, Cardinal Archbishop of Sydney Patrick Francis Moran, that the Catholic church would fare much better in a South Africa united under British rule than it would under the "bigotry" of a Boer government.[82] As Colin Barr has noted, the Catholic hierarchy in Cape Colony itself was by the turn of the twentieth century "wholly Irish" and openly supported the British side.[83] Cleary and Moran understood that where the British empire expanded, the "Hiberno-Roman" spiritual empire followed. The primacy of the Catholic interest colored the *Tablet*'s reporting on imperialism elsewhere, too. While condemning the American campaign in the Philippines for its "savage disregard" for life and property (especially in the looting of Catholic churches), Cleary romanticized Spanish rule for its role in spreading the Catholic faith.[84] By the same token, he supported the eight-nation alliance's suppression of the Boxer rebellion in China, likening the Boxers' treatment of Catholic missions to mid-nineteenth century American nativism.[85]

Like James Grattan Grey, Cleary preferred not to explicitly link his Irish nationalism with his opinion of the war. But when faced with what he felt were "sneaking insinuations" of Irish disloyalty in the colonial press, he responded forcefully. What "conquered country" except Ireland, he asked, had "rendered such conspicuous and faithful military service to its conqueror"? He listed past and present Irish contributions to British military exploits, emphasizing the enlistment of Irish volunteers in colonial contingents and the prominent role of Irish generals and regiments such as the Dublin Fusiliers in the fighting—all rendered despite "galling political disabilities."[86] Cleary also echoed Grey in claiming that the Australasian press and public were markedly less tolerant of dissent than their British counterparts.[87]

Support for the empire as it stood was virtually ubiquitous among Irish nationalists in New Zealand. On St. Patrick's Day in Dunedin, one speaker told assembled "Irishmen" that the war, "much as it was to be regretted, would do much to bring not alone England, Ireland

and Scotland much nearer to each other, but would bind in a closer union the most remote parts of the Empire."[88] Even Grey's fulminations against jingoism and militarism should not be confused with criticism of empire. He was opposed only to its unnecessary expansion. Unlike many nationalists in Ireland and the United States, he championed the idea of an Anglo-American alliance. In a *New York Times* article of December 1899, he attacked the British decision to allow Germany a foothold in Samoa as it imperiled the safety of the empire in the Pacific.[89] Samoan sovereignty apparently did not deserve the same protection as Boer sovereignty. Indeed, Grey could comfortably outstrip the white supremacism of his jingo opponents. When Seddon proposed including Maori volunteers in a New Zealand contingent, Grey wrote in the Dublin *Freeman's Journal* a hysterical screed on what he called Maori "savagery" and "cannibalism." "Surely civilised nations," he entreated, "will not quietly acquiesce in a black and more than half savage race being put in the field against the bravest white race in the world's history."[90] Cleary, too, expressed anxiety—widely shared by Irish nationalists and others throughout the English-speaking world—at the prospect of African "dark-skinned pagans" bringing "the methods of barbarian or savage warfare into the struggle between the two white races."[91]

Given the abundant common ground between them, it might seem surprising that the *Tablet* did not rally to Grey's defense when the scandal surrounding his dismissal broke. But Grey's posturing as a victim of jingoism failed to persuade Cleary, who was fully informed of the antecedents of his case. The *Tablet* avoided weighing in at all until 26 July 1900. Cleary calmly explained to readers that Grey had been reprimanded before, and that his firing was not for his criticism of the war; rather, "the question was whether Parliament should rule its officers, or should the officers control Parliament."[92] Grey was too strong a pro-Boer for Cleary and in any case seemed quite determined to go out in flames. Tying the *Tablet* to his lost cause would do nothing to advance Cleary's project of Irish Catholic advancement and integration.

In New Zealand then, Irish nationalist responses to the war fell somewhere within a relatively narrow spectrum. On the one end were those like the Wellington and Christchurch HACBS, who made a conspicuously loyal display of saluting the Queen and the colonial contingents and cheering Lord Roberts. In the middle were those like Father Cleary and the subscribers to the *Tablet*, who felt the war was unnecessary but who nevertheless got behind the imperial war effort and held no truck with pro-Boerism. Then there were the Boer sympathizers like James Grattan Grey whose views were broadly in line with those of the moderate nationalists at home. It is exceedingly difficult to gauge their relative proportions. In a remote colony where, as James Belich has argued, "Better Britonism" was in the ascendant, and where organized Irish nationalism had lapsed for a decade, there were few forums or organs for the expression of anything but a loyalist or clerically mediated line.[93] What remained of the INF disappeared again from 1902 until January 1906 when at a Wellington meeting it was asked whether, with a single branch, it could reasonably call itself a "federation" anymore. It opted instead to reconstitute as a branch of the United Irish League. Remarkably, this was the first ever to be established in New Zealand despite thriving organizations having existed for almost six years in North America and Australia.[94] With even mainstream Irish nationalism at such a low ebb, it is hardly surprising that there remains no evidence of Fenian activity or sentiment in New Zealand during the South African War.

6

"Strictly Constitutional"

Australia's Irish Nationalists Juggle Loyalty and Dissent

James Grattan Grey's opposition to the war may have made him persona non grata in the eyes of some New Zealand loyalists, but the Dunedin *Evening Star* was wrong to conflate his position with "rank republicanism."[1] Grey, like most Irish nationalists in Australasia, made his disdain for contemporary Fenianism abundantly clear. After spending two weeks enjoying the *Exposition Universelle* at Paris, he and Jane traveled to Dublin, having been contracted by Patrick Ford to report on the Irish National Convention at the Rotunda. They described their visit in "Ireland and the Irish as we found them," serialized in twenty-six parts for the Melbourne *Advocate*.[2] Their accounts heaped praise on the UIL and the reunified Irish Party, whose success made it clear that "the dismemberment of the British Empire [. . .] forms no part of the Irish plan of campaign."[3] Fenianism they dismissed as "a movement alike senseless in its conception and harmful to the true cause of Ireland," an "egregious folly" that was "far worse than no patriotism at all."[4] They expounded with great satisfaction on John Dillon's pro-Boer resolution at the Convention and the "indescribable" response from attendees.[5] The "generous, unselfish and magnanimous" Irish people, they claimed, knew that the Boer "struggle for national existence is precisely what their own has been, in days gone by, and is today."[6]

The Greys were entertained once at dinner by John Dillon, and their story and presence were noted by the nationalist press, but they made little impact in Ireland besides.[7] In early 1901 they took up temporary residence in London, where James completed a book: *Australasia: Old and New*. It received mixed reviews. Some felt it was a thinly veiled diatribe against the premiership of Richard Seddon. One reviewer called it "the verbose raving of a heated partisan" and suggested alternate titles such as "*Wicked Richard And His Naughty Men*" or "*Australasia . . .*

More or Less.[8] Another found it "hopelessly muddled" in its facts and cobbled together "in the slipshod phrases dear to minor orators at public banquets."[9] Grey's decision to credit the Catholic explorer Pedro Fernandes de Quiros with Australia's discovery ahead of the Protestant Tasman or Cook did not help its prospects. This dubious interpretation—the Australian front of contemporary efforts to jam a Catholic cross in the founding myths of white settler nationalities—had already been championed by leaders like Cardinal Moran.[10] It gave Grey's critics reason to dismiss his book on sectarian grounds.

The strongest reviews of *Australasia: Old and New* came from another Ulster-born Australasian. John Laurence Rentoul was a Presbyterian minister and professor of biblical languages and Christian philosophy at the University of Melbourne's Ormond College. Rentoul supported Home Rule and land reform and, despite his evangelical leanings, was respected and admired by the Irish Catholic community in Melbourne.[11] In May 1900 he launched the Peace and Humanity Society, Australasia's first ever anti-war movement. At its inaugural public meeting, Rentoul moved a resolution of sympathy with James Grattan Grey and his wife on their "courageous loyalty to the principles of freedom, and condemnation of the despotism and narrow-mindedness of the Seddonite Parliament."[12] Rentoul respectfully disagreed with Grey's belief that de Quiros had discovered Australia, but argued that this was a small and inconsequential passage being used by hostile reviewers to unfairly discredit an otherwise valuable book. The real reason that the "Jingo press of Australia" was enforcing a "practical boycott" of the book, he alleged, was because of Grey's position on the South African War. As proof he provided extensive extracts from positive British and American reviews and asked how suffocating must Australian public discourse be if the Melbourne dailies dismissed out of hand a book that even the Tory *Irish Times* could praise.[13]

A marginally less hostile literary scene was not sufficient to make life in London agreeable to the Greys. James complained at length to the *Irish World* about the epidemic of female drunkenness surrounding him—clear evidence of "England's downward tendency." His account of the street celebrations marking the return of the City Imperial Volunteers from South Africa provided an opportunity for a broadside against Anglo-Saxon superiority. "As I watched that besotten, howling mob," he wrote, "I could not help thinking how thin their veneer of civilization actually is."[14] Jane, for her part, was unhappy about the price of a bath and the resulting uncleanliness of the people.[15] By the autumn of 1901 the Greys had left London to take up a grand tour of Europe, collecting material and photographs for another jointly authored travel series.[16] They claimed that they were often met with hostility when Europeans mistook them for an English couple, yet "with open arms and all sorts of apologies" when they explained they were Irish. They told the *Irish World* that English tourists had taken to passing themselves off as Irish, because Irishness had become "a passport all over Europe since the robber war began."[17]

With their European tour complete in late 1901, the Greys decided to move to Melbourne. They had gained a friend and admirer there in Rentoul, and James was known professionally in the city as a longtime New Zealand correspondent of the daily *Age*.[18] That paper now took a dim view of Boer sympathizers like him, but the weekly *Advocate* was sufficiently impressed with James to appoint him editor following his arrival in the city in 1902.[19]

As Irish nationalists and opponents of the war, the Greys found the atmosphere in Australia more congenial than that in New Zealand. In the urban centers of Melbourne and Sydney, larger concentrations of Irish Catholics possessing closer ties to political leaders in Ireland and a more active ethnic newspaper press participated in a more robust nationalist culture than could be found across the Tasman. The Irish nationalist revival in Australia was nevertheless slower to unfold and ultimately less dramatic than that in Ireland and the United States. Aside from the obvious obstacle posed by distance, Irish nationalists in Australia were confronted with the same wave of jingoism that crashed through other parts of the British world. A decade of nationalist decline and a growing identification with a fledgling Australian nationality— encouraged by the imminent creation of the federated Commonwealth of Australia—tempered anti-war sentiment among Irish Catholic communities. Some expressed strong Boer sympathies but took care to repudiate Fenianism, asserting that support for the Irish Party and opposition to an unjust war were both consistent with loyalty to Australia and the empire. The difficult case of Arthur Lynch, as we shall see, placed this position under no small strain. Others saw pro-Boerism as a serious liability to the advancement of the Irish Catholic interest, and urged self-censorship. The tension between nationalist impulses and Catholic integration was particularly evident in debates among clergy in New South Wales, where the war exposed cracks in the clerical nationalism propagated by the colony's Cullenite hierarchy.

* * *

Founded in 1868, the *Advocate* was the organ of Melbourne's large and established Irish Catholic community.[20] It was managed by the Home Rule activist Joseph Winter (a groomsman at John Redmond's wedding), and edited for over three decades by Limerick-born Catholic convert William Gunson until his death in December 1901.[21] Winter and the *Advocate* had a close relationship with Michael Davitt, who had most recently visited Melbourne in 1895, and who had since 1883 contributed a fortnightly column to the paper.[22] As Davitt turned his attention to the war—describing it in his column as "unjust, uncalled for, and [. . .] waged for dishonest purposes against a brave and small nation defending its liberty"—the *Advocate* stood firmly behind him and the Irish Party.[23] Unlike the *New Zealand Tablet*, the *Advocate* openly admired the "extraordinary heroism" of the Boers.[24] Gunson's editorials praised Rentoul's Peace and Humanity Society for holding forth against the tide of jingoism and condemning the "felonious attack" on Boer independence.[25]

In 1901 Melbourne's population was over half that of the entire colony of New Zealand. Organized opposition to the war and support for Irish nationalism were both easier to sustain among a minority concentrated in one city rather than scattered across two islands.[26] James Grattan Grey enjoyed a standing ovation when he addressed the Peace and Humanity Society's celebration of the war's end in June 1902. In his speech he openly praised the "brave, gallant, noble" Boers and denounced "colonial Jingoism and imperialism" (as ever missing no opportunity for a jibe at its "arch-priest," Richard Seddon).[27] The Peace and Humanity Society provided a platform for opponents of the war and a forum for supporters of international arbitration, but its public impact was limited. Despite winning the support of select journals like the *Advocate*, it failed to attract a large membership. Its anti-war petition, submitted to the Australian federal parliament in January 1902, garnered only 800 signatures.[28] This was still impressive compared with the society's small New Zealand offshoot quietly established in Wellington in August 1900. "Who Are They?" the *New Zealand Herald* scoffed in a headline of April 1902, having only just learned that the society existed.[29]

While Home Rulers were often represented at Melbourne's Peace and Humanity Society meetings, it was never an explicitly Irish nationalist affair.[30] In May 1902 Grey was the special guest speaker at a meeting of the Melbourne branch of the United Irish League. Introducing him, Dr. Nicholas O'Donnell, the state president of the UIL, praised Grey's "martyrdom" for refusing to support "the extinction of the two little brave republics." New Zealand's loss, he argued, was Melbourne's gain.[31] The establishment of the UIL in Victoria had been driven by O'Donnell himself, a medical doctor and energetic Gaelic scholar, who set the process in motion in June 1900.[32] O'Donnell distributed over two hundred advance circulars "to the clergy and laity" announcing that the League's inaugural meeting in Melbourne was to be held on 13 July. Despite these efforts, the excitement on the day was dampened by disappointingly poor attendance.[33] Some of those who did show up expressed more enthusiasm about the proposal for a "White Rose League"—a cross-national organization that would encourage devolution and Gladstonian principles throughout the empire.[34] Although it deliberately made its subscription fees "exceedingly small" so as to attract "extensive membership among the working classes," for much of 1900 the Melbourne branch of the UIL struggled to grow.[35] By the end of the year it had sent just £200 to the Irish organization—half of which came from the endowment of one deceased supporter.[36] The greatest obstacles appeared to be lingering uncertainty about whether the Irish Party's new experiment in unity would hold, and whether the UIL in Ireland could prove itself a worthy successor to the Land League. But after the Irish Party's strong showing in the "Khaki Election" of September–October 1900 and the cementing of unity at the November National Convention (Healyites excepted), the Melbourne UIL's fortunes began to improve. A summer excursion to Mornington in February 1901 was an unexpected success; the local leaders scrambled to hold an impromptu meeting at the pavilion wharf to promote league membership—open to "both sexes"—before thousands of waiting

Figure 6.1. Dr. Nicholas O'Donnell and his son, 1897, O'Donnell Family Photographs, State Library of Victoria.

excursionists. In an improvised speech, Joseph Winter posed a constitutionalist version of the "England's difficulty" mantra to stress the importance of supporting a strong and united nationalist organization at home. Had the Irish Party been united "when the South African War commenced," he argued, "the Tory Government would have thought twice before it would have refused" a demand for Home Rule.[37]

Any common ground with Fenianism ends there. In colonial society the charge of Fenianism could be damaging to the standing of Irish Catholics, especially in wartime. Irish communities' respectable leadership—lay and clerical—was deeply sensitive to accusations of disloyalty and always ready to dismiss physical force republicanism as having no place in their nationalism. For example, in October 1900 during a debate over a proposed referendum on women's suffrage in the Victoria Legislative Assembly, the pro-suffrage liberal independent Henry Bournes Higgins was attacked by Cork-born Catholic Tory Frank Madden for allegedly being inconsistent in his opinions. Madden declared that, unlike Higgins, he personally would never "go to a meeting of Fenians and support their disloyal language, and then come to Parliament and take the oath of allegiance when there was £300 a year hanging to it. ('Shame' and laughter.)"[38]

Henry Bournes Higgins was born to a Wesleyan family in Co. Down. He emigrated to Melbourne in 1870 where he trained as a barrister, entering state politics in the 1890s. Higgins was prominently involved in Home Rule activism throughout his career—from sharing a platform with the first Irish Party delegation in 1883 to introducing and passing the Australian federal parliament's resolution in favor of Home Rule in 1905.[39] A patron of the Peace and Humanity Society, the UIL, and Melbourne's Shamrock Club, Higgins was outspoken in his opposition to the South African War and the dispatching of colonial contingents. This position, and his idiosyncratic opposition to federation (he had been one of Victoria's ten delegates to the federal constitutional convention), almost ended his political career in 1900.[40] Madden's (spurious) imputation of Fenianism caused Higgins's Irish nationalist friends in Melbourne to leap to his defense.[41] Nicholas O'Donnell wrote to the *Age*, challenging Madden to be specific. "If ever a Fenian meeting has been held in Victoria, the circumstance is unknown to the great majority of Irishmen," he pointed out. "[S]uch a thing has never occurred here." The city's Shamrock Club, a fraternal association with Home Rule sympathies, published a resolution in the *Advocate* condemning Madden and stating that its members "emphatically deny that any action has been taken by the Irish Nationalists of Melbourne other than in a strictly constitutional manner."[42] Some of the rank and file, however, may have been less concerned with appearances. Miss H. J. MacNamara of St. Kilda told the *Advocate* that if Frank Madden was right and the UIL was "synonymous" with Fenianism, "then I do gladly hasten to become a member of that 'Fenian League,' for which please find enclosed 5s."[43]

Numbers afforded some safety to Irish nationalist critics of the war in Melbourne and parts of rural Victoria, but there were limits.[44] Wartime popular culture was dominated by patriotic loyalism, a phenomenon that only intensified following the reverses suffered by British forces during "Black Week" in mid-December 1899. As Craig Wilcox has shown, the peril faced by besieged British garrisons at Ladysmith and Mafeking, and by the empire as a whole should any rival power declare for the Boers, "somehow made the war seem a defensive one."[45] Suspected "disloyalists" faced possible ostracism or dismissal. Edward Seitz, a Swiss-born officer of the Melbourne Metropolitan Board of Works, was known to have pro-Boer leanings. While his colleagues celebrated the relief of Mafeking, Seitz and two German officers were "goaded" with a Union Jack and ordered to sing "God Save the Queen"; they refused and tore down the flag. Seitz was singled out as the ringleader and several commissioners moved to have him sacked for disloyalty in public office; others defended him. As a compromise, he was suspended for three months.[46] William Watt, Postmaster General of Victoria, at first expressed cautious skepticism about dispatching a colonial contingent to South Africa, but soon recanted this position.[47] Mrs. J. C. Jardine, a self-described "thorough Britisher," was not persuaded by Watt's about-face. When he denied a postal worker leave of absence to join the Australian Imperial Regiment in South Africa, Mrs. Jardine needed no further convincing that Watt was a "pro-Boer." On 30 April 1900 she interrupted a cabinet meeting and assaulted him with a horsewhip.[48] In an atmosphere like this, the adventures of one of their native sons, Arthur Lynch, posed a problem to the Irish nationalists of Victoria.

* * *

Lynch was born in Smythesdale, near the gold-rush city of Ballarat, in 1861. His father was a radical Irish veteran of the Eureka Rebellion.[49] He was a voracious learner, studying engineering, philosophy, psychology, and medicine at institutions in Ballarat, Melbourne, Berlin, and Paris. In his thirties he turned to journalism and Irish nationalist politics. After failing to secure election as a Parnellite in Galway in 1892, he drifted into the Irish National Alliance circles of Mark Ryan in London and Maud Gonne in Paris.[50] In December 1899 Lynch traveled to South

Africa as a war correspondent.[51] By January, however, he had taken up Transvaal citizenship and, with the support of prominent Johannesburg Irish nationalist Solomon Gillingham, was appointed to lead a second Irish brigade at the rank of colonel.[52] Whether he had gone to South Africa with the intention of fighting or had, as he later claimed, enlisted in a fit of righteousness, is not clear.

The existence of Lynch's unit gave Irish pro-Boers the impression that the number of Irish combatants flocking to join the Boer fight was too great to be accommodated by a single brigade. The reality was quite different. Colonel John Blake and Major John MacBride, leaders of the first brigade, were opposed to the scheme, believing it "an unnecessary and a foolish move" as they "had not enough men" themselves.[53] The core of Lynch's commando appears to have been comprised of a handful of men who had either deserted or been ejected from the first brigade, and who may have had personal grudges against MacBride. They had that (if little else) in common with Lynch; he and MacBride had been acquainted in London during the 1890s and did not get along.[54] Their forces generally kept their distance, though the two men greeted one another stiffly on the retreat from Johannesburg to Pretoria in June.[55] Few of the other men Lynch managed to scrape together were even Irish—despite his published appeals to Irish and Australian *uitlanders* in the Johannesburg papers.[56] Members of MacBride's brigade disparaged Lynch's commando as "fifty or sixty soreheads, greasers, half-breeds and dagos [. . .] a gang of hobos whom no man in his sober senses would call Irishmen."[57] Whatever their makeup, they did not cover themselves in glory. The commando acquired a reputation for ill-discipline, looting, and horse theft. One of their few notable contributions to the fighting was stalling the advance of Australian troops through part of Johannesburg.[58]

Michael Davitt encountered Lynch near the front and was impressed by his intellect.[59] Partly for this reason and partly because, as he explained to MacBride, he wanted to suppress "the troubles of the Brigade" and "the division which took place," Davitt made a point of writing admiringly of Lynch and his commando.[60] He exaggerated its size and its exploits, much as he did for Blake and MacBride's group.[61] Solomon Gillingham understood this impulse but felt that Davitt went too far in his boosting of the Irish contribution to the fighting,

COL. ARTHUR LYNCH

3664·6

Figure 6.2. Arthur Lynch, ca. 1910–1915, Bain News Service, Library of Congress.

worrying at the embarrassment that any leaking of the less glamorous truth might cause. Gillingham added he had personally been "greatly deceived in Mr. Arthur Lynch" and regretted ever supporting him.[62] By the time the Australian press learned that Lynch was fighting with the Boers (June 1900), Pretoria had fallen, his commando had disbanded, and he was on his way back to Paris. It seems most Irish Australians were unsure what to make of Lynch and his behavior. Only the *Catholic Press* of Sydney, known for its Boer sympathies, offered anything resembling editorial comment, and this was relatively restrained. An article pointed out that the intellectual credentials of Lynch, "a chevalier of literature," challenged the impression given in the Australian newspapers that the Boer Irish Brigade was "composed solely of the worthless hangers-on of the Johannesburg bars." "If," the *Press* supposed, "he escapes the perils of battle and the provost-marshal afterwards, Arthur Lynch may be safely put down for perhaps the most interesting book on the present war."[63] That may have been his intention. Like James Grattan Grey, Lynch was not above using his journalism to make himself the hero of his own story. After returning to Paris, he announced he would be embarking on a lecture tour of the United States.

That tour never quite took off. He arrived in New York on 30 September to at best a lukewarm welcome—although he could at least boast of lunching with fellow gentleman-adventurer Theodore Roosevelt at the Governor's Mansion in Albany.[64] Aside from a few scattered cameos and a flurry of articles on the war, his visit made little impact.[65] Crucially, the leadership of the Clan na Gael was close to his rival John MacBride and deliberately froze Lynch out. He found temporary allies in John Finerty and William Bourke Cockran.[66] However, it appears he alienated them by sailing to Paris to invite the exiled President Paul Kruger to tour the United States under the sponsorship of William Randolph Hearst's *New York Journal.* Not only was Lynch working for the imperialist millionaire "yellow press" baron, but in doing so he was technically competing with the similar efforts of organizations like the Boer Relief Fund and the Anti-Imperialist League in which Cockran was prominently involved.[67] "Lynch's tour," noted Major Gosselin, "is a source of trouble to those 'running' it."[68]

The Irish nationalists of Melbourne were conspicuously quiet on the exploits of the war's most prominent Irish Australian. From October

1900 onward, the *Advocate* occasionally published accounts of Lynch's commando written by Lynch himself or by Michael Davitt, but avoided offering any editorial comment.[69] It was only when Lynch publicly repudiated Fenianism and finally secured nomination as an Irish Party candidate that he became palatable to them. Still smarting from his defeat in 1892, Lynch had been lobbying for another nomination since at least May 1900. "I do not desire to make a point of my action in the Boer war," he explained to John Redmond in a rather audacious letter written from the front line while serving as a colonel in the Boer army.[70] He renewed the pressure in September 1900, telling Redmond that while he would no doubt be popular with the "Extreme Section" in Ireland and America, he was committed to the party's constitutional methods.[71] He failed to get on the party ticket for the "Khaki Election," however, and his subsequent visit to the United States helped dispel any illusion of popularity with the radicals. But the fortuitous elevation to the Lords of the member for Galway North in September 1901 meant a by-election would be held in late November. This time Lynch managed to secure his nomination—but not before publicly affirming that he did "not think that armed force can accomplish the liberation of Ireland" and that he was "against any movement in that direction."[72]

Lynch's conversion to constitutionalism did much to soothe the apprehensions of Irish nationalists in Australia. Where previously they nervously maintained their distance lest he, by association, taint them with the stigma of Fenianism, now they were ready to embrace him as one of theirs. Nicholas O'Donnell, on behalf of Victoria's United Irish League, cabled John Redmond: "Victoria delighted on the selection of Arthur Lynch as candidate for Galway." The *Advocate* acknowledged Lynch as an Irish Australian and "wish[ed] him success."[73] When the *Age* reprinted an extract from Arthur Griffith's *United Irishman* mocking Lynch as a pathetic figure whose sham colonelcy was the laughing stock of advanced nationalists, the *Advocate* drew on Davitt's praise of Lynch to hit back.[74] There were many instances of current or ex-felons being elected to Irish seats, the paper argued. If Lynch had proven himself good enough for the Redmonds, Davitt, and the Irish Party as a whole, he should be good enough for all Irish Australians.[75]

Campaigning from Paris, Lynch beat the Unionist candidate Horace Plunkett by a significant margin without even stepping foot in Ireland.

Whether his success was aided more by his record in South Africa or his endorsement by the Irish Party is unclear, but his military adventure evidently had not hurt his chances with Irish voters.[76] It remained to be seen, however, whether the British government would permit him to take his seat. Despite Lynch's assurance to Redmond that there wasn't "any danger of the Govt. troubling us," most observers expected Lynch to be arrested as soon as he arrived in England.[77] He waited until June 1902 before leaving Paris for London, hoping that the end of the war and the celebrations surrounding Edward VII's coronation would improve his odds at forgiveness. It did not work. He was arrested immediately upon disembarking at Newhaven and was charged with high treason. His would be the first such trial in England since William Smith O'Brien's in 1848.[78]

Lynch's defense rested on his having been sworn as a Transvaal citizen before he enlisted to fight with the Boers, as well as some uncertainty about whether offenses committed outside British territory could legally be considered high treason. His legal team suggested that Lynch ought to be tried by his own peers in Victoria, rather than England. Lynch himself had tentatively injected an Australian dimension to his case in a letter to the Speaker of the House of Commons written on his return to England. Justifying his actions in South Africa, he claimed, rather unconvincingly, that "I was greatly impelled by my Australian sentiments"—specifically his worry about the "detrimental effects" of jingoism, which he called "a reactionary movement." "I would rather have burned my right hand," he insisted, "than have raised it against Australia."[79] But raise it he did—quite literally against Australian soldiers in Johannesburg. Statements from his wife Annie and his former employer, Alfred Harmsworth of the *Daily Mail*, sought to excuse this by emphasizing that Lynch was "a most unpracticable person" who always had "his head in the clouds." If he committed treason, it was an accident of his "romantic, impracticable, poetical nature" rather than a deliberate betrayal of his subjecthood. He was no Fenian diehard. Annie pointed to how he had publicly "disclaimed" physical force ahead of his election. In this her husband went further than many sitting Irish Party MPs, who liked to remain "either silent, or they coquette mildly with Fenianism."[80]

Annie may have had a point, but these desperate arguments did little to mitigate the irresistible case against Lynch. His own published writing on his South African swashbuckling left Crown Solicitor Edward Carson's prosecution with little work to do. Michael Davitt sheepishly told the *Advocate* that his own accounts also, regrettably, provided abundant evidence against his friend.[81] Lynch's defense was hopeless; the jury took twenty-six minutes to return a verdict against him. The senior presiding judge threw Lynch's Australian identity back in his face: Australia "has nobly shown its devotion to its parent country [. . . but] you have indeed taken a different course from that which was adopted by her sons."[82] He was sentenced to death by hanging but, as was universally expected, this was commuted to imprisonment for life.

Lynch's trial received little attention in Australia. It was completely overshadowed by the controversy surrounding the court martial and executions of Bushveldt Carbineers Harry "Breaker" Morant and Peter Handcock over their roles in the murder of unarmed prisoners in northern Transvaal.[83] In fact, observers like Grey preferred to talk about the Morant case—for them it neatly "complete[d] the picture" of a "disastrous" war that would "cause future generations a pang of shame."[84] The Lynch case was more awkward. During his successful North Galway election campaign in November 1901, the Irish nationalists of Victoria had been fleetingly content to claim him as their own. But with his arrest and trial they fell silent once again—even as those in Ireland, Britain, and the United States rallied behind him.[85] The only attempt to stir Irish Australians to speak out against Lynch's sentence came in the form of a letter written in May 1903 to James Grattan Grey as editor of the *Advocate*. Joseph Walsh of Coburg complained that the silence surrounding the "atrocious sentence" handed to Lynch was "a blot upon the Irish people of Australia," and he proposed that a petition for amnesty be presented to the parliament of Victoria. "I will leave this suggestion for the judgment of yourself, sir," Walsh wrote, "and the leaders of the Irish societies of Australia to see what action can be taken in the matter."[86] Tellingly, no action was taken.[87]

Annie Lynch similarly failed to persuade John Redmond to make Lynch's release a platform for agitation.[88] But her constant correspondence made certain that Lynch was not forgotten. Backroom lobbying by Redmond and Davitt eventually secured his conditional release in January 1904.[89] In 1907 he received a full pardon, and immediately turned to Redmond again seeking another Irish Party nomination.

Redmond was reticent. "Are you really serious in wanting to come back here," he asked, "and are you wise in this?"[90] By 1909 Lynch had won an election in West Clare, and finally took his seat at Westminster. But he was unpopular with his Irish Party colleagues and despised by Fenians. By 1914 Tom Clarke was still calling Lynch a "S—of a B—."[91] The *Advocate* welcomed his election for West Clare as evidence of a maturing attitude towards political prisoners in Britain, but was cool on Lynch himself, merely observing that "Probably no other native of Victoria has had any personal experience so strangely varied."[92] Melbourne's Shamrock Club mentioned Lynch's good fortune only as evidence of the magnanimity of King Edward VII.[93]

* * *

It took less than a charge of high treason to cause some Australian Irish nationalists to feel embarrassed by the behavior of their own. For Patrick McMahon Glynn, even moderate Boer sympathies and Home Rule activism were, in time of war, cause for mortification. Born in Galway, Glynn was one of Adelaide's most prominent Irish Catholics and a delegate to the federal constitutional convention. In May 1900 he told his mother that he found the "temper" of the Irish press and of "leading Irish politicians" to be in "bad taste to put it mildly." He complained about his own "blessed countrymen here [in Adelaide]" for mentioning Home Rule in a telegram to the Queen congratulating her on her wartime visit to Dublin. Finding that his advice against this "useless" insertion of the national question fell on deaf ears, Glynn took it upon himself to quietly soften the wording and address the telegram to the Lord Mayor of Dublin instead. He confided he was "glad" to learn it had been ignored.[94]

When the 1798 Memorial at Sydney's Waverley Cemetery was officially unveiled on Easter Sunday, 15 April 1900, Glynn was in attendance. This was "not really by desire," he told his mother, "but to avoid giving offence to good natured enthusiasts."[95] The memorial project had originated in 1898, when the gravesite of the transported Catholic '98 rebel leader Michael Dwyer and his wife Mary was to be disturbed by construction. Following a hugely attended procession, the Dwyers' remains were reinterred at Waverley cemetery, and a fund was commenced to construct a monument at the new burial site. The project was extraordinarily successful. Subscriptions from across Australia raised over £2600—enough to erect a thirty-foot Celtic cross on a substantial twenty-four-foot plinth lined with bronze plaques depicting busts of leading United Irishmen.[96] It was one of only two '98 monuments constructed outside of Ireland during the centenary period. As Ruan O'Donnell has noted, the Fenian presence on memorial committees meant that most of those built in Ireland also prominently acknowledged the rebellions of 1848 and 1867.[97] That the Waverley monument bucked this trend points to the weakness—if not the absence—of any such Fenian influence in Australia.

Whether purged of Fenian symbolism or not, unveiling a monument to a violent wartime Irish rebellion just six weeks after the relief of Ladysmith was a difficult proposition for the respectable leaders of Irish nationalism in Australia. Patrick McMahon Glynn was among the speakers at the ceremony. His oration was only slightly more tepid than the others. All stressed that the rebellion had been a defensive response to intolerable persecution by the "Protestant Parliament" of Dublin. The United Irishmen "were not rebels from choice," Glynn reminded the crowd pointedly. They had not the privilege of representation in parliament or the guidance of a free church that Irish Catholics enjoyed a century later. The speakers carefully avoided mentioning the South African War—except Glynn, who briefly alluded to the battle of Colenso when praising the bravery of the "Irish race" before going on to propose imperial federation. At an overflow event at Botany the following day, however, the men of the committee delivered speeches that were less guarded (the Ladies' Committees were praised but were denied the same privilege). T. E. Healy of Melbourne could not resist mentioning the war. If the British government would go to South Africa to ensure representative government for the *uitlanders*, he asked in a speech tinged with sarcasm, why not peacefully grant autonomy to Ireland next door?

> England professes to the world that she upholds the banner of freedom, and proclaims that she had gone to South Africa to vindicate the claims of those Uitlanders who ought to have the right to vote. We admit that claim (cries of No, no.) for the sake of argument. (Laughter.) We would not believe England had gone there for the sake of plunder, that it was a war of the Stock Exchange, or at the instance of the Jews [. . .] (Laughter.) We would

admit their claim to be fighting for freedom to the Uitlanders to have the liberty of voting—and after that invite the British Government to follow the Queen of England in a ten hours' trip across the channel, and establish a Home Rule Government there. (Applause.) The Irish people did not want separation from England, nor did the Irish wish to give up their share of the Empire they had assisted to build.[98]

Behind (or perhaps embedded in) the jocularity of Healy's speech there is much that reveals the complex position of Irish nationalists in the colonies. The anti-Semitic jibe at capital's role in the war was a common refrain of labor movements—in which Irish workers were strongly represented. The historian C. N. Connolly found that in Australia, Irish emigrants "were clearly at the heart of Labor opposition to the war."[99] As Arthur Hill Griffith, the Irish-born Labour MLA for Waratah in Newcastle and vice president of the Anti-War League, complained: "[t]oday we see Australian working men burning out Dutch farmers in the interests of London Jews and howling for the scalps of Labour members who dare to lift their voices against such infamy."[100] The widespread suspicion that British control of the Rand would mean flooding the mines with cheap native labor resonated with the anxieties of colonial trade unionists who fought bitterly to exclude nonwhite competition on their own turf.[101] These concerns were not sufficient to override the patriotic impulse among a significant portion of Australia's labor movement, however, which was frequently divided on the war question.[102] As for physical force republicanism, Healy's audience at Botany could strongly oppose it in the present while admiring it in the past (an enduring trait of Irish nationalist politics). Similarly, opposition to the war in South Africa and disdain for the British government could sit comfortably alongside pride in the empire and in Ireland's contribution to it. Sydney nationalist leader Dr Charles McCarthy saw no contradiction in condemning "robbery on a gigantic scale" in Ireland while encouraging the audience to build "a greater Ireland" in colonial Australia at the expense of its original inhabitants.[103] Gunson's *Advocate* editorials, while condemning the dispossession of the Boers, were seemingly oblivious to any analogies with settler colonialism in Australia. In one, he pondered over the "very puzzling" decline in the aboriginal population of Victoria and suggested that an overabundance of "kindness" shown by settlers had diminished Indigenous self-reliance.[104] It was perhaps their own role in this process that made any such analogy unappealing to Irish Australian nationalists. They were, as several historians have pointed out, either "actively involved in violently dispossessing and dispersing Indigenous communities" or, at the very least, "inescapably complicit" in it.[105] Arthur Hill Griffith, to his credit, showed some awareness of imperial double standards. Challenging Britain's purported role as the defender of native South Africans from Boer mistreatment, he countered:

> The less we in Australia say about the treatment of the blacks, the better for our self-respect. The blackfellows in the Transvaal are increasing in number. Here we exterminated them with rum and syphilis.[106]

Nonetheless Griffith, as his unsympathetic language belies, was more interested in scoring points against the jingoes than he was in offering a genuine, or indeed accurate, critique of settler colonialism.

* * *

The position of the largely Irish Catholic church in New South Wales was similarly complex. Conspicuous by his absence from the unveiling of the '98 monument was Patrick Moran, Cardinal Archbishop of Sydney. Moran was a prelate in the mold of his powerful uncle, Cardinal Cullen, whose icy attitude towards popular Irish nationalism Moran shared. For Moran it was most tolerable when it could be harnessed to advance the interests of the Hiberno-Roman hierarchy that had come to dominate the church across the Anglo-world. Moran had been openly opposed to the Waverley memorial project since 1898, and although his position softened somewhat in response to criticism, he maintained a passive resistance—preventing, for example, the use of St. Patrick's Day funds, and outdoing the Dwyer procession with a massive funeral to pioneer Irish priests in 1901.[107] On the question of the war, however, Moran took a greater interest than Archbishop Thomas Carr of Melbourne, and dissented from the pro-war line of Herbert Vaughan, Cardinal Archbishop of London, whose brother Roger had been Moran's predecessor at Sydney. An innocuous joke about "annexing goldfields" that Moran cracked at a November 1899 bazaar caused

Figure 6.3. Patrick Francis Cardinal Moran, ca. 1900. Public Domain.

some controversy. While he subsequently made clear that he supported the British effort for the sake of the Catholic interest and some serving relatives, he maintained he did not believe the *uitlander* issue was the real reason behind the war and was skeptical of the decision to send colonial contingents to South Africa.[108]

Priests were unusually prominent in war-related controversies in New South Wales.[109] Perhaps the most famous pro-Boer Irish priest, alongside Father Peter Yorke of San Francisco, had once been based at Waverley's Franciscan Friary: Patrick Fidelis Kavanagh. Best known for his "faith and fatherland" history of the 1798 rebellion which lionised rebel priests like Father John Murphy of Wexford, Kavanagh had spent six years in Sydney before his nationalist zeal caused him to fall afoul of Moran in 1885.[110] Following his return to Ireland he became a clerical talisman of advanced nationalism. During the war he moved in Transvaal Committee and Young Ireland Society circles.[111] Moran's coadjutor at Sydney, Michael Kelly, gravely reported how at one Cork meeting attended by Maud Gonne, Kavanagh had described the war as "organised murder promoted by the insatiable greed of the vampire Empire," and claimed that Irishmen fighting in the British army were guilty of homicide and probably damned to eternity in hell.[112] Kelly and Moran both knew Kavanagh's enduring influence in New South Wales.[113] The Sydney *Freeman's Journal*, one of New South Wales's leading Irish and Catholic weeklies, carried a letter from Kavanagh in February 1900 explaining how Irish sympathy for the Boers came from more than just "hatred" for England. "What came over the generous heart of Australia," he asked, "to unsheathe her virgin sword to smite these struggling freemen whose cause is so undeniably just?"[114] In June 1900 the Sydney branch of the United Irish League condemned Dublin Castle's suppression of Arthur Griffith's *United Irishman*, and thanked Maud Gonne "for her self-sacrificing efforts on behalf of the Irish people."[115] Moran must have been perturbed to find that some in his own flock appeared to share Kavanagh's sympathies with advanced nationalists.

Some New South Wales priests went considerably further than Cardinal Moran to dispel any pall of disloyalty that hung over Irish Catholics. Father Patrick Dunne of Albury wrote frequently in defense of the imperial war effort and to insist that the pro-Boer sentiments frequently found in the columns of the *Freeman's Journal* and *Catholic Press* were not representative of Irish Catholic opinion in the colonies. Dunne argued that Irish Australians should be grateful the Catholic church enjoyed more freedom in the British Empire than it did in majority-Catholic countries like France or Italy and certainly more than it did under the "bigoted and intolerant" Boers who, he added (with some bigotry of his own), had "no more idea of morality than a tom-cat." Pro-Boerism, he warned, "created a bad feeling amongst our fellow-citizens against Irishmen and Catholics."[116] He professed himself a Home Ruler, but urged that the opinions of a minority of "irreconcil-ables" should not be permitted to give "our enemies the opportunity of branding the Irish in Australia as a disloyal body."[117] But even Dunne, whose critics in the *Freeman* accused him of "pandering to the anti-Irish element," agreed with Moran that there had been "no pressing neces-sity" to send colonial contingents when Britain was "well able to settle business with the Boers without their assistance."[118]

The danger of which Father Dunne had warned appeared to come true in the town of Nowra, where two priests were targeted for their suspected disloyalty. In early February "Pan-Britannic" wrote a letter to the editor of the *Shoalhaven News* titled "REBELS IN OUR MIDST." "Irishmen," he warned, "either of birth or descent must be brought to recognize, however unwillingly, that England's time of danger is not quite Ireland's opportunity." Among the examples of "the spouting of seditious treason" by "Pro-Boer foreigners" in the town of Nowra, the author mentioned "a gentleman of the cloth at a recent sports gathering [who] wished it were British men and not insensate targets he was aim-ing at." Two local priests—James Joseph Gunning and Father Dalton—each brought a libel suit against the owner of the *Shoalhaven News*. Alleging they had been defamed as disloyalists by the publication of the letter, they demanded their names be cleared. But their strategy may have been misguided. In a jocose argument that greatly amused the jury, the counsel for the defense portrayed the plaintiffs as two priests on the make. "The whole business is ridiculous," he exclaimed. Before pressing their respective charges, "[t]he two clergymen should have set-tled between themselves in their presbytery [. . .] to which of them the words objected to had reference. (Laughter.)" The judge leaned in favor of Gunning and Dalton. He was visibly surprised when the jury, after a few minutes' deliberation, found against them. "What a pity," one member of the gallery observed of Gunning, "that he isn't a Protestant parson instead of an Irish priest. What thumping damages he'd have got!"[119] It wasn't just priests who fell afoul of loyalist juries. Arthur Hill Griffith, the Irish-born Labour MLA for Newcastle, experienced his own courtroom upset in 1902, when he sought £1,000 in damages from the pro-war *Newcastle Morning Herald* for libel. The defense counsel argued that he really deserved 1,000 kicks as "a traitor of the highest degree," and the presiding judge called his criticism of the British government "sedition of the highest form." Unsurprisingly, the jury found against him after just ten minutes.[120]

From December 1900 onward Moran's circle and the Catholic church in Australia were entangled in a legal case unrelated to the war but far graver than anything faced by Gunning and Dalton. Moran's private secretary, Monsignor Denis O'Haran, was named as a co-respondent in a divorce suit brought by the Australian Test cricketer Arthur Coningham. The Australian church closed ranks to defend O'Haran against the allegations of adultery. Though the jury ultimately found against Coningham, the scandal provoked bitter sectarian antagonism across Australia that frequently overshadowed the smoldering guerrilla conflict in South Africa.[121]

Nevertheless, interest in the war continued in certain quarters, notably in the columns of the Sydney *Catholic Press*. This was sustained, in part, by the contributions of its special correspondent, Agnes Macready. Born in County Down, Macready came to New South Wales in 1867. After converting to Catholicism, she trained as a nurse, and wrote regularly for the *Catholic Press* under her penname "Arrah Luen." Macready traveled immediately to South Africa following the outbreak of the war with a commission from the newspaper—making her Australia's first female war correspondent. She found her first posting at a field hospital near Pietermaritzburg.[122] Through 1900 and 1901 she transmitted mournful accounts of the horrors of the Tugela campaign and of bleak civilian life under "Kitchener's War."[123] Macready's moving prose and her scathing portrayal of the war were invaluable to the *Press*, which of all the Irish and Catholic papers in New South Wales was most strongly sympathetic to the Boers. Its editorials called the war "the most unjustifiable perhaps in the history of the world," attacked Irish members of colonial parliaments who had voted in favor of dispatching contingents, and lamented the "hysterical emotion" that had overtaken the colonies at the encouragement of an "utterly insane" press.[124] The paper printed anti-war essays by Olive Schreiner, Father Peter Yorke of San Francisco, and Professor George Arnold Wood of the University of Sydney.[125]

Although its board of directors was made up of priests, the *Press* was edited by a layman: Tipperary-born John Tighe Ryan. Ryan would later earn a mix of praise and notoriety during the Great War for defying Archbishop Kelly and taking the side of Archbishop Daniel Mannix of Melbourne in the crusade against conscription.[126] Ryan's pro-Boer position on the South African War probably also rankled Kelly, but the editor retained the enthusiastic support of his board and was in March 1902 banqueted in Sydney by "over 50 priests and three prelates" (Kelly excepted).[127] It was instead a cofounder and regular contributor to the *Press*, Father Joseph Bunbury of the suburban Sydney parish of Forest Lodge, who became the target of Kelly's displeasure. Bunbury subtitled his series of essays for the *Press* on the life of John Mitchel "Why Irishmen Sympathise With the Boers," and condemned Father Patrick Dunne's support for "the present disgraceful war of greed and cupidity in Africa."[128] The final straw appears to have been Bunbury's behavior at the annual meeting of the New South Wales HACBS in February 1902. Following a speech from Cardinal Moran, Kelly rose to urge those present to "leave [Irish] politics alone" and "fight the battle of domestic improvement." "[U]nless patriotism was kept always under the control of religion," he warned, "it was likely to go mad." Bunbury spoke later in the day and took a rather different position. In a strongly nationalist speech referencing the famine, "700 years" of conquest, and the civilian death toll of the South African War, he condemned "Irishmen [. . .] who stood up to glorify an Imperialism that sucked the life-blood out of humanity." It was only through rejecting imperialism, he argued, that a federated Australia could become "an Australian nation."[129] Kelly had Bunbury reassigned to the rural parishes of Appin and Camden before ultimately defrocking him "on account of his eccentricity." In May 1903 Bunbury was found dead in a hotel room in Sydney, having ingested strychnine. The coroner recorded a verdict of suicide.[130]

* * *

The South African War, in combination with the rise of the United Irish League, contributed significantly to the reunification of the Irish Parliamentary Party and the reenergization of constitutional Irish nationalism in the Atlantic world. The war's unpopularity in Ireland and the United States provided nationalist leaders from all factions with a flag around which to rally. This feature of the nationalist revival complicated its export to Australasia, where popular support for the war could at times reach fever pitch. For decades, Irish Catholics had been encouraged by their church and their middle-class leadership to stake a place in colonial society as loyal Catholics, and to make the case for Irish Home Rule through their own model subjecthood.[131] Through the 1890s, integration with emerging Australian, New Zealand, and imperial identities progressed under a clerical leadership whose influence expanded as popular nationalist activism and migration from Ireland both declined. When the machine of global Irish nationalism rattled back to life in 1899, many in Australasia found themselves caught between their loyalties to Ireland and their adopted countries. How could they show themselves to be loyal Home Rulers when William Redmond was fraternizing with Maud Gonne in the Dublin Transvaal Committee? How could they convince their neighbors that the United Irish League was not subversive when Michael Davitt was hobnobbing with Paul Kruger? How could they dismiss Fenianism when two Irish brigades, one of them led by an Irish Australian, were shooting at British troops in South Africa? As a consequence, their responses to the war were more complex than those of their counterparts in Ireland and the United States.

Pro-Boer sentiments are hardest to detect in New Zealand, where Irish communities were smaller, more scattered, and underrepresented in the newspaper press. James Grattan Grey's sacking may not technically have been owing to his Boer sympathies, but the response to his utterings and the reports of harassment directed at suspected disloyalists suggest that dissenting from the pro-war consensus could be hazardous. Irish associations there were selective in their engagement with home politics, welcoming the Queen's visit to Dublin but avoiding any public identification with the Irish Party's position on the war. The UIL's overt support for the Boers made it so unpalatable to the New Zealand Irish that its extension to the colony was delayed six years.

Henry Cleary's Dunedin *Tablet* and Cardinal Moran of Sydney both carefully sidestepped awkward developments at home, rejected pro-Boerism, and regretted the outbreak of the war. They made clear, however, that since the empire was now in it, it was in the Catholic interest for them to win it. As Patrick O'Farrell argued, Moran and his followers had by the turn of the century succeeded in making the Church "the arbiter of Ireland's destinies in Australia."[132] But as the debates between New South Wales clergy show, even this "Irish Empire" with its priest "officers" was not immune from the divisive impact of the war. Nevertheless, there was a line that could not be crossed; P. F. Kavanagh and Peter Yorke could attack imperialism all they liked from Ireland and California, but when Father Joseph Bunbury tried to do the same in New South Wales, he was punished for it. A respect for the empire prevailed throughout Irish Catholic colonial communities—something that distinguished their response to the war from that of advanced nationalists in Ireland and the United States. Colonial Irish nationalists were free to criticize jingoism; free to advocate for a more pluralist, less centralized, and less expansionist imperialism. Very few were inclined to question the continued existence of the empire itself, or of Ireland's and the colonies' futures within it. Even for pro-Boers, noisily condemning the conquest of a white people was compatible with quiet support for the continued annexation of other overseas territories and the ongoing expropriation of Indigenous land in white settler colonies. As Dianne Hall and Elizabeth Malcolm have pointed out, to the Irish in Australia "[p]olitical rights were the domain of white people."[133]

In March 1904 James Grattan Grey left Melbourne to take up editorship of the Perth *Western Australian Record*.[134] Among his first public appearances in his new home was a rousing speech he delivered at a Home Rule meeting. He gave the crowd a practiced account of his experiences and travels over the previous years. "[I]s it needed for me to remind you," he asked, "that I have been a Home Ruler ever since I attained the age of reason?"[135] Within a month he had opened a subscription fund in the *Record*—not, however, for Home Rule. He had encountered in Perth Thomas Duggan, an eighty-two-year-old resident of the Old Men's Refuge, and James Keilley, a seventy-six-year-old living in a tent. Both had been Fenians in 1865, transported to Western Australia on the *Hougomont* with John Boyle O'Reilly and other radical nationalist exiles. The *Advocate* gladly agreed to accept subscriptions from any in Melbourne willing to help keep these old patriots out of the poorhouse.[136] Whereas for many Irish Americans Fenianism remained the truest form of Irish patriotism, for Irish Australians it was a relic of the past.[137] In Canada, much to the frustration of loyal Home Rulers, Fenianism had a habit of intruding on the present.

7

"A Few Idiots"?

Irish Nationalists in Canada Mention the War

On 10 October 1899, a day before the South African War commenced, Division No. 1 of the Ancient Order of Hibernians (AOH) in Montreal met to pass a resolution of sympathy with the Boers:

> Whereas Ireland has been persecuted for the past three hundred years, and denied the right of self-government, and has suffered the gibbet, the rack, and all sorts of cruelties to obtain that right; therefore, be it resolved that Division No. 1 extend their fullest sympathy to those brave people, the Boers, who are at present struggling to maintain that right against our most cruel and unjust enemy, the British Government, and we strongly condemn the sending of a Canadian contingent to the Transvaal to fight against a people with whom we have no quarrel; and, be it further resolved, that a copy of these resolutions be forwarded to President Kruger and the press for publication.[1]

Not everyone agreed. A reporter for the Montreal *Gazette* sought comment from "one of the best known Irish Catholics of the city," who lamented "the stigma which a few idiots in this city have cast upon the Irish race."[2] The AOH was only one among many Irish societies active in any given Canadian city, but at the turn of the century it was the most dynamic and influential of them in the sphere of nationalist agitation. While the organization in Ireland was dismissed by Cardinal Logue as "a simple recrudescence of Ribbonism," in North America the Hibernians were a force to be reckoned with.[3] In 1900 more than fifteen hundred branches and fifty-five military companies across the United States and Canada shared a total membership in good standing of over 110,000 and growing.[4] Founded in 1892, Division No. 1—the "Pioneers" behind the pro-Boer resolution—was the oldest, largest, and most prosperous in

Montreal and, they claimed, in all of Canada.[5] They represented only a segment of Irish Canadian Catholic opinion; but whether they should be written off as "a few idiots" is far from certain. The Irishman interviewed by the *Gazette* suggested that the names of the officers responsible for the resolution should be published. It is perhaps a measure of their influence that he did not wish for his own name to be revealed.[6]

What is certain is that the Montreal AOH did not speak for all of Canada's Hibernians. The organization in New Brunswick moved quickly to "vigorously repudiat[e]" the Montreal resolution. The County Board of Saint John, representing five divisions, organized an emergency meeting to counter the damage it might cause to the "good feeling existing between all classes and creeds" in their province. County President John C. Ferguson rose to defend the loyalty of Irish Catholics. Canada, he insisted, was "the greatest colony of the greatest empire the world has ever yet seen." Irish Catholics had been instrumental in building both, and "if the safety of Her Majesty Queen Victoria required it," they would gladly "fight under the red cross of England."[7] The Moncton Division echoed the sentiments of the Saint John Board.[8] The *Gazette* printed these speeches and counter-resolutions with no small satisfaction, asking why the Montreal Hibernians should insist on making "outlanders" of themselves.[9] Noting the role of the Dublin Fusiliers in the fighting at Talana Hill (Glencoe), the *Gazette* asked sarcastically: "Can it be that they did not hear of that Montreal Hibernian resolution?"[10]

Ferguson of Saint John felt sure that the Montreal resolution could not be representative of Irish Catholic opinion in Quebec, and that it must have slipped through a poorly attended meeting. Yet his critics from outside New Brunswick were just as adamant that his sentiments could not possibly reflect those of the Order in that province. The *Irish World* of New York was predictably outraged by the Saint John protest. The name Ferguson, it observed, "smacks more of Caledonia than Hibernia."[11] The AOH of Jersey City accused Ferguson of being "a traitor to Ireland and an enemy of human liberty" and called on National President John T. Keating to expel him from the organization.[12] Hugh McCaffrey of Toronto, the Provincial Secretary of Ontario's AOH, also weighed in. He told the *Irish World* that Ferguson was no more than a "degenerate" office seeker toadying to his friends in local government. Keating, he urged, should not waste his time ejecting "such trash" from the organization, as it was plain that the Order in Canada did not share his views. "I thank God," McCaffrey added, "that in the Belfast of Canada—Toronto—there is not one Hibernian who is not an open sympathizer with the Boers."[13] But these dismissals of the New Brunswick protest were no more convincing than Ferguson's account of the passage of the Montreal resolution. Ad hominem attacks on the County President failed to explain the fact that a majority of five divisions in Saint John and one in Moncton were clearly opposed to the Canadian AOH expressing pro-Boer sentiments.

Canada's Irish Catholics were, at the turn of the twentieth century, in the middle of a decades-long process of integration in Canadian society. This broad arc of increasing identification with Canada and imperial subjecthood was intermittently disrupted by external stimuli—most spectacularly, the Irish revolutionary decade. The South African War was a miniature instance of this phenomenon. Opposition to the war and sympathy for the Boers generated a short spike in nationalist sentiment more pronounced than that seen in New Zealand, but more divisive than its Australian equivalent. Many Irish Catholics and nationalists were committed to supporting the war effort, both in spirit and through enlistment in Canadian volunteer contingents. Others followed the example of nationalist leaders in Ireland and elsewhere by criticizing jingoism and sympathizing with the Boer underdogs. Regional distinctions are evident in the varying intensity of nationalist responses throughout the Dominion, and the proximity of the United States was a significant factor that marked Canada out from Australasia. In places such as Montreal, where pressure from loyalists and clergy were less keenly felt, the influence of Irish American publications, polemicists, and organizations such as the AOH could embolden local Irish nationalists to express strong opposition to the war. In other places, such as those experiencing (rightly or wrongly) Fenian scares, Irish communities were careful to distance themselves from the extreme Anglophobia of their cousins south of the border and were more ambivalent on the question of the war.

* * *

The *True Witness and Catholic Chronicle* was founded in 1850 to represent the interests of English-speaking Catholics in Montreal. By 1899 it doubled as the official organ of the Hochelaga (Montreal) County Board of the AOH. Under the managing editorship of Cornelius A. McDonell, the *True Witness* showed a marked reluctance to weigh in on the South African War.[14] This stance caused friction between the paper and members of the organization it technically represented. The paper did not print Division 1's pro-Boer resolution. Instead, it referred to it obliquely in an editorial, expressing regret that some "individuals of our race may be carried away by an enthusiastic spirit of nationalism, which finds expression in language calculated to militate against their very best interests." The Irish were, the *True Witness* contended, "the most loyal race in the world."[15] The County Board evidently shared the management's concern over the damage that openly disloyal sentiments could do to the reputation of the Irish Catholic community. They worked together to curtail the freedom of local divisions to publicize their proceedings. In future, all meeting reports and resolutions intended for publication would need to be submitted to, and vetted by, the County Board, who would publish them exclusively in the *True Witness*.[16] Any divisions that sent press material to other papers first would find themselves boycotted by the official organ.[17]

McDonell's *True Witness* took a "both sides" approach to debates over the war—deploring "the volcanic loyalism of some" and the "extreme anti-loyalism of others."[18] The middle path was the way forward for Canada, Ireland, and the Empire: loyalists must support the just demands of the French and Irish minorities, while Irish nationalists must demonstrate "external evidence of all the qualities required in a self-governing people." There was nothing to be gained by "[a]buse, vindictiveness [and] ungoverned animosities."[19] Some subscribers were evidently dissatisfied with this policy of treading softly. Editorials in November and December 1899 complained that the paper had recently come under fire for being "not sufficiently radical, nor sufficiently aggressive." The paper retorted that its mission was to defend and advance "the Irish Catholic element in Canada," not to "wage an eternal warfare" against those who did not see things their way.[20] Instead, the *True Witness* frequently tried to divert the attention of its readers away from the distant war and toward local politics.[21] Montreal's Irish Catholics, McDonell urged, should "exercise their rights to benefit themselves instead of others"—in other words: forget about the Boers.[22]

No other Irish Catholic weekly examined for this study was more cautious in its coverage of the war than the *True Witness*. It is quite possible that in its careful moderation the paper was deliberately compensating for the prevalence of advanced nationalist sentiments within its constituency. Perhaps the most extraordinary example of this was the visit to Montreal, on 15 January 1900, of John Devoy.[23] He came at the invitation of the Hibernian Knights, a military company attached to the local AOH. They were known for their weekly drills to Irish language commands at the landmark Bonsecours Market. Devoy was to be the special guest speaker for their fourth annual concert. The speech he delivered on the night was a detailed and unambiguous disquisition on the doctrine of physical force Irish nationalism during the time of "England's difficulty." In his opening remarks, he assured his audience that he had not come "to twist the lion's tail [. . .] nor have I come to threaten Canada with invasion." Any rumors they had read to that effect should be dismissed, he advised, as "[w]hatever plans the Irish leaders may have you may rest assured they are not going to give warning to the British Government in advance through the newspapers." Indeed, by this point, as Devoy almost certainly knew, the dynamite plots targeting Welland and Esquimalt were already secretly underway.

Devoy expressed his appreciation for the resolutions in support of Home Rule that had been passed by the Canadian Parliament in 1882 and 1886.[24] But Irish Canadians, he warned, should not be misled into believing that England would ever concede anything to Ireland purely on the strength of argument or justice. Pointing to the campaigns of the United Irishmen, Daniel O'Connell, the Fenians, and Parnell, he argued that England "will give Ireland nothing unless the Irish people make it very inconvenient and uncomfortable for them to refuse it." The stronger the British Empire became, however, the more difficult it would be for Irish nationalists to generate sufficient pressure to wrest from Westminster their demands. It was only sensible, therefore, to hope that the Boers would prevail:

England defeated and humiliated, sinking in prestige and influence and in fear of combinations that threaten the existence of her empire, will be in a mood to make concessions to Ireland and it is only a question of judgment for the Irish people to determine whether it would be wiser to accept those

Figure 7.1. John Devoy, 1916, Bain News Service, Library of Congress.

concessions or join the hostile combination and earn a right to a share in
the fruits of victory. Every piece or chunk chopped off the British Empire
lightens the weight which presses down upon Ireland, and gives her new
strength to continue her struggle. These considerations are strong enough to
make Irishmen sympathize with England's enemies and to aid them wherever possible. And in the case of the Dutch Republics of South Africa we
have that and a higher motive as well. The very principle of self-government
is at stake . . .

Devoy went on to describe the injustice of the war in terms that
would by then have been familiar to Irish audiences throughout the
world—blaming "stock-jobbers" and "speculators," vilifying Salisbury
and Chamberlain, and warning of the "fatal precedent" set by the colonial contingents. There was a racial dimension to his criticism of the
uitlander issue, but unusually it was not explicitly directed at provoking
white anxieties—rather at highlighting British hypocrisy. "There is not
a solitary native of India that has a right to vote or a voice in the government of his country," Devoy argued, but Salisbury had wanted to
enfranchise "lascars" in the Transvaal—along with working class white
men who would not even qualify for the vote in England—just to overthrow a republican government. Echoing Goldwin Smith, he warned
that Canadians of all people should be wary of endorsing the *uitlander*
cause as "Canada imposes much heavier taxes on the American miners
in the Klondike."[25] The Dominion would be in trouble, he implied, if
the United States were to imitate Britain's belligerence on behalf of its
own gold-diggers.

There is no indication that Devoy's audience was left shocked by his
undisguised Fenianism. Instead, the concert was followed by a banquet
in Devoy's honor at the Albion Hotel, attended by the leading men of
the city's Irish societies—including the Hibernian Knights, the AOH, the
St. Patrick's Society, the Gaelic Society, and the Young Irishmen's Literary
and Benevolent Society. Even the *True Witness* printed Devoy's speech
in full, though not without offering a half-apology for its contents in
an editorial note. "Irishmen in Canada enjoy the most perfect Home
Rule," it explained, "and are unwilling to take second place to any other
section of the Canadian community in their devotion to the institutions
under which they are privileged to live." Devoy, who knew little of these

Canadian privileges and who had "suffered greatly for the cause of Ireland," should be forgiven for holding "strong opinions."[26] It is safe to assume, however, that it was not with the intention of forgiving him that Montreal's Irish nationalists invited the most famous member of the united Clan na Gael executive to their city at the height of the war.

Devoy was not the only notorious Fenian to be feted in the city during the early months of 1900. Edward O'Brien Kennedy was given the honor of delivering the lecture of the evening at the Montreal AOH St. Patrick's Day concert. Kennedy was better known by his alias: Timothy Featherstone. A member of Jeremiah O'Donovan Rossa's United Irishmen splinter group in the early 1880s, Cork-born Featherstone had been trained in the manufacture of explosives in New York. He was one of a Fenian cell responsible for bombings in Glasgow and London in 1883. In the summer of that year, while recruiting men and establishing a bomb-making "factory" in Cork, Featherstone was duped and betrayed by the informer James "Red Jim" McDermott, on whose information he was intercepted by detectives while in possession of dynamite. His party was found guilty of treason felony and sentenced to life in prison.[27] He was among over twenty dynamiters to serve time in the infamous Chatham prison, where their widely reported mistreatment resulted in three deaths and four cases of insanity.[28] Featherstone was, alongside Tom Clarke, among the last of the dynamiters to be released in 1898.[29]

His lecture to the Montreal Hibernians was titled "Sixteen Years in English Prisons" and appears largely to have dealt with the sufferings of the incarcerated dynamiters.[30] Featherstone was not a speaker of Devoy's caliber; he opened his lecture with an apology, claiming that "the conditions in a British prison all combine to destroy the power of public speech." Only brief summaries of his speech were reported. The *Gazette* disparaged the lecture, claiming that nobody at the back of the hall could hear it, and those at the front who could were distinctly "uncomfortable." Featherstone, it reported, "did not certainly represent the feelings of the audience, who did not applaud but once, when Home Rule was spoken of."[31] The summary of the speech given in the *True Witness* noted that Featherstone spoke of his dynamiting career and the "active part he played in the struggle," but it did not report a lack of enthusiasm from the audience. There was a lower than expected attendance, but this was owing to the confusion caused by the destruction of the concert's original venue in a fire some weeks previously.[32] It is easy to imagine Featherstone as an uninspiring speaker—Michael Davitt once described him as "not strong intellectually."[33] Whether the *Gazette*'s report of the audience's distaste for his politics should be trusted is less clear—especially considering the warm reception given to John Devoy. Either way, the decision to mark St. Patrick's Day with a speech from a convicted dynamiter reveals the lingering Fenian sympathies among a section of Montreal's Irish nationalists.

Advanced nationalism historically held a more consistent appeal to Irish Catholics in the province of Quebec than elsewhere in Canada. It has been suggested that their "double minority" status—as a religious minority among the province's English speakers and a linguistic minority among its overwhelmingly French Catholic population—had a ghettoizing effect that produced an "ultra-Irish" identity especially prevalent in the working-class neighborhoods of Montreal and Quebec City.[34] It seems equally likely that the French majority within Quebec acted as a buffer between the province's Irish nationalists and the loyalist Anglo majority within Canada. Take, for example, the residents of Irishtown Road in the remote village of Percé at the tip of the Gaspé peninsula. In his memoir, the prominent Irish Catholic Conservative journalist and senator Grattan O'Leary recalled the nationalist feeling that permeated the area during his childhood at the turn of the twentieth century.

> My father talked of Parnell and Gladstone more than he did of Macdonald or Laurier; and of the wrongs and sorrows of Ireland, Dublin with its "memoried sorrow and old renown" more after his heart than Ottawa, Quebec, or Montreal.

The community of self-described Irish "exiles" learned of events beyond the Gaspé through the *Irish World* and the Fenian-run *Gaelic American* of New York, as well as the liberal *Montreal Star*. During the South African War "[t]he Irish of Gaspé," O'Leary remembered, "lined up solidly with the gallant people who dared to stand up to the Empire's might":

> Brave General De Wet,
> Sure you lick all creation;

To the redcoats you're causing
The utmost vexation
And bringing such shame
On the great British nation!
More power to your elbow
Brave General De Wet!

Thus, the gossoons of the Irish settlement chanting the rhymes that showed there was never a friend of the redcoats along the Irishtown Road.[35]

During the first year of the South African War, concerns over the loyalty of French Canadians loomed much larger in mainstream political debate than the concerns about the comparatively small numbers of Irish Catholics actively expressing pro-Boer sympathies. The highest-profile critics of the war in Canada were prominent French Canadian Liberal MPs. In a gesture similar to that of Michael Davitt, the nationalist intellectual Henri Bourassa resigned his seat in protest in October 1899. Israel Tarte, Minister for Public Works in Laurier's cabinet, also criticized the Prime Minister's decision to embroil Canada in the conflict. For this perceived treachery to the empire, Tarte was burned in effigy by soldiers at Toronto's old fort, and by students of Queen's College at Kingston.[36] When news of the relief of Ladysmith caused the student body of Montreal's Anglo-loyalist McGill University to take to the streets in a fit of patriotism on 1 March 1900, they did not parade their loyalism before the city's Irish Catholics. Instead, they attacked the offices of several French Canadian newspapers before marching on l'Université Laval de Montréal. When the French students fought back, three days of rioting ensued until the militia were deployed to suppress the disturbances.[37] It was unusual in Britain's white settler colonies for Irish Catholics to find themselves on the margins of tensions surrounding ethnicity, nationality, and loyalty. In Quebec, the larger question of French Canadians' position within the Dominion of Canada occupied the spotlight, leaving Irish nationalists with somewhat more freedom to cultivate and express advanced views than was the case in other places.

Still, Irish nationalists in Quebec were not entirely isolated from the loyalist scrutiny prevalent throughout the rest of Canada. In fall 1900,

Canadian customs intercepted and destroyed a parcel of literature mailed to the Montreal AOH from a division in New Haven, Connecticut, because it allegedly contained pro-Boer and disloyal materials.[38] A national initiative to commemorate the Canadian militia veterans of the Fenian Raids with medals was also celebrated in Montreal—an event which a local correspondent to the *Irish World* felt was calculated to insult Irish nationalists, even if amounted to little more than "doddering specimens of a foretime warriordom bracing themselves up to look martial."[39] Some of the "jingoistic intolerance" which in Australasia had resulted in the targeting of individuals suspected of disloyalty was also in evidence in Montreal—an American pastor was in June 1900 ousted by the members of the Zion Congregational Church for refusing to pray for the Queen or give thanks for British victories against the Boers.[40]

Since at least 1848, Irish observers in the United States had tended to exaggerate the tension between French Canadian nationalism and Canadian imperialism. Irish Canadians, who were far better informed, typically met this American commentary with exasperation. When a Buffalo *Times* article claimed that the riots in Montreal were evidence that French Canadian "restiveness" may soon "culminate in rebellion," the *Catholic Register* and the *True Witness* were quick to dismiss this speculation as nonsense.[41] Americans, complained the *True Witness*, "certainly hazard most extraordinary and purely imaginary opinions concerning passing events on this side of the line."[42] Yet ironically, in 1900 as in previous decades, the speculation was partly fueled by disinformation originating from advanced Irish nationalist sources within Canada. The *Irish World*'s regular Montreal correspondent, "MONRO-VIA," appears to have played a significant part in framing the riots as the latest sign of the long-anticipated collapse of British authority in Quebec. "The confederation of the Canadian provinces is hanging in a balance," he wrote on 4 March in the immediate aftermath of the riots:

> It is an open boast of the French Canadians that Quebec will secede, become an independent state, or throw in its fortunes with the Southern Republic. What are the Irish societies of the States doing? Will they assist in accomplishing the ruin of England's power in America? Will they let their greatest chance slip by for striking its deadliest blow at this hereditary enemy of their race?[43]

MONROVIA'S appeal echoed Irish Montrealer Bernard Devlin's 1848 call for the revolutionary New York Irish Republican Union to "pay us a visit." Devlin had claimed that both Irish and French in Canada East were ready to throw off the British yoke, and that "if 10,000 men invaded Canada, they would walk through it in a week."[44] In both cases the estimation of French Canadian disaffection was very wide of the mark. In the early months of the war the liberal and nationalist press in Quebec had indeed been openly critical of the conflict and of Laurier's executive decision to dispatch a Canadian contingent without first seeking parliamentary approval. By the close of 1899, however, the province's Catholic hierarchy had come out explicitly in support of the war effort, and in the following months most of the leading French newspapers of Quebec fell in with the Liberal party line—as did Israel Tarte. There remained some, notably Bourassa and his supporters, who held out strongly against the war in principle, but the issue was far from the focal point for French Canadian grievances, and secessionism was seldom discussed. As the *Catholic Register* explained in a sententious rebuttal of the American reports: French Canadians may not have been "enthusiastic supporters" of the war, but they were "staunch Catholics, and as such know their duty as citizens."[45]

Contrary to nationalist fantasies of another Fenian invasion, it was Irish Canadian paramilitaries who, in reality, ended up marching on American soil during the South African War. The funds raised by the Montreal concerts at which Devoy and Featherstone spoke helped to defray the cost of sending the Hibernian Knights to Boston, where the biennial "national" convention of the AOH was held in May 1900. Traveling with Emmanuel Berchmans Devlin—brother of Charles Ramsay Devlin and nephew of Bernard Devlin—the Hibernian Knights were hosted by the local Clan na Gael.[46] In fact, practically the entire executive of the united Clan na Gael attended the AOH convention.[47] In his keynote address John T. Keating railed against any future American alliance with "the blood-clotted cesspool of British imperialism," the "despoiler of weaker nations." Once the AOH had won the sympathy of the American people for Irish freedom, it was "but a question of time until their active help will follow," and "the aid given to Cuba is extended to Erin."[48] Keating was reelected National President by acclamation. The Hibernian Knights were not the only Canadians present to soak up this anti-British invective. At least sixteen other delegates representing Ontario, Quebec, and New Brunswick were there to mingle with Fenian luminaries such as John Devoy, William Crossin, and Jeremiah O'Donovan Rossa.[49] Among them was Hugh McCaffrey of Toronto—considered a strong candidate for one of four National Directors had he not withdrawn from the race.[50] Another was Jeremiah Gallagher of Quebec City, a civil engineer with decades-long Fenian connections, then spearheading a drive to erect a memorial to the victims of "ship fever" at the infamous immigrant quarantine station on Grosse Ile.[51] But the Hibernian Knights were by far the standout Canadian contribution to the event. They competed against other military companies (some of whom flew the Transvaal flag) in the convention's parade drill. Their striking green uniforms, Irish language commands and their *pièce de résistance*—marching in the shape of a cross—delighted spectators and earned them the top prize.[52]

It is difficult to say with certainty just how far the Canadian Hibernians shared their American brothers' pro-Boer and anti-imperial views, or how representative they were of Irish Canadian nationalist opinion. Neither John C. Ferguson of Saint John nor any of the other divisional leaders named as having spoken out against the Montreal pro-Boer resolution attended the convention—but other New Brunswick delegates did. Perhaps these were dissenters; or perhaps attendance at the convention did not equal endorsement of the views expressed there. In fact the Saint John Hibernians had already declared themselves "unalterably opposed to the stand taken by their American brethren on the Anglo-Boer war" when, in mid-January, the national organization had announced plans to raise funds to assist the Boers.[53] The only other division to come out against the plan was one in Springfield, Missouri, where reservations were expressed over the potential violation of American neutrality laws.[54] As Patrick Mannion has argued, the AOH was "an essential mechanism for the cross-border transfer of Irish culture and identity from the United States into Canada."[55] With the American organization bossed by the Clan na Gael, radical nationalism and anti-imperialist ideas came as part of the package. But this transfer was not frictionless and could at times be met with outright rejection—most spectacularly during the Great War when the Canadians threatened to secede over American support for Germany. For Irish Canadians, decades of experience in cross-border Irish nationalist activism meant they were well accustomed to taking, leaving, or moderating as needed the generally more extreme views of their Irish American neighbors.

In Canada as in Australasia, the Irish nationalist tendency to sympathize with the Boers was mitigated by local factors. Some rejected pro-Boerism out of a genuinely felt loyalty to the empire, some out of pressure from clergy and elites to perform loyalty, and some out of reluctance to invite scrutiny and opprobrium from their loyalist neighbors. There was, as Mark McGowan has shown, a general and growing desire amongst Irish Catholics to identify as Canadians.[56] In New Brunswick these forces combined were strong enough to eclipse pro-Boer feeling within the AOH. In Quebec, where loyalist pressure was not as keenly felt, respectable community leaders struggled with limited success to contain the Fenian sympathies of the nationalist rank and file. In Ontario, pro-Boerism found occasional expression in Toronto and Ottawa, urban areas possessing a critical mass of Irish Catholics, but nationalist commentary on the war was more commonly exhibited as vigorous criticism of jingoism couched in protestations of Irish loyalty.

* * *

In March 1900, dissension surfaced at the Toronto AOH St. Patrick's Day Concert at Massey Hall. The honor of chairing the proceedings had been given to veteran newspaperman Patrick Boyle. Born in County Mayo in 1832, Boyle was best known as the editor of Toronto's *Irish Canadian*, founded in 1863, which for years represented the Fenian interest in Ontario. The paper survived for three decades but its diminishing fortunes and increasingly moderate outlook reflected the dwindling of its base. By 1893 it had merged with the *Catholic Weekly Review* to form the clerically managed *Catholic Register*.[57]

In his speech to the audience at Massey Hall, Boyle welcomed the spectacle of the Irish flag flying that day for the first time over the Ontario legislature and Toronto city hall. The Queen's endorsement of the wearing of the shamrock by Irish soldiers seemed, he remarked, to have made it more popular than ever among civilians from all backgrounds. He regretted, however, that the shamrock concession sullied the national symbol by associating it with Irish soldiers fighting against the Boers. "[T]here were thousands" he said, "who would wear the shamrock with a very different purpose than that of doing honor to hirelings for slitting the throats of men fighting for their independence."[58] Boyle's remarks appear to have split both the crowd and the platform. The Rev. Dr. Burns rose and pointedly "deprecated the use of the term hireling." Charles McCabe hoped the contribution of Irish soldiers in South Africa would bring forward the cause of Home Rule and make Irishmen and their neighbors "brothers within the empire."[59] The sparring comments reportedly solicited "cheers and counter-cheers" from the audience.[60] Boyle's pro-Boer remarks were notably cleansed from the *Catholic Register*'s account of the concert, but were produced elsewhere in the press. In response to criticism, the AOH concert committee released a statement strongly endorsing Boyle's speech. Boyle "not alone voiced the sentiments of the great majority of the large audience present," the statement insisted, "but the sentiments of the Irish people at large."[61] Yet the mixed response on the night made it clear that Toronto's Hibernians were not as unanimous in their sympathy for the Boers as Hugh McCaffrey had claimed in his October letter to the *Irish World*. Ottawa was similarly divided; there, Laurier's Secretary of State, the Canadian-born Irish Catholic Sir Richard Scott, failed in his attempt to pass a pro-Boer resolution through the city's Irish Literary Society.[62]

The underwhelming return of Patrick Boyle's *Irish Canadian*, which he revived in June 1900, also suggests that his opinions were not so widely reciprocated. However, Boyle died in August 1901 and many issues of the new run have not survived; what impact it had, or may have had, is therefore difficult to assess. We do know that the moderate *Register* welcomed its return, and surviving issues point to a tone that was far from the uncompromising *Irish Canadian* of old. Instead, like McDonell at the *True Witness*, Boyle was forced to answer criticism from some subscribers who felt his revived weekly was too timid.[63] These men probably turned instead, like Grattan O'Leary's community in the Gaspésie or "J. O'C." of North Gisborne in New Zealand, to papers like the *Irish World* to represent their opinions. Joseph Rutledge, secretary of Division No. 1 of the Toronto AOH, is a good example. In April 1900 he sent Patrick Ford a contribution of $9.25 to the United Irish League fund with a letter expressing hope that the League would help Ireland "to break asunder from the ties of English tyranny and

rule." Like many other contributors to the UIL fund, he took the opportunity to vent his views on the war in South Africa:

> [M]ay we not forget to pray that Divine Providence will strengthen the arms
> of the brave Boers, now fighting a trouble equal to ours, and may success
> crown their efforts, never to have the flag of that abominable old Empire
> which is noted for its plunder and robbery of weak nations to fly over South
> Africa.[64]

The reluctance of Canadian Catholic papers to print what the *True
Witness* called "red hot letters" like the above is understandable when
we consider that even the suspicion of disloyalty could result in harassment, particularly in provinces with large Anglo-Protestant majorities.[65]
Swedish and Belgian residents of Victoria, British Columbia, were reportedly harassed and boycotted for their pro-Boer sympathies.[66] Captain Victor Jacobsen sued the local *Colonist*, alleging the newspaper's
hostile reporting about his opinion on the war had inspired loyalist
vandals to bore and scuttle his sloop.[67] Harry Helmcken, MPP for Victoria, asked the Attorney General of the province to launch a criminal investigation into reports that patrons of one of the city's saloons
had torn down and trampled upon a picture of the Queen.[68] Popular
paranoia could be heightened in regions subject to Fenian threats—as
southwest British Columbia was in 1900. The *Seattle Times* mockingly
reported on a scare in New Westminster in June, when a package discovered on the street was briefly suspected to be a Fenian bomb—until
police found its contents to be mainly sugar and soap. The *Vancouver
Daily World* snapped back, contending that "[t]he most timid girl in
Canada has nothing but contempt for your Fenian bogie," and pointing
to the swift justice doled out to the Welland Canal dynamiters as proof
that Canadians were unphased by their neighbors' "Fenian friends of
explosive propensities."[69]

There was truth to the *Daily World's* contention. But the response
to some events in Ontario, another province threatened by Fenian dynamiters, suggests that there still existed a certain tendency to see, as
the *Seattle Times* joked, "ogre-eyed Fenians in the bushes."[70] We have
already seen how the Canadian authorities took seriously the potential
nuisance that Fenian activity on the border could cause, particularly in

the aftermath of the Welland Canal bombing. There is some evidence to suggest the public mind was rattled by the revival of Fenian danger. When a catastrophic fire destroyed swaths of Ottawa and the adjacent city of Hull on 26 April 1900, just three days after the Welland Canal bombing, rumors spread that the disaster was the work of Fenian arsonists.[71] Fenians or Boer sympathizers had already been suspected of an arson attack on Toronto's Stanley Barracks in October 1899.[72] Amid reports of a planned Fenian invasion, in late December 1899 the Ottawa AOH was forced to publicly deny rumors that it had voted unanimously in support of a raid by Irish Americans.[73] In most places the talk of an invasion subsided quickly after the first week of January 1900, but it lingered in the columns of Ontario newspapers until March. In mid-January the Toronto *Globe* carried a letter of warning from two Canadian women living in San Francisco about the intensity of Fenian and pro-Boer feeling there: "'Canadians laugh at the idea of a Fenian invasion,' we read. It is nothing to laugh at."[74] The *Globe* was evidently not persuaded. "Out of deference to the ladies," it commented, "we shall try not to laugh."[75]

A month later the *Globe* changed its tune when it claimed to have received reports that the "commanding officers of the Toronto garrison" were taking seriously the possibility of a Fenian raid and were planning war games on the American border. "Curiously enough," the article in question observed, "the troops of the Toronto military district and other sections of Canada will assemble on the frontier for ostensible tactical operations just about the time when the Fenians, according to the report, would be making their attempt to cross."[76] Even when a Colonel told a reporter that "[t]here is nothing in it" and that the games were to be standard exercises against a purely "imaginary" enemy, the *Globe* remained adamant in its reporting that consideration of the Fenian threat did feature in the orders given to officers.[77]

The Toronto *Catholic Register* did not hide its exasperation at such stories. Managed by Father John R. Teefy, Superior of St. Michael's College, and edited by the Irish-born Patrick Francis Cronin, the *Register* offered its modest readership of Irish Catholics in southern Ontario a similar mix of integrationism and moderate nationalism as publications like the Sydney *Freeman's Journal* and the *New Zealand Tablet*. Cronin criticized the *Globe* for printing "foolish drivel" and "mischievous trash" designed, it claimed, to excite ethnic tensions and militarist feeling.[78] "The Fenian scare," he charged, "is the pet scare of [. . .] Ontario."[79] Fenianism in Canada, he claimed, existed largely in the imaginations of loyalists, while Fenianism in America was misguided and unrepresentative of true Irish opinion. Both the *Register* and *True Witness* heaped praise on a speech to this effect delivered at a UIL meeting in Ireland by Edward Blake, former Premier of Ontario and leader of the federal Liberal Party, now turned Irish Party MP. Blake noted reports that "some Irish Americans propose to accomplish Home Rule for Ireland by invading Canada." Given the Canadian parliament's repeated expressions of support for Irish Home Rule, Blake joked that threatening the country "with war and devastation" seemed "rather an odd way of stimulating the sympathy of Canadians." He dismissed the threats as bluster, and announced that if he had any reason to believe them, he would arm himself with a Mauser and return to Toronto to defend his home.[80]

Words such as these from the respectable Blake were useful to the *Register* in its constant rearguard against the tendency to brand Irish deviation from the imperialist mainstream as Fenian treachery. The Toronto *Sentinel and Orange and Protestant Advocate*, the organ of Canada's powerful Loyal Orange Association, was naturally the most enthusiastic propagator of this perspective. The *Sentinel* routinely muddied distinctions between constitutional and physical force Irish nationalism. The "idiotic ravings" of the "Clan na Gaels" and the "Home Rule traitors" all sounded like the same disloyal "childish petulance" to the *Sentinel*.[81] The paper was quick to label echoes of Irish nationalist sympathy for the Boers in Canadian Catholic newspapers as "treason"—challenging, for example, the "Romish hierarchy" to condemn the Kingston *Canadian Freeman* for criticizing the war.[82] Canadian Catholic papers generally knew better than to lend the *Sentinel* attention in their columns but when these sentiments seeped into the dailies, Catholic editors were quick to quash them. When in February 1900 "the Flaneur," a columnist for the Toronto *Mail & Empire*, called Gladstone's conversion to Home Rule a "capitulation to Fenianism," Cronin's *Register* called him an "unmitigated bigot" and pointed to the "practical loyalty" demonstrated by the presence of thousands of Irish soldiers in South Africa.[83] He asked sharply: were they Fenians too?

Distancing Irish Canadian Catholics from Fenianism and highlighting the Irish contribution to the imperial war effort did not, however,
mean that Cronin advocated unconditional support for the empire.
When in November 1899 Charles Fitzpatrick, Irish-descended Liberal
MP for Quebec and Solicitor-General of Canada, gave a speech in Toronto urging Canadian Catholics to commit themselves fully to the
empire in its struggle with the "intolerant and robber-like" Boers, the
Register was irate. Cronin charged him with trying to "make jingoes
out of Catholics." He rebuked Fitzpatrick's argument that the Boers
deserved conquest for having persecuted Catholics and *uitlanders* by
pointing to the Manitoba schools question and coercion in Ireland.
Fitzpatrick claimed there was a moral duty to "protect" native Africans
from the Boers; Cronin asked whether arming and sending them to the
front showed British rule to be any more benign. Even if all Britain's
accusations about Boer intolerance were true, Cronin argued, "bigotry
only could conceive the horrible idea of redressing them with lyddite
shells."[84]

Nevertheless, Fitzpatrick's position on the duty of loyalty to the
empire was popular with many Irish Canadian Catholics. This deeply
irked those who shared the Boer sympathies of the nationalist leaders
at home. A correspondent calling himself "Clan-na-Gael" of Tillson-
burg, Ontario, in a letter to the *Register*, warned his countrymen against
trusting career politicians like Fitzpatrick. "[A] new species of Irishism
[has] lately arisen in Canada" he complained, the "aim" of which was
"to address the galleries—the *Globe* and *Mail and Empire* readers as a
means to an end." These "Irish orators" won't praise "the brave men
of 1798," but "Lord Roberts and Kitchener will be meanly claimed as
Irishmen when there is as much Irishism in both as in my boots."[85]
During the war, Cronin identified more closely with prominent figures
in the Irish Party than with the leading Irish Catholic politicians of
Canada. Of Michael Davitt and William O'Brien—two high-profile
Boer sympathizers—Cronin wrote "there are probably no Irishmen
living for whose opinions the Irish people at home and abroad have
greater respect or in whom they place more implicit confidence."[86] Edward Blake, in the same speech that Cronin praised for the willingness to shoot invading Fenians with a Mauser, explained that even if
the present exponents of physical force were foolish, the principle was

Figure 7.2. Charles Fitzpatrick, ca. 1890–1902, Montminy & Cie, Quebec, P551, Archives of the Law Society of Ontario.

nevertheless sound. Ireland, he claimed, "has never lost the supreme right of resistance to its conquerors and of rising for its freedom"— provided that constitutional efforts were first "exhausted" and there was some hope of success. Irish nationalists also retained the "right," Blake asserted, "freely to express their views in opposition to the present unjust, unnecessary, calamitous and most ill-advised war."[87] Indeed, Cronin showed little hesitation in exercising this right.

From the beginning of the war the *Register* strongly opposed Canadian participation "in the extirpation of the Dutch settlers of South Africa," and complained of the "nauseating silliness" of the "spree of Canadian jingoism" that the war had sparked.[88] Cronin praised Henri Bourassa as the "one honest independent in Canadian politics," reprinted stories about the defiant nationalist gestures of Irish troops shipping off to South Africa, and even reproduced Sannie Kruger's article on Boer women from *Harper's Bazaar*.[89] Pro-Boer op-eds by W. T. Stead and Montagu White were given space in the paper's columns.[90] The specter of a possible British defeat raised by December's reverses did little to alter the *Register*'s position. In the middle of "Black Week," Cronin described the conflict as "the most deplorable event since the fruitless and equally unnecessary war that deluged the Crimea with blood."[91] Cronin felt that open pro-Boerism was ill-advised in Canada, but explained that Irish nationalists could hardly be expected to rally behind the empire simply because of a few Boer victories—that would require "superhuman generosity."[92] If the *uitlander* grievances were sufficient to merit a war, he argued, then those of Irish Catholics certainly gave them a "*casus belli*" of their own.[93] In February he explained that "Greater Ireland" naturally sympathized with the Boers for several reasons. First was an "honest conviction," based on decades of "sad experience," that Britain's motivation for war was unjust. Next was a sympathy for the Boers' "heroic struggle for independence" against a powerful empire. Finally, there existed "the ingrained idea—whether mistaken or well-founded—that 'England's need is Ireland's opportunity.'" In Cronin's eyes, only Home Rule could have secured for Britain the goodwill of Greater Ireland, but in failing to grant it her government had deprived the empire of the united front it now desperately sought.[94] "[T]here cannot be a United Empire with Ireland still discontented," he explained in a St. Patrick's Day editorial.[95]

As with moderate nationalists in Australasia, the *Register*'s criticism of the war did not amount to anti-imperialism. Rather, it represented a combination of the desire for Irish autonomy within the empire, and distaste for an unnecessary war of aggression against "a nation of farmers."[96] Unlike advanced nationalists who hoped for a British defeat, the *Register* and other Catholic newspapers in the Dominions balanced their objection to the war in principle with the hope that an imperial victory would come quickly and with minimal bloodshed—especially when the "Toronto lads" arrived at the front.[97] For Cronin there was no contradiction in venting a sustained attack on jingoism and militarism while printing glowing reports of the bravery of Irish and Canadian troops on the veldt. Even the Irish brigade on the Boer side received an occasional sympathetic mention in the *Register*'s columns.[98] For Cronin, both proved the nationalist case. Home Rule would be a fitting reward for the sacrifices made by Irish soldiers fighting for the empire, while "Greater Ireland's" Boer sympathies showed the urgent necessity of solving Irish disaffection by meeting nationalist demands. Other Canadian Irish nationalists echoed the idea that Irish loyalty existed on a quid pro quo basis. Charles Murphy of Ottawa, an attorney and future Liberal cabinet minister, told the *Ottawa Journal* that "[d]espite all their sacrifices for England, the Irish are not admitted to equal partnership in the affairs of the Empire."[99] D'Arcy Scott asked attendees at the Ottawa St. Patrick's Day celebration whether there was "not to be some recompense for the Irish blood that stains the sands of Africa?"[100] In the principal oration at the Toronto Irish Catholic Benevolent Union's St. Patrick's Day event, Ontario's Minister for Public Works, Frank R. Latchford, pointed out that Ireland "gives her best blood and bravest hearts for the cause of her ancient enemy, fighting in Africa for liberties which she has always refused and still refuses to grant to Irishmen in their own land."[101] What Cronin called Irish Catholics' duty of loyalty to "constituted authority" did not necessarily translate into unconditional loyalty to England or the empire. "The Green Isle is not loyal," he wrote in August, "but it is England and the English policy that has made her what it is."[102]

* * *

If these considerations made a coherent case for Irish nationalists in Ontario to criticize the war, it was less clear how their faith should inform their opinion. It is possible that the strident imperialism of Cornelius O'Brien, Archbishop of Halifax, had some influence on the pro-war position of the New Brunswick AOH and the Saint John *Freeman*.[103] In Quebec, the French Canadian Catholic hierarchy's decision to rally behind the war from December 1899 appears to have had more of an influence on the French population than the Irish minority—although it may have reinforced the cautious approach of the *True Witness*, which made a weekly point of advertising its episcopal approval.[104] Elsewhere in Canada, as Mark McGowan has shown, clear episcopal guidance on the question of the war was lacking—although the influence of clerical nationalism militated, as in Australasia, against the spread of more radical pro-Boer views.[105] The absence of an outspoken figure of equivalent stature to Australasia's Cardinal Moran meant that in parts of English-speaking Canada, Catholic newspapers were left to make their own cases for the appropriate Catholic response to the conflict. The *Register*, despite its supposed commitment to "constituted authority," appears to have been as willing to reject jingoism from church leaders as from politicians. Herbert Vaughan, Cardinal Archbishop of Westminster, campaigned more vigorously in favor of the war than perhaps any other primate. For Cronin, it was all very well for Vaughan, as an Englishman, to support his government—but "he has no right to saddle the Church with responsibility for his opinions."[106]

The critical question was the treatment of Catholics in the Transvaal. But the constant stream of conflicting reports meant that no real consensus emerged in the first year of the war. Those who supported the war and those who opposed it each found various correspondents who claimed to have witnessed Catholics on the receiving end of persecution or generosity. Correspondence between John Redmond and the Boer envoy in Europe, Willem Johannes Leyds, was widely cited in the newspaper press to prove either case. Leyds explained that there had historically been restrictions on Catholics' right to vote or hold office in the Transvaal, but that these had been repealed by 1896.[107] The *Register* was insistent that Catholics need not be concerned for the faith in South Africa, and to be wary of misleading reports emanating from the jingo press:

> This paper has repeatedly placed on record, as against the libels of the jingoes, the unvaryingly kind treatment which Catholics in the Transvaal have received from the Boers.[108]

The Winnipeg *Northwest Review*, another anti-war Catholic newspaper, was similarly confident that religious restrictions in the

Transvaal, if they existed at all, were a "dead letter."[109] In November it carried an article from the *South African Catholic* magazine by Rev. Dr. F. C. Kolbe complaining that claims of Boer mistreatment of Catholics had been grossly exaggerated, and that Catholics in South Africa never asked for a war on their behalf.[110] The paper carried other pieces on how the Oblate Fathers had helped to soften anti-Catholic prejudice in South Africa and now commanded the respect and admiration of the Boers.[111] It echoed the *Register*'s distaste for the pro-war remarks of Charles Fitzpatrick and Cardinal Vaughan.[112] The *Review* scoffed when the *Tablet* of London (England), which it regarded as Vaughan's mouthpiece, claimed to have proof that Leyds was lying about the employment of Catholics in the Transvaal government. The *Tablet* in turn accused the *Northwest Review* of being partly responsible for the defeat of the Liberals in the Manitoba election because it was too busy "championing the Transvaal" to properly organize "the Catholic vote."[113]

The *Catholic Record* of London, Ontario, was also deeply skeptical of reports of anti-Catholicism in the Boer republics during the opening months of the war. Edited jointly by Father George R. Northgraves and Thomas Coffey, the *Record* was not as bullish as Cronin's *Register* on the war and the Irish question and was not inclined to pick fights with other Catholic journals like the *Northwest Review* was, but weighed in on sensitive issues more readily than the *True Witness*. Its outlook was closer to Cleary's *New Zealand Tablet* than to its Canadian competitors. On the war, the *Record*'s tune was mournful: "Blood has been spent needlessly; wives and mothers mourn the loss of dear ones, and brave men have taken their last look at the sun, to make a holiday for Chamberlain."[114] The exploits of the Canadian contingent's Catholic chaplain were cheered in the columns, and the shamrock concession was appreciated—though not without a jibe at a government that praised Ireland's "brave guardians of the empire" yet "frustrate[d] every effort for legislative independence."[115] The *Record* similarly welcomed the Queen's visit, but complained of the resulting deluge of asinine "taffy" puff-pieces intended to flatter Irish readers, and reminded its own that "bones are rotting in the Transvaal."[116] Northgraves and Coffey initially treated allegations of Boer religious intolerance as the product of the same jingoistic "yellow journalism" that habitually denigrated Irish and French Canadian loyalty. Without endorsing pro-Boerism, the *Record*'s editorials admitted the Boers were "brave and not inhumane people" who were "entitled to the privileges of truth and charity."[117]

Yet when evidence of persisting religious restrictions in the Transvaal appeared in the Canadian dailies, seemingly contradicting the assurances of Leyds, Irish Catholic papers awkwardly adjusted their positions. The *Record*, once satisfied of the facts, reprimanded pro-Boer wishful thinking and pared back its defense of the Boer character.[118] The *Register* sheepishly dropped the subject, claiming it was too ambiguous to settle. "The truth probably lies somewhere midway between the two extremes," Cronin shrugged. It would likely show the Boers "to be a very ordinary people—not much worse than the general ruck."[119] This was not the only issue on which the *Register* assumed an attitude of denial when its position was threatened. Cronin repeatedly downplayed the significance of Queen Victoria's visit to Ireland, insisting that the interest it excited in the colonies was not reciprocated by "the overwhelming majority" of Irish people.[120] He dismissed the celebrations as being "almost entirely due to the efforts of the loyalists as distinguished from the true and solid body of the people," and even reprinted Maud Gonne's searing "Famine Queen" article.[121] He was careful, however, not to appear to be repeating the charge that Victoria was acting as a "recruiting sergeant," stating instead that "we believe that the purpose emanated from Her Majesty's own goodness and womanliness of heart [. . .] until the contrary is demonstrated."[122] The *Register* was similarly in denial about the Welland Canal bombing. Cronin, clearly worried about the danger of backlash against his Irish Catholic constituency, shot back angrily at suggestions from police and press that it was a Fenian undertaking.

> [W]e condemn and strongly protest against the reckless way in which the good name of the Irish people and good citizenship are besmirched upon every and the slightest provocation by many of our Canadian journals.[123]

The *Register* rather desperately held to the unlikely explanation that Dallman, Nolan, and Walsh were acting on behalf of the grain handlers of Buffalo.[124]

* * *

By 31 May 1900 the *Register* decided that the South African War had reached "the beginning of the end." Irish nationalist interest in the war sharply declined everywhere from the summer of 1900. In the United States, the intensity of pro-Boer sentiment and the anti-imperial awakening of advanced Irish nationalists, combined with the visit of the Boer envoys, meant that a certain level of interest lingered. In Australasia, the controversy generated by the stories of James Grattan Grey and Arthur Lynch, and the anti-war activism of groups like the Peace and Humanity Society, kept the war relevant to nationalist interests longer. In Canada, where anti-war sentiment was never especially strong, the process of disengagement happened sooner. From June onwards the crisis precipitated by the Boxer rebellion in China eclipsed the South African War as the most pressing foreign news item. Montreal's Irish societies stopped inviting Fenian speakers to their concerts almost as suddenly as they had started. Irish nationalist energies in Canada gradually became absorbed by the reunification of the Irish Parliamentary Party and the global spread of the United Irish League. But in promoting this new agitation, Cronin seems to have sensed a wariness among the Irish nationalists in Canada, borne of a decade of inactivity, the painful divisions over the South African War, and the reputational damage done by the return of the Fenian specter. He attempted to assuage it.

> There is, just at the present time, an inclination on the part of Irishmen in Canada to yield to the stress of the moment, and not to extend to Mr. Redmond and his colleagues that moral and other support which they formerly gave to the leaders in the National movement. [. . . Our] struggle is legitimate and carried along legitimate and constitutional lines, and therefore the Irish Nationalists, fighting for the rights of their people, should not be read out of the pale of citizenship and even true loyalty to the Empire. We in Canada have had our troubles, but so long as a burning question is fought out on strictly constitutional lines there was no cry of disloyalty, treason and kindred characterizations. [. . .] If these rights of citizenship cannot be respected, and that without insult, then the British constitution had better be flung to the winds [. . . I]t is this same rank, domineering spirit, the

denial of the right of British subjects to seek redress of grievances, that has irritated the Catholic minority in Manitoba. In this respect Canada is far more intolerant than is the mother country.[125]

There is much in this passage that is revealing about the position of Irish nationalists in Canada at the turn of the twentieth century. The value they placed on meeting the perceived obligations of Canadian citizenship and loyalty had them hesitant about supporting a revived campaign for Home Rule and land reform. There was a deep sensitivity to accusations of disloyalty, and a feeling that the loyalist culture of Canada afforded little room for dissent. Yet there was also a conviction that the nationalist position was legitimate, and a determination that Canada ought to accommodate the national and religious interests of Irish Catholics. All this helps to explain the mixed response of Irish nationalists in Canada to the South African War, and why they turned to the reunited constitutional movement with some relief once it had proven itself to be a popular and respectable force.[126]

The visit of John Redmond to Montreal and Ottawa in November 1901 was a significant step in this direction. At lectures in both cities organized by local Irish societies, Redmond made the case for responsible government in Ireland along Canadian lines.[127] In Ottawa, Wilfrid Laurier and two members of Governor General Minto's staff attended a luncheon for Redmond—a gesture which irked Chamberlain for the legitimizing effect it had on the constitutional nationalist movement in Canadian eyes.[128] The visit was carefully managed by local Irish leaders such as D'Arcy Scott. He wrote to William Bourke Cockran of New York the week before Redmond's arrival:

> At first some of our people were a little nervous that Mr. Redmond would say something about the South African War that might not be well received here, but I have assured them that Mr. Redmond is too skilful a politician to say anything that would embarrass us.[129]

Redmond's successful visit was the catalyst for the establishment of UIL branches in the major cities of Canada.[130] Here was "practical action" at last, said the *True Witness*. This was far better than the "explosions of sentiment which almost immediately evaporate, leaving an exhaustion of energies"—a reference, thinly veiled, to the explosion of Boer sympathy.[131] Cronin's *Register* shared this enthusiasm for the establishment of a new nationalist organization in Canada, but its Boer sympathies had not evaporated entirely. In response to the news of the Treaty of Vereeniging, it published at length the response of the prominent British anti-war campaigner, Viscount John Morley.[132] Cronin himself continued to praise the Boers as "the bravest in all the history of the human race" and to describe the war as "unnecessary from the beginning." "Three hundred millions of pounds and nearly twenty-five thousand lives is the sacrifice made to the god Jingo," he wrote, all so that "Mr. Chamberlain's teeth" could be "sewn broadcast in the red earth of the veldt."[133]

* * *

Idiots or not, those who shared the views of Irish and American pro-Boers were among a minority of Irish Canadian Catholics. Most identified more closely with the Canadian and Irish troops fighting on the British side than with the Boer commandos and the Fenian adventurers in their ranks. Some, such as the AOH of New Brunswick, were quite adamant about this. Nevertheless, many who maintained an active interest in nationalist politics probably shared, to varying degrees, the reservations expressed in papers like the *Catholic Register*. Unlike those south of the border, however, most did not see the war's unsavory aspects as intrinsic to imperialism. The empire in which they believed upheld the autonomy of colonies and of small (white) nations, but a combination of unscrupulous statesmen and the jingo press were now steering it in the wrong direction. This conviction was seemingly confirmed by remarks made by Lord Salisbury in a speech to the annual convention of the Primrose League, the Conservative party's grassroots organization in Britain, in May 1900. "The disloyalty of the Transvaal Republic in secretly arming," he declared, "has suggested an earnest lesson, and one which will not be forgotten. We know better now than we did a decade ago the risks of giving perhaps a disloyal government in Ireland a similar opportunity."[134]

Salisbury's comments were met with groans by Irish communities throughout the empire.[135] One Canadian rebuke set out an argument for Home Rule rooted firmly in a pro-imperial and anti-Boer position:

> In the first place there is no parallel whatsoever between the case of the Transvaal and that of Ireland. The former is situated half round the globe from England, occupied by a race entirely alien . . . and under a Republican form of government practically independent of any other power; the latter is at the very door of England, within a twelve hours' sail: is inhabited by a race distinct from the Saxon, but one which has for centuries contributed— either through compulsion or from good will—to the building up of the British Empire, and, while Great Britain's most insignificant colonies have enjoyed local legislation, or Home Rule, Ireland . . . has been kept in a state of virtual servitude by a power which owes her most of its ubiquity and strength. Consequently, it is illogical and politically dishonest—if not entirely false—for Lord Salisbury to give as a reason for his opposition to Home Rule, the suddenly discovered genius of the Boers for gathering arms and amassing ammunition.

And yet Salisbury, the author went on, had the gall to praise the Irish soldiers fighting in South Africa and "in the same breath" inform them that on their return home they "may look forward to a perpetuation of the state of servile dependence to which the Act of Union had reduced them."[136] This argument was made in the editorial section of the usually tepid Montreal *True Witness*, on the same week that the city's Hibernian Knights paraded under Transvaal flags in Boston. Irish nationalism in Canada had long been, and would continue to be, defined by a diversity consistent with its many Irish, Canadian, American, imperial, and regional influences. The South African War years were no exception.

PART FOUR

Fenians, Spies, and the Legacy of War

"Ha! Ha!"

Unmasking Agent Z (and Uncaging Luke Dillon)

Joseph McGarrity was a substantial man in several respects. The writer Padraic Colum described him as "a Donegal gallowglass ready to swing a battleaxe with his long arms."[1] McGarrity was, in fact, from Tyrone farming stock, but Colum's flattery nevertheless captured both his impressive stature and his romantic commitment to the cause. He had emigrated to Philadelphia in 1892, aged 18, and joined the Clan na Gael within a year of his arrival. Recognized as a hardworking organizer and a dedicated revolutionist by William Crossin, McGarrity took over as District Organizer (D.O.) for the city in 1904, while making his fortune as a liquor wholesaler. In the years that followed he became close to John Devoy, and by 1912 had ascended to a seat on the Clan's executive.[2] He was described by an informant as "doubtful of every man" and a believer in "individual exertion and close work, circles within circles, so as to safeguard against leakage."[3] McGarrity was a firm supporter of the IRB faction spearheaded by men such as Seán Mac Diarmada and Tom Clarke (who returned to Ireland in 1907), which set about purging the old guard and bringing the organization under the control of a tight-knit, militant executive. Their circle within a circle would, with the assistance of McGarrity and Devoy, eventually plan and instigate the Easter Rising of 1916. The commitment to secrecy that elevated McGarrity to one of the architects of the rebellion plot had been reinforced a few years earlier by the fortuitous discovery of what he called "the active spy system of the British" in his own backyard. The origins of this revelation can be traced to the South African War.

In Philadelphia on 11 June 1912, McGarrity received a telephone call from a local Clan na Gael man informing him that "something serious" had arisen. Bernard "Barney" McNello had died at home, aged 64. An Irish-born railway foreman, McNello was a well-known Philadelphia Fenian who had frequently served as his camp's delegate to Clan conventions. Upon his death, a colleague visited his home and made a disturbing discovery. McGarrity went to see for himself. He later wrote that he was "aroused to a great pitch of excitement" when he opened the dead man's bedroom trunk and saw the papers inside. "[H]ere was real proof of the importance of our Organisation and of its danger to the Great British Empire." He took the papers home and shut himself in a room for a day and a night. "[M]y wife thought something had affected my mind." To his astonishment, he discovered the papers contained more than five hundred letters written by a British handler.[4] McNello, it seemed, had been spying on McGarrity's district for over twelve years. But despite explicit orders to destroy every letter he received from his boss, McNello had kept them all. His sudden death brought the cache into the hands of the Clan na Gael executive—and with it an unprecedented glimpse into the workings of the British counter-Fenian intelligence operation in the United States.

At first McGarrity was furious. He returned to McNello's house to see the spy's body lying "like a great dead fat hog." He had the corpse propped against a wall and photographs taken, intending to publish them in the newspapers with an exposé of McNello's treachery. But he thought better of it. He spoke with McNello's daughter, who tearfully admitted that she knew about her father's secret career as an informant. She had been instructed to write to her father's handler, "Wilcox," to notify him in the event of Barney's death. McGarrity persuaded her to hold off, to pass on any correspondence her father continued to receive, and to keep for herself any money enclosed. She agreed to keep quiet about the discovery while the Clan "put on an attitude of sorrow" and paid for McNello's funeral (though McGarrity made sure to advertise this event too late for many to attend lest the dead man be mourned better than he deserved). McNello's treachery was to be kept secret and Wilcox's letters studied closely.[5] The clues uncovered in them sparked an investigation that would lead to the unmasking of Britain's top spy in the United States: Agent Z.

* * *

Figure 8.1. Joseph McGarrity, ca. 1910, OM II 5/25/4, Joseph McGarrity Collection, Digital Library@Villanova University.

Hiring Agent Z was one of Major Nicholas Gosselin's first actions as head of the Special Branch. It was to be his crowning achievement. He visited New York personally in 1891 to assess the state of the intelligence network in America. Vigilance, it seems, had lapsed in the post-Le Caron era. Gosselin found "that the whole system was rotten" and "well-known to the extremists" it was intended to monitor. He identified only one agent actually embedded in a secret society, and promptly discharged the rest. Gosselin hand-picked Agent Z to establish a "fresh counter organisation" reporting directly to Palace Street, and assigned five trusted spies to his command. "[F]our of these," Gosselin boasted, "managed to worm their way into the very heart of the American conspiracy." Agent Z subsequently added recruits of his own.[6] It was Z's network that penetrated William Lyman's inner circle and proved instrumental in frustrating his attempted outrages. One of Z's spies, Thomas Meric Jones, earned the nickname "Le Caron the second" for the damage he wrought on Lyman's organization through his dramatic testimony from the witness stand in 1897.[7] Gosselin was keenly aware that Z's assignment was "a most delicate and difficult business." "We are keeping up a secret bureau in a friendly country," he reminded Sir Kenelm Digby, Permanent Under-Secretary at the Home Office. "A country where the men we are supervising possess a large share of political power; and in the event of it coming to light it would to say the least cause trouble." Agent Z's "life," for a start, "would be in great danger."[8]

The acerbic major, who seldom had a kind word to say about his colleagues and subordinates, was fulsome in his praise of Agent Z. He was confident that his man possessed the "tact and astuteness" necessary to avoid discovery.[9] He was anxious, however, that a parsimonious Home Office would scupper the system Z had helped to build. The American network, Gosselin stressed, amounted to "a thoroughly effective Secret organization in the hands of a most capable man, holding such a unique position that you might spend thousands in trying to establish a similar organization and fail."[10] Should Z be deprived of the funds necessary to maintain his network—and his interest—any advantage the Special Branch had gained during his tenure might be lost. Gosselin even proposed reducing his own salary by £300 per year so that Z's could be increased by the same amount. Were Z to retire, he explained, "we should be face to face with a very troublesome affair. I don't know how I could replace him."[11] By 1902 Z's agency had transmitted over "15,000 original papers" on Fenian activities to the Home Office.[12] The system had proven so effective, Gosselin explained to his superiors, that although "more than one" dynamite plot had been attempted, "during these 12 years not even a brick has been displaced."[13]

Gosselin meant British bricks. As we have seen, bombs exploded in Dublin during the 1890s, and in Thorold and New Orleans during the South African War. The reunification of the Clan na Gael at the War's outbreak had set Agent Z's operation scrambling to adapt. The old United Brotherhood (UB) stronghold of Philadelphia assumed a new importance in the united organization, and the Welland Canal affair seemed to prove it to be a hotbed of extremism. William Crossin, who appeared to have a hand in both the Welland and *Mechanician* explosions, needed watching. To this end, Barney McNello was recruited to Agent Z's network in 1900. Little is known of his antecedents. He was probably from Drogheda, Co. Louth. According to a man later claiming to be his half-brother, Barney was born in the poorhouse, one of his father's four illegitimate children ("Blood will out even in a bastard," spat McGarrity). By the 1890s, McNello was in Pennsylvania working as a laborer and was a member of a defunct Clan na Gael camp. "Wilcox" brought him to Mexico City, where it seems the terms of his employment were negotiated before he was dispatched to Philadelphia in February 1901. He was given money to pay his back dues and secure a transfer to an active camp in the city, so that he could begin his work.[14]

Wilcox wrote McNello weekly. The letters were typed and usually short, but dense and tonally dissonant. They switched abruptly between cajoling, encouraging, scolding, and flattering, often within the space of a single letter. For the first few months Wilcox took care to coach his agent. "[J]ust be friendly and let the other boys talk," he advised. "[T]he fellows love a good listener."[15] He reminded McNello that he expected "many years of good and loyal work," and that he "[took] care of the men who work true and loyally for me."[16] He bombarded McNello with questions, broad and specific, about individual Fenians, camp elections, local events, feeling about Irish affairs, and gossip or rumors he encountered. Securing election to the Clan's biennial convention could net McNello a $100 bonus.[17] Barney's chief assignment, however, was to work his way up the ranks and get close to the leading men—just as spies such as Thomas Meric Jones had done in New York the decade before. "Cultivate [William] Crossin all you can as he is *most important*," Wilcox urged. "[O]nly always remember he is very sharp and sleek [. . .] don't let him think that you are pushing yourself on him."[18]

Wilcox cleverly acted his dual role as Barney's stern boss and closest friend. He took pains to combat complacency, always keeping his man a little off balance. Though his pay was technically a fixed $40 per month, it came in erratic instalments apparently at Wilcox's pleasure. But Wilcox was generous with praise when McNello's courage needed a boost. This could produce strangely tender passages:

> I think that you have as much and more brains than the men you are meeting and that if you had more confidence in yourself and pushed yourself forward more and gave yourself more importance that you would go to the front.[19]

McNello's responses, of course, were not in his trunk and have not survived. Wilcox's letters do contain some clues as to the information his agent provided, but what they chiefly reveal are the matters in which Agent Z's intelligence network took a special interest. We can use them to track the legacy of the South African War for the Clan na Gael over the decade that followed.

*　*　*

Early on, the Clan's ties to Boer agents and sympathizers were of interest to Wilcox. He asked specifically about Samuel Pearson in November 1901.[20] Whether McNello ever came across him is unclear. Pearson's activism and his connection to Irish nationalists did not cease with the Peace of Vereeniging. Late in 1902 he was busy drumming up investment for a proposed Boer colonization scheme in Texas and Mexico. He caused a stir when he told a reporter in Monterey, Mexico, that he had been involved in a plan to invade Canada with an army of 3,000 pro-Boers. The plan, he claimed, was called off only when its financier Edward Van Ness, a New York pro-Boer activist, died unexpectedly.[21] The colonization scheme appears to have been no more successful than this filibuster. In 1904 Pearson was jailed for his part in an attempt to blackmail a former assistant secretary of the interior. Webster Davis, who had resigned his office in sympathy with the Boers in 1898, was harassed and threatened with death unless he paid Pearson and his accomplice $40,000 in gold bullion they alleged was owed by him to "the Boer government."[22] After 1914 Pearson's "pro-German and pro-Irish activities" became the subject of extensive Bureau of Investigation (BOI) surveillance.[23] In 1915 he attempted to assist the Germans in much the same way as he had the Boers during his campaign against the remount service. He went to court, claiming that arms sales to Britain violated American neutrality and damaged American citizens' property in Germany. His lawsuit failed, but he was suspected of fomenting strikes at munitions factories.[24] In 1917 he was believed to be working as a German spy. BOI Agent Florence Skadden, an "intelligent and prepossessing woman," was assigned to cultivate "a most intimate and confidential relationship with Pearson (of just the right character)," and if possible have him incriminate himself by duping him into a scheme involving a bogus pro-German military corps.[25] After the 1916 Rising he was observed to be "constantly in touch with the Sinn Féiners," and later added sympathy with the Bolsheviks to his list of causes.[26] Hatred of Britain was the constant theme of Pearson's otherwise erratic career, making him a longstanding—if somewhat unreliable—friend to American Fenianism.

Wilcox asked McNello to report on pro-Boer meetings in Philadelphia through 1901 and 1902, but during these years Fenian interest in the South African War was gradually eclipsed by the war brewing within their own ranks.[27] McNello kept Wilcox apprised of the chaos afflicting the Philadelphia rank and file as leading Fenians were expelled from the Clan na Gael over their willingness to support the United Irish League. As the home city of Michael J. Ryan, one of the preeminent secessionists, Philadelphia was a key battleground in the emerging split. On Valentine's Day of 1902 Ryan's followers seized the Irish American Club—the headquarters of the Philadelphia Clan na Gael—and locked out those loyal to the executive. A court battle ensued, which eventually resulted in victory for the loyalists; McNello's name was listed among them.[28] For the spy, this schism was fortuitous. He had narrowly failed to secure election as Junior Guardian (JG) of his camp—a position akin to Vice President. But when his rival vacated the office to join Ryan's side, the position once again came up for grabs. Crossin, desperate for allies, supported McNello's candidacy. "This split has been your opportunity," Wilcox wrote. "[A]vail yourself of it to the full."[29] By May 1902, McNello had secured a seat at the Clan Convention, and his $100 bonus.[30]

This was not the only Fenian convention to be held in the United States that year. Days before the inauguration of the new United Irish

League of America (UILA) in Boston in October 1902, a secret one took place. Fenians expelled from the Clan na Gael, including John Finerty, Patrick Egan, Michael J. Ryan, and Roderick Kennedy, formally organized a rival secret society to coordinate the new New Departure.[31] The leading constitutional nationalists of the day addressed the Boston UILA convention: John Redmond, John Dillon, Edward Blake, and Michael Davitt (who "eulogized the Boers in their great struggle"). William Bourke Cockran and Michael J. Ryan also spoke.[32] But it was the secret society men who would dominate the American organization. Finerty was unanimously re-elected national president of the UILA, and his allies occupied various important offices in the years that followed.[33] This did not represent a sudden embrace of pure constitutional politics. As the secessionists explained in a secret circular of December 1902, it was instead a rejection of the intransigent policy of the "physical farce party" dominating the Clan, and a belief that an alliance between secret society men, land agitators, and the parliamentary party was the only "real revolutionary combination."[34] When it was suggested in the English papers that Finerty's involvement with the UIL meant the return of dynamite, they insisted that the League's "methods" were those of "O'Connell and Parnell."[35] Both knew the value of a big tent.

As the latest struggle between agrarian reformers and the government escalated in Ireland, Finerty kept Redmond informed of the "war" being waged between the Clan and the UILA.[36] In 1903 chief secretary for Ireland George Wyndham's proposals for a comprehensive land purchase bill won the support of William O'Brien, who helped steer it through Parliament. The Clan, which opposed this and every move of the UIL as "West Britonism," found itself accidentally aligned with Dillon and Davitt, who disliked O'Brien and felt the bill did not go far enough. Finerty urged Redmond that it was essential that the bill should pass, or the momentum might shift in favor of the Clan and the IRB.[37] "Gonne, MacBride & Co will shout 'we told you so,'" he warned. Kenelm Digby at the Home Office had the same concern.[38] When the bill passed, Finerty reported with satisfaction that the victory had left the Clan "desperate" and "going from bad to worse."[39] But the ordeal of the bill's passage hurt the UIL in Ireland and the United States just as much. Bitter at Davitt and Dillon's opposition, William O'Brien dramatically resigned from the League and the Irish Party.

"Hold O'Brien retirement disastrous," Patrick Ford glumly cabled Redmond.[40] Damaged by this controversy, and with the land settlement causing agitation to subside, the League declined. Finerty urged Redmond to immediately press for Home Rule if he wanted to keep the League alive in America. "You know that I am a separatist, but I can recognize the logic of circumstances," he wrote. The Irish Party's policy may be "less advanced than ours," but Home Rule was all that was on the table for Ireland at present, "and she could afford to wait for the rest."[41] The League was brought into line as the Irish Party's grassroots machine, and though it survived well into the next decade, it never recovered its popularity.

Nevertheless, the conflict with the Clan persisted. William Bourke Cockran found himself caught up in the feud in September 1903. He had agreed to speak at the centenary commemoration of Robert Emmet's execution, set to be hosted by the New York UILA at Carnegie Hall. When Daniel Cohalan, Devoy's New York protégé, told him that the honor of commemorating Emmet rested rightfully with the Clan na Gael, and that competing events would create a spectacle of disunity, Cockran backed out. He suggested to the leaders of the New York UILA that they work with the Clan. They refused to even entertain the thought. The Clan na Gael, they explained to Cockran, was controlled by "a little knot of unscrupulous designing men" who:

> while England was fighting for her very existence in South Africa, held down the members of their organization here in America, and prevented them from taking a single step that might aid the gallant Boers or the Irish at home, or embarrass England, and who acted throughout the entire period of England's most deadly difficulty as if they had been the hired agents of the British government . . . Their inexplicable inaction during the Boer war drove out of the Clan na Gael nearly all the good and earnest men of that organization . . . Those men never have accomplished, and never intend to accomplish anything against England and should be treated by every Irishman who understands the situation as wreckers and enemies.[42]

In the eyes of their opponents, the leadership of the Clan na Gael and the IRB had squandered the opportunity afforded by the South African War, and in so doing had forfeited any claim to leadership of the nationalist movement. Just as damning, their exclusive commitment to the policy of revolution with foreign intervention led them to actively undermine the UIL's efforts to achieve meaningful change. Whereas the Clan had nothing to show for its obstinacy, the passage of the Land Act appeared to vindicate the position of Finerty, Ryan, and their secessionist friends.

Within eight months, however, the authors of the letter to Cockran themselves came under attack—not from the Clan, but from moderate nationalists within the New York UILA. A pamphlet was published exposing the secret society of expelled Fenians who controlled the organization, and providing evidence of how they stacked committees, bossed proceedings, silenced dissent, and misappropriated funds. Among those named were Roderick Kennedy and John Purroy Mitchel, author of the letter to Cockran, grandson of the Irish revolutionary John Mitchel, and future mayor of New York City.[43] The same year, Redmond himself was warned by other channels that the UILA was "absolutely in the power of a small group of men, all of whom were expelled" from the Clan na Gael.[44] But Redmond the old Parnellite was unmoved. No stranger to working with Fenians, he knew all along the background of the men who had come to control his party's American wing. Finerty and his allies ultimately survived the revolt of the moderates. Although they were hurt by the decline of the League, they remained in a stronger position than their rivals in the Clan.

The Clan na Gael's attempts to fight back saw mixed success. In September 1903, in the midst of the Land Act and Emmet centenary controversies, the *Gaelic American* was launched in New York, with John Devoy as its editor. The weekly paper was intended to present the revolutionist case in the US, and to counter the dominance of pro-UIL papers like Finerty's *Chicago Citizen* and Ford's *Irish World*. In this it served as a complement to Griffith's like-minded *United Irishman*, which was frequently on life-support until its collapse and re-emergence as *Sinn Féin* in 1906.[45] Editorials in its opening issues criticized Redmond's actions during the South African War—especially his welcoming of the royal visit and the "shamrock concession." This, they claimed, was evidence that Redmond was a mere "provincialist," not a nationalist.[46] Alongside a cultural mission to propagate the Gaelic revival in America, the *Gaelic American*'s political goal was to justify the Clan's new anti-parliamentarism by cultivating a mythology of an Irish revolutionary tradition that was distinct from—and purer than—its supposed constitutional antagonist. The popular appeal of this philosophy remained limited for now, but it would gain considerable purchase after its symbolic expression in the revolutionary street theater of Easter 1916.

* * *

Although the coordinated action sought by John Devoy and others had failed to materialize during the South African War years, British intelligence remained concerned about the Clan na Gael's continued interest in collaborating with rival great powers. Wilcox asked McNello to "repeat fully even if only gossip" anything he heard about the Clan's dealings with the French and Russian governments.[47] The Clan's policy of courting Britain's enemies—at least before 1914—proved ill-fated. The Anglo-French *entente cordiale*, formalized in April 1904, closed one such door for good. For a time, the Russian option remained. Fenian cooperation with Russian emissaries in the United States had been ongoing since the Lyman years.[48] During the South African War, chairman of the united Clan executive judge O'Neill Ryan met with the Russian Ambassador Count Cassini.[49] Rumors of cooperation with the Russian government circulated through IRB meetings; Gosselin and John C. Ardagh believed there was truth in them.[50]

The most persistent friend of the Fenians was the Russian Vice Consul at New York and then Chicago, Baron Albert Schlippenbach.[51] The Baron was a handsome bachelor better known as a doll collector and for employing—as his private secretary of thirteen years—a man who was born a woman. Nicolai De Raylan, born Anna Terlessky, married twice in Chicago and caused a scandal when on his death it was discovered that he wore a chamois leather and duck-down prosthetic penis. Schlippenbach claimed to have been none the wiser.[52] He was also for a time—though he certainly didn't know this—an acquaintance of Agent Z, who was fully aware of his Fenian connections.[53]

When in February 1904 war broke out between Russia and Britain's ally, Japan, Irish American opinion was strongly pro-Russia. Given that the conflict stemmed from rival imperial aspirations over Manchuria and Korea, a rather more tortuous case had to be made for supporting Russia than had been necessary for the embattled Boer underdogs. The *Gaelic American* relied heavily on whataboutism to justify its sympathy for the autocratic empire. The problem of Russian despotism was deflected with reference to the treatment of African Americans in the US. Imperial Russia's suppression of national minorities was dismissed as no worse than Britain's occupation of Ireland. According to the newspaper, the war with Japan was analogous to Anglo-American policies of Asian exclusion, but with greater justification because of Russia's unique proximity to the "Yellow Peril." That William Randolph Hearst's newspaper empire took the Japanese side was seized upon as grounds for predictable "yellow press" puns.[54] Anti-Semitism was also employed: it was charged that Anglo-American business interests were using Japan to keep Russia out of China. "The Anglo-American alliance is a misnomer" read one *Gaelic American* editorial. "It should be called the Anglo-Hebrew alliance."[55] The Clan had reason to generate goodwill toward its potential foreign ally, but its rivals at the *Irish World* and the *Chicago Citizen*, as well as Michael Davitt, also sympathized with Russia. Some of the admirable principles expressed in the anti-imperialist outpourings during the South African and Philippine wars could evidently be superseded by a cross-partisan desire to see Britain frustrated.[56]

At the 1904 convention, Clan delegates congratulated themselves on their work in stemming "the pro-English and anti-Russian tide," as well as the "tide of gush and flapdoodle" over the Land Act—legislation which they agreed was "intrinsically worthless or at least fatally bad."[57] They were clutching at straws. Though imperfect, the Wyndham Land Act in fact revolutionized the land system in Ireland, transferring millions of acres into the hands of tens of thousands of peasant proprietors. The Russian alliance meanwhile proved a chimera. The Japanese achieved what the Boers could not. Russia suffered a humiliating defeat, humbling her prestige and throwing the country into turmoil. By 1907 the Anglo-Russian entente put an end to this particular Fenian fantasy. Only Germany remained. Meanwhile, Clan and IRB membership continued to decline. This was rationalized as a positive thing at the 1904 convention. "We recognize," read the secret typed report, "that this work has to be done in face of a police and spy system that is nearly perfect, and therefore can be better done by a small, compact and carefully selected organization."[58] Barney McNello, one of the carefully selected delegates to the convention, provided the Special Branch with a copy of the report.[59] Someone there scribbled three red exclamation points next to the words "nearly perfect."

* * *

Gosselin would no doubt have been pleased at the compliment. This was the impression he liked to convey to his superiors at the Home Office. A year earlier he had explained to Kenelm Digby that his "method of conducting the Secret Service has had not a little to do with the present disorganization & collapse of Secret Societies."[60] There was some truth to this, but Gosselin had good motivation for boosting his own record. After twenty years at the Special Branch, and over a decade at its head, he was preparing for retirement. His shadowy position made his pension entitlements uncertain. His bête noire, Robert Anderson, had retired from the LMP in 1901 to a pension, a knighthood, and a series of book contracts. John Mallon retired in 1902 to a magistracy, a generous pension, and in 1910 published a rather opaque, ghostwritten memoir.[61] Gosselin's secret position precluded him from being lauded as a "great detective" in print, but he lobbied hard to ensure he would not be denied the reward of a pension and title. Digby expressed reservations about "whether a secret agent can properly receive any of the usual rewards for public services," but personally believed that Gosselin's work had been sufficiently valuable that the rules might justifiably be bent.[62]

With Gosselin on his way out and secret societies in disarray, serious consideration was given to the question of whether the Special Branch should continue to exist at all. Digby observed how two decades of failure had chipped away at Fenianism's culture of skirmishing:

[The] tendency to outrage was I believe successfully crushed by the convictions which followed the dynamite outrages of 1882 and 1883—the disunity and arrests which followed the "Antwerp" plot of 1896—the detection and prevention of the plot against M. Chamberlain in the same year, and the conviction for the attempt to blow up the Welland Canal in 1900. It may I think perhaps be said that an organization which talked so much, and notwithstanding ample opportunities did so little during the Boer War cannot be very formidable.[63]

Gosselin warned against complacency. He conceded that Ireland was essentially loyal, but presciently insisted that "the political scum which has risen in the past 25 years will not evaporate without many an effort to show Ireland that at last her 'opportunity' has come."[64] It was settled that the Special Branch's operations in England could safely be scrapped and that its Irish responsibilities could be offloaded to Dublin Castle. Digby agreed, however, that "if there is any danger at all it is in America."[65] Agent Z was considered indispensable by all concerned at the Home Office, the embassy at Washington, DC, and the consulate at New York. The Special Branch would be retained as essentially a one-man outfit, a go-between to manage the correspondence with Agent Z. Digby hoped Gosselin could be persuaded to stay on in a reduced capacity.[66] But Gosselin, set on retirement, proposed his clerk of 20 years as his successor.[67] Instead, C. A. Wilkins, a man about whom little is known, was chosen to run the reduced operation for less than half Gosselin's old salary.[68] Wilkins, though tasked with cutting costs wherever possible, was just as adamant as Gosselin that Agent Z should be retained at no reduction in salary. A visit to the United States in 1905 convinced him of the importance of Z's work. "The Volcano," Wilkins reported, "if not active, is by no means extinct."[69]

Agent Z agreed to let some of his informants go, helping Wilkins shave £600 off the American operation's £3000 annual budget.[70] His approach remained the same: get spies close to the leading members of the Clan, and use them to provoke and prolong disunity. Barney Mc-Nello's success in befriending William Crossin saved him from the chop in 1905. Z's work was made lighter by the continued faction fighting in Irish America, which had a momentum all of its own. In addition to squabbles over parliamentarism and the commemorative calendar, the Clan and the UIL continuously wrestled for control over the Ancient Order of Hibernians (AOH). James Dolan, National President of the AOH in 1903, had tried to introduce a policy of neutrality in the war between the two blocs.[71] But this proved impossible to enforce. Local AOH elections became regular battlegrounds between opposing factions of Irish nationalists for at least a decade.[72] Crossin was in the thick of the struggle in Philadelphia, which could often turn nasty—sometimes with a nudge from Agent Z.

Since the early days of the split at the end of the South African War, a rumor took hold in Philadelphia that Crossin had betrayed Luke Dillon and was responsible for his arrest in Canada. This rumor was almost certainly false—but it helped to widen the schism in the city. At the Clan's convention of 1902 the supporters of Michael J. Ryan, in a petition outlining their grievances, stopped just short of openly accusing Crossin of informing:

> [H]e is utterly destitute of honor, decency or character, and [. . .] his whole career of malevolence has been attended with disgrace and dishonour to the Irish cause, and personal misfortune to the victims of misplaced confidence in his patriotism.[73]

Agent Z appears to have encouraged the revival of this rumor at inopportune times for Crossin—notably during AOH and Clan elections.[74] Joseph McGarrity's papers contain two anonymous threatening letters to Crossin in which he is accused of treachery. Both Crossin and McGarrity believed the letters to have been the work of British spies. "Yes you will be a State Secretary [of the AOH] like hell," read one of them. "A man who would sell out his friends for gain is a son of a bitch and hell will be his bed. Good by you dirty yellow dog."[75] Another, more sinister for its restraint and detail, warned Crossin that his "action in regard to Luke can never be forgotten." "[Y]ou let him go from your city that evening only to turn upon your heel and have your friend [. . .] send a cable to London," it charged, adding: "Rowan was on to you too and told Jack [Nolan] to be careful of you."[76] Whether there was any truth to these accusations is unclear, but unlikely. What we do know is that the second letter was posted by Barney McNello, acting under orders from Wilcox.[77]

* * *

Three hundred miles to the north, in Kingston Penitentiary, Luke Dillon found himself caught up in these rumors and the faction feud they helped to aggravate. He was visited in 1904 by Charles Ramsay Devlin, a Canadian-born Irish nationalist who had served as both a Liberal MP in Ottawa and an Irish Party MP at Westminster.[78] Devlin assured Dillon that everything possible was being done to persuade the Canadian government to secure his early release. He was also visited by Pat O'Brien, another Irish Party MP, who gravely told him that his friends in the Clan had betrayed him.[79] Both Devlin and O'Brien were leading figures in the UIL. When word got out that Dillon had been speaking with the other side, his old colleagues in the Clan na Gael were deeply concerned that he had jumped ship. His friend John Revens of Providence, Rhode Island, wrote to Kingston to ask Dillon to explain.

By this time, Dillon had convinced the prison chaplain to smuggle occasional letters to and from his friends south of the border. "You seemed to think my mind was poisoned," he replied to Revens. He explained that he was completely ignorant of the war going on between the UIL and the Clan when he met with Devlin and O'Brien. He and his fellow dynamiters, Nolan and Walsh, had been confined for their first three years in the so-called "prison of isolation," Kingston penitentiary's highest-security wing, owing to concerns that the Clan was planning to break them out. Each was locked in a two-foot by seven-foot cell and denied contact with other prisoners. Dillon later wrote that one third of those who spent time in the prison of isolation lost their minds.[80] "How," he asked Revens, "could I imagine M[ichael] J. R[yan] twirling his shillalah in Billy [Crossin]'s back yard?" Both had been Dillon's close friends before 1900. He assured Revens that he had not been persuaded by any rumors of treachery. "I am entirely responsible for the imprisonment I am undergoing, no body betrayed me," he wrote. "No language can be too strong to denounce any attempt to smear any of my old friends with the foul crime of informer." He made it clear, however, that he was disappointed with the Clan's lackluster efforts on his behalf and that he would not prevent Charles Ramsay Devlin or any UIL man from lobbying the Canadian government if it improved the odds of his early release.[81]

Dillon's letter does not appear to have been enough to persuade all of his old friends of his loyalty to them. That the UIL side was also in contact with Dillon's family in Philadelphia deepened their concern.[82] John Devoy in particular seems to have hardened in his attitude toward his old ally.[83] Joseph McGarrity later wrote that Devoy quietly frustrated efforts to secure Dillon's release for many years. "Leave him stay there," he claimed Devoy had spat. "This was one of the most disappointing moments of my life," McGarrity wrote. "Here was the individual whom

Figure 8.2. John Nolan (left) and Luke Dillon (right) in Kingston Penitentiary, 1910. Correctional Service of Canada fonds, RG73-C-6, Vol. 558, e010995338 & e010995296, Library and Archives Canada.

I had looked upon as an old patriot and hero—revealing himself to me as a heartless, cruel, selfish, jealous old man."[84]

By 1904 Dillon had been transferred from the prison of isolation to a newer building with more comfortable cells. He was given daily clerical work and then, befitting his old trade, was assigned to shoemaking. Although all work was done under enforced silence, this increased human contact, along with the possibility of visitors and his developing friendship with his chaplain, made prison life somewhat more tolerable for him.[85] "It takes brains to go buggo," he joked with Revens, "so I am perfectly safe on that score."[86] Word of the death of his eldest son in 1905 wounded him deeply, however. He blamed himself, believing that had he not been in prison he might have been able to detect the illness before it was too late. Alone with his grief, he felt the torment of confinement acutely. "I long not only to hear," he wrote, "but also to see and to feel. To love and be loved."[87] His family grieved too— for the loss of a father and a husband. His wife Mary wrote one of his old friends: "I feel some times as though I would go insane thinking about [Luke] and longing to see him."[88] Still, Dillon fared better than his co-conspirators. Nolan, after becoming defiant, was sent to the prison "dungeon" for twenty days, and had to be hospitalized on his emergence. John Walsh, the youngest of the three, was broken by imprisonment. His health failed, and after months of illness he died in 1907. Dillon described the funeral service as "a lonesome looking affair." Only he, Nolan, and the chaplain attended.[89]

Detective John Wilson Murray, who had worked on the Welland case, and his friend the Buffalo journalist Victor Speer, had publicly revealed "Karl Dallman" to be Luke Dillon in 1902. The story was told again in Murray's *Memoirs of a Great Detective* (1904), authored by Speer.[90] But Dillon's enduring silence meant an air of mystery still surrounded the Welland plot, and the newspapers occasionally retold versions of Speer's account whenever new crumbs of information about Dillon's conduct in prison or his antecedents emerged.[91] This infuriated Dillon, who charged Murray with deliberately misrepresenting his character to paper over the holes in his investigation. "I have never in all my life read of a more contemptable villain than I have been pictured," he wrote in 1907. "Murray knew nothing about me [. . .] but as he has finally done one decent act in his long span of life (died) I forgive him."[92] Dillon received from his friends in the United States occasional remittances, which he sometimes shared with Nolan. He claimed the money helped "lighten my imprisonment in this cold hole."[93] For ten years he remained generally in good health, and entered his sixty-third year at 190 pounds' weight.[94] But in 1911 he suffered a months-long bout of dysentery.[95] After Merna and Walsh, it looked as though Dillon might be the third of the Welland Canal plotters to meet his end.

Rumors of an imminent escape attempt had circulated from virtually the moment Dillon first arrived in Kingston in May 1900. The prison authorities took some of these rumors seriously, but there was generally little to substantiate them. However, in April 1904, accounts of a supposedly real attempt appeared in the newspapers. A "bogus nun" from Rochester, New York, reportedly "duped" the sisters in Kingston, and joined them on a visit to the prisoners in the penitentiary. There she passed a package to one of the dynamiters containing $1,000 intended for use in bribing prison guards to facilitate their escape. The prison authorities only recovered a small amount of this cash hidden in the lining of one of the dynamiters' clothing.[96] It is unlikely that this story is true; there is no other evidence to corroborate it. We know that letters and money—for Dillon's comfort—were smuggled to him through the prison chaplaincy. It is possible that guards stumbled upon cash received in this manner and that from there, the story grew in the telling.

From 1905 onward, Dillon's friends in the Clan na Gael were working to petition for his release through legitimate channels. William Crossin took the lead in the first efforts. He rehired Dillon's defense team—attorneys Daniel V. Murphy of Buffalo and William Manley German, Liberal MP for Welland—to do the lobbying.[97] In February 1905, Murphy and German met with Charles Fitzpatrick, who had risen to the office of Minister for Justice in Laurier's cabinet. The wartime champion of Irish Catholic loyalty to the empire had intimated his willingness to consider Dillon's early release. However, just three days before this meeting, Fitzpatrick received a telegram from the Home Office in London warning him that the Clan was plotting to break Dillon out "by other methods." He explained to Murphy and German that this report made it impolitic for him to act in Dillon's favor until time could prove it to be without foundation.[98] The timing of this telegram from the Home Office, and its effect, may not have been a coincidence. Wilcox constantly reminded Barney McNello to report everything he heard about Luke Dillon—especially information on attempts to secure his release.[99] With McNello close to Crossin, who was coordinating the Clan's efforts on this front, word likely reached the Home Office through Agent Z that something was afoot. What is unclear is whether the telegram to Fitzpatrick was a genuine warning based on incomplete information, or a deliberate attempt to sabotage the meeting with the Minister. Either way, Fitzpatrick was spooked, and the negotiations stalled.

Later in 1905 a proposal was made—from which side is uncertain—that Dillon's prospects of release would be enhanced if he would write an account of his career. Dillon gave this some thought, but ultimately decided he could not do it. He was uncomfortable with the idea of celebrating his own life and "endeavouring to impress future generations [that I] was a very goody, goody boy indeed, as well as a very wise old man." An even greater obstacle was his suspicion that he was really being asked to sell his friends out. "If I ever get out of here it must be without cringing on my part," he explained.

> The position that I now occupy reminds me of the boast of the English press, that, if they put an Irishman on a spit they could get another to turn him. They will turn me until this life is extinct e'er I will do anything that in my judgment is unmanly in order to obtain my freedom.[100]

So much for that plan. Another, probably around the same time, was for Crossin to visit Ottawa and revive the old "grain-handler" story as an explanation for Luke Dillon's actions. According to this story, Dillon was hoodwinked by the shovelers "and he being on a long spree did not know what he was doing." The story was to be sweetened by one thousand dollars in bribes, some of it for an unnamed "minister."[101] Crossin did visit Kingston on at least one occasion, but whether any part of this plan was followed through remains unclear.

In 1908 the Clan leadership, this time with Devoy's support, decided to pursue a different approach. Through backroom lobbying, a promise was secured from President Theodore Roosevelt to press Dillon's case with the British Ambassador James Bryce—a Belfast-born Presbyterian and former Chief Secretary for Ireland. Roosevelt thought it best to raise the matter with Bryce as an ordinary act of clemency, rather than appear to be doing the Clan a favor. He suggested that Dillon's wife write him a personal plea, leaving politics out of it entirely.[102] The letter he eventually received was, naturally, drafted by the Clan and vetted by Devoy and Crossin. "I am sure you will not be offended at a poor woman asking you to help her to get back her husband," wrote "Mary," pleading that her children "may have a father's advice as they go on in life" and that she be restored her "husband's protection and care."[103] The request was followed with a series of references in support of Dillon's character from prominent Philadelphians.[104] Chief among them was Wharton Barker, a federal political powerbroker and former populist presidential candidate. These efforts successfully reopened the question in Ottawa. Barker wrote personally to Wilfrid Laurier urging Dillon's "immediate liberation so that in his old age he can return to his family."[105] Dillon himself felt optimistic as 1909 drew to a close. But Laurier's cabinet again decided to kick the matter down the line.

Another push was made in 1911, this time from multiple fronts. Dillon's friends in Providence enlisted the Quebec-born Governor of Rhode Island, Aram J. Pothier, to raise the matter with President William Howard Taft.[106] Michael J. Ryan and Charles Ramsay Devlin pressured Laurier's cabinet and appear to have received assurances.[107] Some Canadian friends encouraged Dillon to write a letter in which he should "acknowledge guilt and petition for mercy." He did write a letter, but it was characteristically unapologetic and thus entirely unhelpful. "There was no Kowtowing" he explained afterwards. "[T]he rest of my life would not be worth such a surrender of principle."[108] While Dillon's letter annoyed the handful of his supporters who saw it, most were unaware and undeterred. The Montreal AOH held a public meeting at which they announced their intention to campaign for amnesty for both Dillon and Nolan.[109] Yet Laurier's government remained slow to move on its assurances.[110] John Gannon, the Clan's treasurer, suspected that Canadian ministers "must be holding up [Luke's] case for the dough."[111] It was more likely that, in a year dominated by controversies over Canada's place in the empire and its relationship with the United States, pardoning a stubbornly unrepentant Irish American dynamiter was not a risk worth taking. The debate over ratifying a reciprocity treaty with the United States triggered an early election in September—which Laurier's Liberals lost. With a new Conservative government in power, Dillon's friends would need to start over. Wilcox, who had been following developments closely, asked Barney McNello: "What will your people do now?"[112]

1912 proved to be a turning point in the fortunes of both the Clan na Gael and Luke Dillon. The introduction of the Third Home Rule Bill in April and the fierce opposition it aroused among Unionists in Ulster reinvigorated physical force nationalist sentiment in Ireland. In 1913 the "Irish Volunteers"—established in name only by the Clan na Gael during the South African War—became a reality as Irish nationalists, at the encouragement of the IRB, responded to the rise of paramilitarism in Ulster.[113] A growing alliance between Irish nationalists and German Americans also began to bear fruit in 1912. Since 1899 both had voiced strong opposition to the ongoing "great rapprochement" between the United States and Britain; negotiations between the two governments over an arbitration treaty in 1911–12 galvanized them further.[114] By July 1912 President Taft, struggling to get the treaty ratified in the Senate, resolved that something needed to be done to placate organizations like the Clan and the AOH. He explained to Whitelaw Reid, the US Ambassador in London, that securing the release of Luke Dillon was of "far reaching importance" and could help to "remove the serious opposition" in Congress that was holding up the treaty. Reid was instructed to meet with the new Conservative Canadian Prime Minister Robert Borden, then on a visit to London, to press the case for Dillon's release.[115]

There was reason to be hopeful that Borden's government, generally eager to uphold imperial interests, would cooperate. Even John Devoy struck what was, for him, a cheery note. "There are some Irishmen in the new Ministry," he told Crossin, "who could not be worse than those in the last one."[116] The new Minister for Justice was Charles Joseph Doherty, a Montreal-born Irish Catholic and a Home Ruler. Reelected in 1911 by the Montreal riding of St. Anne, where the Irish Catholic vote was typically decisive, Doherty could perhaps be swayed by pressure from Irish nationalist organizations. Doherty was with Borden in London, and when approached by Ambassador Reid on the Dillon question he indicated that he was favorably disposed to an early release.[117] Back in Canada, meanwhile, the change in government meant that a new set of advocates emerged to take up Dillon's cause. The Liberals Charles Ramsay Devlin and William Manley German stepped back. Charles J. Foy of Perth, Ontario, national director of the AOH in Canada and a Vice President of the North American organization, instead became increasingly involved.[118] So, too, did Rev. Alfred Edward Burke, the conservative-minded editor of the *Catholic Register* since 1908.[119] Though a firm imperialist, Burke took it upon himself to act as the intermediary between the Canadian government on one side, and the Taft administration and the Clan na Gael on the other. Remarkably, Burke carried out a warm correspondence on the subject with John T. Keating and Joseph McGarrity—two of America's leading Fenians.[120] Amnesty campaigns had a long tradition of creating strange bedfellows from across the Irish political spectrum: this new combination of a Canadian imperialist priest and the Clan na Gael executive was the latest iteration. By late November it looked as though it had worked: newspapers reported that Dillon's pardon was expected by Christmas.[121]

This publicity may only have stalled the matter, however. The question was just as toxic for the Conservative government as it had been for the Liberals. While C. J. Doherty was strongly in favor of a pardon, and had the backing of Charles Fitzpatrick—by then Chief Justice of the Supreme Court of Canada—Borden and others in his cabinet would only go ahead with it if it could be done quietly.[122] With the Home Rule Crisis rendering the Irish question again a sensitive issue, the Conservatives were loath to antagonize Orange and loyalist sentiment in Canada over one man. Rev. Burke, in his enthusiasm, appears to have made things worse. By late October Borden was growing frustrated with him. "He is a most foolish and dangerous man," Borden wrote in his diary, complaining that Burke "visits my office altogether too frequently" and was "so stupidly indiscreet as to be impossible."[123] It seems Burke, on a visit to New York, may have let some details of the plan slip—an indiscretion that forced the already hesitant cabinet to delay acting on Dillon's case.[124] In a sheepish letter to Keating, Burke explained that Doherty had warned him "the Orange men were watching to make trouble" and that Luke would "have to lie quiet."[125] It was at least now a case of when, not if. But Borden was in no hurry. By December 1913 he was still convinced that "the release would undoubtedly raise a storm."[126] As an added obstacle, Kingston Penitentiary was under the spotlight in 1913 and 1914 owing to an ongoing Royal Commission inquiry on penitentiaries. But Dillon's friends kept up the pressure. Burke heard from Doherty in January 1914 that the chances were good so long as there was not "a single murmur . . . Mum's the word."[127] Keating visited Ottawa himself in May 1914 and there the final assurances were given by the government; Dillon would be released at the soonest opportunity, on condition of strict silence. "Let him be forgotten," Keating warned Devoy. "A whisper may betray or awaken suspicion."[128]

On 11 July 1914, as the world's attention was seized by the crisis unfolding in Europe, an order arrived at Kingston Penitentiary authorizing Luke Dillon's release on parole.[129] He stepped outside of the prison walls for the first time in fourteen years the following day. Outside, a crowd of prison staff were celebrating the "Glorious Twelfth." They called out to him, asking him would he join their picnic. "I'll come," he responded, "if I can get a bomb big enough." The "Orange fellows" appreciated the joke. They shook Dillon's hand and wished him well. Dillon told a reporter that he walked away from that friendly exchange wondering what all the fighting was about and "why we can't be like other people. But there's no telling that."[130]

He crossed the border by ferry, landing at Cape Vincent, New York, and making his way south from there.[131] He had for years promised his wife that upon his release he would meet her at his old friend Charles McGlade's hotel at Atlantic City. On his arrival, however, he discovered that McGlade had been dead nine years, and his hotel torn

Figure 8.3. Luke Dillon interviewed in Atlantic City, *Washington Times* (DC), 26 Jul 1914, Chronicling America, Library of Congress.

down. He found his family all the same, but the story greatly amused the reporters who interviewed him. They portrayed Dillon as a sort of time traveler and pressed him for his reaction to having seen automobiles, cinema, and airplanes for the first time. "It is a wonderful age," he admitted, but countered why it was only technology that should advance: "Tell me that. They ought to give women the vote—they ought to give them whatever they want that's reasonable seeing what they are to the world." He spoke at length about the misery of prison, his joy at seeing his family again and meeting his grandchildren for the first time—even agreeing to pose for a photograph with two on his lap. He provided characteristically frank responses to questions about the Welland Canal bombing and its intended effect of tying Canadian troops down on the US border so that they could not be shipped to South Africa.[132]

Luke's joy at returning home was cut short by the death of another of his sons, Robert Emmet Dillon, from an intestinal fever in September 1914.[133] William Crossin was gone, too. His health had begun to fail in August 1911, and deteriorated steadily until his death in June 1912.[134] His deathbed wish, expressed to Keating and McGarrity, had been for them to complete his efforts to liberate his old friend in Kingston.[135] Barney McNello never got to meet Luke Dillon. He died two weeks before his old mark, Crossin.

* * *

McNello had been lagging in his duties through 1911. Once Senior Guardian of his camp, now he was infrequently attending meetings and rarely socializing. He was out of work, no longer close to Crossin, and unable to provide any news about the ongoing efforts to release Luke Dillon. Wilcox grew increasingly frustrated, chastising him for his "absolute neglect of business." He shamed McNello by acting deeply aggrieved. "I really think I am one man in a thousand," he wrote. "I have been very lenient with you because I have a personal regard for you . . . I have time after time tried to do my best for you."[136] He hectored McNello to "buck up and go among your old friends."[137] It was essential that he find a job—men with means but no visible work were always objects of suspicion in Clan circles. McNello's tardiness on this front forced Wilcox to call in a favor with a potential employer in April 1912. "[S]ee Mr. Barton," he instructed, "and say that you know Mr. Armstrong will regard it as a personal matter if he can see you fixed."[138] McNello never did get the job. The last letter to arrive before his death in June concluded: "Don't lose your spirit and things will come right."[139]

As McGarrity sifted through the dead spy's letters, here was a clue. Who was Mr. Armstrong? Were he and "Wilcox" the same person? The correspondence contained other disturbing revelations. Wilcox frequently seemed to have known about certain developments in the Philadelphia Clan even before McNello did. McGarrity copied the letters and shared them with John Devoy. Both agreed: McNello was not the only spy in Philadelphia. There must have been a second man—one still alive and working. Suspicion fell immediately on J. J. Carew, a man who had been seen taking camp minute books home with him. Carew had been suspected before. In 1896 he was living in New York with no apparent employment; while drunkenly attempting to woo a young woman, he hinted that he was involved in secret work. The woman raised the alarm, and the U. B. assigned a man to watch him. They found that he was a member of William Lyman's circle and drank at the same saloon. After the Antwerp affair of that year, he disappeared for a time, and when he reemerged he managed to get a transfer to Philadelphia. Devoy urged that a private detective should be assigned to watch Carew.[140]

In providing so vivid a picture of how British intelligence had penetrated the Clan, McNello's letters equipped the executive to better detect other spies. Devoy believed he had found a man in New York employing the same tricks as McNello.[141] Keating made efforts to root out similar behavior in Chicago.[142] McGarrity put a team of private investigators—one a former postal inspector—on the Carew case.[143] But Carew began to suspect he was being watched. The death of his wife added to his mental strain, and in February 1913 he suffered a psychotic episode. He boarded a train to New York and was found writhing on the floor of a Brooklyn post office at three in the morning, half undressed, crying "Help! They're after me!"[144] A patrolman tried to calm him:

> "They've been shooting at me," said [Carew], piteously, "and they've got me at last."
> "Who?" asked the policeman.
> "The agents of the Irish Republican Brotherhood," he replied.[145]

The incident removed any doubt as to Carew's guilt in the minds of the Clan leadership. Carew tried in vain to explain his actions as the product of drink and grief, on which "undeserved constructions" had been placed.[146] He was expelled from the organization in March 1913.[147] In the preceding months, McGarrity's detectives had been able to trace his mail and identified in the process a P.O. Box in New York registered under the name "E. C. Wilcox." The address associated with his account was a derelict building; Wilcox, they concluded, did not exist. But a "sponsor" listed in his registration was a familiar name: Mr. Armstrong.[148] As the investigation progressed, the detectives discovered that correspondence routed through Wilcox's P.O. Box found its way to the offices of Harry Gloster Armstrong of the Manchester Ship Canal Company—or as his colleagues in London knew him: Agent Z.

Harry Gloster Armstrong was born in 1861 to an Irish Protestant family in Belturbet, Co. Cavan. His father was a prominent local solicitor. After attending the Queen's Service Academy in Dublin, Armstrong joined the Cavan Militia—then being reformed as the volunteer 4th Battalion of the Royal Irish Fusiliers—where he rose to the rank of captain and published several well-regarded drill manuals.[149] It seems he made a positive impression on the adjutant of his battalion: Major Nicholas Gosselin. In 1884, shortly after Gosselin was seconded to secret service duty in England, Armstrong retired from the army and began working in the London theater scene, although whether he was also working for Gosselin at this time is not clear. Armstrong made little impact as a stage actor, but thrived as a producer. He was praised for his "energy and go-ahead style" while manager of the Royal Strand Theatre, and was behind a sell-out run of George Manville Fenn's farcical comedy *The Balloon* in 1889.[150] Despite this success, Armstrong uprooted himself to New York in 1890 when Gosselin, newly promoted to chief of the Special Branch, selected him (for reasons never specified) as the man who would reform the anti-Fenian intelligence network in the United States. His official cover, at first, was his position as the newly appointed American commercial agent for the Mexican Land and Colonization Company, a land speculation venture that held around sixteen million acres in the border state of Baja California and in the southern coffee-growing region of Chiapas. The Company, just prior to Armstrong's arrival, had been mired in controversy following a failed filibuster plot by a San Diego-based "council of fifteen" who sought to annex Lower California to the United States, with the probable connivance of the Company's manager on the ground—a Scottish railway engineer on loan from the Indian Civil Service. Armstrong, tasked in part with smoothing over the company's American image in the aftermath of this fiasco and with representing the interests of investors including J. P. Morgan and Lord Rothschild, must have winced when *Collier's* New York magazine joked that "[s]ome day that vast place may become an independent state, with Gloster Armstrong of Cavan as its president or king."[151] Armstrong's career switch from managing West End dramas to representing a controversial Mexican colonization scheme may seem an implausibly bizarre cover story for a secret agent's relocation to New York. But the explanation is, in fact, straightforward. The chairman of the Mexican Land and Colonization Company was Edward George Jenkinson—the first head of the Special Branch, and Gosselin's old mentor.[152] Armstrong's hire, it seems, was a favor to Gosselin from an old friend who knew the business of spycraft.

Neither his change of public career nor his new secret role dented Armstrong's interest in showmanship. During his first years at New York, he imported British plays for production in the United States, and was behind an unsuccessful scheme to construct a ninety-foot replica of the Tower of London for display at the Chicago Exposition of 1893.[153] By 1894 it appears he switched roles again, taking on what would, alongside his relatively modest £1,500 salary from the Home Office, become his most secure source of employment: the commercial directorship of the Manchester Ship Canal Company in New York.[154] While from this point his responsibilities at Jenkinson's Mexican company were wound down, he appears to have retained an ongoing connection to Mexico—something that may explain Barney McNello's sojourn there at the time of his recruitment. He also remained connected to Gosselin years after the Major's retirement from the Special Branch. In a 1912 encyclopedia of *Distinguished Successful Americans of Our Day*, Armstrong gave as his address Gosselin's seventy-acre estate at Aughnamullen in County Monaghan.[155] For most of the year, though, Armstrong lived with his wife and three children on Long Island. In 1905 he converted to Catholicism and became a prominent member of Catholic lay organizations in New York (much to Joseph McGarrity's disgust).[156] Alongside Armstrong's public reputation as an upstanding member of New York club and society life, as Agent Z he was held in high esteem at Whitehall and the British Consulate for his expertise, experience, and discretion. "It takes an Irishman to deal with Irishmen," wrote Percy Sanderson, the British Consul General at New York in 1905. With Armstrong, he believed, "you have a man who can be thoroughly trusted and who makes no difficulty about risking his life from time to time."[157] For over twenty years as Agent Z, Armstrong had helped to frustrate and humiliate American Fenianism by exposing its secrets and fomenting distrust. But with the death of McNello and the breakdown of Carew, the veil of secrecy had lifted again. The Clan na Gael executive had found its nemesis, and he was a stage manager from Cavan. What would their people do now?

* * *

We know a little of what came next. Armstrong was evidently eager to replace the Philadelphia assets he had lost in McNello and Carew. In August 1914 he approached local Clan na Gael man James MacGuinness with an offer to pay for information. "[Y]ou may just as well earn this money as someone else," Armstrong wrote. MacGuinness took the letter straight to McGarrity, who saw an opportunity to use him as a double agent. The arrangement fell through, however. McGarrity noted briefly that MacGuinness was unable to carry out Armstrong's instructions, and as a result Armstrong "lost interest and dropped away from him."[158] By January 1915, however, a more promising arrangement had materialized. Armstrong was in correspondence (at whose instigation is not clear) with Liam Pedlar, McGarrity's friend and brother in the Clan. Born in Belfast, Pedlar grew up in Glasgow and emigrated to Philadelphia, where he worked in McGarrity's liquor business.[159] Promising a monthly salary and extras for "special work," Armstrong asked Pedlar to provide the particulars of his standing in Irish nationalist circles and to describe what he was "in a position to do."[160] Pedlar consulted with McGarrity over the response he should give. Their plan was to draw Armstrong in without giving "more away than would be prudent for our own good."[161] They decided to let Armstrong know that Pedlar was Junior Guardian of D.195 of the Clan na Gael, and a member of the AOH and the Irish National Foresters. They then dangled some carefully worded bait that they knew would be irresistible to Armstrong:

I have the confidence of men well to the fore in the Clan such as J. McGarrity, Luke Dillon and F. Reilly who is my superior officer in my own club and who I have reason to think are all members of what might be termed the Inner Council in this locality the knowledge of which does not exist amongst the rank and file of the organisation. I have hopes of getting admittance to their councils . . .[162]

Armstrong bit. He offered Pedlar a starting stipend of $40 per month and asked for a complete list of the clubs and officers he knew, and the content of the most recent circulars.[163] Pedlar forwarded the offer to McGarrity. "The damned stuff in it," he snorted. "[T]hey want a cheap fool . . . Will I kick for more money?"[164] Whether to enhance Pedlar's credibility or to drain Armstrong of his budget, McGarrity advised that he insist on no less than $25 per week.[165] In a series of exchanges Pedlar complained to Armstrong that the terms offered were "entirely unsatisfactory" because his "discovery would mean loss of present position and future prospects and much more perhaps."[166] As the negotiations wore on, Pedlar confided to McGarrity that he worried he had been "too strong," but it looked like "the hounds are too anxious to take any setback."[167] Armstrong agreed to start at $60 per month—"Gloster must be dumb," muttered McGarrity.[168] When pushed again, Armstrong caved and offered $100—"Ha! Ha!" McGarrity scribbled.[169] But after this it appears Pedlar pushed too hard. The final surviving letter from Armstrong acknowledged their failure to agree on terms "at the moment" but left the door open to make a higher offer "later on."[170] After that the trail runs cold.

It is possible that Pedlar's correspondence with Armstrong continued later, but it seems more likely that McGarrity scuppered his chance at placing a Fenian mole in Agent Z's network of spies. It is also possible that McGarrity never intended what he called "our game" to go that far. McGarrity was sensitive to the risks. He advised Pedlar to refuse any request to travel to New York to meet with Armstrong and was cagey about providing the information bluntly sought in the letters. "Remember you cannot fool them," he had warned Pedlar.[171] Given the regular arrangement upon which Armstrong insisted, any pill of false information they might hope to slip him would need to be sugared with a much greater amount of real and sensitive detail about the members of the Clan and their activities. Faced with so costly a bargain, it may have been sufficient to know how the spy system operated and how it might be shirked or manipulated.

It was an auspicious time to have gained the upper hand over Agent Z. Since September 1914 most nationalists in Ireland and the Dominions had heeded John Redmond's call to cement Home Rule by assisting Britain in defeating the Central Powers and defending Catholic Belgium. Irish American opinion, however, was at best ambivalent about the British Empire's latest war. Nationalist organizations such as the AOH, which had for years cultivated an alliance with German Americans for precisely this contingency, tended to be openly pro-German. The split in the Volunteer movement and the decline of the UIL effectively placed the machinery of Irish American nationalism back in the hands of the extremists.[172] In September 1914 Armstrong reported rumors that "the C.N.G. in the U.S. are anxious to organize a force to menace Canada."[173] Later reports received by Canadian military intelligence also pointed to the potential for border raids by Irish and German American militias.[174] This was no more likely during the Great War than it had been during the South African War. But Canada was not entirely safe. Franz von Papen, wartime military attaché to the United States and future Chancellor of the Weimar Republic, worked closely with the Clan na Gael in plotting a campaign of sabotage and diversion against the Entente's war effort and its American benefactors. Buffalo lawyer and President of the Clan's Executive Council, John T. Ryan, advised von Papen and his agent, Horst von der Goltz, in a fresh conspiracy to blow up the Welland Canal in September 1914. The logic behind the idea, which was apparently proposed by "Irishmen" at New York, was precisely the same as had motivated Luke Dillon in 1900: tie down Canadian troops to defend the border and create tension in Anglo-American relations. The Canadians had, however, learned from their experiences during the South African War; the canal was too closely guarded for von der Goltz and his men to find an opening. In another incident—one that bore close resemblance to the Esquimalt and New Orleans plots—a barge containing fifteen tons of dynamite intended for shipment to the Eastern Front via Vladivostok was exploded off Harbor Island in Seattle. The San Francisco-based German–Indian–Irish conspiracy behind this and other plots—including one to destroy Canadian railway tunnels and another to foment an uprising in India—was broken partly with the help of the British Consul General's "makeshift intelligence network," which included a Dutch double agent and the attorney T.E.K. Cormac (who, as we have seen, had some experience in these matters). Joseph McGarrity had a hand in an unsuccessful German plot to ship American arms to Indian revolutionaries in 1915, one that led to the sensational courtroom assassination of Ghadar Party leader and Clan na Gael ally, Ram Chandra, in San Francisco.[175]

Irish revolutionaries were happy to assist their German and Indian allies in any scheme that would frustrate Britain, but these were sidelights to the main event. In March 1915, a few weeks after McGarrity and Pedlar's "game" with Harry Gloster Armstrong had concluded, Sean T. O'Kelly was dispatched from Dublin by Tom Clarke and Sean MacDermott. In New York he met with John Devoy and Daniel Cohalan, before traveling to Philadelphia to see Joseph McGarrity and Luke Dillon. At these meetings he was also introduced to Franz von Papen and Liam Pedlar. The purpose of his secret visit was to explain the plans for a rebellion in Ireland and to request funding to support it. He left with £2,000 in banknotes.[176]

In December 1915, John Nolan was released from Kingston Penitentiary.[177] He was warmly welcomed home by his old boss, Fred Allan, the man who had bought his ticket to Philadelphia sixteen years before. Allan set him up with a job at Dublin Corporation. Neither Nolan nor Allan participated in the German-assisted rebellion when it came in Easter 1916, but other prominent pro-Boers of their generation did. Among those executed for their leading role were Clarke, Connolly, and "Major" John MacBride, who joined in the fighting after stumbling across Thomas MacDonagh's column. Nolan's old friend "Willie" T. Cosgrave was also "out"; he survived to carry the coffin at Nolan's funeral in October 1920 and, two years later, to become the first President of the Irish Free State.[178] Liam Pedlar was there too—O'Kelly credited him as the only man to have traveled from America to fight.[179] Pedlar later served as Éamon de Valera's secretary during his second tour of the United States, and became quartermaster general of the IRA in 1923.[180]

Watching Pedlar ascend, Armstrong, if he did not realize he had been hoodwinked by McGarrity in 1915, must have regretted letting such an asset slip through his net. We cannot say for sure how far the discoveries that followed Barney McNello's death in 1912 contributed to his apparent failure to frustrate the plans for the rebellion of 1916. In any case, the responsibility was not Armstrong's alone. The Great War transformed British intelligence, and new agencies such as the Secret Intelligence Service (later MI6) had already begun to gradually supersede the old Special Branch system. The United States' entry to the Great War on the side of the Entente in April 1917 accelerated this transformation. This was a double blow for American Fenianism: for one thing, it made the dreaded Anglo-American alliance a reality at last. For another, it precipitated the fulsome cooperation of the Bureau of Investigation (later FBI) in British efforts to contain the Clan na Gael, whose cozy ties with the German enemy had become suddenly intolerable. As new systems emerged to monitor a new generation of revolutionaries, the Special Branch system that had been built by Jenkinson, refined by Gosselin, and inherited, in part, by Armstrong, was finally dismantled. In 1917 Agent Z's "American Correspondence," the long series of over 1,300 numbered memos that had kept Whitehall and Dublin Castle informed since 1892, was replaced by a "New Series" from a new agent, now reporting directly to the Commissioner of the Dublin Metropolitan Police. The new system was if anything less secure—McGarrity somehow got his hands on at least the first three memos.[181]

What we do know is that Armstrong did not end his career in disgrace. Instead, he was rewarded for his service with a Consul Generalship—first at Boston in 1919, then at New York from 1920 to 1931. He was awarded a knighthood in 1923. On his death in 1938, the *Times* of London noted in an obituary that "[t]o the people of New York he seemed one of themselves." A secret agent could hardly hope for higher praise.[182]

The release of Luke Dillon and John Nolan and the unmasking of Agent Z marked the end of an era in the relationship between Irish revolutionaries and British secret intelligence. They were also among the last ripples of the South African War. Other important legacies included the fragmentation of the Clan na Gael and the widening chasm between physical force and constitutional nationalists. During these years the seeds of later events were planted: events that would ultimately grow to overshadow the South African War. 1914 entangled Britain in the great power conflict that Fenians and pro-Boers had hoped in vain that 1899 would bring. Frustratingly for them, the Great War proved to be a far more popular war among the Irish nationalist mainstream; the political gulf between Irish Americans and their counterparts in the empire became wider than ever. But for the determined minority, Ireland's opportunity had returned. This time they would not let it pass.

Conclusion

The "Beginning of the End"?

In James Joyce's *Ulysses*, an imagined James "Skin-the-Goat" Fitzharris resurfaced as the keeper of a cabman's shelter, during a scene set four years after his humiliation in the shadow of the Statue of Liberty. "[A] day of reckoning was in store for the mighty England," Joyce's Skin-the-Goat prophesied to the shelter's patrons. "The Boers were the beginning of the end." Britain's "downfall would be Ireland, her Achilles heel," with a helping hand from "the Germans and Japs" who, he explained "were going to have their little lookin."[1] Fenian hopes were, notably, no longer vested in French assistance. "The French!" scoffed another of Joyce's nationalist firebrand characters, "the citizen," in an earlier complaint about their new *entente cordiale* with "perfidious Albion"—"[t]hey were never worth a roasted fart to Ireland."[2] Back in the cabman's shelter, Skin-the-Goat's prognostications were challenged by one of his audience, who pointed out that "the Irish Catholic peasant" was "the backbone of the empire." An onlooking Leopold Bloom noted "the interesting point" raised in the ensuing argument that "Irish soldiers had as often fought for England as against her, more so, in fact." It seemed to Bloom that the sensible course of action in Anglo-Irish relations was "to try to make the most of both countries, even though poles apart." The intransigent revolutionary Skin-the-Goat had "transparently outlived his welcome"—a relic of "very ancient history" who "ought to have either died naturally or" as a certain nationalist anthem would have it, "on the scaffold high."[3]

In the years following the South African War, it increasingly looked as though physical force separatism would indeed be consigned to "very ancient history." As this book has revealed, the war's initial impact on transatlantic Fenianism was dramatic, but in the immediate aftermath it appeared to have done more harm than good. When the prospect of war first appeared on the horizon, it was hailed as an oasis in the desert for revolutionary nationalism. England's difficulty had come; now was Ireland's "hour of destiny." By tying its fortunes to the Boer cause, Fenianism rode the wave of Boer fever through 1899–1900. But when that wave crashed, Fenianism crashed with it. The Clan na Gael and the IRB, despite their newfound vigor and the advantage of surprise over a scrambling Special Branch, failed to overcome the burden of a decade of disorganization in time to prove their relevance before the nationalist public. In the uncertain days of January 1900, Under-Secretary for Ireland Sir David Harrel worriedly warned the Lord Lieutenant of the "probabilities of difficulties in the perhaps very near future" posed by Fenians planning "some offensive movement in or upon Ireland."[4] By the war's end, the failure of extremists to present any serious difficulty to the empire seemed evidence that Fenianism was moribund. It was, at the very least, severely demoralized. The "heroic" Boer resistance during the early months of the war may have inspired the advocates of Irish revolution. But in the two years that followed, the grinding defeat inflicted by Britain's overwhelming military force had the opposite effect on many. It convinced even the champion of the Boers, Arthur Griffith, that secret societies were a dead end and that advanced nationalists should probe alternative roads to meaningful independence. Pragmatic Fenians such as John Finerty, meanwhile, deserted the seemingly obsolescent Clan na Gael to join forces with the United Irish League and the reunited Irish Parliamentary Party.

Moderate nationalists navigated the war years more deftly than their Fenian cousins. In Ireland and the United States, they funneled pro-Boer energies into the United Irish League and from there into the new campaign for land reform. In most parts of Britain's Dominions, they were effectively the only show in town. Although the opposition could be fierce, they found ways to express their distaste for the war while defensively asserting their support for a more decentralized empire. A year after the war's end, the resurgent Irish Party and the growing UIL could claim some credit for the advent of a transformative Land Purchase Act. Their momentum dwindled for a time thereafter, as there was little to do but resume the Home Rule waiting game. But those keeping an eye on postwar South Africa found reason to be hopeful. The former *bittereinder* Louis Botha led Boer nationalists into a rapprochement with Britain that culminated in the creation of a united white South African Dominion. Home Rulers increasingly came to see the Boers as a model of détente and self-government within the empire, rather than one of violent resistance against it. In 1910, the same year that the Union of South Africa came into being, a constitutional crisis in the United Kingdom precipitated a pair of dramatic elections which made the Irish Party kingmakers in Commons. The Liberal alliance returned, and Home Rule shot suddenly to the top of the legislative agenda. John Redmond, described by some as "the Irish Louis Botha," adopted an increasingly conciliatory approach to empire and the Anglo-Irish relationship as the finish line came within sight.[5] With the Ulster question threatening to derail the Home Rule project, it became more expedient than ever for nationalist Ireland to demonstrate its reliability as a partner in empire, and to find common ground with unionists. Redmond's maiden speech as Irish Party leader may have been an attack on the injustice of the South African War, but his most famous speech, delivered at Woodenbridge in September 1914, struck a very different note. The war against Germany, he explained, was one "undertaken in the defense of the highest principles of religion and morality and right." In defense of these principles, Irishmen must be prepared to go "wherever the firing line extends."[6] A minority of hardliners split from the Irish Volunteers over the question of enlistment—a development that was mirrored by a Boer rebellion in October 1914, led by former Generals Christiaan De Wet and Koos De La Rey, in protest against South African participation in Britain's Great War.[7] But this episode appears to have received relatively little attention or sympathy from Irish nationalists. Indeed, the popular response in Ireland and the Irish communities of the Dominions to the outbreak of war with Germany was strikingly different to that almost fifteen years earlier.

There are few more dramatic examples of this shift than Arthur Lynch. From 1914 he acted as a liaison between the British and French governments, placing his formerly subversive Parisian connections at the disposal of the country that had quite recently sentenced him to death for high treason. Later in the war he was once more honored with the rank of colonel—this time in return for his services as a British Army recruiting agent in Ireland. His requests to raise another Irish brigade—one that would fight for, rather than against, the British—were politely declined.[8] Another onetime Irish Australian Boer sympathizer who went beyond the call of duty during the Great War was Arthur Hill Griffith, whose advocacy for conscription saw him expelled from the Australian Labour Party in 1916.[9]

A war in defense of small nations was an easier sell than a war to annex them. But in parts of the diaspora, support for the war was just as often suffused in the language of Irish Catholic duty to empire. Canadian Catholic journals such as the *Northwest Review* went as far as to raise the South African War as a precedent for Irish Canadians fulfilling this duty of service—neglecting to mention the widespread antipathy to that conflict that its own columns once recorded.[10] James Grattan Grey did not grandstand as an opponent of the Great War. In 1916 the writing of his fourteen-year-old granddaughter, Florence Stafford, attracted attention of a rather more favorable sort than Grey's had sixteen years earlier. Her essay on the war was awarded the top prize in a national competition held by the Navy League of New Zealand, and a poem she wrote was printed with glowing praise by her grandfather's old employer, the Irish nationalist *Advocate* of Melbourne. The contrast with Grey's complaints about sending colonial contingents to fight the empire's battles is clear:

> Oh, why are some men shirking,
> While others go away,
> And fight in those awful battles
> Or in a more cruel fray?
>
> Oh, why are some men shrinking,
> When they could go as well
> As those who are now in the firing line
> Out in that living hell?
>
> . . .
>
> Now, let us give three mighty cheers
> For our King and our country too,
> And ask our God when we pray to-night
> To help our Empire through![11]

After 1916, global Irish nationalism would be turned on its head. Revolutionary republicans seized the reins. Even in the loyal Dominions, mainstream Irish nationalists came out eventually in support of revolutionary Sinn Féin—albeit through the euphemistically-styled "Self Determination Leagues." The causes of this transformation are obviously numerous and complex. There was nothing inevitable about the Irish "revolution"—insofar as that label applies to the upheavals of 1916–1923. Nevertheless, as Aidan Beatty has argued, portraying it as an "ostensibly sudden rupture" obscures the "long arc of development" that helped to create the conditions for the collapse of the Anglo-Irish relationship.[12] The legacy of the South African War must be counted among the factors that explain its origins. Not all Fenians were deterred by the Boer defeat. As the slouch hats atop the heads of rebels "out" in Easter 1916 show, some still clung to the vanquished Boer commandos as icons of anti-imperial defiance. Their disappointment at the failure to make good on England's difficulty at the turn of the century left certain key players determined not to let Ireland's next opportunity slip. This "get it right next time" attitude underpinned the Clan na Gael's exclusive commitment to an insurrectionary policy from 1900 onwards. Although this prompted an exodus that led the Clan to become eclipsed by the UILA in peacetime, it left a leaner and more effective secret organization to pursue conspiracy by the return of "England's difficulty." Tom Clarke, who was among the Fenians most profoundly affected by the South African War, played a central role in reshaping the IRB in the new Clan's image after 1907, and in instigating the rebellion that was to be the fruit of this revived transatlantic partnership. It would be wrong to suggest that Clarke and the military council on one side of the ocean, and McGarrity and Devoy's Clan on the other, enjoyed anything resembling a free hand. But the "veil of secrecy" under which they operated benefited from the aging out of the Special Branch system. Seeing the Fenian conspiracies of the South African War go out with a whimper helped to justify budget cuts and the retirements of key spymasters John Mallon, Robert Anderson, and Nicholas Gosselin. Harry Gloster Armstrong—Agent Z—remained watchful, but the man he hired to infiltrate the Philadelphia Fenians behind the Welland Canal plot ended up compromising his network right as the Great War broke out.

Certain features of the revolutionary decade can also be seen, in part, as repetitions of patterns evident during the South African War years. The Irish and German American partnership kindled in 1899 was sustained by opposition to Anglo-American rapprochement and flourished between 1914 and 1917 as a sizeable constituency of Irish nationalists in the United States embraced imperial Germany as their enemy's enemy.[13] The Clan na Gael's secret lobbying failed to win material assistance from the French, Russian, and Boer governments at the turn of the century, but the same strategy won them "gallant allies" in the Germans. The results of this alliance during the Great War looked rather familiar: arms-smuggling, a new plot against the Welland Canal, a cross-ethnic conspiracy out of San Francisco, and an attempt to raise an Irish Brigade from POWs in German camps. As had been the case during the South African War, the crisis of the Great War helped thrust a hardcore anti-imperialist minority into the center of the action. The challenge they had hoped to mount in 1900 appeared sixteen years late. That failed insurrection was dismissed by many at first as the latest unwelcome intrusion of the "physical farce" party. But the fortuitous combination of the heavy-handed British response, war weariness, the looming threat of conscription, and the spectacular success of the Sinn Féin political machine had a delayed legitimizing effect on transatlantic Fenianism's insurrectionary policy. A fondness, even a protectiveness, for the men and women of action—and especially the martyred—was seldom far beneath the surface of popular Irish nationalism. As Joyce's Leopold Bloom conceded, "he certainly did feel, and no denying it . . . a certain kind of admiration for a man [like Skin-the-Goat] who had actually brandished a knife, cold steel, with the courage of his political convictions."[14]

The New York-born Éamon de Valera, a man who had brandished a gun during Easter Week, drew crowds of tens of thousands of admirers on his US tours as President of Dáil Éireann during 1919–1920. But official American support for an Irish republic, sought as earnestly during that tour as at the Paris Peace Conference of 1918, proved no more forthcoming than it had been for the Boer republics. The Irish nationalist lobby once again failed to challenge the primacy of the Anglo-American special relationship. The broken promise of the "Wilsonian moment" left radicals—suddenly the mainstream force in Irish nationalism yet increasingly isolated on the international stage—searching for allies among other groups left out in the cold by the Versailles settlement: notably Indian and Egyptian nationalists. This was not the first such identification, and it was not without significant limitations, but de Valera's widely publicized February 1920 declaration to the New York Friends of Freedom for India that "our cause is a common cause" was an extraordinary development for an extraordinary time.[15] It did not, however, signal a wholesale reappraisal of Irish nationalists' imperial double standards. When de Valera, that same month, suggested in an interview that "Britain do thus with Ireland as the United States did with Cuba," John Devoy countered that it "would be suicidal to give England in Ireland" the interventionist rights the United States claimed over Cuba since its "liberation" from Spain. Many Irish nationalists sided with Devoy in angrily rejecting de Valera's Cuban analogy—without necessarily questioning whether it was right that Cuba be a "vassal state" of the United States in the first place.[16] Nevertheless, diasporic agitation successfully directed American and Dominion attentions to Britain's counterinsurgency policy in Ireland. This level of public scrutiny and the political influence of Irish communities made it impolitic to subject the IRA and its civilian backers to the scorched earth and concentration camps that had exhausted the Boer resistance, or indeed the military crackdown that stunned the Punjab in 1919. The result was that by 1922, twenty years after the Empire absorbed one Free State in South Africa, it created another in Ireland.

The willingness to compromise that made the Anglo-Irish Treaty possible, and the counterrevolutionary impulse that enforced the settlement, can also be identified in the developments of the South African War years. Although the "revolution" was driven by transatlantic Fenianism with all its republican and anti-imperial trappings, it culminated in a Dominion status settlement that more closely resembled the measure long desired by the moderate imperial Irish of Britain's colonies. In April 1921 Maurice Moore, the veteran Connaught Ranger who had two decades earlier secretly connived from the front with the anti-war press, returned to South Africa as an envoy of Dáil Éireann. He was received warmly by his old adversary Jan Smuts, then Prime Minister of South Africa, who lent his public support for a resolution of the Irish troubles that would give Ireland a measure of independence no less than that exercised by South Africa.[17] Just as the pragmatic Fenians deserted the intransigents after 1900, pro-Treaty Sinn Féin and a swath of the IRA embraced the Dominion compromise after December 1921. Just as separatists such as Finerty could, in 1903, "recognize the logic of circumstances" and pursue Home Rule because Ireland "could afford to wait for the rest," so could the supporters of Michael Collins accept the Treaty as "the freedom to achieve freedom."[18] This realignment and the schisms it produced followed a familiar pattern. But the stakes were higher than ever, and Ireland was awash with weapons; infighting devolved this time into a bloody civil war. The hardline minority lost—as it usually did—and subsequent events seemed again to vindicate the moderate position. Irish and South African cooperation within the imperial conference system helped to bring about the enshrinement of the voluntary principle in imperial relations. It was through the privileges conferred by the resulting Statute of Westminster that the returning anti-Treatyites would peacefully dismantle the imperial connection during the 1930s—further isolating the extremists in the process. And it was on a state visit to Canada in 1948 that the successors of the Treaty-ites would announce their intention to formally proclaim Ireland a republic. But the six northern counties remained a focal point for Fenian energies. In the late 1960s, simmering radical republicanism erupted again, driven this time by northern Catholic grievances, sustained in part by transatlantic connections, and carrying an anti-imperial veneer. It even boasted an African backer—this time in the shape of Muammar Gaddafi's Libya (Irish nationalist affinity for the Boers having by then evaporated over the apartheid issue). A host of factors including infiltration by British intelligence and a failure to achieve its stated objectives eventually led this latest iteration of Fenianism to transition, in its turn, to constitutional politics.

* * *

"Ireland's destiny," historian Paul Townend has argued, "was fundamentally dependent on its relationship to the outside world."[19] To understand Irish nationalism, we must look beyond the Irish Sea and consider the imperial worlds that Ireland and its diaspora inhabited. The movements that spanned these worlds were, as Niall Whelehan reminds us, not "singular transnational entities, supported by a unitary people," but rather represented a sort of "polyphonic activism."[20] As this book has shown, global Irish nationalism was the product of "reciprocal interactions" between the homeland and heterogeneous diaspora communities, each distinguished by particular local interests, pressures, and conflicts.[21] The transnational and comparative approach required to trace these interactions also highlights the importance of imperialism in popular nationalist thought. The rejuvenating effect of events in remote South Africa on both physical force and moderate Irish nationalism around the world shows how deeply intertwined were empire and Irish politics. Boer fever, especially in the United States, excited an anti-imperial impulse already present in Irish nationalism—albeit one that tended to be limited, self-serving, and unevenly felt. The ambivalent response of Irish nationalists in the Dominions, taken together with the postwar direction of mainstream nationalism, demonstrates how the desire to advance Irish interests from within the empire could be at least as pronounced as the drive to resist it. Ireland and its diaspora were, like the Boer republics, products of empire after all; active participants in, and beneficiaries of, what Donald Harman Akenson has described as "the greatest single period of land theft, cultural pillage, and casual genocide in world history."[22] Perhaps the outstanding feature of the outpouring of Irish nationalist sympathy for the Boers is how emphatically it surpassed the comparatively lethargic interest in the struggles of nonwhite victims of imperial violence before (and, arguably, after) 1919. For Irish nationalists to permit anything beyond the loosest analogy between themselves and Indians, Zulus, Filipinos, or others would, by the imperial standards of the day, be to tacitly admit their own unfitness for self-government. To identify with the Boer republics, however, was to defend the principal to which they had committed themselves: that as an ancient and civilized white, Christian nation, Ireland had a legitimate entitlement to sovereignty.[23] It is for reasons such as these that Alvin Jackson has described Ireland as "simultaneously a bulwark of the Empire, and a mine within its walls."[24]

In recent years, at the encouragement of scholars, certain institutional initiatives, and President Michael D. Higgins, Irish society has begun to show a willingness to grapple with its imperial legacies, not merely in Ireland's historic role as a victim of empire at home, but as an agent of empire abroad. There remains, nevertheless, a popular inclination both in Ireland and overseas to see Irish nationalism as an uncomplicatedly anti-imperial tradition. But as President Higgins, while publicly criticizing "imperial amnesia," rightly pointed out: "anti-imperialist struggles weren't free of the traits of empire either."[25] Confronting this "Janus-like" character of Irish nationalism, in all its global varieties and with all its selective sympathies, will be a vital part of Ireland's imperial reckoning.[26]

ACKNOWLEDGMENTS

This book emerged from my PhD research at the University of Toronto. It is difficult to overstate the debt I owe to my supervisor, David A. Wilson. His brilliant scholarship inspired me to attempt this project and his supportive and compassionate mentorship helped me get it across the line. This book has benefited greatly from his advice and his keen editorial eye over many drafts. I am grateful to my dissertation committee members Mark McGowan and Paula Hastings, to my examiners Max Mishler and Kevin Kenny, and to my anonymous peer reviewers. Their insightful comments helped me understand what this book was really about when I had lost sight of the wood for the trees.

Research across many continents is time consuming and expensive. This project was made possible by doctoral and postdoctoral fellowships from the Social Sciences and Humanities Research Council of Canada; by the Ontario Graduate Scholarship; and by various travel grants and supplemental funding awarded through the University of Toronto's Department of History, including the Jeanne Armour Graduate Scholarship in Canadian History, and the Jerome Samuel Rotenberg 7To Memorial Graduate Scholarship in British History. During the postdoctoral phase of this project, Glucksman Ireland House at New York University allowed me valuable library access, and the History Department at McMaster University generously provided me with an office and much-needed conviviality. I am grateful to Danny and Christine Vickers, Marianne and Tom Smith, Kevin Lynn, and Deirdre Lynn, for their hospitality in various parts of the world; to the Mealy-O'Farrelly family without whose generosity I would never have made it through my undergraduate studies; and to the Ravensbergen-Hodginses who welcomed me into their family the moment I arrived in Canada. I prevailed upon librarians and archivists almost as much as friends and family, and benefited also from the generous support and advice of many scholars. These included, but are not limited to, my postdoctoral advisor Kevin Kenny, Ciaran O'Neill, Donald Harman Akenson, Dianne Hall, Elizabeth Malcolm, Val Noone, Anne-Maree Whitaker, Rory Sweetman, Malcolm Campbell, William Jenkins, Peter Toner, Barry Kennerk, and others. Thanks to Eric Anderson of Arc Indexing for providing the index. I would also like to thank my friends and colleagues in Toronto, Hamilton, Oxford, New York, Ireland and elsewhere whose good company sustained me in what can be a lonely endeavor.

Above all, I am indebted to Léa Ravensbergen, who has been at my side for every step of this adventure even as she navigated (and excelled in) one of her own. Without her I would be utterly lost.

NOTES

INTRODUCTION

1 *Times* (London), 20 Jan 1900.

2 Quoted in McCracken, *Forgotten Protest*, 90.

3 Lowry, "'The Boers Were the Beginning of the End'? The Wider Impact of the South African War"; Mommsen, "Introduction"; Kuitenbrouwer, *War of Words*.

4 J. A. Hobson, *Imperialism: A Study* (London: Nisbet & Co., 1902); V. I. Lenin, *Imperialism, the Highest Stage of Capitalism* (London: Martin Lawrence, 1934).

5 Saunders and Smith, "Southern Africa, 1795–1910," 617.

6 Nasson, *The Boer War*, 258–65.

7 Foster, *Modern Ireland*, 448.

8 See Kelly, *The Fenian Ideal*, 99, 130, 137, 153, 156–60; Maume, *The Long Gestation*, 29; King, *Davitt*, ch. 14; Whelehan, *Dynamiters*, 86, 130; McGee, *IRB*, 294–9; idem, *Arthur Griffith*, ch. 2; McGarry, *The Rising*, 26, 37, 40, 56, 96, 129; Coogan, *Michael Collins*, 13, 54; Ó Broin, *Revolutionary Underground*, 111, 112, 118; Ward, *Ireland and Anglo-American Relations*, 32–3; aan de Wiel, *The Irish Factor*, 125–9. Dedicated studies are rare and typically short. See Strauss, "God Save the Boer"; Ní Bhroiméil, "The South African War, Empire and the *Irish World*"; Mathews, "Stirring Up Disloyalty."

9 See McCracken, *Forgotten Protest*; idem, *MacBride's Brigade*; "Odd Man Out: The South African Experience"; "'Fenians and Dutch Carpetbaggers': Irish and Afrikaner Nationalisms, 1877–1930"; "Irish Settlement and Identity in South Africa before 1910"; "Michael Davitt's Wartime Visit to South Africa."

10 Fitzpatrick, "Emigration, 1871–1921," 607.

11 Kenny, "Irish Emigration, *c.*1845–1900," 666–8.

12 See for example Akenson, *The Irish in Ontario*; Campbell, *Ireland's New Worlds*.

13 See Wilson, *United Irishmen, United States*; Lynn, "Friends of Ireland: Early O'Connellism in Lower Canada"; idem, "Before the Fenians: 1848 and the Irish Plot to Invade Canada."

14 On exile, see Miller, *Emigrants and Exiles*. On Famine legacy, see Wilson, *Canadian Spy Story*, 22–3, 26–7; on Home Rule see McGowan, *The Imperial Irish*, 32–3.

15 See McGowan, *The Waning of the Green*. On its habitual "resurgence," see Mannion, *A Land of Dreams*. On opposition, see Wilson, ed., *The Orange Order in Canada*; Lynn, "Osmond Esmonde's Dominion Odyssey."

16 Delaney, "Our Island Story"; English, "History and Irish Nationalism"; Mannion and McGarry, eds., *The Irish Revolution: A Global History*; Delaney and McGarry, "Introduction: A Global History of the Irish Revolution"; Barr, *Ireland's Empire*; Carey and Barr, eds., *Religion and Greater Ireland*; Janis, *A Greater Ireland*.

17 *Vindicator and Canada Advertiser* (Montreal), 1 Apr 1831.
18 See Ballantyne, *Webs of Empire*; Crosbie, *Irish Imperial Networks*.
19 Howe, *Ireland and Empire*, 110. The most notorious being the Fenian raids. See Wilson, *Canadian Spy Story*.
20 Lake and Reynolds, *Drawing the Global Colour Line*, 9.
21 Pocock, "The Limits and Divisions of British History," 317.
22 See Kenny, "Diaspora and Comparison"; Lambert and Lester, eds., *Colonial Lives across the British Empire*; Bender, *The 1857 Indian Uprising and the British Empire*.
23 O'Brien, *The Shaping of Modern Ireland*, 13.
24 Nelson, *Irish Nationalists*, 146; McCracken, *Forgotten Protest*, 145.
25 Nelson, *Irish Nationalists*, 145–7.
26 Ibid.; Lowry, "'A Fellowship of Disaffection'"; idem, "Making John Redmond 'the Irish [Louis] Botha.'"
27 McGarry, *The Rising*, 96.
28 James Quinn, "Clarke, Thomas James ('Tom')," in *Dictionary of Irish Biography* (*DIB*), www.dib.ie.
29 See Whelehan, *Dynamiters*.
30 Ibid., 163, 188.
31 Clarke to Kathleen Daly, 21 Jan 1900, MS 49,351/2/14, Tom Clarke and Kathleen Clarke Papers, National Library of Ireland (NLI).
32 Clarke to Kathleen Daly, 5 Nov 1899, MS 49,351/2/1, Clarke Papers, NLI.
33 "Well if they have and they send him to Africa he will fight I know, but it won't be for the English." This fear passed by early January. His brother declined the offer to join him. Clarke to Kathleen Daly, 28 Nov, 24 Dec 1899, 9 Jan 1900, MS 49,351/2/2, 11, 13, Clarke Papers, NLI.
34 Quinn, "Clarke," *DIB*.
35 Clarke to Jim Bermingham, 28 Jan 1900, MS 49,353/1, Clarke Papers, NLI.
36 John E. Redmond, Speech to the House of Commons, 7 February 1900. United Kingdom *Hansard Parliamentary Debates*, Commons Series 4, Vol. 78 (1900), cols. 830–41.
37 For other examples see Lowry, "The Wider Impact of the South African War," 214–8; Douma, "Dutch American Reaction to the Anglo-Boer War"; Martin Bossenbroek, "The Netherlands and the Boer War: Their Wildest Dreams: The Representation of South African Culture, Imperialism and Nationalism at the Turn of the Century," in Wilson, ed., *The International Impact of the Boer War*; William N. Tilchin, "The United States and the Boer War," in ibid.; Martin Kröger, "Imperial Germany and the Boer War: From Colonial Fantasies to the Reality of Anglo-German Estrangement," in ibid.
38 Akenson, *God's Peoples*.
39 Nasson, *Boer War*, 22–3.
40 Smith, *Origins of the South African War*, 17–29.
41 Townend, *The Road to Home Rule*, 31–2.
42 Nelson, *Irish Nationalists*, 127–8.
43 See O'Leary, Ireland and Empire, 25–9, 48–65, 78–9, 87.

44 McGee, *Arthur Griffith*, 37–8; Van Onselen, *Masked Raiders*, ch. 8.

45 Smith, *Origins of the South African War*, 45–7.

46 Saunders and Smith, "Southern Africa, 1795–1910," 611–5.

47 McCracken, *Forgotten Protest*, 32–3; Galbraith, "The British South Africa Company and the Jameson Raid"; *Irish Republic* (New York), 18 Jul 1897, in CBS/13989/S, National Archives of Ireland (NAI).

48 Early studies assigned the blame to capital: see Hobson, *Imperialism* (1902); Lenin, *Imperialism* (1917). Ronald Robinson and John Gallagher emphasized strategic thinking in *Africa and the Victorians* (1963). P. J. Cain and A. G. Hopkins suggested a different sort of economic interpretation in *British Imperialism* (1993): 374–81. A strong case against gold mining as a factor is made in Porter, *The Origins of the South African War* (1980) and Smith, *The Origins of the South African War* (1996). The difficulty of separating gold from strategy is highlighted in Shula Marks, "Rewriting the South African War" (2003).

49 Judd and Surridge, *The Boer War*, 47–50.

50 Nasson, *Boer War*, 53.

51 Mommsen, "Introduction."

52 Nasson, *Boer War*, 258–65.

53 Ibid., 242–7.

54 Ibid., 22, 309.

55 Ibid., 310.

56 Pretorius, "Boer Attitudes to Africans in Wartime"; Nasson, *Abraham Esau's War*, 93–103.

57 Mbenga, "The Role of the Bakgatla of the Pilanesberg in the South African War"; Genge, "The Role of the EmaSwati in the South African War."

58 Tamarkin, "The Cape Afrikaners and the British Empire from the Jameson Raid to the South African War."

59 Judd and Surridge, *The Boer War*, 2–3.

60 McCracken, "Michael Davitt's Wartime Visit to South Africa"; Nelson, *Irish Nationalists*, 128–47; Lowry, "The Wider Impact of the South African War," 211; King, *Michael Davitt*, 472–3; Davitt, *The Boer Fight for Freedom* (1902).

61 Nelson, *Irish Nationalists*, 147; Howe, *Ireland and Empire*, ch. 4.

62 Townend, *Road to Home Rule*, 9.

63 Beatty, *Masculinity and Power in Irish Nationalism*, 4–5.

64 Lowry, "The Wider Impact of the South African War," 209.

65 Clarke to Kathleen Daly, 11 Mar 1900, MS 49,351/2/16, Clarke Papers, NLI.

66 Clarke to Jim Bermingham, 28 Jan 1900, MS 49,353/1, Clarke Papers, NLI.

67 The circular was leaked and printed in *Times*, 20 Jan 1900.

68 Ibid.

69 Ibid.

70 Kelly, *The Fenian Ideal*, 99–102; Funchion, ed., *Irish American Voluntary Organizations*, 80–82.

71 Clarke to Kathleen Daly, 25 Nov 1900, 15 Apr 1901, MS 49,351/2/5&7, Clarke Papers, NLI.

72 "I've a strong hankering during the past month—since I found how your people felt—to go down there." Clarke to Kathleen Daly, 12 May 1900, MS 49,351/2/19, Clarke Papers, NLI.

73 Clarke to Kathleen Daly, 11 Mar 1901, MS 49,351/2/32, Clarke Papers, NLI.

74 MacBride proposed to her that spring, but she did not accept until later. Despite the protests of Gonne's friends, including Yeats and Griffith, they married in 1903. Foster, *Apprentice Mage*, 284–7.

75 Clarke to Kathleen Daly, 11 Mar 1900, MS 49,351/2/16, Clarke Papers, NLI.

76 Convention 1902, OM I 3/2/5, Joseph McGarrity Papers, Digital Library @ Villanova University (DL@VU), 26–7.

77 Ibid.

78 McCracken, *Forgotten Protest*, xx.

79 Belich, *Paradise Reforged*; Berger, *The Sense of Power*.

80 See McGowan, *Waning of the Green*; idem, *The Imperial Irish*; Mannion, *Land of Dreams*; Jenkins, *Between Raid and Rebellion*; Davis, *Irish Issues in New Zealand Politics*; O'Farrell, *The Irish in Australia*.

81 See Ian McGibbon, "The Origins of New Zealand's South African War Contribution," in Crawford and McGibbon, eds., *One Flag, One Queen, One Tongue*, 1–11.

82 For more see Doyle, *Irish Americans, Native Rights and National Empires*.

83 Sean McGarry, WS 368, Bureau of Military History Witness Statements, Military Archives, Dublin (BMH): 10, 14. Quoted in McGarry, *The Rising*, 96.

1. "THE HOUR OF DESTINY"

1 Monthly report, 12 May 1899, in Crime Branch Precis 29 May 1899, CBS/19369/S, NAI.

2 See monthly reports in Crime Branch Precis 21 Apr 1899, CBS/19172/S; 29 May 1899, CBS/19369/S; 21 Jun 1899, CBS/19485/S, NAI.

3 Crime Branch Precis, 21 Jun 1899, CBS/19485/S, NAI.

4 Gosselin's brief comprised the northern half of Britain. On the Special Branch in the 1880s, see Porter, *Origins of the Vigilant State*, 43–8, 50–51, 61, 72, 78, 85–6; Kenna, *War in the Shadows*, 108–114, 210–11; McGee, *The IRB*, 119–121, 132–3. Robert Anderson, best known for his connection with Henri Le Caron and Richard Piggott, was particularly keen to implicate Parnell in Fenian conspiracy. See Campbell, *Fenian Fire*; Porter, *Origins of the Vigilant State*, 88–92; McGee, *IRB*, 181–2; Whelehan, *Dynamiters*, 128; Kenna, *War in the Shadows*, ch. 11; Margaret O'Callaghan, *British High Politics and a Nationalist Ireland*, 111–13; idem, "Richard Pigott, the Fringe-Fenian Press and the Politics of Irish Nationalist Transition to Parnellism," in McGarry and McConnel, eds., *The Black Hand of Republicanism*, 150–59; Ó Broin, *Revolutionary Underground*, 43; idem, *The Prime Informer*, 50–92.

5 Porter, *Origins of the Vigilant State*, 66.

6   His predecessors were Edward George Jenkinson, James Monro, and Robert Anderson. The latter two held the position while simultaneously working as head of the London Metropolitan Police's (LMP) Criminal Investigation Department (CID).

7   These included the Royal Irish Constabulary (RIC), Dublin Metropolitan Police (DMP), Dublin Castle, the CID—which had its own "Special Irish Branch"—British consulates in the United States, an American spy network run by "Agent Z" (who answered to Gosselin), and the ad hoc cooperation of military intelligence and local British and Dominion police forces. The Special Branch was the spider at the center of this sprawling web.

8   Crime Branch Precis, 22 Oct 1899, CBS/20270/S, NAI.

9   Crime Branch Precis, 20 Nov 1899, CBS/20529/S, NAI.

10 Crime Branch Precis, 22 Oct 1899, CBS/20270/S, NAI.

11 Thynne admitted that while there was "very little prospect" of these contingencies arising, the "unsettled state of feeling" was cause for concern. "Activity of suspect F. Dorr as IRB organizer," CBS/21028/S, NAI.

12 David Harrel to Cadogan, 6 Jan 1900, PRO 30/60, G. W. Balfour Papers, The National Archives, Kew (TNA).

13 See O'Brien, *Blood Runs Green*; McGee, *IRB*, 185–6.

14 "Statement of Meyrick Jones," 14 Oct 1896, HO 317/39, Home Office Private Papers, TNA; *Chicago Tribune*, 27 Sep 1895, 5; Gosselin to Matthew White Ridley, 18 Nov 1895, PRO 30/60/13/2, TNA.

15 Gosselin to Mathew White Ridley, 5 Oct 1896, HO 317/39, TNA; McGee, *IRB*, 219–20; Agent Z, "An Argument in favor of a full and complete exposure of the Lyman Wing of the Secret Organisation in the United States of America," HO 317/39, TNA.

16 Gosselin to Mathew White Ridley, 5 Oct 1896, HO 317/39, TNA.

17 *Irish Republic*, 6 Sep 1896, in CBS/121631/S, NAI.

18 "Re-organisation of the IRB," 30 Nov 1894, CBS 9317/S, NAI; Memo by Gosselin re: Secret Societies, 15 Oct 1894, CBS 9117/S, NAI; Memo by John Lowe, 16 Aug 1894 in Reorganisation of Extreme Nationalists, CBS 8882/S, NAI; The Irish National Alliance, CBS 11921/S, NAI; McGee, *IRB*, 241–2. Notable converts included Dr. Mark Ryan, the chief physical force organizer in London; Australian-born Arthur Lynch; organizer James Egan; Anna Johnston and Alice Milligan of Belfast's *Shan Van Vocht*; Maud Gonne and W. B. Yeats; and John MacBride, who likely established an INB circle in Johannesburg. See Ó Broin, *Revolutionary Underground*, 63–5; Clipping from the *Nation*, 13 Jul 1897, in "Irishmen of the Transvaal on British Rule," CBS/11637/S, NAI; Gosselin to Matthew White Ridley, 18 Nov 1895, HO 317/37, Home Office Private Papers, TNA.

19 The assassin was reported to be Patrick "the Fox" Cooney, who was among the men believed to have murdered P. H. Cronin. Gosselin to Sanders, 13 Aug 1896, HO 317/39, TNA. On the Dublin bombings, see Chapter 2 of this book.

20 See Gosselin to Matthew White Ridley, 5 Oct 1896, HO 317/39, TNA; Gosselin to Sanders, 16 Sep 1896, GD433/2/32/20, Arthur J. Balfour Papers, National Records of Scotland (Edinburgh); Robert Anderson to Kenelm Digby, 15 Sep 1896, HO 317/39, TNA; "An argument in favour of a full and complete exposure of the Lyman Wing of the Secret Organisation in the United States of America," 14 Oct 1896, HO 317/39, TNA; *Irish World*, 21 Nov 1896.

21 He was forced to decline the nomination. *New York Times*, 27 Feb 1897, 2.

22 Crime Branch Precis, 8 Jun 1899, CBS/19425/S, NAI.

23 On advanced nationalists' hopes, see Memo by Gosselin to Kenelm Digby, 25 Jan 1898, HO 317/37, TNA; Fred Allan to John Devoy, 29 Dec 1897, MS 18,000/2/3, John Devoy Papers, NLI.

24 King, *Davitt*, 438–9; McGee, *IRB*, 263.

25 John Devoy was among the statement's signatories. *New York Times*, 2 May 1898, 9. Lyman offered President McKinley volunteer brigades from INB ranks. *Tyrone Daily Herald* (Tyrone, PA), 5 May 1898, 11.

26 See *New York Times*, 2 May 1898, 9; Martin Organ to unknown recipient, 24 Apr 1898, CBS/16247/S, NAI; Doyle, *Irish Americans, Native Rights and National Empires*, 183.

27 Crime Branch Precis, 22 Feb 1899, CBS/18696/S, NAI; Kelly, "The End of Parnellism and the Ideological Dilemmas of Sinn Féin," 143–4.

28 Fred Allan to John Devoy, 29 Dec 1897, MS 18,000/2/3, Devoy Papers, NLI.

29 Bull, "The United Irish League"; Maume, *The Long Gestation*, 30–39; O'Brien, *William O'Brien*, chs. 5 and 6.

30 Crime Branch Precis, 16 Jul 1900, CBS/22369/S, NAI; Report of Mr. Waters, C.I. in Crime Branch Precis, 3 Oct 1900, CBS/23008/S, NAI.

31 Crime Branch Precis, 22 Feb 1899, CBS/18696/S, NAI; 21 Apr 1899, CBS/19172, NAI; McGee, *IRB*, 267–8; Kelly, *The Fenian Ideal*, 144–9.

32 Others included Gonne's *L'Irlande Libre* and the Belfast *Shan Van Vocht*. Ó Broin, *Revolutionary Underground*, 98–101; Crime Branch Precis, 22 Mar 1899, CBS/18948/S, NAI.

33 Crime Branch Precis, 21 Apr 1899, CBS/19172, NAI.

34 *Times*, 20 Jan 1900, 4.

35 *Buffalo Times*, 29 May 1899.

36 *Times*, 20 Jan 1900, 4.

37 Ibid.

38 Joseph V. Lawless, WS 1034, BMH, 8–9.

39 Frank Henderson, WS 249, BMH, 1.

40 Hugh Hehir, WS 683, BMH, 16.

41 Seumas Robinson, WS 156, BMH, 2.

42 Mary Clancy, WS 806, BMH, 4.

43 *Irish Times*, 20 Oct 1899; *Daily Nation*, 20 Oct 1899. "Magic lantern exhibition at *Independent* offices," CBS/20191/S, NAI; "Pro Boer and Anti Boer demonstration in College Green," CBS/20202/S, NAI; "Magic Lantern displays and the Boer demonstration in College Green," CBS/20225/S, NAI.

44 "Beresford Place Meeting on Sunday 17 Inst." CBS/20751/S, NAI; McCracken, *Forgotten Protest*, 54–6.
45 *Nation*, 18 Dec 1899; *Independent*, 18 Dec 1899.
46 Kevin O'Shiel, WS 1770, BMH, 60–63.
47 *Freeman's Journal* (Sydney), 3 Mar 1900, 5. Original story in *Irish People*, 20 Jan 1900.
48 *Irish World* (New York), 17 Feb 1900, 12.
49 *Freeman's Journal* (Dublin), 26 Jul 1900, 5; *Irish World*, 18 Aug 1900, 4.
50 Crime Branch Precis, 5 Mar 1900, CBS 21361/S, NAI.
51 Thirty thousand is the more commonly quoted number, though Luke Diver has recently proposed the higher figure. See Diver, "Ireland's South African War 1899–1902."
52 McCracken, "John Ardagh."
53 Ó Corráin, "'A Most Public Spirited and Unselfish Man,'" 74–6.
54 "IRB Meeting—Longford," CBS/20899/S, NAI.
55 "Irish Transvaal Committee—Seditious Placards," CBS/20142/S, NAI.
56 "Seditious Placards," CBS/20244/S, NAI.
57 "Irish Transvaal Committee—Seditious Placards," CBS/20142/S, NAI.
58 Transvaal Committee Minute Book, MS 19,933, NLI; Crime Branch Precis, 20 Nov 1899, CBS/23367/S, NAI.
59 McCracken, *Forgotten Protest*, 42.
60 Lowry, "Nationalist and Unionist Responses" 162.
61 Ibid., 161.
62 Margaret O'Callaghan and Caoimhe Nic Dháibhéid, "MacBride, (Edith) Maud Gonne," in *Dictionary of Irish Biography* (*DIB*), www.dib.ie.
63 Foster, *The Apprentice Mage*, 223.
64 "Conduct of the daughters of Mr McGillicuddy I.R. in distributing seditious leaflets," CBS/20698/S, NAI.
65 See Senia Pašeta, "Nationalist Responses to Two Royal Visits."
66 *United Irishman*, 7 Apr 1900.
67 Levenson, *Maud Gonne*, 169–74; Pašeta, *Irish Nationalist Women*.
68 Pašeta, "Nationalist Responses to Two Royal Visits," 495.
69 Foster, *The Apprentice Mage*, 222–3.
70 Crime Branch Precis, 31 Jul 1900, NAI CBS/22489/S.
71 Sir William Everett to Sanderson, 5 Jan 1901, HO 317/39, TNA.
72 John C. Ardagh, "Irish Defence Schemes, and the Irish Disloyalists, and the Anti-Government Parties in France," 17 Jan 1901, HO 317/39, TNA.
73 aan de Wiel, "French Military Intelligence and Ireland, 1900–1923," 50–52.
74 King, *Davitt*, 473–4.
75 Foster, *The Apprentice Mage*, 227–9; Lowry, "Nationalist and Unionist Responses," 168.
76 Kenny, "Frank Hugh O'Donnell: A Virulent Anti-Semite."
77 Foster, *The Apprentice Mage*, 227.
78 Ibid., 190.

79 *United Irishman,* 30 Jun 1900; Crime Branch Precis, 31 Jul 1900, CBS/22489/S, NAI; Kenny, "Frank Hugh O'Donnell," 31.

80 aan de Wiel, *The Irish Factor,* 128.

81 "Summary of Gonne's activities," 3 Apr 1900, CO 904/202/166, Colonial Office, Irish Papers, TNA.

82 King, *Davitt,* 468.

83 Pašeta, "Nationalist Responses to Two Royal Visits," 493; Ó Broin, *Revolutionary Underground,* 112–4; Lowry, "Nationalist and Unionist Responses," 169.

84 *Freeman's Journal,* 5 May 1900.

85 *Freeman's Journal,* 14 May 1900; McCracken, *Forgotten Protest,* 70; Levenson, *Maud Gonne,* 164–7.

86 Crime Branch Precis, 19 Jan 1900, CBS/20989/S, NAI.

87 Gosselin to Harrel, 20 Nov 1900, CBS/23136/S, contained in TNA CO 904/202/166, TNA.

88 Kenelm Digby to Ritchie, 5 Dec 1900, HO 317/42, TNA.

89 Hugh McCalmont to D.A.G. Ireland, 1 Jan 1900, CBS/20869/S, NAI.

90 "Boer Ambulance party," CBS/21085/S, NAI; "Boer Agents in Ireland," CBS/21069/S, NAI.

91 Minute Book of the Irish Transvaal Committee, MS 19,933, NLI.

92 Report of John Mallon, 19 Jan 1900, CBS/20957/S, NAI.

93 Michael S. Walsh to "Phil," 7 Mar 1900, MS 18,287, Michael S. Walsh Papers, NLI.

94 Anna Johnston to John MacBride, 21 Feb 1900, MS 26,755, Frederick J. Allan Papers, NLI.

95 Kelly, *The Fenian Ideal,* 130.

96 Crime Branch Precis, 21 May 1900, CBS/21888/S, NAI; 15 Jun 1900, CBS/22189/S, NAI.

97 Crime Branch Precis, 16 Jul 1900, CBS/22369/S, NAI.

98 McCracken, *Forgotten Protest,* 42.

99 Andrew Reed to David Harrel, 6 Jan 1900, PRO 30/60, TNA; "Mullingar District Council Sympathy with the Boers," CBS/20754/S, NAI; *Freeman's Journal,* 17 Oct 1899; Lowry, "Nationalist and Unionist Responses," 164–5.

100 "The Dublin Corporation and the Boers," CBS/20684/S, NAI; *Daily Nation,* 12 Dec 1899; *United Irishman,* 16 Dec 1899.

101 On the Liberal Party and the war, see Price, *An Imperial War and the British Working Class.*

102 King, *Davitt,* 469.

103 King, *Davitt,* 477–82; Davitt, *The Boer Fight for Freedom.*

104 *Irish World,* 23 Dec 1899.

105 *Irish World,* 16 Dec 1899.

106 *Irish World,* 23 Dec 1899, 13 Jan, 3 Feb 1900.

107 King, *Davitt,* 445, 449.

108 See Bull, "The United Irish League."

109 McCracken, *Forgotten Protest,* 48.

110 Bull, "The United Irish League," 63.

111 Davis, *Arthur Griffith and Non-Violent Sinn Féin*, 39–40.

112 *Freeman's Journal*, 21 Feb 1900.

113 Ibid.

114 King, *Davitt*, 470; Davis, *Arthur Griffith*, 40.

115 McCracken, *Forgotten Protest*, 144.

116 *United Irishman*, 13 Jan 1900, quoted in Levenson, *Maud Gonne*, 160.

2. "PHYSICAL FARCE"

1 According to the testimony of the Superintendent of the Canal and a civil engineer. *Globe* (Toronto), 26 May 1900; Murray, *Memoirs of a Great Detective*, 461–2.

2 A connection that was otherwise impossible owing to Niagara Falls. The canal had recently been enlarged at the cost of $20 million. *The Canada Year Book 1909*, 351–3.

3 Report of Sergeant Michael Lynch, 1 Nov 1899, CBS 25132/S, NAI; Alun Hughes, "Terrorist Attacks on the Welland Canal," 6–10.

4 Murray, *Memoirs of a Great Detective*, 462–3.

5 *Trenton Evening Times*, 23 Jul 1914.

6 Lynn, "Before the Fenians."

7 *Times*, 20 Jan 1900.

8 Memo by Gosselin re: Secret Societies, 5 Jun 1900, HO 317/37, TNA.

9 *Times*, 20 Jan 1900.

10 The insult became common in UIL circles. King, *Davitt*, 459; *Patriots or Impostors: Which? The Case of the Erin's Hope Branch against the New York Municipal Council of the United Irish League of America* (June 1904), MS 15,236/6, John E. Redmond Papers, NLI, 35.

11 The Patriot War awaits a modern book-length scholarly study. See Allan Greer, "1837–38: Rebellion Reconsidered," *Canadian Historical Review* 76.1 (1995): 1–18, 15; Andrew Bonthius, "The Patriot War of 1837–38: Locofocoism with a Gun?" *Labour/Le Travail* 52 (2003): 9–43.

12 *Hartford Courant*, 15 Sep 1841; *Baltimore Sun*, 23 Sep 1841; Chris Raible, "Benjamin Lett: Rebel Terrorist," *Beaver* (Winnipeg) 82, No. 5 (Oct/Nov 2002): 10–15; Allan J. MacDonald, "Lett, Benjamin," in *Dictionary of Canadian Biography* (*DCB*), www .biographi.ca.

13 Lynn, "Before the Fenians," 83; Belchem, "Nationalism, Republicanism and Exile."

14 William E. Leonard to Thomas William Sweeny, 9 Apr 1866, MssCol 2934, Thomas William Sweeny Papers, New York Public Library (NYPL). I am indebted to David A. Wilson for this excerpt.

15 Vronsky, *Ridgeway*; Wilson, *Canadian Spy Story*.

16 Typescript biographical article about Luke Dillon upon his death by Joseph McGarrity with manuscript annotations, 1930, MS 17,448/17, Joseph McGarrity Papers, NLI.

17 Luke Dillon's Military Record, 27 Aug 1870, MS 17,448/25, McGarrity Papers, NLI; *U.S. Army, Register of Enlistments, 1798–1914*, ancestry.com.

18 Biographical article about Luke Dillon, MS 17,448/17, McGarrity Papers, NLI.

19 Wilson, *Canadian Spy Story*, chs. 14–16.

20 See Le Caron's testimony to the *Times* Special Commission: *Times*, 9 Feb 1889, 8.

21 Biographical article about Luke Dillon, MS 17,448/17, McGarrity Papers, NLI.

22 Desmond McCabe and Owen McGee, "Dillon, Luke," *DIB*. On skirmishing, see Niall Whelehan, "'Cheap as Soap and Common as Sugar': The Fenians, Dynamite and Scientific Warfare," in McGarry and McConnel, eds., *The Black Hand of Republicanism*, 105–120; Máirtín Ó Catháin, "'The Black Hand of Irish Republicanism'? Transcontinental Fenianism and Theories of Global Terror," in ibid., 135–148; Kenna, *War in the Shadows*, ch. 1.

23 *Times*, 31 May 1884, 7.

24 *Times*, 27 Jan 1885, 10; Biographical article about Luke Dillon, MS 17,448/17, McGarrity Papers, NLI.

25 *Times*, 15 Dec 1884, 10; 24 Apr 1886; Devoy, *Recollections of an Irish Rebel*, 212; Desmond McCabe and Owen McGee, "Lomasney, William Francis Mackey," *DIB*.

26 *Times*, 24 Apr 1886.

27 Kenna, *War in the Shadows*, ch. 5.

28 Notes by Joseph McGarrity regarding Luke Dillon's republican career, 1930, MS 17,448/22, McGarrity Papers, NLI; *Times*, 15 Sep 1886, 5.

29 Kelly, *The Fenian Ideal*, 100–102.

30 See Campbell, *Fenian Fire*; Porter, *Origins of the Vigilant State*, 88–92; McGee, *IRB*, 181–2; Whelehan, *Dynamiters*, 128; Kenna, *War in the Shadows*, ch. 11.

31 See O'Brien, *Blood Runs Green*; McGee, *IRB*, 185–6.

32 *Buffalo Express*, 28 Mar 1902, 12.

33 Owen McGee, "Nolan, John," *DIB*.

34 Owen McGee, "Nally, Patrick William," *DIB*.

35 Ó Broin, *Revolutionary Underground*, 53–4.

36 Mallon had made his name breaking the Invincibles. See Donal P. McCracken, "Mallon, John," *DIB*; McCracken, *Inspector Mallon*.

37 Memo by Mallon, 5 Nov 1894, "Movements of John Merna since his return to Dublin," CBS 9204/S, NAI.

38 Memo by Mallon, 1 Mar 1895, "Alleged intention to assassinate Ed. Downes," CBS 9632/S, NAI.

39 "Reports on Exchange Court Explosion," CBS 6234/S, NAI. The Nally Club and the Independent Labourer's Club were also believed to have been behind a series of lesser explosions and attempts at arson in Dublin since October 1891. See Report by Mallon, 28 Jan 1893, CBS 6234/S, NAI.

40 *Freeman's Journal*, 25 Mar 1893, 5; 27 Apr 1893, 6.

41 Gosselin to Under Secretary, May 1894, CBS 8454/S, NAI.

42 *Freeman's Journal*, 28 Nov 1893, 5.

43 Subsequent comments by Gosselin and Mallon suggest that Reid may indeed have been an informant. See Comment by Gosselin on Memo from Mallon, 12 Apr 1894,

CBS 8351/S, NAI; Report of John Mallon, undated (probably 29 Jan 1894), "The Explosives Act Enquiry at the Castle," CBS/8008/S, NAI.

44 *Weekly Independent*, 21 Jan 1894.

45 See *Freeman's Journal*, 28, 29 Nov, 15, 23 Dec 1893, 6, 13 Jan 1894. Walter Sheridan's trial also collapsed amid controversy. *Freeman's Journal*, 10 Feb, 18 Apr, 8 Jun 1894.

46 Ó Broin, *Revolutionary Underground*, 54.

47 Statement of Meyrick Jones, HO 317/39, TNA; Whelehan, *Dynamiters*, 130.

48 Gosselin to Under Secretary, 14 Oct 1894, "John Merna's Arrival," CBS 9103/S, NAI.

49 Gosselin to Mathew White Ridley, memo on the "Dynamite Conspiracy of 1896," 5 Oct 1896, PRO/30/60/13/2, TNA.

50 Statement of Meyrick Jones, PRO/30/60/13/2, TNA.

51 Crime Branch Precis, 22 Mar 1899, CBS 18948/S, NAI.

52 Crime Branch Precis, 21 May 1900, CBS 21888/S, NAI.

53 Crime Branch Precis, 6 May 1899, CBS 19257/S, NAI; 29 May 1899, CBS 19369/S, NAI; 15 Jun 1900, CBS 22189/S, NAI. Gosselin was less confident "that Allan had changed the opinion of a life time."

54 Report of Sergeant Patrick Gaffney, Manchester, 1 Nov 1899, CBS 25132/S, NAI; Report of Sergeant Michael Lynch, 1 Nov 1899, CBS 25132/S, NAI; "John Nolan, John Merna, John Rowan and John Walsh gone to America," 10 Nov 1899, CBS 20420/S, NAI.

55 CBS 25132/S, NAI.

56 *Times* (Philadelphia), 18 Nov 1899, 4.

57 Manifest of *S. S. Rhynland*, Passenger Lists of Vessels Arriving at Philadelphia, Pennsylvania, The National Archives at Washington, DC, RG 85, T840, ancestry.com.

58 Addresses found on John Nolan, CBS 21857/S, NAI.

59 *Brooklyn Daily Eagle*, 30 Apr 1900, 1; *Daily Nation* (Dublin), 21 May 1900.

60 *Evening Star* (Washington, DC), 1 May 1900, 11.

61 McGee, *IRB*, 214.

62 Articles of Union between the T. H. and the U. B., Philadelphia, Monday 4 September 1899, OM I 3/1/2 McGarrity Papers, DL@VU.

63 William Crossin to John Nolan, 19 Mar 1900, CBS 21857/S, NAI.

64 John Walsh to Mary Walsh, 26 Mar 1900, (Private collection of P. Earls)—courtesy of Dr. Barry Kennerk.

65 J. McInerney to John Nolan, 20 Mar 1900, CBS 21857/S, NAI.

66 CBS 21857/S, NAI; *Trenton Evening Times*, 23 Jul 1914, 11.

67 Dillon to Devoy, 12 Dec 1894, MS 18,003/9/3, Devoy Papers, NLI.

68 Biographical article about Luke Dillon, MS 17,448/17, McGarrity Papers, NLI.

69 James O'Sullivan to John Devoy, 15 Apr 1897, MS 18,010/22/4, Devoy Papers, NLI.

70 *Philadelphia Inquirer*, 13 Jun 1897, 20; 23 May 1898, 5; 28 Nov 1899, 3. He also organized a major "Irish Fair" in aid of the Irish Political Prisoners' Fund, but controversy erupted when "genuine soil from Ireland" on which visitors were charged

10 cents to walk turned out to have been "common Philadelphia hothouse soil." *Philadelphia Inquirer*, 24 Dec 1898, 2.

71 Articles of Union, OM I 3/1/2, McGarrity Papers, DL@VU.

72 *Globe*, 31 May 1900.

73 *Buffalo Express*, 28 Mar 1902.

74 The men were also noticed by US Immigration Agent O'Meara. *Globe*, 25 May 1900.

75 Murray and Speer, *Memoirs of a Great Detective*, 465.

76 *Globe*, 26 May 1900, 20.

77 "Four persons on whom I can rely to a very considerable extent say that no one could vouch for Nolan so long as he can get money and drink." Mallon to J. J. Jones (undated, probably 9 Apr 1895), in "Death of James Boland, Movements of John Nolan," CBS/9789/S, NAI.

78 *Globe*, 25 May 1900.

79 *Globe*, 31 May 1900.

80 *Buffalo Express*, 22 Apr 1900, 9.

81 Murray is now best known as the inspiration for the titular protagonist of *Murdoch Mysteries*, Canada's longest-running hour-long drama series.

82 *Buffalo Express*, 28 Mar 1902.

83 Murray, *Memoirs of a Great Detective*, 463.

84 Dillon made similar complaints when he later read Murray's *Memoirs* in prison. "Laurence Brennan" (Luke Dillon) to "Friend Curran," 4 May 1907, MS 17,438/19, McGarrity Papers, NLI.

85 *Trenton Evening Times*, 23 Jul 1914, 11.

86 Ibid.

87 *Buffalo Express*, 28 Mar 1902, 14; *Globe*, 26 May 1900.

88 That the attack was done in "revenge for the establishing of grain elevators at Port Colborne and Montreal by the Conners syndicate" was the "more generally accepted theory" for several days. *Globe*, 23, 24 Apr 1900.

89 *Buffalo Express*, 23 Apr 1900, 1.

90 *New York Tribune*, 24 Apr 1900.

91 CBS 21899/S, NAI; Sherwood, Memorandum for the Deputy Minister of Justice, 1 May 1900, RG18-E, Vol. 3106, Reel C-13857, Dominion Police Letterbooks, Library and Archives Canada (LAC).

92 A. P. Sherwood, Memorandum for the Deputy Minister of Justice, 1 May 1900, RG18-E, Vol. 3105, Reel C-13856, LAC, 155–6.

93 Murray and Speer, *Memoirs of a Great Detective*, 466–70.

94 Ibid., 471.

95 A. P. Sherwood to R. A. Pinkerton, 27 Jan 1900, RG18-E, Vol. 3104, Reel C-13855, LAC.

96 A. P. Sherwood to R. A. Pinkerton, 30 April 1900, RG18-E, Vol. 3105, Reel C-13856, LAC.

97 *Globe*, 18 May 1900.

98 A. P. Sherwood to E. F. B. Johnson, 18 May 1900, RG18-E, Vol. 3106, Reel C-13857, LAC.

99 *Globe*, 24 May 1900, 4.

100 Ibid.

101 *Globe*, 26 May 1900, 15, 20, 25.

102 Ibid.

103 *Kingston Whig*, 28 May 1900, 2.

104 Ó Broin, *Revolutionary Underground*, 115–6.

105 Report by John Mallon, 28 Jan 1893 in CBS/6234/S, NAI; "The Transvaal War &c." CBS/20957/S, NAI.

106 "Alleged intention to injure army barracks," CBS/21056/S, NAI; Crime Branch Precis, 21 May 1900, CBS/21888/S, NAI.

107 Mallon to Harrel, 19 May 1900, in "Visit of Joe Mullet and Fitzharris to America," CBS/21880/S, NAI.

108 J. F. McCarthy to Arthur Griffith, undated, in "Visit of Joe Mullet and Fitzharris to America," CBS/21880/S, NAI. Gosselin queried whether the letter was intended for the police to read, but Mallon insisted there was "no doubt" it was "genuine."

109 *Glasgow Herald*, 24 Nov 1899.

110 Mallon to Harrel, 19 May 1900, in "Visit of Joe Mullet and Fitzharris to America," CBS/21880/S, NAI.

111 Crime Branch Precis, 31 Jul 1900, CBS/22489/S, NAI; 21 Aug 1900, CBS/22648/S, NAI; 8 Sep 1900, CBS/22758, NAI.

112 *Sun* (New York), 25 May 1900.

113 *Brooklyn Daily Eagle*, 27 May 1900; *Sun* (New York), 28 May 1900.

114 *Sun* (New York), 28 May 1900; *Brooklyn Daily Eagle*, 29 May 1900; *Buffalo Weekly Express*, 31 May 1900; *Buffalo Courier*, 11 Jun 1900.

115 *Irish World*, 16 Jun 1900.

116 *Brooklyn Daily Eagle*, 21 Jun 1900.

117 *Irish World*, 9, 16, 30 Jun 1900.

118 *Brooklyn Daily Eagle*, 23 Jun 1900.

119 *Globe*, 7 Jul 1900, 21; 31 Jul 1900, 4; A. P. Sherwood to E. M. Platt, Warden of Kingston Penitentiary, 4 Jul 1900, RG18-E, Vol. 3105, Reel C-13856, LAC, 399; Percy Sanderson to Lord Salisbury, 15 Jun 1900, CBS 22222/S, NAI.

120 A. P. Sherwood, Dominion Police—Supplementary Estimates, 11 Jul 1900, RG18-E, Vol. 3105, Reel C-13856, LAC, 465–6.

121 See for example Carpenter & Crowe to A. P. Sherwood, 15, 25 Jul 1900, RG18-E, Vol. 3105, Reel C-13856, LAC, 452, 528.

122 *Globe*, 8 May 1900, 4; 30 Jul 1900, 10.

123 *Globe*, 30 Jul 1900, 10.

124 *Globe*, 10 Jul 1900.

125 Ibid.

126 This convention is mentioned obliquely in the report of the following convention, which survives. Report of Clan na Gael Convention, Washington, DC, 1902, OM I 3/2/5, McGarrity Papers, DL@VU. See also Crime Branch Precis, 21 Aug 1900, CBS 22648/S, NAI.

127 *Ottawa Journal*, 13 Jul 1900.

128 *Globe*, 19 May 1900, 21.

129 Crime Branch Precis, 2 Jul 1900, CBS 22283/S, NAI.

130 By October 1901 he described the "apathy and want of life in secret societies" as "a state of affairs for which I take some credit." Gosselin to Kenelm Digby, 17 Oct 1901, HO 317/41, TNA.

131 Gosselin to Sir Andrew (surname unknown), 23 Apr 1900, in "Information from Major Gosselin as to an attempt to blow up the Welland Canal," 24 Apr 1900, CBS 21675/S, NAI.

132 *Trenton Evening Times* (Trenton, NJ), 23 Jul 1914, 11; Luke Dillon to John Revens, 17 Dec 1904, MS 17,438/8, McGarrity Papers, NLI.

133 Clan na Gael circular on death of Luke Dillon, 17 Jan 1930, MS 17,448/16, McGarrity Papers, NLI.

134 Biographical article about Luke Dillon, MS 17,448/17, McGarrity Papers, NLI.

135 Articles of Union, OM I 3/1/2, McGarrity Papers, DL@VU.

136 Nolan and Walsh's wives were given pensions. Crime Branch precis, 31 Jul 1900, CBS 22489/S, NAI.

137 Contemporaries didn't think so either. A widely reprinted story noted that they "were despatched from Ireland to America almost simultaneously with the departure of the *Sardinian* [the vessel carrying the Canadian contingent to South Africa] from Quebec." *Sun* (New York), 29 May 1900.

138 *Trenton Evening Times* (Trenton, NJ), 23 Jul 1914, 11.

139 *Buffalo Express*, 23 Apr 1900, 1.

140 A. P. Sherwood, Dominion Police—Supplementary Estimates, 11 Jul 1900, RG18-E, Vol. 3105, Reel C-13856, LAC, 465–6.

141 David Omissi and Andrew Thompson, "Introduction: Investigating the Impact of the War," in Omissi and Thompson, eds., *The Impact of the South African War*, 8.

142 Whelehan, *Dynamiters*, 86.

3. "EITHER IRISH OR GERMAN, OR A VERY BAD MIXTURE OF BOTH"

1 *Call*, 29 Oct 1899.

2 Úna Ní Bhroiméil, "Anti-Imperial Rhetoric in the *Chicago Citizen*, 1898–1902," in McMahon, de Nie, and Townend, eds., *Ireland in an Imperial World*, 246.

3 Ibid., 259.

4 *Call*, 22 Sep 1899.

5 *Chronicle*, 24 Oct 1899l *Los Angeles Times*, 1 Nov 1899; see also Kuitenbrouwer, *War of Words*.

6 *Chronicle*, 4 Nov 1899.

7 *Chronicle*, 24 Nov 1899.

8 *Chronicle, Call,* 24 Nov 1899.

9 *Chronicle, Examiner,* 30 Nov 1899.

10 *Chronicle,* 4 Mar 1900.

11 *Chronicle,* 27 Dec 1899; *Call, Examiner,* 3 Jan 1900; Report of Agent X, 18 Jan 1900, FO 115/1176, TNA.

12 *Chronicle,* 10 Feb 1900.

13 *Examiner,* 28 Oct, 20 Nov 1899; *Call,* 4 Nov 1899.

14 Fennell and King, *John Devoy's Catalpa Expedition,* 84–6, 181; *Chronicle,* 17 Feb 1900.

15 *Call,* 17 Feb 1900; *Chronicle,* 4 Mar 1900.

16 *Chronicle,* 11 Nov 1899, 4 Mar 1899; *Examiner,* 17 Feb 1900.

17 *Call,* 3 Mar 1900.

18 Miller, *Chants for the Boer,* 8, 17, 23, 27.

19 *Chicago Tribune,* 28 Feb 1900, 10.

20 See Walsh and Foley, "Father Peter C. Yorke, Irish-American Leader"; Shott, *Mediating America.*

21 *Call,* 14 Mar 1900.

22 "Distribution of printed copies of speech by Father Yorke on Robt. Emmet," 31 Jul 1900, CBS 22441/S, NAI; "Seditious Pamphlets," 30 Jul 1900, CBS 22478/S, NAI.

23 Convention 1902, Washington, DC, OM I 3/2/5, McGarrity Papers, DL@VU.

24 *Chronicle, Call,* 24 Nov 1899.

25 *Call,* 24 Dec 1899.

26 *Call, Examiner,* 7 Jan 1900.

27 *Examiner,* 18 Mar 1900; *Semi-Weekly Spokesman Review* (Spokane, WA), 1 Apr 1900. In the east a translation was provided for performance at pro-Boer meetings— including one attended by John Devoy—by Professor Ernest Held of Syracuse. See *Wilkes-Barre Record* (PA), 17, 20 Mar 1900.

28 *Examiner,* 18 Mar 1900.

29 *Chronicle,* 4 Mar 1900.

30 Laidlaw to Pauncefote, 10 Jan 1900, FO 115/1174, TNA.

31 *Chronicle,* 11 Jan 1900.

32 *Seattle Post-Intelligencer,* 8, 9 Jan 1900; *Colfax Gazette,* 26 Jan 1900; 1900 United States Census, Huntsville, Washington, digital image s.v. "Paul Kruger," ancestry .com.

33 *Chronicle,* 11 Jan, 4 Mar 1900; *Call,* 14 Jan, 9 Feb 1900; *Oakland Tribune,* 25, 26 Jan 1900; Laidlaw to Pauncefote, 31 Jan 1900, FO 115/1175, TNA.

34 *Los Angeles Times,* 11 Dec 1901.

35 Laidlaw to Pauncefote, 7 Jun 1900, FO 115/1178, TNA.

36 Laidlaw to Pauncefote, 11 Dec 1899, FO 115/1173, TNA; Laidlaw to Pauncefote 10, 31 Jan 1900, FO 115/1174, TNA.

37 *Oakland Tribune,* 27 Jan 1900.

38 *Call,* 21 Jun 1900. Leach subsequently persuaded the state judge to transfer the case to federal court as it took place on federal government property. *Chronicle,* 13, 19 Jul 1900. However, the federal court judge refused to consider and sent it back to the

state court. *Chronicle, Call,* 3 Aug 1900. Reports of the case stop there. Either Leach paid the full amount, settled out of court, or O'Brien let the matter drop. In 1901 a supposedly unconnected scandal broke when it was discovered that $30,000 had been stolen from the Mint. The Chief Clerk was held responsible. In 1907 Theodore Roosevelt appointed Leach Director of the United States Mint. See Leach, *Recollections of a Newspaperman.*

39 Report of Agent X, 15 Feb 1900, FO 115/1176, TNA; *Call,* 13 May 1900.

40 *Chronicle,* 30 Nov 1899; *Examiner,* 30 Nov 1899, 17 Feb, 3 Mar 1900.

41 *Chronicle,* 30 Nov 1899, 7 Apr 1900.

42 *Call,* 24 Oct 1898.

43 *Evening Post* (San Francisco), 22 Nov 1899, clipped in Pickersgill to Pauncefote, 25 Nov 1899, FO 115/1173, TNA.

44 Pickersgill to Pauncefote, 25 Nov 1899, FO 115/1173, TNA.

45 Pickersgill to Pauncefote, 20, 21 Dec 1899, FO 115/1173, TNA; Pickersgill to Pauncefote, 6 Jan 1900, Laidlaw to Pauncefote, 10 Jan 1900, FO 115/1174, TNA.

46 The case of Agent X was first written about by Graeme S. Mount and Michael D. Stevenson, whose work was brought to my attention by David A. Wilson. See Mount, *Canada's Enemies,* ch. 2, "Agent X and the Boer War, 1900."

47 Pickersgill to Pauncefote, 28 Apr 1900, FO 115/1177, TNA.

48 Pickersgill to Pauncefote, 26 Mar 1900, FO 115/1176, TNA.

49 Report of X, 18 Jan 1900, FO 115/1176, TNA; Cormac, Donohoe & Baum to Pickersgill, 11 May 1900, FO 115/1178, TNA.

50 Report of X, 16, 18 Jan, 15 Feb 1900, FO 115/1176, TNA.

51 Cormac, Donohoe & Baum to Pickersgill, 7 Mar 1900, FO 115/1176, TNA; 11 May 1900, FO 115/1178, TNA; Pickersgill to Pauncefote, 26 Mar 1900, FO 115/1176, TNA.

52 On illicit shipments, see Pickersgill to Pauncefote, 25 Jan 1900, FO 115/1174, TNA; 26 Mar 1900, FO 115/1176, TNA; 30 Mar 1900, FO 115/1177, TNA.

53 *New York Tribune,* 26 Dec 1899, *Chronicle,* 1 Jan 1900.

54 *Democrat and Chronicle* (Rochester, NY), 27 Dec 1899.

55 *New York Times,* 27 Dec 1899; *Ottawa Citizen,* 26 Dec 1899.

56 *New York Times,* 27 Dec 1899.

57 Sherwood to Robert A. Pinkerton, 13, 27 Jan 1900, RG18-E, Vols 3106, 3128, LAC.

58 *Seattle Post-Intelligencer,* 5 Jan 1900; Laidlaw to Pauncefote, 8, 10 Jan 1900, FO 115/1174, TNA.

59 *Seattle Post-Intelligencer,* 5 Jan 1900.

60 Report of X, 16 Jan 1900, FO 115/1176, TNA.

61 Pickersgill to Pauncefote, cable, 18 Jan 1900, FO 115/1176, TNA.

62 Note by Pickersgill in Report of X, 7 May 1900, FO 115/1177, TNA.

63 Pickersgill to Pauncefote, cable, 2 Feb 1900, FO 115/1175, TNA; Report of X, 28 Jan 1900, FO 115/1176, TNA.

64 J.F.M. to Pickersgill, 5 Feb 1900, FO 115/1176, TNA.

65 Cormac, Donohoe & Baum to Pickersgill, 8 Feb 1900, FO 115/1175, TNA.

66 Report of X, 15 Feb 1900, FO 115/1175, TNA; *Call*, 4 Mar 1896, 6 Jan 1900; *Chronicle*, 4 Nov 1899; *Examiner*, 31 Mar 1900.

67 Cormac, Donohoe & Baum to Pickersgill, 17 Feb 1900, FO 115/1175, TNA.

68 Undated note by Pickersgill at foot of J.F.M. to Pickersgill, 6 Feb 1900, FO 115/1175, TNA; F.S. Hussey to Pickersgill, 10 Mar 1900, FO 115/1175, TNA; Pickersgill to JFM, 16 Mar 1900, FO 115/1175, TNA; Pickersgill to Pauncefote, 26 Mar 1900, FO 115/1176, TNA.

69 Undated note by Pickersgill at foot of J.F.M. to Pickersgill, 6 Feb 1900, FO 115/1175, TNA; T.E.K. Cormac to Pickersgill, 1 Mar 1900, FO 115/1175, TNA.

70 JFM to Pickersgill, 22 Mar 1900, FO 115/1175, TNA. Pickersgill apparently felt JFM might still reach out again. See Pickersgill to Pauncefote, 16 May 1900, FO 115/1177, TNA.

71 Word had previously been sent to Esquimalt after Agent X's report on 18 Jan 1900. Lieutenant Governor T. R. McInnes to Provincial Secretary, 19 Jan, 2 Feb 1900; McInnes to Captain Fagen, 9 Feb 1900, GR-0443.A, Vol. 3, Lieutenant Governor's Papers, British Columbia Archives (BCA).

72 *Chronicle*, 27 Feb 1900.

73 Cormac to Pickersgill, 1 Mar 1900; Report of X, 4 Mar 1900, FO 115/1175, TNA.

74 *Victoria Daily Colonist*, 22 May 1900.

75 *Evening Sentinel* (Santa Cruz), 5 Apr 1900.

76 *Call*, 8 Apr 1900; Sgt. William R. Atkins to Attorney General of B. C., 9 Apr 1900; P. Boynes Reed, J. P., to Attorney General of B. C., 12 Apr 1900, GR-0429, Box 5, File 4, Attorney General Correspondence, BCA.

77 *Los Angeles Times*, 20 May 1900; *Plain Speaker* (Hazleton, PA.), 21 May 1900; *Globe* (Toronto), 23 May 1900. The *Victoria Daily Colonist* disputed these stories, alleging the incident Bennett claimed took place in mid-May actually occurred months earlier. See 22 May 1900.

78 *Inter-Ocean* (Chicago), 23 May 1900.

79 *Atlanta Constitution*, 22 Apr 1900.

80 Pickersgill to Pauncefote, 18 May 1900, FO 115/1177, TNA.

81 Report of X, 4 Mar 1900, FO 115/1176, TNA.

82 Louis Cnopius was "indignant" with Van Baggen, complaining "he has nothing to risk, he has not even any property in this country." By late March the "Cnopiae" were "badly frightened." Reports of X, 5, 23 Mar 1900, FO 115/1176, TNA.

83 Report of X, 13 Mar 1900, FO 115/1176, TNA; 22, 24 Mar 1900, FO 115/1177, TNA.

84 Report of X, 24 Mar 1900, FO 115/1177, TNA.

85 See JFM's description in Cormac, Donohoe & Baum to Pickersgill, 8 Feb 1900, FO 115/1175, TNA.

86 Report of X, 27 Apr 1900, FO 115/1177, TNA.

87 Report of X, 7 May 1900, FO 115/1177, TNA.

88 Report of X, 19 Jun 1900, FO 115/1178, TNA.

89 Report of X, 28 Mar 1900, FO 115/1177, TNA.

90 Cormac, Donohoe & Baum to Pickersgill, 25 Apr 1900, FO 115/1177, TNA.

91 Wellesley Moore to Pauncefote, 18 Jul 1900, FO 115/1179, TNA.

92 Copies of Agent X's reports are enclosed in F. S. Hussey to Maclean, 1 May 1900, GR-0429, Box 05, File 05, BCA.

93 Report of X, 24 Apr 1900, FO 115/1177, TNA.

94 Report of X, undated (probably 19 Jun 1900), FO 115/1178, TNA.

95 Cormac, Donohoe & Baum to Wellesley Moore, 20 Jun 1900, FO 115/1178, TNA.

96 Cormac, Donohoe & Baum to Wellesley Moore, 14 Jul 1900, FO 115/1179, TNA.

97 Cormac, Donohoe & Baum to Wellesley Moore, 16 Jul 1900, FO 115/1179, TNA.

98 Pickersgill to Pauncefote, 18 May 1900, FO 115/1177, TNA.

99 A. P. Sherwood to Donald Ross, 2 Aug 1900, RG18-E, Vol. 3105, Reel C-13856, LAC.

100 Hussey to Maclean, 2, 23 May 1900, GR-0429, Box 05, File 05, BCA.

101 Wellesley Moore to Pauncefote, 20 Jul 1900, FO 115/1179, TNA.

102 Report of X, 22 Mar 1900, FO 115/1177, TNA.

103 Hussey to Maclean, 2 May 1900, GR-0429, Box 05, File 05, BCA.

104 Report of X, 4 Mar 1900; Cormac, Donohoe & Baum to Pickersgill, 7 Mar 1900; Pickersgill to Pauncefote, 26 Mar 1900, FO 115/1176, TNA. Cora Driffield and her lodgers are listed in 1900 United States Census, San Francisco, California, digital image s.v. "Cora Driffield," ancestry.com. One, Gerard J.M.E. D'Aquin seemed to have been chiefly occupied in training fox terriers for dog shows. Report of X, 28 Jan, 15 Feb, 13 Mar 1900, FO 115/1176, TNA. *Call*, 24 Aug 1899, 23 Apr 1900; *Examiner*, 17 Mar, 23 Apr 1900. The other, E.J.F. Penninck, may have been related to James Penninck, former member of the Netherlands Society and the US Marine Corps, reported to be fighting on the Boer side in South Africa. *Call*, 9 Mar 1891, 24 Oct 1899.

105 Carrie Cnopius was one of them. See for example *Examiner*, 3 Jan, 3 Mar 1900. Helen Edith Grey was mentioned twice in connection with Transvaal Committee meetings, and Flora Langhead once. See *Call*, 27 Dec 1899; *Sacramento Record-Union*, 8 Feb 1900. Mrs. Theodore Richards and the wives of Transvaal Committee members Charles Flanagan and Jeremiah Donovan were active in the ladies' AOH and the pro-Boer themed St. Patrick's Day preparations but were not named at any Transvaal Committee meetings. See *Chronicle*, 27 Feb 1900; *Call*, 19 Feb 1900, 1 Jul 1900, 8 Apr 1901.

106 *Chronicle*, 4 Mar 1900.

107 She was born Susanna Vogel but went by her own mother's maiden surname. *Examiner*, 17 Apr 1900; Birch, *History of the War in South Africa*, 161–5.

108 1891 England Census, Croydon, Surrey, digital image s.v. "Lincoln D. W. Woodford"; "Washington W. Woodford," ancestry.com.

109 *Salt Lake Tribune*, 16 Dec 1910; *Evening World* (New York), 18 Jan 1913; *Call*, 19 Jan 1913.

110 *Kansas City Gazette*, 2 Apr 1900; *Herald* (Los Angeles), 6 May 1900. The family lived at 1543 York St. *Ballenger & Richards Twenty-Fifth Annual Denver City Directory*, 1166.

111 They were married at Tucson on 3 June 1897. See *Chronicle*, 28 Sep 1900; *Examiner*, 5 Jul 1900.

112 The mine was at Helvetia, Arizona. *Arizona Daily Star* (Tucson), 14 Jan 1900; 1900 United States Census, Helvetia, Arizona, digital image s.v. "Lyman [sic] Woodford," ancestry.com. Working as fireman: *City of Tucson General and Business Directory for '99–1900*, 52.

113 *Examiner*, 5 Jul, 28 Sep 1900.

114 Her first mention in the local newspapers was in the *Call*, 27 Oct 1899. She appears in a tableau as a Tivoli performer in *Examiner*, 12 Nov 1899.

115 *Chronicle*, 4 Jul 1900.

116 Cormac, Donohoe & Baum to Pickersgill, 7 Mar 1900, FO 115/1175, TNA; *Chronicle, Call*, 24 Nov 1899.

117 1900 United States Census, San Francisco, California, digital image s.v. "Mercedes E. Newsam," ancestry.com. She is listed as a boarder in the Cnopius's building at 727 Pine.

118 See for example Reports of X, 16 Jan, 15 Feb, 4, 5, 13 Mar 1900, FO 115/1176, TNA. *Examiner*, 7 Jan, 23, 24, 25 Feb, 18 Mar 1900; *Chronicle*, 4 Mar 1900; *Call*, 17 Feb 1900.

119 Report of X, 15 Feb 1900, FO 115/1176, TNA.

120 The lyrics were translated into English by Charles D. South. *Examiner*, 18 Mar 1900; *Call*, 24 Mar 1900; *Semi-Weekly Spokesman Review*, 1 Apr 1900.

121 "Stage-door Johnnies" were the obsessive male fans of female theatrical performers. *Examiner*, 24 Mar 1900.

122 Pickersgill to Pauncefote, 26 Mar 1900, FO 115/1176, TNA.

123 *Call*, 1 Apr 1900; *L.A. Herald*, 6 May 1900. See also *News-Journal* (Mansfield, OH), 10 Apr 1900 and *Times* (Streator, IL), 24 May 1900 for examples of how far the story spread.

124 *Hayward Review*, 6, 13 Apr 1900. She was on the program for a pro-Boer concert at San Francisco's Mission Music Hall on 4 April, but whether she performed is unclear. *Examiner*, 5 Apr 1900.

125 *Call*, 21 Apr 1900; *Chronicle*, 21, 25 Apr 1900; *Examiner*, 25 Apr 1900.

126 Cormac, Donohoe & Baum to Pickersgill, 11 May 1900, FO 115/1178, TNA.

127 On Woodford and the Macrum controversy, see *Buffalo Times*, 15 Feb 1900; *Napa Journal*, 21 Mar 1900; *Examiner*, 16 Feb 1900; Another supporter of Macrum was Charles F. Grote, who was welcomed in San Francisco by the Transvaal Committee. See *Call*, 16 Feb 1900.

128 *Examiner*, 17 Apr 1900.

129 *Examiner*, 1 Apr 1900.

130 *Examiner*, 17 Apr 1900.

131 In January her mother told a reporter in Tucson that she intended eventually to join her daughter "Mrs Frank Newsam" in San Francisco. Luckily for Sannie Kruger this news did not leave Tucson. *Arizona Daily Star* (Tucson), 14 Jan 1900.

132 See for example Report of X, 24 Apr 1900, FO 115/1177, TNA: "When he leaves on the train I will telephone to R.3451 this message which you will understand. 'Mary is better' which will mean that you can see the man on the arrival of the boat which has just left for the city."

133 Cormac, Donohoe & Baum, "Precis of a conversation held with Agent X by telephone," 2 Jul 1900, FO 115/1178, TNA.

134 Report of X, undated (probably 19 June 1900), FO 115/1178, TNA.

135 Accounts attached to Pickersgill to Pauncefote, 26 Mar 1900, FO 115/1176, TNA; Cormac, Donohoe & Baum to Pickersgill, 8 Feb 1900, FO 115/1176, TNA.

136 *Call*, 9 Feb 1900; *Sacramento Record-Union*, 8, 9 Feb 1900. Hotel registers printed in the *Record-Union* and the *Sacramento Bee* the week of the meeting are similarly devoid of any recognizable names.

137 "[O]n one or two occasions we have authorised X to entertain Mr and Mrs Cnopius, Mrs Dreffield [sic], Mr Van Baggan, etc., at luncheon and at theatre when we were informed by X that these social meetings would doubtless be productive of less guarded conversation, and hence we might obtain information of importance. We would add that X's opinion on this subject has been justified by the result." Cormac, Donohoe & Baum to Pickersgill, 7 Mar 1900, FO 115/1176, TNA. Note they do not mention Sannie Kruger here.

138 *Call*, 20, 22 Jun, 3 Jul, 20 Oct 1901; *Chronicle*, 12, 14, 24 Jun 1901.

139 *Call*, 11 Feb 1902, 1 Oct 1905; *Union and Daily Bee* (San Diego), 26 Jun 1905.

140 *Ukiah Daily Journal*, 2 May 1957, 1 Dec 2008.

141 *New York Tribune*, 16 Dec 1910; *Call*, 19 Jan 1913; *Evening World* (New York), 18 Jan 1913.

142 *Ukiah Daily Journal*, 2 May 1957; *Examiner*, 28 May 1959.

143 *Examiner*, 28 Sep 1900.

144 *Call*, 12 Oct 1901; *Examiner*, 3 Apr 1901.

145 *Call*, 11 Dec 1901, 21 Feb 1902.

146 *Call*, 26 Feb, 13 Mar, 11 Dec 1901.

147 See for example *Irish World*, 21 Jul, 4, 18, 25 Aug, 1, 8, 15, 29 Sep 1900.

4. "PETTY INJURIES"

1 John Finerty, Register of Suspects (American), CO 904/19, TNA.

2 "The Irish National Alliance," CBS/11921/S, NAI.

3 John Corrigan, "United Irish Societies of Chicago (UISC)," in Funchion, ed., *Irish American Voluntary Organizations*, 276–82; Owen McGee, "Finerty, John Frederick," *DIB*.

4 Ní Bhroiméil, "Anti-Imperial Rhetoric in the *Chicago Citizen*, 1898–1902."

5 *Chicago Tribune*, 26 Dec 1899.

6 *Inter Ocean* (Chicago), 19 Nov 1899, 17 Jan 1900; *Chicago Tribune*, 24 Dec 1899, 6, 13 Jan 1900.

7 *Irish World*, 24 Feb 1900.

8 *Chicago Tribune*, 19 Nov 1900; Strauss, "God Save the Boer," 21; McCracken, "Michael Davitt's Wartime Visit to South Africa," 60.

9 Articles of Union, OM I 3/1/2, McGarrity Papers, DL@VU; CBS/1389/S, NAI.

10 Funchion, ed., *Irish American Voluntary Organizations*, 57.

11 *Chicago Tribune*, 19 Nov 1900.

12 Strauss, "God Save the Boer," 2.

13 Paul Rouse, "Cockran, William Bourke," *DIB*; Andrews, "Winston Churchill's Tammany Hall Mentor."

14 Alfred Chasseaud to Bourke Cockran, 16 Mar 1900, MssCol 582, Series 1, A, b. 1 f. 8, William Bourke Cockran Papers, NYPL.

15 Patrick Ford to Bourke Cockran, 20 Mar 1900, MssCol 582, Series 1, A, b. 1 f. 8, Bourke Cockran Papers, NYPL.

16 *New York Times*, 5 Mar 1900.

17 Bourke Cockran to Edwin Burrit Smith, 14 Aug 1900, MssCol 582, Series 1, A, b. 1 f. 9, Bourke Cockran Papers, NYPL.

18 Doyle, *Irish Americans, Native Rights and National Empires*, 263, 266–8, 287, 308; Strauss, "God Save the Boer," 13–15.

19 *Inter-Ocean*, 11 Jun 1900.

20 Dye, "Irish-American Ambivalence toward the Spanish-American War," 104–5, 112.

21 Finerty, *War-Path and Bivouac*, iii; Ní Bhroiméil, "Anti-Imperial Rhetoric in the *Chicago Citizen*, 1898–1902," 257.

22 *Inter-Ocean*, 28 Oct 1901.

23 *Irish World*, 21 Oct 1899.

24 *Indian Chieftain*, 1 Feb 1900.

25 *Freeman* (Indianapolis), 28 Oct 1899; *Irish World*, 6 Oct 1900.

26 *Irish World*, 3 Mar 1900; also 17 Feb, 7, 21 Apr, 9 Jun 1900; *Richmond Planet* (VA), 11 Nov 1899, 7.

27 *Irish World*, 10 Mar 1900.

28 Quoted in Levenson, *Maud Gonne*, 161–2.

29 *Irish World*, 21, 28 Jul, 29 Sep 1900.

30 James A. O'Gowan to John Redmond, 17 May 1900, MS 15, 236/20, Redmond Papers, NLI.

31 See for example references to pro-British meetings and fundraising in Laidlaw to Pauncefote, 11 Dec 1899, 10, 31 Jan, 8 Mar 1900, Pickersgill to Pauncefote, 24 Jan 1900, FO 115/1173, 1174, 1175, 1176, TNA; Wellesley Moore to Pauncefote, 31 Aug 1900, FO 115/1180, TNA. The British embassy sought to aid them through the distribution of pro-British literature. See Pauncefote to Salisbury, 12, 17 Feb, 7 Mar, 10, 20 May 1900, and accompanying enclosures, FO 115/1172, TNA. Some meetings are mentioned in *Examiner* (San Francisco), 31 Mar 1900; *Irish World*, 20 Jan 1900.

32 *Philadelphia Bulletin*, 24 Mar 1900, clipping in "An American Woman" to Bourke Cockran, MssCol 582, Series 1, A, b. 1 f. 8, Bourke Cockran Papers, NYPL.

33 H. Montague Vickers to Bourke Cockran, 14 May 1900, MssCol 582, Series 1, A, b. 1 f. 8, Bourke Cockran Papers, NYPL.

34 Elbert B. Hamlin to Bourke Cockran, 19 May 1900, MssCol 582, Series 1, A, b. 1 f. 8, Bourke Cockran Papers, NYPL.

35 Montagu White to Bourke Cockran, 27 Jul 1900, MssCol 582, Series 1, A, b. 1 f. 9, Bourke Cockran Papers, NYPL.

36 Charles L. Wedding to Bourke Cockran, 13 Jul 1900, MssCol 582, Series 1, A, b. 1 f. 9, Bourke Cockran Papers, NYPL.

37 *Irish World*, 1 Sep 1900; Doyle, *Irish Americans, Native Rights and National Empires*, 268–70.

38 Quoted in *Rock Island Argus*, 24 Jan 1900; Ní Bhroiméil, "Anti-Imperial Rhetoric in the *Chicago Citizen*," 255–6.

39 Crime Branch Precis, 16 Oct 1900, CBS/23069/S, NAI.

40 *Irish World*, 17 Nov 1900. Bryan himself said much the same thing.

41 Bull, "The United Irish League," 76–8.

42 *Irish World*, 10, 17, 24 Feb, 17, 24 Mar 1900.

43 *Inter-Ocean*, 11 Jun 1900.

44 *Irish World*, 17 Nov 1900.

45 The controversy is detailed in the report of the Clan's 1902 convention. See Convention 1902, OM I 3/2/5, McGarrity Papers, DL@VU, 17–8, 26–7.

46 See extract of report from Agent Z, CBS/23690/S in John MacBride, CO904/208/258, TNA, 185–6.

47 McGee, *The IRB*, 294.

48 John Devoy to John MacBride, 14 Mar 1901, MS 26,759, Allan Papers, NLI.

49 *Irish World*, 23 Feb, 19 Mar 1900.

50 *Irish World*, 9 Mar 1901.

51 Convention 1902, OM I 3/2/5, McGarrity Papers, DL@VU, 27; King, *Davitt*, 453–4.

52 Letters from Roderick Kennedy to John Redmond, 18 Jun 1900, 2, 16 Jan, 6 Jun 1901, MS 15,236/12, Redmond Papers, NLI.

53 Convention 1902, OM I 3/2/5, McGarrity Papers, DL@VU, 23–5.

54 Ward, *Ireland and Anglo-American Relations*, 36.

55 *Irish World*, 26 May, 7 Jul 1900.

56 *Irish World*, 7 Jul 1900.

57 *Irish World*, 28 Jul 1900.

58 Patrick Ford to William Bourke Cockran, 21 Aug 1900, MssCol 582, Series 1, A, b. 1 f. 9, Bourke Cockran Papers, NYPL.

59 Theodore Roosevelt to Cecil Spring-Rice, 21 Jan 1900, quoted in Ward, *Ireland and Anglo-American Relations*, 38.

60 Pauncefote to Minto, 5 Jan 1900, MG26-G, Vol. 137, Reel C-772, Sir Wilfrid Laurier Fonds, LAC, 40802–4.

61 Military code: adopted, 1900, XM DA954.M55 1900, McGarrity Papers, DL@VU.

62 Robert Redford to F. W. Borden, 26 Dec 1899, CO 42/875, Colonial Office, TNA, 7–10.

63 John Blunt to Pauncefote, 4 Nov 1899, FO 115/1173, TNA.

64 *Times-Democrat*, 20 Nov 1901.

65 *Los Angeles Times*, 27 Nov 1901; *Seattle Star*, 28 Nov 1901.

66 *Irish World*, 18 Nov 1899.

67 Dumonceaux, "The Canadian Response to the Order of the Midnight Sun and the Alaska Boundary Dispute."

68 Percy Sanderson to Lord Salisbury, 15 Jun 1900, CBS/22222/S, NAI.

69 William Wyndham to Pauncefote, 10 Jul 1900, FO 115/1178, TNA.

70 This "ally," he believed, would "play the part [John J.] Breslin did in helping [James] Stephens to escape from Richmond Prison" in 1865. Gosselin to Digby, date unknown (probably December 1900), CO 42/876, Colonial Office, TNA.

71 John Devoy to John MacBride, 31 Mar 1901, MS 26,759, Allan Papers, NLI.

72 Convention 1902, OM I 3/2/5, McGarrity Papers, DL@VU, 21–2.

73 See for example *Irish World*, 28 Oct 1899, 13 Jan, 28 Apr 1900.

74 *Irish World*, 2 Dec 1899, 6 Jan, 21 Apr 1900.

75 For Kansas City see F. H. Tillotson to Wilfrid Powell, 1 Jan 1900, FO 115/1174, TNA; for Boston see Pauncefote to Salisbury, 23 Jan 1900, FO 115/1172, TNA; for Chicago and the Midwest see William Wyndham to Pauncefote, 14 Feb 1900, FO 115/1175, TNA. Sanderson had Pinkerton men interview Clan executive member John J. Teevens of Boston prior to the departure of the Ambulance Corps. See enclosures in Sanderson to Pauncefote, 20 Feb 1900, FO 115/1175, TNA.

76 Wilfrid Powell to Pauncefote, 2, 5 Feb 1900, FO 115/1175, TNA; Sanderson to Pauncefote, 31 Jan 1900, FO 115/1175, TNA.

77 Sanderson to Pauncefote, 9 Feb 1900, FO 115/1175, TNA.

78 Sanderson was satisfied with the assurances he received from the agency. Sanderson to Pauncefote, 15 Feb 1900, FO 115/1175, TNA.

79 Winton, *Horsing the British Army*, 86.

80 *Sun* (New York), 14 Jul 1901.

81 *St. Louis Post-Dispatch*, 8, 13 Apr 1902.

82 *St. Louis Post-Dispatch*, 13 Apr 1902; *Evening Star* (Washington, DC), 4 Apr 1902.

83 *Evening Star*, 14 Jan 1901.

84 *Boston Globe*, 27 Nov 1900. *Buffalo Enquirer*, 18 Apr 1901.

85 *Times-Democrat* (New Orleans), 5 Apr, 7 Jun 1902.

86 *Baltimore Sun*, 14 Dec 1900. He claimed Churchill tricked him by disguising himself as a clergyman.

87 Winton, *Horsing the British Army*, 87.

88 *Washington Times*, 14 Apr 1901.

89 Pearson was frequently in Washington, DC, and had several audiences with President McKinley and subsequently with President Roosevelt. *Buffalo Enquirer*, 18 Apr 1901; *Buffalo Commercial*, 19 Apr 1901; *Washington Times*, 24 Oct 1901; *Times-Democrat*, 13 Dec 1901.

90 *Times-Democrat*, 11 Aug 1901.

91 *Times-Democrat*, 13 Aug 1901.

92 *St. Louis Post-Dispatch*, 13 Apr 1902.

93 *Times-Democrat*, 11 Aug 1901.

94 *Times-Democrat*, 21 Aug 1901.

95 *Times-Democrat*, 12 Aug 1901.

96 Memo by Gosselin re: Secret Societies, 5 Jun 1900, HO 317/37, TNA. Gosselin was referring to the destruction of the *USS Maine* in Havana harbor in 1898 having acted

as a catalyst for the Spanish-American War. In this case it was later found that the explosion was probably caused by a bituminous coal fire igniting the ship's magazine, and not a mine as originally supposed. The *Mechanician* had no explosive material on board.

97 Cronin, *The McGarrity Papers*, 29. By "falls" here he probably means "levee."
98 Samuel Pearson to William Crossin, 14 Dec 1901, MS 17,438/1, Joseph McGarrity Papers, NLI.
99 Agent Z to Bernard McNello, 27 Aug, 6 Nov 1901, MS 17,495/1, Joseph McGarrity Papers, NLI.
100 *Times-Democrat*, 28 Jan 1902.
101 *Brooklyn Daily Eagle*, 11 Jan 1902; *Wilmington Messenger*, 19 Jan 1902.
102 *Tribune* (Scranton, PA), 20 Jan 1902.
103 *Morning Journal-Courier* (New Haven), 12 Mar 1902; *Fall River Daily Herald* (Fall River, Massachusetts), 31 Mar 1902.
104 *Hartford Courant*, 2 Apr 1902.
105 *Times-Democrat*, 13 Apr 1902.
106 *St. Louis Post-Dispatch*, 13 Apr 1902.
107 Samuel Pearson to Theodore Roosevelt, 1 Feb 1902, in U.S. Congress, *Horses, Mules, etc., Shipped to South Africa*, 2–3.
108 W. W. Heard to John Hay, 29 Mar 1902, U.S. Congress, *Horses, Mules, etc., Shipped to South Africa*, 4–5.
109 *Evening Star* (Washington, DC), 4 Apr 1902.
110 Ibid.; *St. Louis Post-Dispatch*, 13 Apr 1902. U.S. Congress, *Horses, Mules, etc., Shipped to South Africa*, 20–22.
111 *Sun* (New York), 14 Jul 1901.
112 *St. Louis Post-Dispatch*, 9, 13 Apr 1902.
113 *Evening Star*, 4 Apr 1902. Colonel E. H. Crowder was appointed to carry this out. *St Louis Post-Dispatch*, 9 Apr 1902.
114 *Times-Democrat*, 22 Apr 1902.
115 *Times-Democrat*, 3, 8, 10, 13 May 1902.
116 *Times-Democrat*, 16 May 1902.
117 *Times-Democrat*, 24 May 1902.
118 Sessions, *Two Years with the Remount Commission*, 280–1, quoted in Winter, *Horsing the British Empire*, 87.
119 Convention 1902, OM I 3/2/5, McGarrity Papers, DL@VU, 26–7.
120 *Times*, 20 Jan 1900.

5. "JINGOISTIC HYSTERIA"

1 *Irish Standard* (Minneapolis), 29 Dec 1900; *Freeman's Journal* (Dublin), 29 Nov 1900.
2 *Chronicle* (San Francisco), 22 Sep 1900; *Hawaiian Star* (Honolulu), 29 Sep 1900. In another account, probably provided by the Greys themselves, Jane denied having insulted the Queen but admitted to telling the British passengers that she

was "ashamed to belong to such a race of cowards and tyrants." *Irish World*, 13 Oct 1900.

3 *Advocate* (Melbourne), 11 Aug 1900.

4 *Examiner* (San Francisco), 28 Sep 1900.

5 M. Cooney to John Redmond, 26 Sep 1900, MS 15, 236/2, Redmond Papers, NLI.

6 *Irish World*, 13 Oct 1900.

7 *Advocate*, 3, 17 May 1902.

8 *New York Times*, 2 Sep 1900.

9 James Grattan Grey to R. J. Seddon, 15 Feb 1900, in J. Grattan Grey, *Freedom of Thought & Speech in New Zealand, No. 1*, 16.

10 Hirst, "Empire, State, Nation," 154; Wilcox, *Australia's Boer War*, 26–7.

11 Until the mid-twentieth century these national and imperial identities were deeply intertwined. See Bell, *The Idea of Greater Britain*; Berger, *The Sense of Power*; Lake, "British World or New World?"; Meaney, "The Problem of Nationalism and Trans-nationalism in Australian history."

12 See O'Farrell, *The Irish in Australia*; McGowan, *The Waning of the Green*; McGowan, *The Imperial Irish*; Belich, *Paradise Reforged*.

13 O'Farrell, *The Irish in Australia*, 243–4.

14 See for example Farrell, "Irish Rebel, Imperial Reformer: Charles Gavan Duffy and Australian Federation."

15 O'Farrell, *The Irish in Australia*, 234–5.

16 Campbell, *Ireland's New Worlds*, 146. Rosalyn Trigger, describing this phenomenon in the Canadian context, has suggested the term "embedded" nationalism to describe clerically led, inward-looking colonial Irish nationalism, which worked to contain "diasporic" nationalism that looked outwards to transnational networks of lay agitators. Trigger, "Clerical Containment of Diasporic Irish Nationalism: A Canadian Example from the Parnell Era."

17 Malcolm and Hall, *A New History of the Irish in Australia*, 142–4; Amos, *The Fenians in Australia, 1865–1880*; O'Keeffe, "Australia's Irish Republican Brotherhood."

18 O'Farrell, "Varieties of New Zealand Irishness: A Meditation," 28.

19 About 23 per cent of the Australian settler population was ethnically Irish, about one quarter of whom were Protestants. Both groups were quite evenly distributed across rural and urban areas, with Irish Catholics slightly overrepresented in hinterland towns. Assuming 17.25 per cent of Melbourne and Sydney's population in 1901 were Irish Catholics gives us figures of roughly eighty-four to eighty-five thousand each. The total Irish Catholic population of New Zealand can be estimated at between 96,251 and 108,282, depending on whether the Protestant portion of the total is calculated at one quarter or one third (estimates vary). The total population of Auckland was approximately 67,000. For Australia, see Fitzpatrick, *Oceans of Consolation*, 14–19; Fitzpatrick, "Irish Emigration to Nineteenth Century Australia." For New Zealand, see Akenson, *The Irish Diaspora*, 66–9; Hearn, "The Origins of New Zealand's Irish Settlers, 1840–1945"; Galbraith, "The Invisible Irish? Re-Discovering the Irish Protestant Tradition in Colonial New Zealand."

20 Hearn, "Irish Migration to New Zealand to 1915," 57, 68. The exile motif, common in the United States and Australia, also seems to have been less pronounced among New Zealand's Irish emigrants who, O'Farrell suggested, largely "did not wish to be apart" from their neighbors. O'Farrell, "Varieties of New Zealand Irishness," 35; Hall and Malcolm, *A New History of the Irish in Australia*, 10.

21 Remarkably, in 1885 the Orange Order and the Hibernian Australasian Catholic Benefit Society celebrated St. Patrick's Day together in Christchurch. Sweetman, "'The Importance of Being Irish': Hibernianism in New Zealand, 1869–1969," 139; O'Farrell, "Varieties of New Zealand Irishness," 34–5; Sweetman, "How to Behave among Protestants: Varieties of Irish Catholic Leadership in Colonial New Zealand," 89–90.

22 MacDonagh, "Emigration from Ireland to Australia: An Overview," 134.

23 Sweetman, "How to Behave among Protestants"; Sweetman, "The Importance of Being Irish"; Sweetman, *Bishop in the Dock*; Brosnahan, "'Shaming the Shoneens': the Green Ray and the Maoriland Irish Society in Dunedin, 1916–1922"; Brosnahan, "Parties or Politics: Wellington's IRA 1922–1928"; O'Farrell, "Varieties of New Zealand Irishness," 34–5.

24 *New York Times*, 26 Nov 1899.

25 *Advocate*, 5 Jul 1902.

26 R. J. Seddon to J. Grattan Grey, 11 Jun 1896, in Grey, *Freedom of Thought & Speech in New Zealand, No. 1*, 10.

27 *Evening Star* (Dunedin), 29 Jan 1900.

28 J. Grattan Grey to R. J. Seddon, 15 Feb 1900, in Grey, *Freedom of Thought & Speech in New Zealand, No. 1*, 16–17.

29 *Evening Star*, 23 Mar 1900.

30 Grey, *Freedom of Thought & Speech in New Zealand, No. 1*, 8.

31 Ibid., 9–10.

32 J. Grattan Grey, *Freedom of Thought & Speech in New Zealand, No. 2*, 14.

33 Ibid., 16.

34 Ibid., 17.

35 Ibid., 29; *Evening Post* (Wellington), 23 Mar 1900.

36 Ibid., 7–8, 29, 33.

37 Ibid., 70–71.

38 Ibid., 73–4.

39 Ibid., 28. "Osmosis" took issue with Blake's criticisms of British colonialism in the *Otago Daily Times* (Dunedin), 12 May 1900. For more on women's opposition, see Hutching, "New Zealand Women's Opposition to the South African War."

40 Grey, *Freedom of Thought & Speech in New Zealand, No. 2.*, 69–70.

41 Ibid., 6–9.

42 Ibid., 36–72.

43 Ibid., 14.

44 Ibid., 20–23, 29–33.

45 G. Maurice O'Rorke to J. Grattan Grey, 20 Jul 1900, ACHW 8633 7/ 28 R11184622, Richard J. Seddon Papers, Archives New Zealand—Te Rua Mahara o te Kāwanatanga, Wellington (ANZ).

46 *New York Times*, 2 Sep 1900.

47 Reprinted in the *Norfolk Landmark* (Norfolk, VA), 20 Nov 1900.

48 *Evening Post* (Wellington), 21 Aug 1900.

49 *Irish World*, 13 Oct 1900.

50 See *New York Times*, 5, 19 Mar, 14 May, 23 Jul 1899; Extract from Hansard, 29 Aug 1899, ACHW 8633 7/ 28 R11184622, Seddon Papers, ANZ.

51 Extract from Hansard, 29 Aug 1899, ACHW 8633 7/ 28 R11184622, Seddon Papers, ANZ.

52 Report of the Reporting Debates Committee, 14 Sep 1899, ACHW 8633 7/ 28 R11184622, Seddon Papers, ANZ.

53 Report of Committee, 17 Jul 1900, ACHW 8633 7/ 28 R11184622, Seddon Papers, ANZ.

54 Extract from Hansard, 19 Jul 1900, ACHW 8633 7/ 28 R11184622, Seddon Papers, ANZ.

55 G. Maurice O'Rorke to J. Grattan Grey, 20 Jul 1900, ACHW 8633 7/ 28 R11184622, Seddon Papers, ANZ.

56 *New Zealand Tablet* (Dunedin), 14 Dec 1899.

57 *Lyttelton Times*, 7, 8 Aug 1900.

58 *Lyttelton Times*, 8 Aug 1900.

59 See for example James O'Neill's comments on how Grey's actions are "explained when his political and other opinions coincide with the 'irreconcilables' in Irish politics" in a letter to the editor of the *Lyttelton Times*, 14 Apr 1900.

60 *Evening Post* (Wellington), 27, 29 Mar 1900.

61 *Auckland Star*, 1 Feb 1901; *Lyttelton Times*, 25 May 1901.

62 *Evening Post* (Wellington), 16 May, 6 Jun 1902.

63 Collombier-Lakeman, "Ireland, New Zealand and Home Rule," 3.

64 *Auckland Star*, 10 Dec 1901, 7 Jan 1902.

65 *Evening Post* (Wellington), 29 Mar 1900; *Auckland Star*, 1 Feb 1901.

66 *New Zealand Herald* (Auckland), 20 Sep, 14 Nov 1900.

67 *The Press* (Christchurch), 2 Apr 1900.

68 *Irish World*, 27 Oct 1900.

69 Sweetman, "The Importance of Being Irish," 143.

70 *New Zealand Times* (Wellington), 15 Mar 1900; *New Zealand Mail* (Wellington), 22 Mar 1900.

71 *Lyttelton Times*, 17 Mar 1900; *Star* (Christchurch), 17 Mar 1900. Similar addresses to the Queen were sent by the "Irishmen" of Dunedin and Invercargill. *New Zealand Tablet*, 22, 29 Mar 1900.

72 *New Zealand Herald*, 17, 31 Mar 1900.

73 *Evening Star* (Dunedin), 10 Aug 1900.

74 Rory Sweetman, "Cleary, Henry William," in *Dictionary of New Zealand Biography* (*DNZB*), www.teara.govt.nz.

75 Hugh Laracy, "Moran, Patrick," *DNZB*; Rory Sweetman, "Kelly, James Joseph," *DNZB*.

76 For more on the *Tablet* and its editors, see Sweetman, "'How to Behave among Protestants"; Molloy, "Victorians, Historians and Irish History: A Reading of the *New Zealand Tablet*, 1873–1903"; McNamara, "The *New Zealand Tablet* and the Irish Catholic Press Worldwide, 1898–1923."

77 Sweetman, "Cleary, Henry William," *DNZB*; Barr, *Ireland's Empire*, 460–62.

78 *New Zealand Tablet*, 19, 26 Oct 1899.

79 *New Zealand Tablet*, 16 Nov 1899; also 23 Nov 1899; 12 Apr, 26 Jul 1900.

80 See for example *Catholic Register* (Toronto), 10, 24 Nov, 1 Dec 1899, 11, 18 Jan 1900; *Northwest Review* (Winnipeg), 21 Nov, 5 Dec 1899; 9, 16 Jan 1900; *Freeman's Journal* (Sydney), 28 Oct, 4, 11 Nov 1899, 6 Jan 1900.

81 *New Zealand Tablet*, 5, 19 Oct 1899; 11 Jan, 8 Feb, 7 Dec 1900.

82 *New Zealand Tablet*, 15 Feb 1900.

83 Barr, *Ireland's Empire*, 202–3.

84 *New Zealand Tablet*, 4 Jan 1900.

85 *New Zealand Tablet*, 12 Jul 1900.

86 *New Zealand Tablet*, 8 Mar 1900.

87 *New Zealand Tablet*, 8 Mar 1900.

88 *New Zealand Tablet*, 22 Mar 1900.

89 *New York Times*, 24 Dec 1899.

90 Reprinted in *Advocate* (Melbourne), 16 Feb 1901, dated 29 Dec 1900. Grey later favorably contrasted the German treatment of Samoans with the "policy of spoliation" endured by Maori. In New Zealand this was dismissed as more anti-Seddon crankery. The implied sympathy with Maori dispossession is indeed difficult to reconcile with his earlier comments. *New Zealand Mail* (Wellington), 24 Jul 1901.

91 *New Zealand Tablet*, 19 Oct 1899.

92 *New Zealand Tablet*, 26 Jul 1900.

93 Belich, *Paradise Reforged*.

94 *New Zealand Times*, 30 Jan 1906.

6. "STRICTLY CONSTITUTIONAL"

1 *Evening Star*, 23 Mar 1900.

2 *Advocate*—the first appeared 3 May 1902, the last 25 Oct 1902.

3 *Advocate*, 3 May 1902.

4 *Advocate*, 10 May 1902.

5 *Advocate*, 31 May 1902.

6 *Advocate*, 31 May 1902.

7 See interview with the *Irish People*, reprinted in *Advocate*, 26 Jan 1901.

8 *New Zealand Herald*, 22 May 1901.

9 *New Zealand Times*, 13 Jul 1901.

10 A. E. Cahill, "Moran, Patrick Francis (1830–1911)," *Australian Dictionary of Biography* (*ADB*), adb.anu.edu.au. The argument echoes others made by Irish Catholics in the late nineteenth century that the Irish had first discovered North America. See Carey and Barr, "Introduction: Religion and Greater Ireland" in idem, eds., *Religion and Greater Ireland*, 17.

11 Stuart Macintyre, "Rentoul, John Laurence (1846–1926)," *ADB*.

12 *New Zealand Tablet*, 9 Aug 1900; *Advocate*, 11 Aug 1900; Saunders and Summy, *The Australian Peace Movement*, 13.

13 See his three-part review in *Advocate*, 24, 31 May, 7 Jun 1902. Rentoul may have been swayed by Grey's decision to present him as the authority on Australasian literature, basing the entirety of his chapter on that subject on an interview Rentoul gave to the Perth *West Australian*. James Grattan Grey, *Australasia: Old and New*, 197–210.

14 Reprinted in *Irish Standard*, 9 Nov 1901. Grey also had much to say about indecent theater productions and mammon worship.

15 From the *Irish World*, reprinted in *Advocate*, 18 Jan 1902.

16 "Our Chief Pro-Boer on his Travels," reported the Dunedin *Evening Star*, 25 Sep 1901.

17 Reprinted in *Advocate*, 25 Jan 1902.

18 See Grey's obituary, *Advocate*, 28 May 1931.

19 On the *Age*'s attacks on Michael Davitt, see *Advocate*, 7 Oct 1899. For mentions of Grey as editor of the *Advocate*, see his obituary in *Advocate*, 28 May 1931; James, "From beyond the Sea: the Irish Catholic Press in the Southern Hemisphere," Table 4.1, 83.

20 Patrick Naughtin has argued that it was Australia's most important Irish national-ist journal. See Naughtin, "*The Melbourne Advocate*, 1868–1900: Bastion of Irish Nationalism in Colonial Victoria."

21 Geoffrey Serle, "Winter, Joseph (1844–1915)," *ADB*; Sally O'Neill, "Gunson, William Henry (1828–1901)," *ADB*.

22 King, "Michael Davitt and Australia 1895," 26.

23 *Advocate*, 18 Nov 1899.

24 *Advocate*, 16 Dec 1899.

25 *Advocate*, 23 Jun 1900.

26 The comparison is 493,956 in Melbourne versus 815,862 in New Zealand. *Age*, 27 Apr 1901; "Report on the results of a census of the colony of New Zealand taken for the night of the 31st March, 1901," Statistics New Zealand, stats.govt.nz.

27 *Advocate*, 21 Jun 1902.

28 Saunders and Summy, *The Australian Peace Movement*, 15.

29 *Evening Post* (Wellington), 21 Aug 1900; *New Zealand Herald*, 9 Apr 1902.

30 At the meeting mentioned above, for example, the speakers included Grey, Rent-oul, Co. Down-born Protestant Home Ruler Henry Bournes Higgins MP, and Australian-born Catholic Labour MLA Dr. William Maloney. *Advocate*, 21 Jun 1902.

31 *Advocate*, 17 May 1902.
32 *Advocate*, 16 Jun 1900. There were already branches in Sydney, Adelaide, and one in Gympie, Queensland, run by the ex-convict John Flood, veteran of the Fenian raid on Chester Castle. Chris McConville, "O'Donnell, Nicholas Michael (1862–1920)," *ADB*.
33 *Advocate*, 21 Jul 1900.
34 Even Morgan Jageurs, one of Melbourne's most prominent Irish nationalist leaders for decades, was among them. *Advocate*, 16 Jun 1900.
35 *Advocate*, 25 Aug 1900.
36 *Advocate*, 2 Feb 1901.
37 *Advocate*, 9 Feb 1901.
38 *Advocate*, 6 Oct 1900.
39 John Redmond to H. B. Higgins, 28 Feb 1883, MS 1057/7, Redmond to Higgins, 1 Nov 1905, MS 1057/118, Archbishop Thomas Carr to Higgins, 22 Sep 1895, MS 1057/8, Henry Bournes Higgins Papers, National Library of Australia (NLA); John Rickard, "Higgins, Henry Bournes (1851–1929)," *ADB*.
40 Higgins lost his state seat at Geelong in November 1900, but was elected to represent North Melbourne in the first federal parliament four months later. J. Laurence Rentoul to Higgins, 19 Nov 1900, MS 1057/73, Higgins Papers, NLA; *Age*, 2 Nov 1900; Rickard, "Higgins," *ADB*.
41 Even the *Age* called it "a stupid calumny" but admitted its likely effectiveness at the Geelong polls. *Age*, 31 Oct 1900.
42 *Advocate*, 6 Oct 1900.
43 *Advocate*, 13 Oct 1900.
44 See McQuilton, "Resisting the Siren Call of Empire? Kelly Country during the Boer War and the First World War"; McQuilton, *Australia's Communities and the Boer War*.
45 Wilcox, *Australia's Boer War*, 26; Connolly, "Australian Attitudes to the Boer War," 219.
46 *Freeman's Journal*, 9 Jun 1900; *Advocate*, 23 Jun 1900. Commissioner Gahan "gave Mr. Seitz credit for having the courage of his opinions, but he would sack him all the same. (Cheers.)"
47 John Anderson and Geoffrey Serle, "Watt, William Alexander (1871–1946)," *ADB*. Watt's mother was Irish.
48 *Advocate*, 5 May 1900.
49 A failed uprising of gold diggers at Ballarat against licensing fees. It assumed radical democratic trappings and comprised a significant Irish cohort. O'Farrell, *The Irish in Australia*, 91–2; Connolly, *On Every Tide*, 159–61.
50 Owen McGee, "Lynch, Arthur Alfred," *DIB*. Gosselin noted in May 1895 that "Lynch is living on his wits and is in the hands of Mark Ryan." CBS 9862/S, NAI. See also CBS 9117/S, NAI.
51 McCracken, "Arthur Lynch at War," 127. McCracken's is the best account of Lynch's involvement in South Africa.

52 Gillingham was known to the Special Branch. "Secret Organization in Co Mayo," CBS/20974/S, NAI; "Irishmen of the Transvaal on British Rule," CBS/11637/S, NAI; Van Onselen, *Masked Raiders*, 185.

53 McCracken, *MacBride's Brigade*, 94.

54 Ibid., 94–6; McCracken, "Arthur Lynch at War," 128.

55 Arthur Lynch to Mark Ryan, 22 Aug 1900, MS 26,757, Allan Papers, NLI; McCracken, "Arthur Lynch at War," 132, 136.

56 McCracken, "Arthur Lynch at War," 129, 131.

57 McCracken, *MacBride's Brigade*, 96; McCracken, "Arthur Lynch at War," 129, 131.

58 McCracken, *MacBride's Brigade*, 97–8; McCracken, "Arthur Lynch at War," 132, 136. McCracken warns that advanced nationalists' dislike of Lynch means that some accusations against his commando's character should be treated with caution.

59 King, *Davitt*, 480–81.

60 Michael Davitt to John MacBride, 30 Apr 1900, MS 26/757, Allan Papers, NLI; McCracken, "Arthur Lynch at War," 133. For more see McCracken, "Michael Davitt's Wartime Visit to South Africa"; King, *Davitt*, ch. 14.

61 *Freeman's Journal* (Dublin), 11 Jun 1900. Between May and June, he revised the combined number in both brigades downwards from 3,000 to 500, but even the lower figure is probably generous.

62 Solomon Gillingham to unnamed (probably Mark Ryan or Michael Davitt), 27 Mar 1900, MS 26,757, Frederick J. Allan Papers, NLI.

63 *Catholic Press* (Sydney), 9 Jun 1900.

64 *Sun* (New York), 1 Oct 1900.

65 On Lynch's tour, see Edward Lauterbach to William Bourke Cockran, 19 Oct 1900, MssCol 582, Series 1, A, b. 1 f. 10, Bourke Cockran Papers, NYPL; *New York Tribune*, 19 Oct 1900; *Buffalo Evening News*, 24 Nov 1900; *Boston Globe*, 10 Oct, 2, 5 Nov 1900.

66 McGee, "Lynch," *DIB*.

67 Arthur Lynch to William Bourke Cockran, 27 Dec 1900, MssCol 582, Series 1, A, b. 1 f. 10, Bourke Cockran Papers, NYPL.

68 CBS/23481/S, NAI.

69 *Advocate*, 6 Oct, 10 Nov 1900, 26 Oct 1901.

70 Arthur Lynch to John Redmond, 22 May 1900, MS 15,202/1, Redmond Papers, NLI.

71 Arthur Lynch to John Redmond, 7, 19 Sep, 12 Oct 1901, MS 15,202/1, Redmond Papers, NLI.

72 Open letter from Lynch to John J. Forde, secretary of the UIL, 10 Oct 1901, published in *Freeman's Journal* (Dublin) and reprinted in *Advocate*, 30 Nov 1901. "Better the meanest Constitutionalist than a turn-coat like this," responded the Irish National Club of London. *Times Union* (Brooklyn), 9 Nov 1901. It also annoyed Davitt, who felt physical force could be useful in certain circumstances. See his special correspondence, dated 31 Oct 1901, to the *Advocate*, 14 Dec 1901.

73 *Advocate*, 2 Nov 1901. Two Sydney Catholic papers echoed the same cautious encouragement: *Freeman's Journal*, 2 Nov 1901; *Catholic Press*, 2 Nov 1901.

74 *Age*, 27 Nov 1901.

75 *Advocate*, 30 Nov 1901.

76 Davitt believed it reflected pro-Boer sentiment, rather than any popular fondness for Lynch himself. King, *Davitt*, 489–90. See also Kelly, "Radical Nationalisms, 1882–1916," 46–7.

77 Arthur Lynch to John Redmond, 12 Oct 1901, MS 15,202/1, John E. Redmond Papers, NLI.

78 Wilcox, *Australia's Boer War*, 267; McCracken, "Arthur Lynch at War," 137–8.

79 *Advocate*, 26 Jul 1902.

80 *Rex v. Arthur Lynch*, Statement of Mrs. Lynch, 25 Jan 1903, MS 15,202/2, Redmond Papers, NLI.

81 *Advocate*, 26 Jul 1902.

82 Quoted in Wilcox, *Australia's Boer War*, 268.

83 See Wilcox, *Australia's Boer War*, ch. 14; Wilcox, "Pardon Me for Being an Historian."

84 *Advocate*, 17 May, 7, 21 Jun 1902.

85 *New York Times*, 1 Feb 1903; *New York Tribune*, 29 Jan 1903; *Advocate*, 21 Mar 1903. Afrikaners and Irish Canadians were also reportedly silent. *Age*, 28 Jan 1903.

86 *Advocate*, 30 May 1903.

87 Annie Lynch claimed to have received a cable from "some Australian nationalists" in August but does not name them. Annie Lynch to John Redmond, 15 Aug 1903, MS 15,202/2, Redmond Papers, NLI.

88 John Redmond to Charles Russell, 15 Oct 1903, Redmond Papers, NLI MS 15,223/5.

89 One story alleges that the crucial factor was Davitt's persuading Sir Thomas Lipton, the millionaire friend of Edward VII, to raise the matter with the king on a yachting trip in December 1903. King, *Davitt*, 490. Donal McCracken, however, finds this "highly unlikely." McCracken, "Michael Davitt's Wartime Visit to South Africa," 61. Certainly Annie Lynch was dogged in her correspondence with John Redmond throughout 1903. Immediately following his release, Lynch wrote to Redmond to say "thank you for all your exertions on my behalf." Arthur Lynch to John Redmond, 25 Jan 1904, MS 15,202/1, Redmond Papers, NLI.

90 John Redmond to Arthur Lynch, 15 Jul 1907, MS 15,202/1, Redmond Papers NLI.

91 McCracken, "Arthur Lynch at War," 139.

92 *Advocate*, 11 Sep 1909.

93 *Advocate*, 4 Dec 1909.

94 Patrick McMahon Glynn to Ellen Glynn, 16 May 1900, MS 4653/1/188, Patrick McMahon Glynn Papers, NLA.

95 Patrick McMahon Glynn to Ellen Glynn, 16 May 1900, MS 4653/1/188, McMahon Glynn Papers, NLA.

96 *Advocate*, 21 Apr 1900.

97 See O'Donnell, "Irish-Australia and the 1798 Centenary in Sydney."

98 *Advocate*, 28 Apr 1900.

99 Connolly, "Australian Attitudes to the Boer War," 218.

100 Graham, "Arthur Hill Griffith and Opposition to the Boer War," 65.

101 P. M. Glynn and H. B. Higgins supported restrictions on non-white immigration. Hall and Malcolm, *A New History of the Irish in Australia*, 98–101.

102 Graham, "Arthur Hill Griffith and Opposition to the Boer War," 57, 60.

103 *Advocate*, 21 Apr 1900.

104 *Advocate*, 11 Nov 1899. For more on Aborigines, race, and the war, see Maynard, "Aborigines and the Boer War"; Karageorgos, "War in a 'White Man's Country.'"

105 Hall and Malcolm, *A New History of the Irish in Australia*, 54; Connolly, *On Every Tide*, 157; McGrath, "Shamrock Aborigines: The Irish, the Aboriginal Australians, and Their Children."

106 Graham, "Arthur Hill Griffith and Opposition to the Boer War," 55.

107 Barr, *Ireland's Empire*, 398; Williams, "Moran, Mannix and St. Patrick's Day.

108 *Freeman's Journal*, 24 Feb 1900; Fowler, "NSW Catholic Clergy and the Boer War," 44–5; McQuilton, "Resisting the Siren Call of Empire?" 60.

109 For a fuller account see Fowler, "NSW Catholic Clergy and the Boer War."

110 See Patrick F. Kavanagh, *A Popular History of the Insurrection of 1798: Derived from Every Available Written Record and Reliable Tradition* (Dublin: M. H. Gill & Son, 3rd ed., 1880).

111 Fowler, "'Firebrand Friar.'"

112 Copy of letter from Michael Kelly to Moran, undated, MS 6265/5/65, Patrick O'Farrell Papers, NLA.

113 Wooding, "The 'Language in Which They Spoke in '98': The Irish Language and the Centenary of 1798 in Ireland and Australia."

114 *Freeman's Journal*, 24 Feb 1900.

115 *Freeman's Journal*, 9 Jun 1900.

116 *Freeman's Journal*, 11 Nov, 9 Dec 1899.

117 *Freeman's Journal*, 10 Mar 1900.

118 *Freeman's Journal*, 11, 25 Nov, 9 Dec 1899, 24 Mar 1900. Dunne died in July 1900, aged 81. For more on Dunne and other pro-war clerics such as the Jesuit John Robert Fagan see Fowler, "NSW Clergy and the Boer War"; McQuilton, *Australia's Communities and the Boer War*, 35.

119 *Freeman's Journal*, 16 Jun 1900.

120 Graham, "Arthur Hill Griffith and Opposition to the Boer War," 69–70.

121 Anthony D'Arcy, "O'Haran, Denis Francis (1854–1931)," *ADB*; Bede Nairn, "Coningham, Arthur (1863–1939)," *ADB*.

122 Baker, *Australian Women War Reporters*, 9–19.

123 See for example *Catholic Press*, 28 Apr 1900, 5 Jan, 9 Feb 1901.

124 *Catholic Press*, 21, 28 Oct, 4 Nov 1899.

125 Wood, an Englishman, later founded and acted as president of the Australian Anti-War League in 1902. When his activism almost cost him his job, he sought advice from Henry Bournes Higgins. He was rescued by the intervention of Prime Minister Edmund Barton and the Labor Party. See Saunders and Sumy, *The Australian Peace Movement*, 13; Field, *The Forgotten War*, 33; R. M. Crawford, "Wood, George Arnold

(1865–1928)," *ADB*; George Arnold Wood to Henry Bournes Higgins, 6 May 1902, MS 1057/85, Henry Bournes Higgins Papers, NLA; Letters from George Arnold Wood to Mrs Holman, Jan-Feb 1902, MLDOC 697, State Library of New South Wales.

126 Michael McKernan, "Ryan, John Tighe (1870–1922)," *ADB*; Patrick O'Farrell, "Kelly, Michael (1850–1940)," *ADB*.

127 *Catholic Press*, 8 Mar 1902.

128 *Catholic Press*, 18 Nov, 2 Dec 1899; Fowler, "NSW Clergy and the Boer War," 47.

129 *Catholic Press*, 1 Mar 1902.

130 He was no older than 38. *Sydney Morning Herald*, 23 May 1903; Fowler, "NSW Clergy and the Boer War," 51–2. Weeks later Patrick O'Shea of Wagga claimed Bunbury was taking strychnine for a heart condition and that his death must have been accidental. *Catholic Press*, 11 Jun 1903.

131 See Cooper, *Forging Identities*, 156–85.

132 O'Farrell, *The Irish in Australia*, 241.

133 Hall and Malcolm, *A New History of the Irish in Australia*, 101.

134 *Advocate*, 12 Mar 1904.

135 *Advocate*, 2 Jul 1904.

136 *Advocate*, 13 Aug 1904.

137 See Gerald Patrick Fitzgerald, "The Last of the Western Australian Fenians, 1869–1918," undated, MLDOC 1804, State Library of New South Wales.

7. "A FEW IDIOTS"?

1 *Gazette* (Montreal), 13 Oct 1899.

2 *Gazette*, 18 Oct 1899.

3 Logue to O'Dwyer, 20 Sep 1900, MS 6265/5/181, O'Farrell Papers, NLA.

4 In the two years before May 1900, the Order had accepted 36,400 new members across the United States and Canada. *True Witness and Catholic Chronicle* (Montreal), 19 May 1900. The AOH grew strongly in the ten years up to around 1905 but declined in the ten years that followed. McGowan, *Waning of the Green*, 154–5; Jenkins, *Between Raid and Rebellion*, 298–9. In 1907, there were 841 members in Quebec and 4,437 across all of Canada. Mannion, "I'm as Good an Irishman as You," 32.

5 *True Witness*, 13 Jan 1900.

6 *Gazette*, 18 Oct 1899.

7 *Gazette*, 19 Oct 1899.

8 *Gazette*, 18 Oct 1899.

9 *Gazette*, 19 Oct 1899.

10 *Gazette*, 21 Oct 1899.

11 *Irish World*, 4 Nov 1899.

12 *Irish World*, 18 Nov 1899.

13 *Irish World*, 18 Nov 1899. In March 1900, McCaffrey's outspoken pro-Boerism earned him mention in Special Branch circulars—a rare distinction among Irish Canadian nationalists. Crime Branch Precis, 16 Apr 1900, CBS 21614/S, NAI.

14 Coffey, "*The True Witness and Catholic Chronicle*."

15 *True Witness*, 28 Oct 1899.

16 *True Witness*, 28 Oct 1899.

17 *True Witness*, 11, 18 Nov 1899. "The daily newspapers may mutilate the reports of their meetings, publish whatever they please in regard to those meetings." *True Witness*, 2 Dec 1899.

18 *True Witness*, 28 Oct 1899.

19 *True Witness*, 4 Nov 1899.

20 *True Witness*, 18 Nov 1899.

21 *True Witness*, 25 Nov 1899.

22 *True Witness*, 2 Dec 1899.

23 The account of Devoy's visit is taken from *True Witness*, 20 Jan 1900. A shorter report is also given in *Gazette*, 16 Jan 1900.

24 Horrall, "Canada and the Irish Question."

25 *Catholic Register* (Toronto), 10 Nov 1899.

26 *True Witness*, 20 Jan 1900.

27 See McKenna, *The Irish American Dynamite Campaign*, 61–7; Whelehan, *Dynamiters*, 123–4, 136, 158, 266, 269, 271.

28 Whelehan, *Dynamiters*, 187.

29 *Freeman's Journal* (Dublin), 3 Oct 1898.

30 Prison narratives had for decades been a staple of the Fenian tradition. See Murphy, "Narratives of Confinement: Fenians, Prisons and Writing, 1867–1916."

31 *Gazette*, 19 Mar 1900.

32 *True Witness*, 24 Mar 1900.

33 McConville, *Irish Political Prisoners 1848–1922*, 347, n. 72.

34 Moir, "The Problem of a Double Minority"; McGowan, *Imperial Irish*, 58.

35 O'Leary, *Grattan O'Leary*, 2–4. I am indebted to David A. Wilson for this reference.

36 *Globe*, 18 Oct 1899.

37 Miller, *Painting the Map Red*, 440–44; Heath, *A War with a Silver Lining*, 82–6.

38 *Irish World*, 6 Oct 1900.

39 *Irish World*, 12 May 1900.

40 *Irish World*, 30 Jun 1900.

41 *Catholic Register*, 10 May 1900.

42 *True Witness*, 5 May 1900.

43 *Irish World*, 17 Mar 1900. See also 10 Mar 1900.

44 Lynn, "Before the Fenians," 83.

45 *Catholic Register*, 10 May 1900.

46 *True Witness*, 19 May 1900; Convention, 1902, OM I 3/2/5, McGarrity Papers, DL@ VU, 5–8. John J. Curley, for example, was delegate for D 72, District 7.

47 *Boston Globe*, 11 May 1900.

48 *Boston Globe*, 10 May 1900.

49 *Boston Globe*, 9 May 1900.

50 *True Witness*, 19 May 1900.

51 See Wilson, "The Fenian World of Jeremiah O'Gallagher."

52 *True Witness*, 19 May 1900; *Boston Globe*, 10 May 1900.

53 *Boston Globe*, 8 Jan 1900; *Gazette*, 15 Jan 1900.

54 *Boston Globe*, 10 Jan 1900.

55 Mannion, "I'm as Good an Irishman as You," 26.

56 See McGowan, *Waning of the Green*; McGowan, *Imperial Irish*.

57 Mark G. McGowan, "Boyle, Patrick," *DCB*.

58 *Globe*, 19 Mar 1900.

59 *Globe*, 19 Mar 1900; *Catholic Register*, 22 Mar 1900.

60 "Cheers and counter-cheers mingled fiercely before the fervor of the audience spent itself." *Catholic Union and Times* (Buffalo), 22 Mar 1900.

61 *Catholic Register*, 12 Apr 1900.

62 McGowan, *Imperial Irish*, 57.

63 *Irish Canadian* (Toronto), 23 May 1901.

64 *Irish World*, 7, 14 Apr 1900.

65 *True Witness*, 18 Nov 1899.

66 *San Juan Islander*, 18 Jan 1900.

67 *Vancouver Daily World*, 7 Feb 1900; *Seattle Post-Intelligencer*, 10 Jan 1900.

68 *Seattle Post-Intelligencer*, 10 Jan 1900.

69 *Vancouver Daily World*, 9, 13 Jun 1900.

70 *Vancouver Daily World*, 9 Jun 1900.

71 *Globe*, 30 Apr 1900.

72 *Globe*, 12, 13, 14 Oct 1899.

73 *Gazette*, 28 Dec 1899.

74 *Globe*, 16 Jan 1900.

75 *Globe*, 18 Jan 1900.

76 *Globe*, 20 Feb 1900.

77 *Globe*, 22 Feb 1900.

78 *Catholic Register*, 1 Mar 1900.

79 *Catholic Register*, 3 May 1900.

80 *True Witness*, 27 Jan 1900; *Catholic Register*, 15 Feb 1900.

81 *Sentinel and Orange and Protestant Advocate*, 5, 26 Oct 1899. On Canadian Orangeism see Wilson, ed., *Orange Order in Canada*; Houston and Smyth, *The Sash Canada Wore*; Smyth, *Toronto, the Belfast of Canada*; Jenkins, *Between Raid and Rebellion*.

82 *Sentinel*, 12 Oct 1899.

83 *Catholic Register*, 1 Mar 1900.

84 *Catholic Register*, 10 Nov 1900.

85 *Catholic Register*, 22 Mar 1900.

86 *Catholic Register*, 1 Mar 1900.

87 *True Witness*, 27 Jan 1900; *Catholic Register*, 15 Feb 1900.

88 *Catholic Register*, 5, 12, 19, 26 Oct 1899.

89 *Catholic Register*, 26 Oct, 17, 24 Nov 1899.

90 *Catholic Register*, 12 Oct 1899; 15 Feb, 1 Mar 1900.

91 *Catholic Register*, 21 Dec 1899.

92 *Catholic Register*, 21 Dec 1899.

93 *Catholic Register*, 28 Dec 1899.

94 *Catholic Register*, 15 Feb 1899.

95 *Catholic Register*, 22 Mar 1900.

96 *Catholic Register*, 14 Jun 1900.

97 *Catholic Register*, 4, 11 Jan 1900; 29 Mar 1900.

98 *Catholic Register*, 25 Jan 1900.

99 *Catholic Record*, 31 Mar 1900.

100 *Catholic Record*, 31 Mar 1900.

101 Granted, Latchford was more effusive than others in his praise for Irish "loyalty in its highest sense." *Catholic Record*, 31 Mar 1900.

102 *Catholic Register*, 9 Aug 1900.

103 McGowan, *Imperial Irish*, 55, 61.

104 "Approved and recommended by the Archbishops, Bishops and Clergy" read the masthead of the editorial page each week.

105 McGowan, *Imperial Irish*, 55–6.

106 *Catholic Register*, 1 Feb 1900.

107 *Irish World*, 25 Nov 1899; 3 Feb, 3 Mar 1900; *Catholic Register*, 10 Nov 1899; 11 Jan, 22 Feb 1900.

108 *Catholic Register*, 1 Dec 1899.

109 *Northwest Review*, 5 Dec 1899.

110 *Northwest Review*, 21 Nov 1899.

111 *Northwest Review*, 9 Jan 1900.

112 *Northwest Review*, 7, 21 Nov 1899; 23 Jan 1900.

113 *Northwest Review*, 5 Dec 1899; 16 Jan 1900.

114 *Catholic Record*, 3 Feb 1900.

115 *Catholic Record*, 24 Mar, 19 May 1900. It was argued that the war should also entitle Ireland to a Catholic University. 5 May 1900.

116 *Catholic Record*, 24 Mar, 21 Apr 1900.

117 *Catholic Record*, 11, 25 Nov, 16 Dec 1899, 13, 20 Jan, 3 Feb 1900.

118 *Catholic Record*, 17 Feb, 10 Mar 1900. Editorials still occasionally piped up to defend Boers from unreasonable jingo attacks. For example, 16, 23 Jun 1900.

119 *Catholic Register*, 1 Feb 1900.

120 *Catholic Register*, 5, 12 Apr 1900.

121 *Catholic Register*, 19, 26 Apr 1900.

122 *Catholic Register*, 5 Apr 1900.

123 *Catholic Register*, 31 May 1900. The *Record* also remarked that Chinese news "now almost envelopes the South African in a total eclipse." 30 Jun 1900.

124 *Catholic Register*, 26 Apr, 3, 24 May 1900.

125 *Catholic Register*, 28 Jun 1900.

126 The *Record* was particularly leery about trusting the factionalists again, suggesting that with a few exceptions "[i]t would be well . . . to make a clean sweep of the

whole lot," and hoping that the UIL groundswell would shake off the deadweight in the party. 10, 17 Feb 1900.

127 *Gazette*, 21 Nov 1901; *Ottawa Journal*, 21, 22 Nov 1901.

128 Miller, *The Canadian Career of the Fourth Earl of Minto*, 58–9; *Ottawa Journal*, 28 Nov 1901.

129 D'Arcy Scott to William Bourke Cockran, 15 Nov 1901, MssCol 582, Series 1, A, b. 1 f. 12, Bourke Cockran Papers, NYPL.

130 *True Witness*, 30 Nov 1901; 22 Mar 1902.

131 *True Witness*, 30 Nov 1901.

132 *Catholic Register*, 26 Jun, 17 Jul 1902.

133 *Catholic Register*, 5 Jun 1902.

134 *New Zealand Tablet*, 21 Jun 1900; *Times*, 10 May 1900.

135 *Freeman's Journal* (Sydney), 19 May 1900; *New Zealand Tablet*, 21 Jun 1900; *Catholic Register*, 24 May 1900.

136 *True Witness*, 19 May 1900.

8. "HA! HA!"

1 Cronin, *The McGarrity Papers*, 17.

2 Francis M. Carrol, "McGarrity, Joseph," *DIB*.

3 Memo by Agent Z, 23 Jun 1914, HO 317/37, TNA.

4 McGarrity narrates the story of the discovery in typescript memoranda by Joseph McGarrity regarding his dealings with Clan na Gael and the Irish Republican Brotherhood, MS 17,550, McGarrity Papers, NLI.

5 Memoranda, MS 17,550, Joseph McGarrity Papers, NLI.

6 Gosselin to Matthew White Ridley, 5 Oct 1896, HO 317/39, TNA.

7 *Irish World*, 21 Nov 1896; "Statement of Meyrick Jones," 14 Oct 1896, HO 317/39, TNA; "An argument in favour of a full and complete exposure of the Lyman Wing of the Secret Organisation in the United States of America," 14 Oct 1896, HO 317/39, TNA; Ó Broin, *Revolutionary Underground*, 77–9.

8 Gosselin to Digby, 10 Dec 1902, HO 317/41, TNA.

9 Ibid.

10 Gosselin to Digby, 10 Sep 1903, HO 317/41, TNA.

11 Gosselin to Digby, 10 Dec 1902, HO 317/41, TNA.

12 Gosselin to Cadogan, 23 Jan 1901, HO 317/41, TNA.

13 Gosselin to Digby, 10 Dec 1902, HO 317/41, TNA.

14 Memoranda, MS 17,550, McGarrity Papers, NLI.

15 Wilcox to McNello, 29 Mar 1901, MS 17,495/1, McGarrity Papers, NLI.

16 Wilcox to McNello, 23 Apr 1901, MS 17,495/1, McGarrity Papers, NLI.

17 Wilcox to McNello, 4 Oct 1901, MS 17,495/1, McGarrity Papers, NLI.

18 Wilcox to McNello, 21 May 1901, MS 17,495/1, McGarrity Papers, NLI.

19 Wilcox to McNello, 13 Jan 1904, MS 17,495/2, McGarrity Papers, NLI.

20 Wilcox to McNello, 6 Nov 1901, MS 17,495/1, McGarrity Papers, NLI.

21 *Buffalo Evening News*, 30 Dec 1902; *Baltimore Sun*, 31 Dec 1902. Van Ness's widow denied the claim.

22 *Star-Gazette* (Elmira, NY), 18 May 1904.

23 Unnamed author to W. R. Bryon, 7 Oct 1918, Old German Files 1909–21, Case number 221041, German Activities—Samuel Pearson, Investigative Case Files of the Bureau of Investigation (BOI), 1908–1922, fold3.com.

24 Ellen Janet Jenkins, "Organizing Victory," 230–2.

25 John M. McCourt to A. Bruce Bielaski, 20 May 1917, Old German Files, 1909–21, Case number 8000–444, Neutrality Matter—Samuel Pearson, Investigative Case Files of the BOI, 1908–1922, fold3.com.

26 Director, Military Intelligence to L. J. Baley, 1 Jun 1920, RG 65, M1085, Case number 202600–622, General Samuel Pearson, Roll 929, Investigative Case Files of the BOI 1908–1922, fold3.com.

27 Wilcox to McNello, 12 Nov 1901, 24 Jan, 26 Feb, 10 Jul 1902, MS 17,495/1, McGarrity Papers, NLI.

28 See OM I 4/13/1, McGarrity Papers, DL@VU.

29 Wilcox to McNello, 19, 23 Nov 1901, 12 Feb 1902, MS 17,495/1, McGarrity Papers, NLI.

30 Wilcox to McNello, 29 Apr, 12 May 1902, MS 17,495/1, McGarrity Papers, NLI.

31 *Patriots or Impostors*, MS 15,236/6, Redmond Papers, NLI, 35.

32 *Boston Globe*, 20, 21 Oct 1902.

33 Patrick Egan served as Vice President, and Michael J. Ryan later served as President.

34 *Patriots or Impostors*, MS 15,236/6, Redmond Papers, NLI, 35.

35 *Boston Post*, 11 Feb 1902.

36 Finerty to Redmond, 23 Jan 1903, MS 15,236/7, Redmond Papers, NLI.

37 Finerty to Redmond, 18 Jun 1903, MS 15,236/7, Redmond Papers, NLI.

38 Memo by Kenelm Digby, 9 Sep 1903, HO 317/41, TNA.

39 Finerty to Redmond, 4 Sep 1903, MS 15,236/7, Redmond Papers, NLI.

40 Patrick Ford to Redmond, 9 Nov 1903, MS 15,236/8, Redmond Papers, NLI.

41 Finerty to Redmond, 28 Oct, 11 Dec 1903, MS 15,236/7, Redmond Papers, NLI.

42 John Purroy Mitchel and John Jay Joyce to William Bourke Cockran, 12 Sep 1903, MssCol 582, Series 1, B, b. 13 f. 20, Bourke Cockran Papers, NYPL.

43 *Patriots or Impostors*, MS 15,236/6, Redmond Papers, NLI.

44 J. P. O'Mahoney to Redmond, 23 Aug 1904, MS 15,236/20, Redmond Papers, NLI.

45 For example, John MacBride to William Crossin, 6 May 1902, MS 17,456/1, McGarrity Papers, NLI.

46 *Gaelic American*, 19, 26 Sep 1903.

47 Wilcox to McNello, 20 May 1902, MS 17,495/1, McGarrity Papers, NLI.

48 C. A. Wilkins to Chalmers, 6 Feb 1906; Memo from Agent Z, 24 Jan 1905, HO 317/37, TNA.

49 Ward, *Ireland and Anglo-American Relations*, 51–3.

50 Gosselin to Harrel, 20 Nov 1900, CBS/23136/S Miss Maud Gonne, etc., in CO 904/202/166, TNA; "Secret Organization in Co Mayo," CBS/20974/S, NAI.

51 Dispatch from Consul Vansittart, Chicago 28 Oct 1895, HO 317/37, TNA.

52 *New York Tribune*, 7 Jun 1908; St. Sukie de la Croix, *Chicago Whispers*, 32–3.

53 Memo from Agent Z, 24 Jan 1905, HO 317/37, TNA.

54 *Gaelic American*, 2, 9 Apr 1904.

55 *Gaelic American*, 2 Apr 1904.

56 Ward, *Ireland and Anglo-American Relations*, 51–3.

57 Report of Clan na Gael Convention, Atlantic City, 20 Jun 1904, HO 317/37, TNA.

58 Ibid.

59 Wilcox to McNello, 26 Jun 1904, MS 17,495/3, McGarrity Papers, NLI.

60 Gosselin to Digby, 10 Sep 1903, HO 317/41, TNA.

61 McCracken, *Inspector Mallon*, 216–29.

62 Memo by Sir Kenelm Digby, 9 Sep 1903, HO 317/41, TNA.

63 Memo by Sir Kenelm Digby, 9 Sep 1903, HO 317/41, TNA.

64 Gosselin to Mackenzie Chalmers, 9 Feb 1904, HO 317/41, TNA.

65 Memo by Sir Kenelm Digby, 9 Sep 1903, HO 317/41, TNA.

66 Ibid.

67 Gosselin to Digby, 10 Sep 1903, HO 317/41, TNA.

68 Secret Service—Irish-American Branch, budget, 21 Jun 1905, HO 317/41, TNA.

69 Report by C. A. Wilkins, 21 Jun 1905, HO 317/41, TNA.

70 Ibid.

71 James E. Dolan to Redmond, 21 Jul 1903, MS 15,236/4, Redmond Papers, NLI.

72 Funchion, ed., *Irish American Voluntary Organizations*, 59.

73 Convention, 1902, OM I 3/2/5, McGarrity Papers, DL@VU, 40–41.

74 Wilcox to McNello, 24 Feb, 1, 4, 9, 23 Mar 1911, MS 17,495/6, McGarrity Papers, NLI.

75 Anonymous to Crossin, undated, with comments by Joseph McGarrity, MS 17,438/44, McGarrity Papers, NLI.

76 Anonymous to Crossin, 25 Mar 1911, MS 17,438/29, McGarrity Papers, NLI.

77 After a series of letters inquiring about Luke Dillon and about Crossin's prospects in the AOH election, Wilcox wrote to McNello on 24 March, "I would be glad if you would post the enclosed letter uptown upon receipt of it. Of course you need not and must not say that you know anything about this matter if you hear it spoken about. Post it anywhere early Saturday [25th]." The envelope containing the letter to Crossin was postmarked Philadelphia, 25 March. Wilcox to McNello, 24 Mar 1911, MS 17,495/6, McGarrity Papers, NLI.

78 Alexander Reford, "Devlin, Charles Ramsay," *DCB*.

79 Dillon to John Revens, 17 Dec 1904, MS 17,438/8, McGarrity Papers, NLI.

80 *Trenton Evening Times* (Trenton, NJ), 23 Jul 1914.

81 Dillon to John Revens, 17 Dec 1904, MS 17,438/8, McGarrity Papers, NLI.

82 John L. Gannon to Crossin, enclosing exchange with Miss Mary Dillon, 8 May 1906, MS 17,438/17, McGarrity Papers, NLI.

83 John L. Gannon of Providence wrote to Devoy, "I hope ye have not stopped trying to do something for Luke on account of that letter Revens received. He does not

know anything about how things have worked for the last few years." Gannon to Devoy, 14 Dec 1904, MS 18,005/13/5, Devoy Papers, NLI.

84 Draft letter by McGarrity to the editor of the *Irish World*, 1930, MS 17,448/19, McGarrity Papers, NLI.

85 *Trenton Evening Times*, 23 Jul 1914; Neufeld, "Kingston Penitentiary, 1890–1914."

86 Dillon to Revens, 17 Dec 1904, MS 17,438/8, McGarrity Papers, NLI.

87 Dillon to Daniel V. Murphy, 27 Oct 1905, MS 17,438/16, McGarrity Papers, NLI.

88 Mary T. Dillon to John L. Gannon, 18 May 1906, MS 18,003/10/5, Devoy Papers, NLI.

89 Dillon to "Friend Curran," 4 May 1907, MS 17,438/19, McGarrity Papers, NLI.

90 *Buffalo Express*, 28 Mar 1902; Murray and Speer, *Memoirs of a Great Detective*.

91 For example, *Ottawa Journal*, 10 Jul 1907.

92 Dillon to "Friend Curran," 4 May 1907, MS 17,438/19, McGarrity Papers, NLI.

93 Ibid., Dillon to John L. Gannon, 14 Aug 1911, MS 17,438/37, McGarrity Papers, NLI.

94 Dillon to John L. Gannon, 14 Feb 1911, MS 17,438/28, McGarrity Papers, NLI.

95 Dillon to John L. Gannon, 2 Jun 1911, MS 17,438/33, McGarrity Papers, NLI.

96 *Ottawa Citizen*, 26 Apr 1904.

97 Daniel V. Murphy to Crossin, 11 Jan 1905, MS 17,438/9, McGarrity Papers, NLI.

98 Daniel V. Murphy to Crossin, 3 Feb 1905, McGarrity Papers, NLI MS 17,438/10, McGarrity Papers, NLI.

99 "Remember what I said about Luke Dillon. Every word be sure and repeat to me and keep your ears open." Wilcox to McNello, 8 Sep 1903, MS 17,495/2, McGarrity Papers, NLI. Questions about Luke Dillon appear at least every few months throughout the hundreds of letters sent by Wilcox over ten years.

100 Dillon to Daniel V. Murphy, 27 Oct 1905, MS 17,438/16, McGarrity Papers, NLI.

101 Unnamed author to unnamed recipient, undated, MS 17,438/43, McGarrity Papers, NLI.

102 Devoy to William Crossin, 6 Nov 1908, MS 17,438/23, McGarrity Papers, NLI.

103 Mary T. Dillon to Theodore Roosevelt, undated, MS 18,003/10/8, Devoy Papers, NLI.

104 These included Dr. William Carroll, veteran Fenian and former lieutenant-colonel in the Union Army; William McAleer, Irish-born former US Congressman; and US Senator Boies Penrose.

105 Wharton Barker to Wilfrid Laurier, 29 Oct 1909, MG26G, 603, Reel C-884, 163792, Laurier Fonds, LAC.

106 Ward, *Ireland and Anglo-American Relations*, 63.

107 Dillon to John L. Gannon, 2 Jun 1911, MS 17,438/33, McGarrity Papers, NLI.

108 "I fear Soggarth [the prison chaplain] took umbrage at the tone of my letter as he has not spoken to me since." Dillon to John L. Gannon, 11 May 1911, MS 17,438/30, McGarrity Papers, NLI.

109 *Montreal Gazette*, 13 Jun 1911.

110 Crossin to James Reidy, 13 Jun 1911, MS 18,001/22/14, Devoy Papers, NLI.

111 John L. Gannon to Crossin, 17 Aug 1911, MS 17,438/38, McGarrity Papers, NLI.

112 Wilcox to McNello, 5 Oct 1911, MS 17,495/6, McGarrity Papers, NLI.

113 Military code: adopted, 1900, XM DA954.M55 1900, McGarrity Papers, DL@VU.

114 Funchion, ed., *Irish American Voluntary Organizations*, 59; Ward, *Ireland and Anglo-American Relations*, 28, 33, 60, 65.

115 Ward, *Ireland and Anglo-American Relations*, 68.

116 John Devoy to William Crossin, 23 Oct 1911, MS 17,438/39, McGarrity Papers, NLI.

117 Ward, *Ireland and Anglo-American Relations*, 68.

118 Dillon to John L. Gannon, 2 Aug 1907, MS 17,438/20; Dillon to John L. Gannon, 22 May 1911, MS 17,438/30, McGarrity Papers, NLI.

119 Mark G. McGowan, "Burke, Alfred Edward," *DCB*.

120 See for example McGarrity to Burke, 26 Jun 1912, MS 17,644/1/18; 28 Dec 1912, MS 17,644/1/24, 31 Dec 1914, MS 17,504/63; Burke to Keating, 13 Nov 1912, MS 17,644/1/23; Burke to McGarrity, 23 Jan 1913, MS 17,645/1, 31 Jul 1913, MS 17,645/4, 14 Dec 1914, MS 17,504/62, McGarrity Papers, NLI.

121 *Victoria Daily Times*, 29 Nov 1912; *Buffalo Sunday Morning News*, 8 Dec 1912.

122 The Diaries of Sir Robert Borden, 9, 17 Oct, 11, 13 Nov 1912; 20, 28, 31 Dec 1913, MG26-H, Vol. 450, Sir Robert Borden Fonds, LAC.

123 Diaries of Sir Robert Borden, 30 Oct, 1 Nov 1912, MG26-H, Vol. 450, Borden Fonds, LAC.

124 Borden wrote of his "unpardonable action in New York," and mentioned that Doherty also "deplores" this "indiscretion." Diaries of Sir Robert Borden, 30 Oct, 1 Nov 1912, MG26-H, Vol. 450, Borden Fonds, LAC.

125 Burke to Keating, 13 Nov 1912, MS 17,644/1/23, McGarrity Papers, NLI.

126 Diaries of Sir Robert Borden, 20 Dec 1913, MG26-H, Vol. 450, Borden Fonds, LAC.

127 Burke to Keating, 14 Jan 1914, MS 17,504/38, McGarrity Papers, NLI.

128 Keating to Devoy, 13 May 1914, MS 18,006/22/5, Devoy Papers, NLI.

129 *Montreal Gazette*, 13 Jul 1914.

130 *Wilkes-Barre Record*, 24 Jul 1914.

131 *Montreal Gazette*, 18 Jul 1914.

132 *Trenton Evening Times*, 23 Jul 1914.

133 *Evening Public Ledger* (Philadelphia), 17 Sep 1914; Dr. William Carroll to Devoy, 21 Sep 1914, MS 18,002/30/14, Devoy Papers, NLI.

134 *Evening Journal* (Wilmington, Delaware), 27 Jun 1912; Wilcox to McNello, undated (probably August) 1911, MS 17,495/6, McGarrity Papers, NLI; Gannon to Devoy, 17 Feb 1912, MS 18,005/16/6, Devoy Papers, NLI.

135 Memoranda, MS 17,550, McGarrity Papers, NLI, 8.

136 Wilcox to McNello, 6, 11 Sep 1911, MS 17,495/6, McGarrity Papers, NLI.

137 Wilcox to McNello, 25 Sep 1911, MS 17,495/6, McGarrity Papers, NLI.

138 Wilcox to McNello, undated (probably Apr 1912) no. 19, MS 17,495/7, McGarrity Papers, NLI.

139 Wilcox to McNello, undated, no. 28, MS 17,495/7, McGarrity Papers, NLI.

140 Devoy to McGarrity, 19 Jun 1912, MS 17,442/7, McGarrity Papers, NLI.

141 The man's name was Barney Quinn. Devoy to McGarrity, 24 Jul 1912, MS 17,442/8, McGarrity Papers, NLI. Another suspect was Sylvester Moore. Sylvester Moore to Matthias Harford, 30 Dec 1912, MS 17,501/40, McGarrity Papers, NLI.

142 Keating to McGarrity, 3 Mar 1913, MS 17,503/8, McGarrity Papers, NLI.

143 D. Miles Rigor, a private investigator from New Jersey, and Thomas M. Reddy, a former postal inspector, then working at a Manhattan firm. On Reddy's colorful career, see *Pittsburgh Press*, 8 Aug 1915.

144 *Times Union* (Brooklyn), 11 Feb 1913.

145 *Brooklyn Daily Eagle*, 11 Feb 1913.

146 J. J. Carew to James Reidy, 10 Jun 1913, MS 17,636/13, McGarrity Papers, NLI.

147 Secretary, V. C., to McGarrity, 3 Mar 1913, MS 17,657/4, McGarrity Papers, NLI.

148 See undated Memorandum, MS 17,501/59, McGarrity Papers, NLI. The records of this investigation are fragmentary but can be found in MS 17,501.

149 *Distinguished Successful Americans of Our Day*, 200–201; *Freeman's Journal*, 23 Nov 1880.

150 *Era* (London), 7 Jan 1893.

151 Reprinted (triumphantly) in *Anglo-Celt* (Cavan), 19 Aug 1893.

152 See Chaput, "The British Are Coming!"; Pinera, *American and English Influence on the Early Development of Ensenada*. Jenkinson purchased the Baja company holdings in 1888 and appointed fellow Indian Civil Service man and Indian Rebellion veteran Buchanan Scott to manage the colony. It does not appear that Jenkinson was aware of the filibuster plot.

153 *Era*, 14 Jan 1893; *Chicago Tribune*, 6 Feb 1892. He later scaled his plans for the Exposition down somewhat, proposing instead an Irish pub "attended by real Irish girls, attired in the picturesque costume of Connemara." *Era*, 28 May 1892.

154 Report by C. A. Wilkins, 21 Jun 1905, HO 317/41, TNA.

155 *Distinguished Successful Americans of Our Day*, 200–201. After Gosselin's death in 1917 Aughnamullen House was purchased by Benjamin Moore, the Brooklyn-based paint manufacturer, who was born in Ballybay. *Dundalk Democrat*, 13 Oct 1917.

156 Memoranda, MS 17,550, McGarrity Papers, NLI.

157 Report by C.A. Wilkins, 21 Jun 1905, HO 317/41, TNA.

158 Armstrong to James MacGuinness, MS 17,482/1, McGarrity Papers, NLI.

159 Seán T. O'Kelly, WS 1765, BMH, 194.

160 Armstrong to Pedlar, 3 Feb 1915, MS 17,482/4/3, McGarrity Papers, NLI.

161 Pedlar to McGarrity, undated 1915, MS 17,482/4/8, McGarrity Papers, NLI.

162 Copy of letter from Pedlar to Armstrong, 3 Feb 1915, MS 17,482/3/1, McGarrity Papers, NLI.

163 Armstrong to Pedlar, 9 Feb 1915, MS 17,482/2, McGarrity Papers, NLI.

164 Pedlar to McGarrity, undated 1915, MS 17,482/4/9, McGarrity Papers, NLI.

165 McGarrity to Pedlar, undated 1915, MS 17,482/3/4, McGarrity Papers, NLI.

166 Pedlar to Armstrong, undated 1915, MS 17,482/3/3, McGarrity Papers, NLI.

167 Pedlar to McGarrity, undated 1915, MS 17,482/4/10, McGarrity Papers, NLI.

168 Armstrong to Pedlar, 15 Feb 1915, MS 17,482/4/4, McGarrity Papers, NLI.

169 Armstrong to Pedlar, 19 Feb 1915, MS 17,482/4/5, McGarrity Papers, NLI.

170 Armstrong to Pedlar, 25 Feb 1915, MS 17,482/4/6, McGarrity Papers, NLI.

171 McGarrity to Pedlar, undated 1915, MS 17,482/3/4, McGarrity Papers, NLI.

172 This outcome Agent Z and his informants felt was likely even before the split. Memos from Z, 17, 24 Jun 1914, HO 317/37, TNA.

173 Memo from Z, 9 Sep 1914, HO 317/37, TNA.

174 "Sinn Féin Party to Attack Canada, 1909–1933," RG24, Vol. 2020, File HQC-965, Department of National Defence Fonds, LAC.

175 See *Buffalo Express*, 18 Apr 1916; "Sinn Fein Movement," Bureau Section Files, 1909–21, fold3.com; McMahon, *British Spies and Irish Rebels*, 110; Hughes, "Terrorist Attacks on the Welland Canal," 6–10; Plowman, "Irish Republicans and the Indo-German Conspiracy of World War I"; Plowman, "The British Intelligence Station in San Francisco during the First World War"; Silvestri, "British Imperial Intelligence and Anticolonial Revolutionaries during and after the Great War."

176 Seán T. O'Kelly, WS 1765, BMH, 183–203.

177 *Gazette*, 8 Dec 1915.

178 Ó Broin, *Revolutionary Underground*, 107.

179 Seán T. O'Kelly, WS 1765, BMH, 194.

180 Pedlar traveled to Glasgow to bring a contingent of IRB men over to fight. He was imprisoned in Frongoch after the surrender, and following his release became deeply involved in drilling and gun-running for the IRA. See MS17,483, McGarrity Papers, NLI; Sean Nunan, WS 1744, BMH, 14; Pat McCormack, WS 339, BMH, 7–8; Edmond O'Brien, WS 597, BMH, 53–4; Patrick McHugh, WS 664, BMH, 42.

181 See MS 17,502, Joseph McGarrity Papers, NLI.

182 *Times*, 7 Feb 1938.

CONCLUSION

1 Joyce, *Ulysses*, 595. Quoted in McCracken, *Forgotten Protest*, 145. See also Lowry, "'The Boers Were the Beginning of the End'? The Wider Impact of the South African War."

2 Joyce, *Ulysses*, 316.

3 Ibid., 595–7. Bloom is unsure whether this was even the real Skin-the-Goat or someone posing as he.

4 David Harrel to Cadogan, 6 Jan 1900, PRO 30/60, TNA.

5 Lowry, "Making John Redmond 'the Irish [Louis] Botha.'"

6 *Freeman's Journal*, 21 Sep 1914.

7 Nasson, "A Great Divide: Popular Responses to the Great War in South Africa."

8 McCracken, "Arthur Lynch at War"; McGee, "Lynch, Arthur Alfred," *DIB*; Maume, *The Long Gestation*, 233–4.

9 Graham, "Arthur Hill Griffith and Opposition to the Boer War," 70. Bede Nairn, "Arthur Hill Griffith (1861–1946)," *ADB*.

10 McGowan, *Imperial Irish*, 74.

11 *Advocate* (Melbourne), 19 Feb 1916.

12 Beatty, *Masculinity and Power in Irish Nationalism*, 3.

13 See the many helpful contributions on this topic in Miriam Nyhan Grey, ed., *Ireland's Allies: America and the 1916 Easter Rising*.

14 Joyce, *Ulysses*, 596–7.

15 Silvestri, *Ireland and India*, 37.

16 Gannon, "Addressing the Irish World," 44, 52.

17 Ó Corráin, "'A Most Public Spirited and Unselfish Man,'" 120–5.

18 John Finerty to John Redmond, 28 Oct, 11 Dec 1903, MS 15,236/7, Redmond Papers, NLI.

19 Townend, "A Cosmopolitan Nationalist: James J. O'Kelly in America," 236.

20 Whelehan, *Changing Land*, 14.

21 Kenny, "Diaspora and Comparison," 149.

22 Akenson, "The Great European Migration and Indigenous Populations," 25.

23 See Nelson, *Irish Nationalists*, 123–5; O'Leary, *Ireland and Empire*, 25–9, 48–65; Beatty, *Masculinity and Power in Irish Nationalism*, 4; Townend, *Road to Home Rule*, 14.

24 Jackson, "Ireland, the Union, and the Empire, 1800–1960," 123.

25 Michael D. Higgins, "Empire Shaped Ireland's Past. A Century after Partition, It Still Shapes Our Present," *Guardian*, 11 Feb 2021.

26 Harkness, "Ireland," 115.

BIBLIOGRAPHY

MANUSCRIPT SOURCES

IRELAND
  Military Archives
    Bureau of Military History Witness Statements
  National Archives of Ireland
    Crime Branch Special "S" files 1890–1910
    Crime Branch Special Précis of Reports 1894–1905
  National Library of Ireland
    Frederick J. Allan Papers
    John Devoy Papers
    John E. Redmond Papers
    Joseph McGarrity Papers
    Michael S. Walsh Papers
    Tom Clarke and Kathleen Clarke Papers
    Minute Book of the Irish Transvaal Committee

UNITED KINGDOM
  The National Archives
    Colonial Office and predecessors: Canada, formerly British North
      America, Original Correspondence (CO 42)
    Colonial Office, Irish Papers (CO 904)
    G. W. Balfour Papers (PRO 30/60)
    Foreign Office: Embassy and Consulates, United States of America: Gen-
      eral Correspondence (FO 115)
    Home Office Private Papers (HO 317)
  National Records of Scotland
    Arthur J. Balfour Papers (GD 433/2)

UNITED STATES
Digital Library @ Villanova University
  Joseph McGarrity Papers (OM I)
New York Public Library
  William Bourke Cockran Papers (MssCol 582)
  Thomas William Sweeny Papers (MssCol 2934)

FOLD3.COM
Investigative Case Files of the Bureau of Investigation 1908–1922 (RG 65)

CANADA
British Columbia Archives
  Attorney General Correspondence (GR-0429)
  Lieutenant Governor's Records (GR-0443)
Library and Archives Canada
  Department of National Defence Fonds (RG24)
  Dominion Police Records (RG18-E)
  Sir Robert Borden Fonds (MG26-H)
  Sir Wilfrid Laurier Fonds (MG26-G)

AUSTRALIA
National Library of Australia
  Henry Bournes Higgins Papers (MS 1057)
  Patrick McMahon Glynn Papers (MS 4653)
  Patrick O'Farrell Papers (MS 6265)
State Library of New South Wales
  Gerald Patrick Fitzgerald, "The Last of the Western Australian Fenians,
    1869–1918" (MLDOC 1804)
  Letters from George Arnold Wood to Mrs Holman (MLDOC 697)

NEW ZEALAND
Archives of New Zealand—Te Rua Mahara o te Kāwanatanga
  Richard J. Seddon Papers (ACHW 8633)

NEWSPAPERS

IRELAND
  Anglo-Celt (Cavan)
  Daily Nation (Dublin)

Freeman's Journal (Dublin)
Independent (Dublin)
Irish Times (Dublin)
United Irishman (Dublin)

BRITAIN
Era (London)
Glasgow Herald
Times (London)

UNITED STATES
Arizona Daily Star (Tucson)
Atlanta Constitution
Baltimore Sun
Brooklyn Daily Eagle
Boston Globe
Boston Post
Buffalo Commercial
Buffalo Courier
Buffalo Enquirer
Buffalo Evening News
Buffalo Express
Buffalo Times
Call (San Francisco)
Catholic Union and Times (Buffalo)
Chicago Tribune
Chronicle (San Francisco)
Democrat and Chronicle (Rochester)
Evening Journal (Wilmington, DE.)
Evening Post (San Francisco)
Evening Public Ledger (Philadelphia)
Evening Sentinel (Santa Cruz, CA)
Evening Star (Washington, DC)
Evening World (New York)
Examiner (San Francisco)
Fall River Daily Herald (MA)
Gaelic American (New York)

Hartford Courant
Hawaiian Star (Honolulu)
Hayward Review (CA)
Herald (Los Angeles)
Inter-Ocean (Chicago)
Irish Republic (New York)
Irish Standard (Minneapolis)
Irish World (New York)
Kansas City Gazette
Los Angeles Times
Morning Journal-Courier (New Haven, CT)
Napa Journal (CA)
New York Times
New York Tribune
News-Journal (Mansfield, OH)
Norfolk Landmark (VA)
Oakland Tribune
Philadelphia Bulletin
Philadelphia Inquirer
Plain Speaker (Hazleton, PA)
Press (Pittsburgh, PA)
Record-Union (Sacramento)
Rock Island Argus (IL)
Sacramento Bee
Salt Lake Tribune
San Juan Islander (WA)
Seattle Post-Intelligencer
Seattle Star
Semi-Weekly Spokesman Review (Spokane, WA)
Star-Gazette (Elmira, NY)
St. Louis Post-Dispatch
Sun (New York)
Times (Philadelphia)
Times (Streator, IL)
Times-Democrat (New Orleans)
Times Union (Brooklyn)
Trenton Evening Times (NJ)

Tribune (Scranton, PA)
Tyrone Daily Herald (PA)
Ukiah Daily Journal (CA)
Union and Daily Bee (San Diego)
Washington Times (DC)
Wilkes-Barre Record (PA)
Wilmington Messenger (NC)

CANADA

Catholic Record (London)
Catholic Register (Toronto)
Daily Colonist (Victoria)
Daily Times (Victoria)
Daily World (Vancouver)
Gazette (Montreal)
Globe (Toronto)
Irish Canadian (Toronto)
Kingston Whig
Northwest Review (Winnipeg)
Ottawa Citizen
Ottawa Journal
Sentinel and Orange and Protestant Advocate (Toronto)
True Witness (Montreal)

AUSTRALIA

Advocate (Melbourne)
Age (Melbourne)
Catholic Press (Sydney)
Freeman's Journal (Sydney)
Sydney Morning Herald

NEW ZEALAND

Auckland Star
Evening Post (Wellington)
Evening Star (Dunedin)
Lyttelton Times
New Zealand Herald (Auckland)

New Zealand Mail (Wellington)
New Zealand Tablet (Dunedin)
New Zealand Times (Wellington)
Otago Daily Times (Dunedin)
Press (Christchurch)
Star (Christchurch)

CONTEMPORARY PUBLICATIONS

Ballenger & Richards Twenty-Fifth Annual Denver City Directory. Denver: Ballenger & Richards, 1897.

The Canada Year Book 1909. Ottawa: C. H. Parmeler, 1910.

City of Tucson General and Business Directory for '99–1900. Tucson: Chas. T. Connell, 1899.

Crocker-Langley San Francisco Directory for Year Commencing: April 1896. San Francisco: H. S. Crocker Co., 1896.

Crocker-Langley San Francisco Directory for Year Commencing: May 1901. San Francisco: H. S. Crocker Co., 1901.

Distinguished Successful Americans of Our Day: Containing Biographies of Prominent Americans Now Living. Chicago: Successful Americans, 1912.

Patriots or Impostors: Which? The Case of the Erin's Hope Branch against the New York Municipal Council of the United Irish League of America. June 1904.

Birch, James H. Jr. *History of the War in South Africa.* Saint John, N.B.: R.A.H. Morrow, 1900.

Davitt, Michael. *The Boer Fight for Freedom.* New York: Funk, 1902.

Devoy, John. *Recollections of an Irish Rebel.* New York: Chas. P. Young Co., 1929.

Finerty, John F. *War-Path and Bivouac: or, The Conquest of the Sioux: a Narrative of Stirring Personal Experiences and Adventures in the Big Horn and Yellowstone Expedition of 1876, and in the Campaign on the British Border, in 1879.* Chicago: M. A. Donohue & Co., 1890.

Grey, J. Grattan. *Freedom of Thought & Speech in New Zealand: A Serious Menace to Liberty, No. 1.* Wellington: Wright & Grenside, 1900.

———. *Freedom of Thought & Speech in New Zealand: A Serious Menace to Liberty, No. 2.* Wellington: Wright & Grenside, 1900.

———. *Australasia: Old and New.* London: Hodder & Stoughton, 1901.

Leach, Frank A. *Recollections of a Newspaperman: A Record of Life and Events in California.* San Francisco: Levinson, 1917.

Le Caron, Henri. *Twenty-Five Years in the Secret Service: The Recollections of a Spy.* London, 1892.

Miller, Joaquin. *Chants for the Boer.* San Francisco: The Whitaker & Ray Company, 1900.

Murray, John W. and Victor Speer. *Memoirs of a Great Detective: Incidents in the Life of John Wilson Murray.* New York: Baker & Taylor, 1904.

Sessions, Harold. *Two Years with the Remount Commission.* London: Chapman & Hall, 1903.

Tynan, Patrick J. P. *The Irish National Invincibles and Their Times.* London: Chatham, 1894.

U.S. Congress. House of Representatives. Committee on Foreign Affairs. *Horses, Mules, etc., Shipped to South Africa: Message from the President of the United States, Transmitting Report and Accompanying Papers Concerning Shipments of Horses, Mules and Other Supplies from Louisiana to the Seat of War in South Africa.* 57th Cong., 1st Session. H. Doc. 568.

ONLINE DATABASES

Ancestry.com
Australian Dictionary of Biography, adb.anu.edu.au
Dictionary of Canadian Biography, www.biographi.ca
Dictionary of Irish Biography, www.dib.ie
Dictionary of New Zealand Biography, www.teara.govt.nz
Statistics New Zealand, www.stats.govt.nz

SECONDARY SOURCES

Aan de Wiel, Jerome. *The Irish Factor 1899–1919: Ireland's Strategic and Diplomatic Importance for Foreign Powers.* Dublin: Irish Academic Press, 2008.
———. "French Military Intelligence and Ireland, 1900–1923." *Intelligence and National Security* 26, no. 1 (Feb 2011): 46–71.

Akenson, Donald Harman. *The Irish in Ontario: A Study in Rural History.* Montreal & Kingston: McGill-Queen's University Press, 1984.
———. *God's Peoples: Covenant and Land in South Africa, Israel, and Ulster.* Ithaca: Cornell University Press, 1992.
———. *The Irish Diaspora: A Primer.* Toronto: P. D. Meany, 1993.
———. "The Great European Migration and Indigenous Populations." In *Irish and Scottish Encounters with Indigenous Peoples: Canada, the United States, New Zealand, and Australia,* edited by Graeme Morton and David A. Wilson, 22–48. Montreal & Kingston: McGill-Queen's University Press, 2013.

Amos, Keith. *The Fenians in Australia, 1865–1880.* Kensington: New South Wales University Press, 1988.

Andrews, James H. "Winston Churchill's Tammany Hall Mentor." *New York History* 71, no. 2 (Apr 1990): 133–71.

Ballantyne, Tony. *Webs of Empire: Locating New Zealand's Colonial Past.* Vancouver: UBC Press, 2010.

Baker, Jeannine. *Australian Women War Reporters: Boer War to Vietnam.* Sydney: New South Publishing, 2015.

Barr, Colin. *Ireland's Empire: The Roman Catholic Church in the English-Speaking World, 1829–1914.* Cambridge: Cambridge University Press, 2019.

Beatty, Aidan. *Masculinity and Power in Irish Nationalism, 1884–1938.* London: Palgrave Macmillan, 2016.

Belchem, John. "Nationalism, Republicanism and Exile: Irish Emigrants and the Revolutions of 1848." *Past & Present* 146, no. 1 (Feb 1995): 103–135.

Belich, James. *Paradise Reforged: A History of the New Zealanders from the 1880s to the Year 2000*. Honolulu: University of Hawai'i Press, 2001.

Bell, Duncan. *The Idea of Greater Britain: Empire and the Future of World Order, 1860–1900*. Princeton: Princeton University Press, 2007.

Bender, Jill C. *The 1857 Indian Uprising and the British Empire*. Cambridge: Cambridge University Press, 2016.

Berger, Carl. *The Sense of Power: Studies in the Ideas of Canadian Imperialism, 1867–1914*. Toronto: University of Toronto Press, 1970.

Boehmer, Elleke. *Empire, the National, and the Postcolonial, 1890–1920*. Oxford: Oxford University Press, 2004.

Bossenbroek, Martin. "The Netherlands and the Boer War: Their Wildest Dreams: The Representation of South African Culture, Imperialism and Nationalism at the Turn of the Twentieth Century." In *The International Impact of the Boer War*, edited by Keith Wilson, 123–39. Chesham: Acumen, 2001.

Brosnahan, Sean. "'Shaming the Shoneens': The Green Ray and the Maoriland Irish Society in Dunedin, 1916–1922." In *A Distant Shore: Irish Migration & New Zealand Settlement*, edited by Lyndon Fraser, 117–34. Dunedin: University of Otago Press, 2000.

———. "Parties or Politics: Wellington's IRA 1922–1928," In The Irish in New Zealand: Historical Contexts and Perspectives, edited by Brad Patterson, 67-88. Wellington: Stout Research Centre for New Zealand Studies, 2002.

Brownrigg, Jeff, Cheryl Mongan, and Richard Reid, eds. *Echoes of Irish Australia: Rebellion to Republic—A Collection of Essays*. Canberra: Paragon, 2007.

Bull, Philip. "The United Irish League and the Reunion of the Irish Parliamentary Party, 1898–1900." *Irish Historical Studies* 26, no. 101 (May 1988): 51–78.

———, Frances Devlin-Glass, and Helen Doyle, eds., *Ireland and Australia, 1798–1998: Studies in Culture, Identity and Migration*. Sydney: Crossing Press, 2000.

Cain, P. J. and A. G. Hopkins. *British Imperialism: Innovation and Expansion, 1688–1914*. London: Longman, 1993.

Campbell, Christy. *Fenian Fire: The British Government Plot to Assassinate Queen Victoria*. London: Harper Collins, 2002.

Campbell, Malcolm. *Ireland's New Worlds: Immigrants, Politics, and Society in the United States and Australia, 1815–1922*. Madison: University of Wisconsin Press, 2008.

Carey, Hilary and Colin Barr, eds. *Religion and Greater Ireland: Christianity and Irish Global Networks, 1750–1950*. Montreal: McGill Queen's University Press, 2015.

Chaput, Donald. "The British Are Coming!" *Journal of San Diego History* 33, no. 4 (Fall 1987): 151–64.

Coffey, Agnes. "*The True Witness and Catholic Chronicle*: Sixty Years of Catholic Journalistic Action." *Canadian Catholic Historical Association Report* 5 (1937–38): 33–46.

Collombier-Lakeman, Pauline. "Applying a Transnational Approach to the Question of Irish Home Rule: Ireland, New Zealand and Home Rule." *French Journal of British Studies* 24, no. 2 (2019).

Connolly, C. N. "Class, Birthplace, Loyalty: Australian Attitudes to the Boer War," *Historical Studies* 71 (1978): 210–32.

Connolly, Sean. *On Every Tide: The Making and Remaking of the Irish World.* New York: Basic Books, 2022.

Coogan, Tim Pat. *Michael Collins: A Biography.* London: Arrow, 1991.

Cooper, Sophie. *Forging Identities in the Irish World: Melbourne and Chicago, c. 1830–1922.* Edinburgh: Edinburgh University Press, 2022.

Corrigan, John. "United Irish Societies of Chicago (UISC)." In *Irish American Voluntary Organizations,* edited by Michael F. Funchion, 276–82. Westport, CT: Greenwood, 1983.

Crawford, John and Ian McGibbon, eds. *One Flag, One Queen, One Tongue: New Zealand, the British Empire and the South African War, 1899–1902.* Auckland: Auckland University Press, 2003.

Cronin, Sean. *The McGarrity Papers: Revelations of the Irish Revolutionary Movement in Ireland and American 1900–1940.* Anvil: Tralee, 1972.

Crosbie, Barry. *Irish Imperial Networks: Migration, Social Communication and Exchange in Nineteenth-Century India.* Cambridge: Cambridge University Press, 2011.

Cuthbertson, Greg, Albert Grundlingh and Mary-Lynn Suttie, eds. *Writing a Wider War: Rethinking Gender, Race, and Identity in the South African War, 1899–1902.* Athens: Ohio University Press, 2002.

Davis, Richard P. *Arthur Griffith and Non-Violent Sinn Féin.* Dublin: Anvil, 1974.

———. *Irish Issues in New Zealand Politics, 1868–1922.* Dunedin: University of Otago Press, 1974.

de la Croix, St. Sukie. *Chicago Whispers: A History of LGBT Chicago before Stonewall.* Madison: University of Wisconsin Press, 2012.

Delaney, Enda. "Our Island Story? Towards a Transnational History of Late Modern Ireland." *Irish Historical Studies* 37, no. 148 (Nov 2011): 599–621.

——— and Fearghal McGarry. "Introduction: A Global History of the Irish Revolution." *Irish Historical Studies* 44, no. 165 (May 2020): 1–10.

Diver, Luke. "Ireland's South African War 1899–1902." *Scientia Militaria, South African Journal of Military Studies* 42, no. 1 (2014): 1–17.

Douma, Michael James. "Ethnic Identities in a Transnational Context: The Dutch American Reaction to the Anglo-Boer War 1899–1902." *South African Historical Journal* 65, no. 4 (2013): 481–503.

Doyle, David Noel. *Irish Americans, Native Rights and National Empires: The Structure, Divisions and Attitudes of the Catholic Minority in the Decade of Expansion, 1890–1901.* Arno Press: New York, 1976.

Dumonceaux, Scott. "The Conspiracy: The Canadian Response to the Order of the Midnight Sun and the Alaska Boundary Dispute." MA dissertation, University of Saskatchewan, 2013.

Dye, Ryan D. "Irish American Ambivalence toward the Spanish-American War." *New Hibernia Review* 11, no. 3 (Autumn 2007): 98–113.

English, Richard. "History and Irish Nationalism." *Irish Historical Studies* 37, no. 147 (2011): 447–60.

Fennell, Phillip and Marie King, eds. *John Devoy's Catalpa Expedition*. New York: New York University Press, 2006.

Field, Laurie. *The Forgotten War: Australia and the Boer War*. Carlton, Vic.: Melbourne University Press, 1995.

Fitzpatrick, David. "Irish Emigration to Nineteenth Century Australia." In *Australia and Ireland 1788-1988: Bicentenary Essays*, edited by Colm Kiernan, 138-144. Dublin: Gill and Macmillan, 1986.

———. "Emigration, 1871–1921." In *A New History of Ireland Volume VI: Ireland Under the Union, II 1870-1921*, edited by W.E. Vaughan, 606–652. Oxford: Oxford University Press, 1989.

———. *Oceans of Consolation: Personal Accounts of Irish Migration to Australia*. Ithaca: Cornell University Press, 1994.

———. *Harry Boland's Irish Revolution*. Cork: Cork University Press, 2003.

Foster, R. F. *Modern Ireland 1600–1972*. London: Allen Lane, 1988.

———. *W. B. Yeats: A Life I: The Apprentice Mage, 1865–1914*. Oxford: Oxford University Press, 1997.

Fowler, Colin. "NSW Catholic Clergy and the Boer War: For and Against," *Journal of the Australasian Catholic Historical Society* 38 (2017): 43–58.

———. "'Firebrand Friar'—Patrick Fidelis Kavanagh OSF (1838–1918)." *Journal of the Australian Catholic Historical Society* 41 (2020): 6–18.

Fraser, Lyndon, ed. *A Distant Shore: Irish Migration & New Zealand Settlement*. Dunedin: University of Otago Press, 2000.

Funchion, Michael F., ed. *Irish American Voluntary Organizations*. Westport, CT: Greenwood Press, 1983.

Galbraith, Alasdair. "The Invisible Irish? Re-Discovering the Irish Protestant Tradition in Colonial New Zealand." In *A Distant Shore: Irish Migration & New Zealand Settlement*, edited by Lyndon Fraser, 37–54. Dunedin: University of Otago Press, 2000.

Galbraith, John S. "The British South Africa Company and the Jameson Raid." *Journal of British Studies* 10, no. 1 (Nov 1970): 145–161.

Gannon, Darragh. "Addressing the Irish World: Éamon de Valera's 'Cuban Policy' as a Global Case Study." *Irish Historical Studies* 44, no. 165 (May 2020): 41–56.

Genge, Manelisi. "The Role of the EmaSwati in the South African War." In *Writing a Wider War: Rethinking Gender, Race, and Identity in the South African War, 1899–1902*, edited by Greg Cuthbertson, Albert Grundlingh, and Mary-Lynn Suttie, 136–58. Athens: Ohio University Press, 2002.

Graham, Morris. "Newcastle Rallies to the Flag, February 1902: Arthur Hill Griffith and Opposition to the Boer War." *Journal of the Royal Australian Historical Society* 89, no. 1 (June 2003): 53–71.

Harkness, David. "Ireland." In *The Oxford History of the British Empire: Historiography, Vol. V*, edited by Robin Winks, 114–33. Oxford: Oxford University Press, 1999.

Hearn, Terry. "Irish Migration to New Zealand to 1915." In *A Distant Shore: Irish Migration & New Zealand Settlement*, edited by Lyndon Fraser, 55–74. Dunedin: University of Otago Press, 2000.

———. "The Origins of New Zealand's Irish Settlers, 1840–1945." In *The Irish in New Zealand: Historical Contexts and Perspectives*, edited by Brad Patterson, 15–34. Wellington: Stout Research Centre for New Zealand Studies, 2002.

Heath, Gordon L. *A War with a Silver Lining: Canadian Protestant Churches and the South African War, 1899–1903*. Montreal: McGill-Queen's University Press, 2009.

Higgins, Michael D. "Empire Shaped Ireland's Past. A Century after Partition, It Still Shapes our Present." *Guardian*, 11 Feb 2021, theguardian.com.

Hirst, John. "Empire, State, Nation." In *Australia's Empire*, edited by Deryck M. Schreuder and Stuart Ward, 141–62. Oxford: Oxford University Press, 2008.

Horrall, Stanley W. "Canada and the Irish Question: A Study of the Canadian Response to Home Rule." MA dissertation, Carleton University, 1966.

Houston, Cecil J. and William J. Smyth. *The Sash Canada Wore: A Historical Geography of the Orange Order in Canada*. Toronto: University of Toronto Press, 1980.

Howe, Stephen. *Ireland and Empire: Colonial Legacies in Irish History and Culture*. Oxford: Oxford University Press, 2002.

Hughes, Alun. "Terrorist Attacks on the Welland Canal." *The Historical Society of St. Catharines Newsletter* (June 2008): 6–10.

Hutching, Megan. "New Zealand Women's Opposition to the South African War." In *One Flag, One Queen, One Tongue: New Zealand, the British Empire and the South African War, 1899–1902*, edited by John Crawford and Ian McGibbon, 46–57. Auckland: Auckland University Press, 2003.

Jackson, Alvin. "Ireland, the Union, and the Empire, 1800–1960." In *Ireland and the British Empire*, edited by Kevin Kenny, 123–53. Oxford: Oxford University Press, 2004.

James, Stephanie. "From beyond the Sea: The Irish Catholic Press in the Southern Hemisphere." In *Ireland in the World: Comparative, Transnational, and Personal Perspectives*, edited by Angela McCarthy, 81–109. New York: Routledge, 2015.

Janis, Ely M. *A Greater Ireland: The Land League and Transatlantic Nationalism in Gilded Age America*. History of Ireland and the Irish Diaspora. Madison: The University of Wisconsin Press, 2015.

Jeffery, Keith, ed. *An Irish Empire? Aspects of Ireland and the British Empire*. Manchester: Manchester University Press, 1996.

Jenkins, Ellen Janet. "'Organizing Victory': Great Britain, the United States and the Instruments of War, 1914–1916." PhD dissertation, University of Northern Texas, 1992.

Jenkins, William. *Between Raid and Rebellion: the Irish in Buffalo and Toronto, 1867–1919*. Montreal: McGill-Queen's University Press, 2013.

Joyce, James. *Ulysses*, prepared by Hans Walter Gabler, Wolfhard Steppe, and Claus Melchior. New York: Garland, 1984.

Judd, Denis and Keith Surridge. *The Boer War*. London: John Murray, 2002.

Karageorgos, Effie. "War in a 'White Man's Country': Australian Perceptions of Blackness on the South African Battlefield, 1899–1902." *History Australia* 15, no. 2 (2018): 323–38.

Kelly, Matthew J. "The End of Parnellism and the Ideological Dilemmas of Sinn Féin." In *Ireland in Transition, 1867–1921*, edited by D. George Boyce and Alan O'Day, 142–58. London: Routledge, 2004.

———. *The Fenian Ideal and Irish Nationalism, 1882–1916*. Woodbridge: Boydell Press, 2006.

———. "Radical Nationalisms, 1882–1916." In *The Cambridge History of Ireland, Volume IV, 1880 to the present*, edited by Thomas Bartlett. Cambridge: Cambridge University Press, 2018.

Kenna, Shane. *War in the Shadows: The Irish-American Fenians Who Bombed Victorian Britain*. Dublin: Merrion, 2014.

Kennedy, Padraic C. "The Secret Service Department: A British Intelligence Bureau in Mid-Victorian London, September 1867 to April 1868." *Intelligence and National Security* 18, no. 3 (Autumn, 2003): 100–127.

Kenny, Colum. "Frank Hugh O'Donnell: A Virulent Anti-Semite." *History Ireland* 28, no. 1 (Jan/Feb 2020): 30–32.

Kenny, Kevin. "Diaspora and Comparison: The Global Irish as a Case Study." *Journal of American History* 90, no. 1 (June 2003): 134–62.

———, ed. *Ireland and the British Empire*. Oxford: Oxford University Press, 2005.

———. "Irish Emigration, c.1845–1900." In *The Cambridge History of Ireland Volume III: 1830–1880*, edited by James Kelly, 666–87. Cambridge: Cambridge University Press, 2018.

Kiernan, Colm, ed. *Australia and Ireland 1788–1988: Bicentenary Essays*. Dublin: Gill and Macmillan, 1986.

King, Carla. "'I Am Doing Fairly Well in the Lecturing Line': Michael Davitt and Australia 1895." *Australasian Journal of Irish Studies* 12 (2012): 25–46.

———. *Michael Davitt after the Land League, 1882–1906*. Dublin: University College Dublin Press, 2016.

Kröger, Martin. "Imperial Germany and the Boer War: From Colonial Fantasies to the Reality of Anglo-German Estrangement." In *The International Impact of the Boer War*, edited by Keith Wilson, 25–42. Chesham: Acumen, 2001.

Kuitenbrouwer, Vincent. *War of Words: Dutch Pro-Boer Propaganda and the South African War (1899–1902)*. Amsterdam: Amsterdam University Press, 2012.

Lake, Marilyn. "British World or New World? Anglo-Saxonism and Australian Engagement with America." *History Australia* 10, no. 3 (2013): 36–50.

——— and Henry Reynolds. *Drawing the Global Colour Line: White Men's Countries and the International Challenge of Racial Equality*. Cambridge: Cambridge University Press, 2008.

Lambert, David and Alan Lester, eds. *Colonial Lives across the British Empire: Imperial Careering in the Long Nineteenth Century*. Cambridge: Cambridge University Press, 2006.

Levenson, Samuel. *Maud Gonne*. New York: Reader's Digest Press, 1976.

Lowry, Donal. "'A Fellowship of Disaffection': Irish-South African Relations from the Anglo-Boer War to the *Pretoriastroika* 1902–1991." *Études irlandaises* 17-2 (1992): 105–121.

———. "'The Boers Were the Beginning of the End'? The Wider Impact of the South African War." In *The South African War Reappraised*, edited by Donal Lowry, 203–246. Manchester: Manchester University Press, 2000.

———. "Nationalist and Unionist Responses to the British Empire in the Age of the South African War, 1899–1902." In *Newspapers and Empire in Ireland and Britain: Reporting the British Empire, c. 1857–1921*, edited by Simon J. Potter, 195–216. Dublin: Four Courts Press, 2004.

———. "Making John Redmond 'the Irish [Louis] Botha': The Dominion Dimensions of the Anglo-Irish Settlement, c. 1906–1922." In *The MacKenzie Moment and Imperial History: Essays in Honour of John M. MacKenzie*, edited by Stephanie Barczewski and Martin Farr, 211–37. Cham: Palgrave Macmillan, 2019.

Lynn, Shane. "Osmond Esmonde's Dominion Odyssey: Irish Nationalism in the British Empire, 1920–21." *Australasian Journal of Irish Studies* 14 (2014): 69–90.

———. "Friends of Ireland: Early O'Connellism in Lower Canada." *Irish Historical Studies* 40, no. 157 (2016): 43–65.

———. "Before the Fenians: 1848 and the Irish Plot to Invade Canada." *Éire-Ireland* 51, nos. 1 and 2 (Spring/Summer 2016): 61–91.

MacDonagh, Oliver. "Emigration from Ireland to Australia: An Overview." In *Australia and Ireland 1788–1988: Bicentenary Essays*, edited by Colm Kiernan, 121–37. Dublin: Gill and Macmillan, 1986.

Malcolm, Elizabeth and Dianne Hall. *A New History of the Irish in Australia*. Sydney: NewSouth Publishing, 2018.

Mannion, Patrick. *A Land of Dreams: Ethnicity, Nationalism, and the Irish in Newfoundland, Nova Scotia, and Maine, 1880–1923*. Montreal & Kingston: McGill-Queen's University Press, 2018.

———. "'I'm as Good an Irishman as You': The Ancient Order of Hibernians and the Construction of Irish Ethnicity in Canada and the United States, 1908–1918." *Journal of American Ethnic History* 41, no. 2 (Winter 2022): 26–57.

——— and Fearghal McGarry, eds. *The Irish Revolution: A Global History*. New York: New York University Press, 2022.

Marks, Shula. "Rewriting the South African War." H-SAfrica, H-Net Reviews, June 2003. www.h-net.org.

Mathews, P. J. "Stirring Up Disloyalty: The Boer War, the Irish Literary Theatre and the Emergence of a New Separatism." *Irish University Review* 33, no. 1 (Spring–Summer, 2003): 99–116.

Maume, Patrick. *The Long Gestation: Irish Nationalist Life 1891–1918*. New York: St. Martin's, 1999.

Maynard, John. "'Let Us Go' . . . It's a 'Blackfellows' War': Aborigines and the Boer War." *Aboriginal History* 39 (2015): 143–62.

Mbenga, Bernard. "The Role of the Bakgatla of the Pilanesberg in the South African War." In *Writing a Wider War: Rethinking Gender, Race, and Identity in the South African War, 1899–1902*, edited by Greg Cuthbertson, Albert Grundlingh, and Mary-Lynn Suttie, 85–114. Athens: Ohio University Press, 2002.

McCarthy, Angela. *Irish Migrants in New Zealand, 1840–1937: "The Desired Heaven."* Woodbridge: Boydell Press, 2005.

———, ed. *Ireland in the World: Comparative, Transnational, and Personal Perspectives.* New York: Routledge, 2015.

McConville, Seán. *Irish Political Prisoners 1848–1922: Theatres of War.* London: Routledge, 2003.

McCracken, Donal P. "Irish Settlement and Identity in South Africa before 1910." *Irish Historical Studies* 28, no. 110 (Nov 1992): 134–49.

———. "'Fenians and Dutch Carpetbaggers': Irish and Afrikaner Nationalisms, 1877–1930." *Éire-Ireland* 29, no. 3 (Fall 1994): 109–125.

———. *MacBride's Brigade: Irish Commandos in the Anglo-Boer War.* Dublin: Four Courts, 1999.

———. "Odd Man Out: The South African Experience." In *The Irish Diaspora*, edited by Andy Bielenberg, 251–71. Florence: Routledge, 2000.

———. *Forgotten Protest: Ireland and the Anglo-Boer War.* Belfast: Ulster Historical Foundation, 2003.

———. "From Paris to Paris via Pretoria: Arthur Lynch at War." *Études irlandaises* 28 (1) (2003): 125–42.

———. *Inspector Mallon: Buying Irish Patriotism for a Five-Pound Note.* Dublin: Irish Academic Press, 2009.

———. "John Ardagh (1840–1907): The Irish Intelligence Scapegoat for Britain's Anglo-Boer War Debacles." *Études irlandaises* 38, no. 1 (July 2013): 55–67.

———. "Michael Davitt's Wartime Visit to South Africa (March–May 1900) and Its Consequences." *Scientia Militaria, South African Journal of Military Studies* 46, no. 2 (2018): 53–76.

McGarry, Fearghal. *The Rising: Ireland: Easter 1916.* Oxford: Oxford University Press, 2010.

——— and James McConnel, eds. *The Black Hand of Republicanism: Fenianism in Modern Ireland.* Dublin: Irish Academic Press, 2009.

McGee, Owen. *The IRB: the Irish Republican Brotherhood, from the Land League to Sinn Féin.* Dublin: Four Courts Press, 2005.

———. *Arthur Griffith.* Dublin: Merrion Press, 2015.

McGowan, Mark G. *The Waning of the Green: Catholics, the Irish, and Identity in Toronto, 1887–1922.* Montreal: McGill-Queen's University Press, 1998.

———. *The Imperial Irish: Canada's Irish Catholics Fight the Great War, 1914–18.* Montreal: McGill-Queen's University Press, 2017.

McGrath, Ann. "Shamrock Aborigines: The Irish, the Aboriginal Australians, and Their Children." *Irish and Scottish Encounters with Indigenous Peoples: Canada, the United States, New Zealand, and Australia*, edited by David A. Wilson and Graeme Morton, 108–43. Montreal & Kingston: McGill-Queen's University Press, 2013.

McKenna, Joseph. *The Irish American Dynamite Campaign: A History, 1881–1896.* Jefferson, NC: McFarland & Co., 2012.

McKinnon, Malcolm. "Opposition to the War in New Zealand." In *One Flag, One Queen, One Tongue: New Zealand, the British Empire and the South African War,*

1899–1902, edited by John Crawford and Ian McGibbon, 28–45. Auckland: Auckland University Press, 2003.

McMahon, Paul. *British Spies and Irish Rebels: British Intelligence and Ireland, 1916–1945*. Woodbridge, UK: Boydell Press, 2008.

McMahon, Timothy G., Michael de Nie, and Paul Townend, eds. *Ireland in an Imperial World: Citizenship, Opportunism, and Subversion*. London: Palgrave Macmillan, 2017.

McNamara, Heather J. "The *New Zealand Tablet* and the Irish Catholic Press Worldwide, 1898–1923." *New Zealand Journal of History* 37, no. 2 (2003): 153–70.

McQuilton, Francis John. "Resisting the Siren Call of Empire? Kelly Country during the Boer War and the First World War." In *Echoes of Irish Australia: Rebellion to Republic—A Collection of Essays*, edited by Jeff Brownrigg, Cheryl Mongan, and Richard Reid, 59–69. Paragon: Canberra, 2007.

———. *Australia's Communities and the Boer War*. Cham: Springer International Publishing, 2016.

Meaney, Neville. "The Problem of Nationalism and Transnationalism in Australian History: A Reply to Marilyn Lake and Christopher Waters." *History Australia* 12, no. 2 (2015): 209–231.

Meleady, Dermot. *Redmond: The Parnellite*. Cork: Cork University Press, 2008.

Miller, Carman. *The Canadian Career of the Fourth Earl of Minto: The Education of a Viceroy*. Waterloo: Wilfried Laurier University Press, 1980.

———. *Painting the Map Red: Canada and the South African War, 1899–1902*. Montreal: Canadian War Museum, 1993.

Miller, Kerby A. *Emigrants and Exiles: Ireland and the Irish Exodus to North America*. New York: Oxford University Press, 1985.

Moir, John S. "The Problem of a Double Minority: Some Reflections on the Development of the English-Speaking Catholic Church in Canada in the Nineteenth Century." *Histoire sociale / Social History* 4, no. 7 (1971): 53–67.

Mommsen, Wolfgang J. "Introduction." In *The International Impact of the Boer War*, edited by Keith Wilson, 1–7. Chesham: Acumen, 2001.

Molloy, Kevin. "Victorian, Historians and Irish History: A Reading of the *New Zealand Tablet*, 1873–1903." In *The Irish in New Zealand: Historical Contexts & Perspectives*, edited by Brad Patterson, 153–70. Wellington: Stout Research Centre for New Zealand Studies, 2002.

Mount, Graeme S. *Canada's Enemies: Spies and Spying in the Peaceable Kingdom*. Toronto: Dundurn Press, 1993.

Murphy, William. "Narratives of Confinement: Fenians, Prisons and Writing, 1867–1916." In *The Black Hand of Republicanism: Fenianism in Modern Ireland*, edited by Fearghal McGarry and James McConnel, 160–76. Dublin: Irish Academic Press, 2009.

Nasson, Bill. *Abraham Esau's War: A Black South African War in the Cape, 1899–1902*. Cambridge: Cambridge University Press, 1991.

———. "A Great Divide: Popular Responses to the Great War in South Africa." *War & Society* 12, no. 1 (May 1994): 47–64.

———. *The Boer War: The Struggle for South Africa*. Stroud: The History Press, 2011.

Naughtin, Patrick. "*The Melbourne Advocate*, 1868–1900: Bastion of Irish Nationalism in Colonial Victoria." In *Visual, Material and Print Culture in Nineteenth-Century Ireland*, edited by Ciara Breathnach and Catherine Lawless, 223–33. Dublin: Four Courts Press, 2010.

Nelson, Bruce. *Irish Nationalists and the Making of the Irish Race*. Princeton: Princeton University Press, 2012.

Neufeld, Robert. "Cabals, Quarrels, Strikes and Impudence: Kingston Penitentiary, 1890–1914." *Histoire sociale / Social History* 31, no. 61 (1998): 95–125.

Ní Bhroiméil, Úna. "The South African War, Empire and the *Irish World*, 1899–1902." In *Newspapers and Empire in Ireland and Britain: Reporting the British Empire, c. 1857–1921*, edited by Simon J. Potter, 195–216. Dublin: Four Courts Press, 2004.

———. "'Up with the American Flag in All the Glory of Its Stainless Honor': Anti-Imperial Rhetoric in the *Chicago Citizen*, 1898–1902." In *Ireland in an Imperial World: Citizenship, Opportunism, and Subversion*, edited by Timothy G. McMahon, Michael de Nie, Paul Townend, 245–60. London: Palgrave Macmillan, 2017.

Nyhan Grey, Miriam, ed. *Ireland's Allies: America and the 1916 Easter Rising*. Dublin: University College Dublin Press, 2016.

O'Brien, Conor Cruise. *The Shaping of Modern Ireland*. London: Routledge & Kegan Paul, 1960.

O'Brien, Gillian. *Blood Runs Green: The Murder that Transfixed Gilded Age Chicago*. Chicago: University of Chicago Press, 2015.

O'Brien, Joseph V. *William O'Brien and the Course of Irish Politics, 1881–1918*. Berkeley: University of California Press, 1976.

Ó Broin, Leon. *The Prime Informer: A Suppressed Scandal*. London: Sidgwick & Jackson, 1971.

———. *Revolutionary Underground: The Story of the Irish Republican Brotherhood, 1858–1924*. Dublin, Gill & Macmillan, 1976.

O'Callaghan, Margaret. *British High Politics and a Nationalist Ireland: Criminality, Land and the Law under Forster and Balfour*. Cork: Cork University Press, 1994.

———. "Richard Pigott, the Fringe-Fenian Press and the Politics of Irish Nationalist Transition to Parnellism." In *The Black Hand of Republicanism: Fenianism in Modern Ireland*, edited by Fearghal McGarry and James McConnel, 150–59. Dublin: Irish Academic Press, 2009.

Ó Corráin, Daithí. "'A Most Public Spirited and Unselfish Man': The Career and Contribution of Colonel Maurice Moore, 1854–1939." *Studia Hibernica* 40 (2014): 71–133.

O'Donnell, Ruan. "Irish-Australia and the 1798 Centenary in Sydney." In *Echoes of Irish Australia: Rebellion to Republic—A Collection of Essays*, edited by Jeff Brownrigg, Cheryl Mongan, and Richard Reid, 1–11. Paragon: Canberra, 2007.

O'Farrell, Patrick. *The Irish in Australia*. Kensington, NSW: New South Wales University Press, 1987.

———. "Varieties of New Zealand Irishness: A Meditation." In *A Distant Shore: Irish Migration and New Zealand Settlement*, edited by Lyndon Fraser, 25–35. Dunedin: University of Otago Press, 2000.

O'Keeffe, Garrath. "Australia's Irish Republican Brotherhood." *Journal of the Royal Australian Historical Society* 83, no. 2 (Dec 1997): 136–52.

O'Leary, Fergal. *Ireland and Empire in the Late Nineteenth Century.* Woodbridge: The Boydell Press, 2023.

O'Leary, Michael Grattan. *Grattan O'Leary: Recollections of People, Press, and Politics.* Toronto: Macmillan of Canada, 1977.

Omissi, David E., and Andrew S. Thompson, eds. *The Impact of the South African War.* New York: Palgrave, 2002.

Pašeta, Senia. "Nationalist Responses to Two Royal Visits to Ireland, 1900 and 1903." *Irish Historical Studies* 31, no. 124 (Nov 1999): 488–504.

———. *Irish Nationalist Women, 1900–1918.* Cambridge: Cambridge University Press, 2013.

Patterson, Brad. ed., *The Irish in New Zealand: Historical Contexts & Perspectives.* Wellington: Stout Research Centre for New Zealand Studies, 2002.

Pinera, David. *American and English Influence on the Early Development of Ensenada, Baja California, Mexico.* San Diego: Institute for Regional Studies of the Californias, San Diego State University, 1995.

Plowman, Matthew Erin. "Irish Republicans and the Indo-German Conspiracy of World War I." *New Hibernia Review* 7, no. 3 (Autumn, 2003): 81–105.

———. "The British Intelligence Station in San Francisco during the First World War." *Journal of Intelligence History* 12, no. 1 (2013): 1–20.

Pocock, J.G.A. "The Limits and Divisions of British History: In Search of the Unknown Subject." *American Historical Review* 87, no. 2 (1982): 311–36.

Porter, Andrew. *The Origins of the South African War: Joseph Chamberlain and the Diplomacy of Imperialism, 1895–99.* New York: St. Martin's Press, 1980.

Porter, Bernard. *The Origins of the Vigilant State: The London Metropolitan Police Special Branch before the First World War.* London: Weidenfeld and Nicolson, 1987.

Pretorius, Fransjohan. "Boer Attitudes to Africans in Wartime." In *The South African War Reappraised,* edited by Donal Lowry, 104–120. Manchester: Manchester University Press, 2000.

Price, Richard. *An Imperial War and the British Working Class: Working-Class Attitudes and Reactions to the Boer War 1899–1902.* Toronto: University of Toronto Press, 1972.

Raible, Chris. "Benjamin Lett: Rebel Terrorist." *The Beaver* (Winnipeg) 82, no. 5 (Oct/Nov 2002): 10–15.

Regan-Lefebvre, Jennifer. *Cosmopolitan Nationalism in the Victorian Empire: Ireland, India and the Politics of Alfred Webb.* London: Palgrave Macmillan, 2009.

Robinson, Ronald and John Gallagher. *Africa and the Victorians: The Official Mind of Imperialism.* London: Macmillan, 1963.

Saunders, Christopher and Iain R. Smith. "Southern Africa, 1795–1910." In *The Oxford History of the British Empire, Vol. III: The Nineteenth Century,* edited by Andrew Porter, 597–623. Oxford: Oxford University Press, 1999.

Saunders, Malcolm and Ralph Summy. *The Australian Peace Movement: A Short History.* Canberra: Peace Research Centre, Australian National University, 1986.

Schreuder, Deryck and Stuart Ward, eds. *Australia's Empire*. Oxford: Oxford University Press, 2010.

Shott, Brian. *Mediating America: Black and Irish Press and the Struggle for Citizenship, 1870–1914*. Philadelphia: Temple University Press, 2019.

Silvestri, Michael. *Ireland and India: Nationalism, Empire and Memory*. New York: Palgrave Macmillan, 2009.

———. "British Imperial Intelligence and Anticolonial Revolutionaries during and after the Great War." In *The Irish Revolution: A Global History*, edited by Patrick Mannion and Feargal McGarry, 237–61. New York: New York University Press, 2022.

Smith, Iain R. *The Origins of the South African War, 1899–1902*. London: Longman, 1996.

Smyth, William J. *Toronto, the Belfast of Canada: The Orange Order and the Shaping of Municipal Culture*. Toronto: University of Toronto Press, 2018.

Strauss, Charles T. "God Save the Boer: Irish American Catholics and the South African War, 1899–1902." *U.S. Catholic Historian* 26, no. 4 (Fall 2008): 1–26.

Sweetman, Rory. "New Zealand Catholicism, War, Politics and the Irish Issue 1912–1922". PhD dissertation, University of Cambridge, 1990.

———. *Bishop in the Dock: The Sedition Trial of James Liston*. Auckland: Auckland University Press, 1997.

———. "'The Importance of Being Irish': Hibernianism in New Zealand, 1869–1969." In *A Distant Shore: Irish Migration & New Zealand Settlement*, edited by Lyndon Fraser, 135–54. Dunedin: University of Otago Press, 2000.

———. "How to Behave among Protestants: Varieties of Irish Catholic Leadership in Colonial New Zealand." In *The Irish in New Zealand: Historical Contexts and Perspectives*, edited by Brad Patterson, 89–102. Wellington: Stout Research Centre for New Zealand Studies, 2002.

Tamarkin, Mordechai. "The Cape Afrikaners and the British Empire from the Jameson Raid to the South African War." In *The South African War Reappraised*, edited by Donal Lowry, 121–39. Manchester: Manchester University Press, 2000.

Tilchin, William N. "The United States and the Boer War." In *The International Impact of the Boer War*, edited by Keith Wilson, 107–122. Chesham: Acumen, 2001.

Townend, Paul A. *The Road to Home Rule: Anti-Imperialism and the Irish National Movement*. Madison: University of Wisconsin Press, 2016.

———. "A Cosmopolitan Nationalist: James J. O'Kelly in America." In *Ireland in an Imperial World: Citizenship, Opportunism, and Subversion*, edited by Timothy G. McMahon, Michael de Nie, and Paul Townend, 223–43. London: Palgrave Macmillan, 2017.

Trigger, Rosalyn. "Clerical Containment of Diasporic Irish Nationalism: A Canadian Example from the Parnell Era." In *Irish Nationalism in Canada*, edited by David A. Wilson, 83–96. Montreal and Kingston: McGill-Queen's University Press, 2009.

Van Onselen, Charles. *Masked Raiders: Irish Banditry in South Africa 1880–1899*. Cape Town: Zeba Press, 2010.

Vronsky, Peter. *Ridgeway: The American Fenian Invasion and the 1866 Battle that Made Canada*. Toronto: Penguin, 2011.

Walsh, James P. and Timothy Foley. "Father Peter C. Yorke, Irish-American Leader." *Studia Hibernica* 14 (1974): 90–103.

Ward, Alan J. *Ireland and Anglo-American Relations, 1899–1921*. London: Weidenfeld and Nicolson, 1969.

Whelehan, Niall. *The Dynamiters: Irish Nationalism and Political Violence in the Wider Worlds, 1867–1900*. Cambridge: Cambridge University Press, 2012.

———. *Changing Land: Diaspora Activism and the Irish Land War*. New York University Press, 2021.

Wilcox, Craig. *Australia's Boer War*. Melbourne: Oxford University Press, 2002.

———. "Pardon Me for Being an Historian." *Australian Historical Studies* 41, no. 2 (June 2010): 233–40.

Williams, Caroline. "Moran, Mannix and St. Patrick's Day." In *Ireland and Australia, 1798–1998: Studies in Culture, Identity and Migration*, edited by Philip Bull, Frances Devlin-Glass, and Helen Doyle, 143–51. Sydney: Crossing Press, 2000.

Wilson, David A. *United Irishmen, United States: Immigrant Radicals in the Early Republic*. Ithaca: Cornell University Press, 1998.

———. "The Fenians in Montreal, 1862–68: Invasion, Intrigue, and Assassination." *Éire-Ireland* 38, nos. 3 and 4 (2003): 109–33.

———, ed. *The Orange Order in Canada*. Dublin: Four Courts Press, 2007.

———, ed. *Irish Nationalism in Canada*. Montreal and Kingston: McGill-Queen's University Press, 2009.

———. *Thomas D'Arcy McGee Volume II: The Extreme Moderate, 1857–1868*. Montreal and Kingston: McGill-Queen's University Press, 2011.

———. "2015 Marianna O'Gallagher Memorial Lecture: The Fenian World of Jeremiah O'Gallagher." *Canadian Journal of Irish Studies* 39, No. 1 (2015): 20–37.

———. *Canadian Spy Story: Irish Revolutionaries and the Secret Police*. Montreal and Kingston: McGill-Queen's University Press, 2022.

——— and Graeme Morton, eds. *Irish and Scottish Encounters with Indigenous Peoples: Canada, the United States, New Zealand, and Australia*. Montreal & Kingston: McGill-Queen's University Press, 2013.

Wilson, Keith, ed. *The International Impact of the Boer War*. Chesham: Acumen, 2001.

Winton, Graham. *Theirs Not to Reason Why: Horsing the British Army 1875–1925*. Solihull: Helion & Company Limited, 2013.

Wooding, Jonathan M. "The 'Language in Which They Spoke in '98': The Irish Language and the Centenary of 1798 in Ireland and Australia." In *Ireland and Australia, 1798–1998: Studies in Culture, Identity and Migration*, edited by Philip Bull, Frances Devlin-Glass, and Helen Doyle, 143–51. Sydney: Crossing Press, 2000.

INDEX

Page numbers in *italics* indicate Figures.

"The Absent-Minded Beggar," 147

Adair House, bombing of, 54

Advocate (newspaper), 153, 155, 156, 159, 163–64; Davitt in, 166; Gunson in, 169; Lynch, Arthur, in, 167

Afrikaner. *See* Boers

Age (newspaper), 155, 159

agent provocateur, 53, 56

Agent X, 88, 89, 98, 100, 276n137; "Donovan" and, 92–94, 99; Ladies' Auxiliary and, 87; Pickersgill and, 85–86, 90, 93, 94–95; Transvaal Committee, of California and, 85, 91, 97

Agent Z, 212, 224, 237, 238, 243, 261n7; Clan na Gael and, 215, 239; Crossin and, 225; Gosselin and, 213–14; Schlippenbach and, 221. *See also* "Wilcox"

Akenson, Donald Harman, 253

Aldborough Barracks, attempted bombing of, 58

Allan, Fred, 28, 29, 38, 58; Crossin and, 65; *Independent* and, 59; Nolan and, 242; Welland Canal and, 72

Ancient Order of Hibernians (AOH), 25, 78, 190, 274n105, 290n4; Clan na Gael and, 191, 224; Dillon, L., and, 231; Germany and, 241; Keating and, 106, 120; in Montreal, 179–81; in New Brunswick, 180–81; in Toronto, 192

Anderson, Robert, 56, 223; Parnell and, 57, 260n4

Anglo-American conflict, 72

Anglo-Irish Treaty, 5, 251–52

Anglo-Saxonism, 113; imperialism and, 76, 111

anti-Catholicism, 31, 202

anti-imperialism, xii, 3, 16, 20, 112–13, 129; Finerty and, 111

Anti-Imperialist League, 109, 163

anti-Semitism, 15, 40, 168–69, 222

AOH. *See* Ancient Order of Hibernians

Ardagh, John C., 38, 39; Gonne and, 42

Armstrong, Harry Gloster, 237–38, 241, 249; Pedlar and, 239–40, 242. *See also* Agent Z; "Wilcox"

Auckland, New Zealand, 146

Aughnamullen House, 299n155

Australasia: Old and New (Grey, J. G.), 153–54

Australia, 19, 21, 136, 138–39; Fenian Brotherhood in, 168, 178; Irish Catholicism in, 155–56, 176, 281n19; Melbourne, 134, 154–55, 167; New South Wales, 175; Nowra, 173; O'Brien, W., in, 146; Sydney, 137, 167–68; Victoria, 164, 169–70

Australian Anti-War League, 289n125

Ballina, 25, 37

Barker, Wharton, 230

Barr, Colin, 150

Barrett, James, 35

Barry, Richard J., 125

Barry, Thomas F., 78, 79

Baum, Alexander R., 85; Agent X and, 86, 97; Pickersgill and, 93, 94–95
Beach, Thomas Billis. *See* Le Caron, Henri
Belich, James, 19; "Better Britonism" and, 152
Beresford Place, 31
bittereinders, 13
"Black Week," 13, 43, 199
Blake, Edward, 12, 196, 197, 198–99
Blake, John, 161
Blake, Louisa, 141
Bloemfontein, Orange Free State, 61
Bloom, Leopold (fictional character), 245, 250
The Boer Fight for Freedom (Davitt), 15
Boer Franco-Irish Committee, 38, 43
BOI. *See* Bureau of Investigation
Borden, Robert, 231–33, 298n124
Botha, Louis, 246
Bourassa, Henri, 188, 190, 199
Bourke Cockran, William, 108–9, *110*, 113, 114, 205, 219–20; Fenian Brotherhood and, 106; Ford and, 118; Lynch, Arthur, and, 163
Boxer rebellion, 150, 204
Boyle, Patrick, 192–93
"The Boys of Wexford," 33
De Brandt (spy), 38, 42
British Cape Colony, 14
British secret police, 17. *See also* Home Office Crime Department—Special Branch
British South Africa Company, 11
Bryan, William Jennings, 109, *115*; Clan na Gael and, 114
Bunbury, Rev. Joseph, 175, 177, 290n130
Bureau of Investigation (BOI), 216–17; Fenianism and, 243
Burke, Alfred Edward, 232–33
Butt, Isaac, 19

California, 81. *See also* San Francisco, California; Transvaal Committee, of California

Call (newspaper), 81, 96
Canada, 52; AOH in, 290n4; Clan na Gael in, 72, 105, 119; Fenian Brotherhood in, 48, 87, 191, 194–96; Irish Catholicism in, 192, 205, 206; jingoism in, 19, 199; Ottawa, 192, 205; Quebec, 188–89, 192, 200–201; Saint John, 180–81; UIL in, 204, 205–6; United States and, 191, 231. *See also* Ontario, Canada
Canadian Freeman (newspaper), 196
Canadian Secret Service Agency, 69
Carew, J. J., 236–37, 239
Carpenter, Grant, 101
Carr, Archbishop Thomas, 170
Carroll, William, 297n104
Carson, Edward, 166
Cassini (Count), 221
Catholicism, 31, 111, 113, 145, 150, 202; Hiberno-Roman hierarchy in, 170. *See also* Irish Catholicism
Catholic Press (newspaper), 163, 172–73, 174–75
Catholic Record (newspaper), 202, 203; UIL in, 293n126
Catholic Register (newspaper), 189, 190, 192–93, 195, 199–200, 204; *Catholic Record* compared to, 202; Fitzpatrick and, 197; jingoism and, 199, 201; on Welland Canal, 203
Cavan Militia, 237
Celtic Union, San Francisco, 78
Chalmette. *See* New Orleans
Chamberlain, Joseph, 11–12, 20, 27–28, 31, 223
Chandra, Ram, 241–42
Chants for the Boer (Miller), 80
Chatham prison, 186
Chicago Citizen (newspaper), 76, 114; Finerty and, 105
Chronicle (newspaper), 82; Kruger, S., in, 96
Churchill, Jennie, 108
Churchill, Winston, 13; Bourke Cockran and, 108; Pearson and, 123

CID. *See* Criminal Investigation Department

City Imperial Volunteers, 154–55

City Mint, San Francisco, 83–84

Clan na Gael, 19, 43, 48, 124, 128, 246; Agent Z and, 214–15, 239; AOH and, 191, 224; BOI and, 243; British secret police and, 17; Bryan and, 114; in Canada, 72, 105, 119; Clarke, T., and, 6; Cronin, P., and, 27, 29; Crossin and, 61, 118, 225; Dillon, L., and, 56–57, 230; Emmet and, 219; Ford and, 117; Free Soil Club of, 53–54; Gaelic League and, 105; Germany and, 250; Hibernian Knights and, 190; IPP and, 116; IRB and, 1, 21, 65; Irish Transvaal Brigade and, 104; Keating and, 106; Kingston Penitentiary and, 226; Knights of the Red Branch of, 78, 87–88, 89; Lyman and, 50; MacBride and, 163; McGarrity and, 71, 211–12, 294n4; McKinley administration and, 120; O'Brien, P., and, 68; Von Papen and, 241; Pearson and, 125–26; Pinkerton Detective Agency and, 121; Russia and, 222; Triangle faction in, 55, 56, 116; UILA and, 219–20; UIL and, 118, 217, 218; Welland Canal and, 52, 70; "Wilcox" and, 221

Clare Militia, 33

Clarke, Tom, *8*, 9, 70, 117, 186, 211; Daly, J., and, 55; Daly, K., and, 7, 19, 258n33, 260n72; IRB and, 6, 249; Lynch, Arthur, and, 167; on MacBride, 18; McGarry on, 21; Merna and, 60; O'Kelly and, 242; racism of, 16

Cleary, Henry William, 147–48, *149*, 150–52, 177

Cnopius, Carrie, 80, 86, 274n105; Agent X and, 95, 99–100; Van Baggen and, 91

Cnopius, Louis Christian, 86, 90, 276n137; Van Baggen and, 91, 273n82

Coffey, Thomas, 202–3

Cohalan, Daniel, 219, 242

Colenso, battle of, 13, 168

College Green, Dublin, 31, *32*

Colles, Ramsey, 41

Collier's (magazine), 237–38

Collins, Michael, 6

Colum, Padraic, 211

concentration camps, 13, 14, 34, 251; Barberton, 123

Coningham, Arthur, 174

Connolly, C. N., 169

Connolly, James, 31, 35

Constable, Euphemia, 49, 63

Cooney, Michael, 80, 102, 134

Cooney, Patrick "the Fox," 261n19

Cormac, T. E. K., 85, 241; Agent X and, 86, 97; Jordan, M. F., and, 88–89, 90; Pickersgill and, 93, 94–95

Cosgrave, "Willie" T., 242

Criminal Investigation Department (CID), 54, 261n6

Cronin, Patrick Francis, 195–97, 199, 203, 204–5; on jingoism, 200

Cronin, Patrick Henry, 27, 29, 55, 116, 261n19; Triangle faction and, 56

Cronin, Sean, 124–25

Crossin, William, 62, 64, 124–25, 229, 230, 235; Allan and, 65; Clan na Gael and, 61, 118, 225; Devoy and, 232; McNello and, 215, 217, 224

Cuba, xii, 28, 190, 251

Curtis, George, 69

Dáil Éireann, 250–51

Dallman, Karl (alias), 50, *51*, 62, 64–66, 70, 92–94; Murray and, 228. *See also* Dillon, Luke

Dalton (Father), 173–74

Daly, John, 6–7, 47, 55, 117

Daly, Kathleen, 18; Clarke, T., and, 7, 19, 258n33, 260n72

Davis, Webster, 216

Davitt, Michael, 1–2, *39*, 137; *The Boer Fight for Freedom*, 15; Cronin, P. F., and, 197; on Featherstone, 187; Finerty and, 117; First Anglo-Boer War and, 44, 45; Gonne and, 41; Gunson and, 156; Kruger, P., and, 176; Lipton and, 288n89; Lynch, Arthur, and, 161, 164, 166; UIL and, 28, 46; on *uitlanders*, 35; Zionism and, 40
Deasy, Jeremiah, 102
De La Rey, Koos, 247
Denver, Colorado, 96
De Raylan, Nicolai, 221
De Villiers, Louis, 125–26
Devlin, Bernard, 190
Devlin, Charles Ramsay, 190, 232; Dillon, L., and, 225–26; Laurier and, 230
Devlin, Emmanuel Berchmans, 190
Devoy, John, 18, 28, 29, 70, *184*, 187; Crossin and, 232; Dillon, L., and, 55, 61–62; *Gaelic American* and, 220; Gannon and, 296n83; Holland and, 116–17; in Irish American Union, 114; MacBride and, 120; McGarrity and, 211, 226, 227, 235–36; in Montreal, 183, 185–86; O'Kelly and, 242; De Valera and, 250–51
De Wet, Christiaan, 6, 95, 247; Kruger, S., and, 75
De Wet, Piet, 95
De Wet, Susanna "Sannie," 95–96, 101
Digby, Kenelm, 42, 120, 214, 218; Gosselin and, 223–24
Dillon, John, 28, 52; Grey, J. G., and, 134, 153; INF and, 146; Sheahan and, 147
Dillon, Luke, 53–55, 59, 71, *227*, 235; AOH and, 231; Clan na Gael and, 56–57, 230; as Dallman, 50, *51*, 62, 64–66, 70, 92–94, 228; Devlin, C., and, 225–26; at Dime Savings Bank, 61–62; McGlade and, 233, 234; McNello and, 229; Ryan, M. J., and, 116; in *Washington Times*, *234*; at Welland Canal, 62–64
Dillon, Mary, 227, 230
Dillon, Robert Emmet, 235

Dime Savings Bank, 61–62
DMP. *See* Dublin Metropolitan Police
Doherty, Charles Joseph, 232, 233, 298n124
Dolan, James, 224
Donohoe, Denis, 85; Agent X and, 86, 97; Pickersgill and, 93, 94–95
"Donovan," 91–94, 95, 99
Dorset Regiment, 33
Dreyfusards, 40
Driffield, Cora, 95
Dublin: College Green, 31, *32*; O'Connell Bridge in, 30; Transvaal Committee of, 35, 176
Dublin Castle, 31, 43
Dublin Corporation, 6, 38; Irish Transvaal Brigade and, 44
Dublin Fusiliers, 34, 150
Dublin Metropolitan Police (DMP), 30–31, 261n7; G Division of, 57
Duggan, Thomas, 177–78
Duke of Connaught's Own Rifles, 90
Dunedin, New Zealand, 139–40
Dungannon, Co. Tyrone, 6
Dunne, Patrick, 172–73, 175
Dwyer, Michael, 167–68
Dynamite War, 6, 54–56

Easter Rising, 1916, 5–6, 138, 211, 221, 242, 249–50
Edward VII (King), 165, 167
Egan, James, 47
Egypt, 11
Emmet, Robert, 81, 108–9, 219
Esquimalt, 87–88, 103, 128; Fenianism and, 90–91
Eureka Rebellion, 160
Evening Post (newspaper), 140
Evening Star (newspaper), 139–40; Grey, J. G., in, 153
Explosives Act, 58

Fagen (Captain), 87, 90; Pickersgill and, 91
"Famine Queen" article, 37, 202

Featherstone, Timothy (alias), 186–87. *See also* Kennedy, Edward O'Brien

Fenianism, xiii, 1, 5, 16–17, 43, 69, 176, 245–46; Agent Z and, 214; Anglo-American conflict and, 72; Anglo-Irish Treaty and, 251; in Australia, 168, 178; BOI and, 243; in Canada, 48, 87, 191, 194–96; Cooney and, 80; Crossin and, 61; Devoy and, 185; Esquimalt and, 90–91; Fenian Brotherhood, 11, 18, 53–54, 72, 87, 105, 189; Gonne and, 37; Gosselin and, 25–26; Grey, J. G., and, 153; IPP and, 19–20, 136–37; Irish Catholicism and, 155, 158–59; Le Caron and, 54, 56; Local Government (Ireland) Act and, 28–29; Lyman and, 29; Lynch, Arthur, and, 164; Nolan and, 65; O'Donnell, J., and, 46; in Paris, 26, 38, 39; P. W. Nally Club and, 57; Roosevelt and, 119; Russia and, 221; UIL and, 18–19, 47–48, 104, 117, 159; Welland Canal and, 52, 53

Ferguson, John C., 180, 191

Fernandes de Quiros, Pedro, 154

Finerty, John F., 76, 108, 109; anti-imperialism and, 111; Bryan and, 114; Davitt and, 117; Home Rule and, 219, 252; Lynch, Arthur, and, 163; Redmond, J., and, 218; UIL and, 116, 246; UISC and, 105–6

First Anglo-Boer War, 10, 14–15; IPP and, 44, 45

Fitzharris, James "Skin-the-Goat," 66, *67*, 67–69, 128; in *Ulysses*, 245

Fitzpatrick, Charles, 197, *198*, 229, 232

Flanagan, Charles B., 80, 95

Ford, Patrick, 45–46, 102; Bourke Cockran and, 106, 118; Clan na Gael and, 117; Grey, J. G., and, 153; in Irish American Union, 114; Redmond, J., and, 219; Rutledge and, 193

Foster, Roy, 2

Foy, Charles J., 232

France, 28, 40; Paris, 26, 38, 39

Franklin, Benjamin, 118

Freedom of Thought & Speech in New Zealand (Grey, J. G.), 140–41

Freeman's Journal (newspaper), 45, 151, 172–73, 195

French Canadians, 188–90

Friends of Freedom for India, 251

Gaddafi, Muammar, 252

Gaelic American (newspaper), 187, 220–21, 222

Gaelic League: of California, 81; Clan na Gael and, 105

Gallagher, Jeremiah, 191

Gandhi, Mohandas K., 13, 14

Gannon, John, 231, 296n83

Gazette (newspaper), 179–80, 186

G Division, DMP, 57

German, William Manley, 64, 66, 232

Germany, xii, 151, 217, 247; AOH and, 241; United States and, 250

Gibbon, Edward, 111–12

Gillingham, Solomon, 161, 163

Gladstone, William, 10, 196

Globe (newspaper), 195–96

Glynn, Patrick McMahon, 167, 168

Gonne, Maud, 18, *36*, 39, 48, 59; Home Office Crime Department-Special Branch and, 41–42; Kruger, S., compared to, 95, 100, 102–3; Lynch, Arthur, and, 160; MacBride and, 117, 260n74; at New York Academy of Music, 112; O'Connell, F., and, 40–41; Redmond, W., and, 176; Transvaal Committee, of Dublin and, 35, 36; UIL and, 172; Victoria (Queen) and, 37–38; Welland Canal and, 70, 72

Gosselin, Nicholas, 25–26, 27, 70–71; Agent Z and, 213–14; Armstrong and, 237; Clan na Gael and, 50, 124; Clare Militia and, 33; Digby and, 223–24; Gonne and, 41–42; Jenkinson and, 238; Kingston Penitentiary and, 120;

Gosselin, Nicholas (*cont.*)
  Lyman and, 29; Lynch, Arthur, and, 163; Merna and, 58, 60; on Reid, P., 266n43; on *USS Maine*, 270n96
"Greater Ireland," 4–5, 200
great rapprochement, 102, 113, 231
Great Trek, 9
The Great War, 33, 191, 242–43, 247–48; United States in, 102
Grey, Helen Edith, 274n105
Grey, James Grattan, 21, 133, *135*, 152, 176, 204; at *Advocate*, 155; *Australasia* of, 153–54; Cleary compared to, 150; *Freedom of Thought & Speech in New Zealand* of, 140–41; The Great War and, 248; IPP and, 137; jingoism and, 134, 151; Lynch, Arthur, compared to, 163; Morant and, 166; in *New York Times*, 138–40, 142–43, 151; Peace and Humanity Society and, 156; Rentoul and, 285n13; Reporting Debates and Printing Committee and, 143–44, 145; on Samoa, 284n90; Transvaal Committee, of California and, 101–2, 134; UIL and, 157; at *Western Australian Record*, 177
Grey, Jane, 133–34, *135*, 155, 280n2
Griffith, Arthur Hill, 11, 169, 170, 246, 247–48; Gonne and, 41; McCarthy, J. F., and, 68; *Newcastle Morning Herald* and, 174; Transvaal Committee, of Dublin and, 35; UIL and, 47; in *United Irishman*, 40
Gunning, James Joseph, 173–74
Gunson, William, 156; in *Advocate*, 169

HACBS. *See* Hibernian Australasian Catholic Benefit Society
Hall, Dianne, 177
Handcock, Peter, 166
Harmsworth, Alfred, 165
Harper's Bazaar (magazine), 199
Harrel, David, 26, 246; Gonne and, 41–42; McGillicuddy sisters and, 37
Harrison, William Greer, 83

Hay, John, 118, 126–27
Healy, T. E., 168–69
Heard, William Wright, 126–27
Hearst, William Randolph, 163, 222
Hehir, Hugh, 30
Henderson, Frank, 30
Hennessy, Mary, 46
Hibernian Australasian Catholic Benefit Society (HACBS), 147, 151–52, 282n21; in New South Wales, 175
Hibernian Knights, 183, 191, 207; Clan na Gael and, 190
Hiberno-Roman hierarchy, 170
Higgins, Henry Bournes, 159, 289n125
Higgins, Michael D., 253–54
high imperialism, xi, 2, 20
Hobhouse, Emily, 13
Hobson, J. A., 2
Holland, John Philip, 116–17
Home Office Crime Department—Special Branch, 25–26, 27, 70–71, 223–24; Gonne and, 41–42; Jenkinson and, 238; Lyman and, 29; Millen and, 56; Nolan and, 57
Home Rule, xiii, 5, 16, 104, 136, 246–47; Blake, E., on, 196; Cleary and, 148; Cronin, P. F., on, 199; Devoy and, 183; Dunne, Patrick, and, 173; Finerty and, 219, 252; Glynn and, 167; Grey, J. G., and, 145, 177; Higgins, H., and, 159; IPP and, 158; Peace and Humanity Society and, 157; Redmond, J., and, 240–41; Rentoul and, 154; Salisbury and, 207; Third Home Rule Bill, 231
Home Rule Party, 10
House of Commons, bombing of, 54
Hudson, Grace Carpenter, 101
Humbert (General), 25
Hussey, Frank, 94
Hutcheson, John, 142, 143

imperialism, xi–xii, 83, 175, 200, 221–22, 253–54; Anglo-Saxonism and, 76, 111;

capital and, 259n48; high, 20; Irish Catholicism and, 177; jingoism and, 2, 137; McKinley administration and, 113–14; in Philippines, 81; of United States, 109; white supremacy and, 15–16

INA. *See* Irish National Alliance

Independent (newspaper), 28, 29, 30; Allan and, 59

Indian Chieftain (newspaper), 111–12

Indian Civil Service, 299n52

Indigenous people, 169–70, 197

INF. *See* Irish National Federation

Inghinidhe na hÉireann (Daughters of Ireland), 38

Inter-Ocean (newspaper), 111

IPP. *See* Irish Parliamentary Party

IRA. *See* Irish Republican Army

IRB. *See* Irish Republican Brotherhood

Irish American Club, 217

Irish American Transvaal Ambulance Corps, 106, *107*, 108

Irish American Union, 114

Irish Canadian (newspaper), 192, 193

Irish Catholic Benevolent Union, 200

Irish Catholicism, 3, 20, 148, 154; in Australia, 155–56, 176, 281n19; in Canada, 192, 205, 206; Fenianism and, 155, 158–59; imperialism and, 177; in Montreal, 179–82, 187; national identity and, 134, 136; in New Zealand, 137–38, 176

Irish diaspora, xi, 3, 4, 137–38, 248, 252–53

Irish Figaro (newspaper), 41

Irish Literary Society, Ottawa, 193

Irish militia companies, 33

Irish National Alliance (INA), 27–28; Finerty and, 105; Lynch, Arthur, and, 160

Irish National Convention, 134; Grey, J. G., at, 153

Irish National Federation (INF), 146, 152

Irish National Invincibles, 57

Irish nationalism. *See specific topics*

Irish National League, 105

Irish Parliamentary Party (IPP), 1, 5, 18, 117, 128, 204, 246; *Advocate* and, 156; Cronin, P. F., and, 197; Fenianism and, 19–20, 136–37; First Anglo-Boer War and, 44, 45; Home Rule and, 158; INF and, 146; Irish Catholicism and, 155; in Khaki Election, 157; Lynch, Arthur, and, 164–65, 166–67; Parnell and, 55; Redmond, J., and, 7, 9; Redmond, J., in, 247; UIL and, 28, 46, 114, 116, 176

Irish Political Prisoners' Fund, 62, 267n70

Irish question, xi, 54, 102, 134, 136, 148, 202, 232

Irish Republic (newspaper), 12, 27, 29

Irish Republican Army (IRA), 18, 300n180; in Canada, 53

Irish Republican Brotherhood (IRB), 27, 34, 246, 300n180; Clan na Gael and, 1, 21, 65; Clarke, T., and, 6, 249; Nolan in, 49; O'Connell, F., and, 40–41; Supreme Council of, 55; UIL and, 46–47; Welland Canal and, 52

Irish Republican Union, 52–53, 190

Irish Socialist Republican Party, 35

Irish Times (newspaper), 154

Irishtown, Co. Mayo, 11

Irish Transvaal Brigade, 35, 42; Clan na Gael and, 104; Dublin Corporation and, 44; Walsh, M., and, 43

Irish Volunteers, of Clan na Gael, 119, 231

Irish World (newspaper), 18, 45–46, 69, 102, 114, 187; on Ferguson, 180; Grey, J. G., in, 134, 154–55; Hay in, 118; "Ho for the Transvaal!" in, 120; McCaffrey in, 193; McGarrity in, 71; "Monrovia" in, 189–90; UIL and, 116; Van Baggen in, 112

L'Irlande Libre (journal), 38

Isandlwana, battle of, 11

Jackson, Alvin, 253

Jackson, Andrew, 127

Jameson, Leander Starr, 11–12

Jameson Raid, 11–12; IPP and, 44

Japan, 221–22
Jardine, Mrs. J. C., 160
Jenkinson, Edward George, 26, 238, 243, 299n152
JFM. *See* Jordan, M. F.
jingoism, 15, 19, 129, 148, 156, 192; *Catholic Register* and, 199, 201; Cronin, P. F., on, 200; Grey, J. G., and, 134, 151; imperialism and, 2, 137
Johnson, E. F. B., 65
Johnston, Anna, 43
Jones, J. J., 30, 35
Jones, Thomas Meric, 214, 215
Jordan, David Starr, 80, 99
Jordan, M. F., 94; Cormac and, 88–89, 90
Joubert, Piet, 95; Kruger, S., and, 75
Joyce, James, 245
Junior Carlton Club, bombing of, 54

Kavanagh, Patrick Fidelis, 172, 177
Keating, John T., 106, 120, 180–81, 190, 232, 233
Keilley, James, 177–78
Kelleher, Patrick, 46
Kelly, Archbishop Michael, 172, 175
Kelly, James, 148
Kelly, M. J., 43
Kennedy, Edward O'Brien, 186
Kennedy, Roderick, 117–18, 220
Khaki Election, 157, 164
Kimberley, 9, 12–13
Kingston Penitentiary, 66, 70, 119–20, 225–26, 227–28, 233
Kitchener, Herbert, 12; scorched earth tactics of, 13, 14, 34
Klondike, 119, 185
Knights of St. Patrick, 78
Knights of the Red Branch, 78, 87–88; Jordan, M. F., and, 89
Know-Nothing movement, 76
Kolbe, F. C., 202
Kruger, Paul, 11, 12, 75, 95, 163; *Chants for the Boer* and, 80; Clare Militia and, 33;

Davitt and, 176; Netherlands Society and, 78; Washington compared to, 16
Kruger, Paul (Reverend), 82–83
Kruger, Sannie, 75, 77, 95, 103; Carpenter and, 101; in *Harper's Bazaar*, 199; Newsam and, 96, 97; Transvaal Committee, of California and, 97, 102; Van Baggen and, 81–82, 100; Woodford, E., and, 98–99. *See also* Agent X

Lachine Canal, Montreal, 69
Ladysmith, 12–13
Laidlaw, James, 83, 87
Land League, 11
Land War, 6, 55
Latchford, Frank R., 200
Latta, Fred, 62–63
Laurier, Wilfrid, 119, 205, 230–31
Lawless, Joseph V., 30
Leach, Frank A., 84, 271n38
Le Caron, Henri, 54, 56, 61
Lenin, V. I., 2
Leonard, William E., 53
Lett, Benjamin, 52
Leyds, Willem Johannes, 40, 41, 48, 84, 201
Limerick Borough Council, 44
Lipton, Thomas, 288n89
LMP. *See* London Metropolitan Police
Local Government (Ireland) Act (1898), 28–29
Logue (Cardinal), 179
Lomasney, William Mackey, 55
London Metropolitan Police (LMP), 261n6
Los Angeles Times (newspaper), 83
Lowry, Donal, 6
Lyman, William, 27–28, 29, 57, 105; Agent Z and, 214; Carew and, 236; Clan na Gael and, 50; Nolan and, 58; Welland Canal and, 58–59
Lynch, Annie, 165, 166, 288n87, 288n89
Lynch, Arthur, 38, 155, 160–61, *162*, 204, 247; Bourke Cockran and, 163; IPP

and, 164–65, 166–67; McCracken on, 287n58

Lyttelton Times (newspaper), 141, 145

MacBride, John, 11, 128, 242; Clan na Gael and, 163; Devoy and, 120; Fenianism and, 18–19; Gonne and, 117, 260n74; Johnston and, 43; Lynch, Arthur, and, 161; UIL and, 46–47
MacDermott, Tom, 59
Mac Diarmada, Seán, 211, 242
MacDonagh, Oliver, 138
MacGuinness, James, 239
MacNamara, H. J., 159
Macready, Agnes, 174–75
Macrum, Charles, 98
Madden, Frank, 159
Mafeking, 12–13, 160
Magee, Edward, 87
Magersfontein, 13
Mahdi, of Sudan, 11
Mail & Empire (newspaper), 196, 197
Maine, *USS*, 124, 270n96
Majuba Hill, 10, 12
Malcolm, Elizabeth, 177
Mallon, John, 57–58, 67–68, 70, 223, 268n77; Merna and, 60; on Reid, P., 266n43
Manchester Ship Canal Company, 237–38
Mannion, Patrick, 191
Mannix, Daniel, 175
Maori people, 151, 284n90
Massey, William, 143
McAleer, William, 297n104
McCabe, Charles, 193
McCaffrey, Hugh, 180–81, 191; in *Irish World*, 193
McCalmont, Hugh, 42
McCarthy, Charles, 169
McCarthy, J. F., 68
McCracken, Donal P., 3, 19, 287n58
McDermott, James "Red Jim," 53–54, 186; Home Office Crime Department–Special Branch and, 55

McDonell, Cornelius A., 182, 193
McGarrity, Joseph, 53, *213*; Burke and, 232; Chandra and, 241–42; Clan na Gael and, 71, 211–12, 294n4; Crossin and, 225; Devoy and, 211, 226, 227, 235–36; on Dillon, L., 61; McNello and, 211–12; Pedlar and, 239–40
McGarry, Sean, 21
McGillicuddy sisters, 37
McGill University, 188
McGlade, Charles, 233, 234
McGowan, Mark, 192, 201
McGuinness, William, 59; Welland Canal and, 72
McInerney, Joe, 60, 61
McKinley, William, 98, 104; Anglo-Saxonism and, 76; Anti-Imperialist League and, 109; Clan na Gael and, 120; imperialism and, 113–14; Pearson and, 126; remount service and, 121
McNello, Bernard "Barney," 211–12, 222–23, 235, 238–39; Crossin and, 215, 217, 224; Dillon, L., and, 229; "Wilcox" and, 215–16, 217, 221, 225, 231, 235, 296n77
Mechanician (steam ship), 123–25, 126, 279n96
Melbourne, Australia, 155; Peace and Humanity Society in, 134; Shamrock Club of, 159, 167; University of, 154
Melbourne Advocate (newspaper), 45
Memoirs of a Great Detective (Speer), 63–64, 228
Merna, John, 60–61; Murray and, 65; Nolan and, 57–59
Mexican Land and Colonization Company, 237–38
Millen, Frank, 56
Miller, Joaquin, 80
Millevoye, Lucien, 37, 38, 40
Milner, Alfred, 12
Mitchel, John, 175, 220
Moana, SS, 133–34
Monitor (newspaper), 81

Monroe Doctrine, 20
"Monrovia," 189–90
Montreal, Quebec: Devoy in, 183, 185–86; Irish Catholicism in, 179–82, 187; Lachine Canal, 69
Montreal Star (newspaper), 187
Moore, Benjamin, 299n155
Moore, Maurice, 34, 251
Moore, Wellesley, 94
Moran, Patrick, 148, 150, 170, *171*, 172, 174, 177
Morant, Harry "Breaker," 166
Morgan, J. P., 237
Morley, John, 206
Morrison, Arthur, 143
Mullett, James, *67*, 67–69, 128
Murdoch Mysteries (drama series), 268n81
Murphy, Charles, 200
Murphy, Daniel V., 229
Murphy, G. T., 83
Murphy, John, 172
Murray, John Wilson, 63–66, 268n81; Dallman and, 228

Napoleonic Wars, 2, 3, 9
Nation (weekly), 80
National Boer Relief Fund Association, 106, 118, 163
national identity, Irish Catholicism and, 134, 136
Native American land, xii
Navy League, of New Zealand, 248
Nelson, Bruce, 6, 15
Netherlands Society, of San Francisco, 76, 78, 80
Newcastle Morning Herald (newspaper), 174
"New Departure" policy, 54, 116, 118, 218
New Orleans, Louisiana, 46, 104, 121–27, 215, 241
Newsam, Frank E., 96, 97
New South Wales, Australia, 175
New York: Irish Republican Union of, 190; United Irish Societies of, 118

New York Academy of Music, 112
New York Journal (newspaper), 163
New York Times (newspaper), 138–40, 142–43, 151
New York World (newspaper), 142
New Zealand, 138, 142–43, 145–46, 281n19, 282n20; Dunedin, 139–40; Irish Catholicism in, 137–38, 176; jingoism in, 19; Navy League of, 248; UIL in, 152; Women's National Council of, 141
New Zealand Herald (newspaper), 147, 157
New Zealand Tablet (newspaper), 148, 150, 151–52, 195, 202; *Advocate* compared to, 156
New Zealand Times (newspaper), 141–42
Niagara Falls, 49
Nolan, John, 49–50, *51*, 52, 60, 70, *227*; Allan and, 242; AOH and, 231; Crossin and, 61; Home Office Crime Department-Special Branch and, 71; Mallon on, 268n77; Merna and, 57–59; Murray and, 65–66; at Welland Canal, 62–63
North Cork Militia, 33
Northgraves, George R., 202–3
Northwest Review (journal), 201–2, 248
Nowra, Australia, 173

O'Brien, Cornelius, 200
O'Brien, Patrick "Rocky Mountain," 68; Dillon, L., and, 226
O'Brien, Thomas, 84, 271n38
O'Brien, William, 28, 47, 165, 219; in Australia, 146; Cronin, P. F., and, 197; Wyndham, G., and, 218
Observer (newspaper), 144
O'Connell, Daniel, 4
O'Connell Bridge, Dublin, 30
O'Donnell, Frank Hugh, 40–41, 48
O'Donnell, John, 46, 47
O'Donnell, Nicholas, 157, *158*, 159, 164
O'Donnell, Ruan, 168
O'Donovan Rossa, Jeremiah, 6, 68

O'Farrell, Patrick, 137, 177
O'Haran, Denis, 174
O'Kelly, Sean T., 242
O'Leary, Grattan, 187–88, 193
O'Leary, John, 35
Omdurman, Sudan, 12
O'Neill (General), 18
O'Neill, Roger, 54
Orange Free State, 9; Bloemfontein, 61; racial hierarchy in, 75; South African Republic and, 12
Orange Order, 196, 282n21
Order of the Midnight Sun, 119
O'Regan, Patrick Joseph, 143
Oregon, Portland, 83
The Oregonian (newspaper), 83
O'Reilly, John Boyle, 178
O'Rorke, George Maurice, 144
O'Shea, Patrick, 290n130
O'Shiel, Kevin, 31
O'Sullivan Burke, Ricard, 106, 108, 119–20
Ottawa, Canada, 187, 192–93, 195, 200, 205, 230, 233
Ottawa Journal (newspaper), 200

Paine, Thomas, 76
Von Papen, Franz, 241; O'Kelly and, 242
Paris, France, 26, 38, 39
Paris Peace Conference, 250
Parnell, Charles Stewart, 1, 5, 10–11, 26; Anderson and, 57, 260n4; IPP and, 55; Phoenix Park Murders and, 56
La Patrie (newspaper), 40, 45
Pauncefote, Julian, 85–86, 88; Agent X and, 94–95
Peace and Humanity Society, 154, 204; Gunson and, 156; Home Rule and, 157; in Melbourne, 134
Pearse, Patrick, 5–6
Pearson, Samuel, 121, 123, 124, 128, 216–17; Clan na Gael and, 125–26; Heard and, 126–27
Pedlar, Liam, 239–40, 242, 300n180

Penrose, Boies, 297n104
Phelan, James Duval, 80
Philadelphia Bulletin (newspaper), 113
Philippines, 81, 109, 111, 150
Phoenix Park, Victoria in, 38
Phoenix Park Murders, 25; Nolan and, 57; Parnell and, 56
Pickersgill, William Clayton, 84, 88, 89; Agent X and, 85–86, 90, 93, 94–95; Fagen and, 91
Pile, Thomas, 38, 59
Pinkerton Detective Agency, 65, 87, 92–93; Clan na Gael and, 121; Jordan, M. F., and, 89
Pinther, Theodore, 102
Plunkett, Horace, 164
Pocock, J. G. A., 4–5
Port Colborne, 268n88
Portland, Oregon, 83
Pothier, Aram J., 230
Press (newspaper), 141–42, 146
Primrose League, 206
Proclamation of the Irish Republic, 4
Protestants, 111, 148
P. W. Nally Club, 57–58

Quebec, Canada, 188–89, 192, 200–201. *See also* Montreal, Quebec

racial hierarchy, 75
racism, 16, 75, 111–13, 151
Reddy, Thomas M., 299n143
Redmond, John, 1, 46, 113, 117–18, 134, 201, 247; in Canada, 205–6; Dillon, L., and, 62; Finerty and, 218; Ford and, 219; Home Rule and, 240–41; IPP and, 7, 9; Lynch, Annie, and, 288n87, 288n89; Lynch, Arthur, and, 164, 166–67
Redmond, William, 35; Gonne and, 176
Reid, Pat, 58, 266n43
Reid, Whitelaw, 231, 232
remount service, 121, 123–24, 127–28
Rentoul, John Laurence, 154, 285n13

Revens, John, 226
Rhodes, Cecil, 11–12, 13
Rhynland, SS, 59–60
RIC. *See* Royal Irish Constabulary
Richmond Prison, 279n79
Rigor, D. Miles, 299n143
Roberts (Lord), 13, 151–52
Robinson, Seumas, 30
Roosevelt, Theodore, 119, 163, 271n38;
    Chalmette and, 127; Dillon, L., and,
    230; Pearson and, 126
Rothschild (Lord), 237
Rowan, John, 59–60; Dallman and, 64–65
Royal Irish Constabulary (RIC), 25–26, 28,
    261n7
Royal Irish Fusiliers, 137
Royal Strand Theatre, 237
Russell, George Warren, 144
Russia, 40, 221–22
Rutledge, Joseph, 193–94
Ryan, John Tighe, 175, 241
Ryan, Mark, 40; Lynch, Arthur, and, 160
Ryan, Michael J., 116, 217, 225, 226; Clan
    na Gael and, 118; Laurier and, 230
Ryan, O'Neill, 221

Saint John, Canada, 180–81
Salisbury (Lord), 119, 206–7
Samoa, 151, 284n90
Sanderson, Percy, 119, 121, 238
San Francisco, California, 75, 82, 134; Celtic
    Union in, 78; City Mint in, 83–84;
    "Donovan" in, 92–93; Tivoli Opera
    House in, 75, 96, 97; Yorke in, 80–81
San Francisco Call (newspaper), 75
"Saunders," 85
Scanlan, Francis, 89, 92
Scannell, Roger F., 87
Schlippenbach, Albert, 221
Schreiner, Olive, 142
scorched earth tactics, 251; of Kitchener,
    13, 14, 34
Scotland Yard, CID of, 54

Scott, Buchanan, 299n152
Scott, D'Arcy, 200, 205
Scott, Reginald, 90
Scott, Richard, 193
Seattle Times (newspaper), 194
Secret Intelligence Service, 242
secret societies, 25, 26, 44, 246; Irish
    National Invincibles, 57; Order of the
    Midnight Sun, 119. *See also* Clan na
    Gael; Fenianism
Seddon, Richard, 139, 140, 151, 284n90;
    Australasia and, 153–54; Grey, J. G., and,
    143, 144–45
Seitz, Edward, 160
"Self Determination Leagues," 249
Sentinel and Orange and Protestant Advocate
    (newspaper), 196
Shamrock Club, Melbourne, 159, 167
Shan Van Vocht (newspaper), 43
Sheahan, M. J., 147
Sheridan, Walter, 58
Sherwood, A. P., 65, 69, 87, 94
Shields, Mary, 53
Shoalhaven News (newspaper), 173–74
Sinn Féin, 31, 138, 249; Anglo-Irish Treaty
    and, 251–52; Pearson and, 217
Sinn Féin (newspaper), 220
Sioux Wars, 109, 111
Skadden, Florence, 217
Smith, Goldwin, 185
Smuts, Jan, 251
Snyman, Willem, 102
"Soldiers of the Queen," 147
South African Catholic (magazine), 202
South African Confederation Act, 10
South African Dominion, 246
South African Republic, 9, 10; Orange Free
    State and, 12; racial hierarchy in, 75;
    Witwatersrand, 11
South African War. *See specific topics*
South Mayo by-election (1900), 18–19,
    46–48, 114, 128
Spanish-American War, 28, 124

Special Commission on Parnellism and Crime, 56
Speer, Victor, 63, 228
Spion Kop, 14
Springfield, Missouri, 191
Stafford, Florence, 248
Stanley Barracks, Toronto, 195
Statute of Westminster, 252
Stead, W. T., 34, 199; Grey, J. G., and, 142
Stephens, James, 279n79
Stop the War Committee, 141
Stormberg, 13
Sudan, 11, 12
Sulzer, William, 127
Supreme Council, of IRB, 55
Swazi Kingdom, 14–15
Sweeny, Thomas William, 53
Sydney, Australia, 137; Waverley Cemetery in, 167–68

Tablet (newspaper), 202
Taft, William Howard, 230, 231
Talana Hill, 180
Tallon, Daniel, 44; Dillon, L., and, 62
Tarte, Israel, 188, 190
Teefy, John R., 195
Third Home Rule Bill, 231
Times (newspaper), 17, 56, 189
Tivoli Opera House, 75, 96, 97
Tone, Theobald Wolfe, 38, 41
Toronto, Ontario, 192, 195, 200; Stanley Barracks in, 195
Townend, Paul, 16, 252
the Transvaal. See South African Republic
Transvaal Committee, of California, 78–80, 81–83, 84, 86–87; Agent X and, 85, 91, 97; Grey, J. G., and, 101–2, 134; Jordan, M. F., and, 88
Transvaal Committee, of Dublin, 35, 36, 37, 42–43, 176; UIL and, 46
"Transvaal National Hymn," 97, 100
Treaty of Vereeniging, 128, 206
Triangle faction, 55, 116; Cronin, P., and, 56

Trinity College Dublin, 30–31
True Witness and Catholic Chronicle (newspaper), 181–83, 185–86, 189, 201, 202, 207; Blake, E., and, 196; "red hot letters" and, 194; on Redmond, J., 205–6
Tugela campaign, 34, 174
Turner, Francis John, 102
Tyrone Place, 58

UB. See United Brotherhood
UIL. See United Irish League
UILA. See United Irish League of America
UISC. See United Irish Societies of Chicago
uitlanders, 11–12, 35, 113, 119, 168–69; Lynch, Arthur, and, 161
Ulster, 231
Ulysses (Joyce), 245
Union of South Africa, 247
United Brotherhood (UB), 55, 57, 215
United Irish League (UIL), 16, 21, 25, 128, 153, 246; AOH and, 224; in Canada, 204, 205–6; in Catholic Record, 293n126; Clan na Gael and, 118, 217, 218; Fenian Brotherhood and, 18–19, 47–48, 104, 117, 159; Gonne and, 172; Grey, J. G., and, 157; INF and, 152; IPP and, 28, 46, 114, 116, 176; Rutledge and, 193–94; in Victoria, Australia, 164
United Irish League of America (UILA), 217–18; Clan na Gael and, 219–20
United Irishman (newspaper), 35, 41, 164, 220; Gonne in, 37, 48; Griffith in, 40
United Irishmen, 4, 186
United Irish Societies of Chicago (UISC), 105–6, 116
United Irish Societies of New York, 118
United States, 3, 21, 48, 69, 113, 185; Anglo-Saxonism in, 76; AOH in, 290n4; Canada and, 191, 231; Germany and, 250; in The Great War, 102; INA in, 27; Macrum in, 98; Philippines and, 81, 109, 111, 150

l'Université Laval de Montréal, 188
University of Melbourne, 154

De Valera, Éamon, 250–51
Van Baggen, L. K. P., 80, 81–82, 91, 100, 273n82; Agent X and, 86, 88, 97; Cooney and, 102; in *Irish World*, 112
Vancouver Daily World (newspaper), 194
Vancouver Island, 21
Van Der Line, 89
Van Ness, Edward, 216
Van Siclen, George William, 118
Vaughan, Herbert, 170, 201
Victoria (Queen), 34, 133, 203; Gonne and, 37–38; HACBS and, 147, 151–52; INF and, 146; Millen and, 56
Victoria, Australia, 169–70; UIL in, 164
Victoria, British Columbia, 159, 194
Von der Goltz, Horst, 241
voortrekker, 9, 112

Walsh, John, 49–50, *51*, 70, 71, 227; McInerney and, 60; Merna and, 61; Murray and, 65–66; Welland Canal and, 59, 62–64
Walsh, Joseph, 166
Walsh, Michael S., 43
War of Independence, 6, 250–51
Washington, George, 16
Washington state, 82
Washington Times (newspaper), *234*
Waters, Samuel, 25, 26, 43–44
Watt, William, 160
Waverley Cemetery, 167–68
"The Wearing of the Green," 147
Welland Canal, Ontario, 21, 49–50, 71–72, 128, 241; Agent X and, 93; *Catholic Register* on, 203; Clan na Gael and, 52, 70; Dillon, L., and, 62–64; Fenian Brotherhood and, 53; Lyman and, 58–59
Wellington, New Zealand, 146

Western Australian Record (newspaper), 177
Westminster Abbey, 56
Westminster Palace, 54
Wexford militia, 33
Whelehan, Niall, 252
White, Montagu, 91, 199
White Rose League, 157
white supremacy, xi, 151; imperialism and, 15–16
Wilcox, Craig, 160
"Wilcox," 212, 215–16, 217, 225, 235, 296n77; Carew and, 236–37; Clan na Gael and, 221; Dillon, L., and, 229, 231
Wilhelmina (Queen), 78
Wilkins, C. A., 224
Winter, Joseph, 156, 158
Witwatersrand, South African Republic, 11
Women's National Council of New Zealand, 141
Wood, George Arnold, 175, 289n125
Woodford, Ethelbert George, 95–96, 101; Kruger, S., and, 98–99
Woodford, Mercedes Estelle. *See* Kruger, Sannie
Wyndham, William, 119–20
Wyndham Land Purchase Act (1903), 218, 220, 222, 246

Yeats, W. B., 35
"yellow journalism," 202–3
"Yellow Peril," 222
Yorke, Peter C., 80–81, 172, 177
Young, Brigham, 95
Young, Caesar, 83
Young, John Willard, 95–96, 101
Yukon goldfields, 119

Zeltner, Fred, 140
Zion Congregational Church, 189
Zionism, 40
Zulu Kingdom, 9, 10, 14–15

ABOUT THE AUTHOR

Shane Lynn is an Irish historian based at McMaster University, Hamilton. He received a Gold Medal from Trinity College Dublin, earned his PhD at the University of Toronto, and held a postdoctoral fellowship at New York University. He has contributed scholarly articles on Irish diaspora nationalism to journals such as *Irish Historical Studies*.